SACRIFICE IN RELIGIOUS EXPERIENCE

NUMEN BOOK SERIES

STUDIES IN THE HISTORY
OF RELIGIONS

VOLUME XCIII

SACRIFICE IN RELIGIOUS EXPERIENCE

EDITED BY

ALBERT I. BAUMGARTEN

BRILL
LEIDEN · BOSTON · KÖLN
2002

This book is printed on acid-free paper.

Cover illustration: Marcus Aurelius Sacrificing before the Capitoline Temple.One of three reliefs from the lost arch of Marcus Aurelius. Rome, Palazzo dei Conservatori © Copyright Alinari/Art Resource, NY.

Die Deutsche Bibliothek – CIP-Einheitsaufnahme

Sacrifice in religious experience /ed. by Albert I. Baumgarten. – Leiden ; Boston ; Köln : Brill, 2002
   (Studies in the history of religions ; Vol. 93)
   ISBN 90–04–12483–7

Library of Congress Cataloging-in-Publication data

Library of Congress Cataloging-in-Publication Data is also available

ISSN   0169-8834
ISBN   90 04 12483 7

CONTENTS

PART TWO

ALTERNATIVES TO SACRIFICE

INTRODUCTION

Albert I. Baumgarten

The essays in this volume are revisions of selected papers presented at two international conferences, one "Sacrifice From a Comparative Perspective," held in 1998, and the second "Alternatives to Sacrifice," held in 1999. The papers from the first conference take up "hard core" sacrifice, instances in which an actual offering is made on an altar. They participate in the on-going discussion of sacrifice that has been so fruitful over the past decades and enriched our understanding of the meaning of this primary religious ritual. Some of the papers aim at expanding the analysis provided by others, Burkert,[1] Detienne-Vernant,[2] Girard,[3] Grotanelli-Parise[4] and Jay,[5] for example, while other papers offer critiques of the work done thus far in the hope of correcting apparent errors. These papers also attest to the rich variety of meaning sacrifice can offer. It is difficult, if not impossible, to reduce sacrifice to one basic archetype without doing injustice to some aspect of the phenomenon somewhere. Yet these many variations on the theme prove the place of sacrificing, indicated etiologically for the Biblical tradition in Genesis, when it ascribes the first offerings to the sons of Adam.

The papers from the second conference take up a topic that has been less intensively discussed from a theoretical perspective. While individual studies have been written on particular topics in the past, the goal of the 1999 conference and of the second part of this volume is to open a broader discussion of alternatives to sacrifice across

---

[1] In a series of monographs, beginning with Walter Burkert, *Homo Necans: The Anthropology of Ancient Greek Sacrificial Ritual and Myth* (Berkeley: University of California Press, 1983).

[2] Marcel Detienne and Jean-Pierre Vernant (Eds.), *The Cuisine of Sacrifice Among the Greeks* (Chicago/London: University of Chicago Press, 1989).

[3] René Girard, *Violence and the Sacred* Baltimore: Johns Hopkins University Press, 1977); *The Scapegoat* (Baltimore: John Hopkins University Press, 1986).

[4] Cristiano Grotanelli and Nicola F. Parise, *Sacrificio e società nel mondo antico* (Roma/Bari: Laterza, 1988). See now also Cristiano Grotanelli, *Il sacrificio* (Bari/Rome: Laterza, 1999).

[5] Nancy Jay, *Throughout Your Generations Forever: Sacrifice Religion and Paternity* (Chicago: University of Chicago Press, 1992).

a number of cultures through a collection of case studies. In both parts of this volume, as in previous Taubes Minerva Center publications, no uniformity of approach was imposed on the authors. We hope that as many voices as possible will be heard, some in harmony, others in counterpoint.[6]

The centrality of sacrifice, as a primary form of religious ritual, emerges from the papers in both sections. Indeed, the diversity and intensity of the alternatives offered to sacrifice (not limited to such obvious examples as prayer), and the role of sacrifice in providing a model for other forms of religious expression, prove the fundamental place of sacrifice. We modern worshippers in the Abrahamic monotheistic traditions may sometimes imagine that sacrifice belongs deep in our past and is practiced today only by those whom we would label as "idolators." As the papers in this volume indicate, sacrifice remains much more a part of the way we worship than we might care to concede. This is true even two thousand years after the "greatest reformer in history," Titus,[7] severed the self-evident connection between the worship of the God of the Hebrew Bible and sacrificing.

This will be the last volume of Taubes Minerva Center essays. The vision of a full series of publications that would "make the point," that is show the value of Religious Anthropology as a window of insight into religious experience, will not be fulfilled. This volume and its three predecessors[8] will have to bear that burden. Responsibility for the termination of this dream lies with the senior administration of Bar Ilan University. Individual scholars will continue, but the particular collective effort represented by the Taubes Minerva Center has come to an end.

Jerusalem
July 14, 2001

---

[6] Compare Dorothy L. Sayers, *Gaudy Night* (London: New English Library, 1974) 439. Lord Peter Wimsey, about to receive the consent of Harriet Vane to his proposal for marriage, pursued across many years and through several novels commented: "anybody can have the harmony if they would leave us the counterpoint."

[7] See Elias J. Bickerman, *The Jews in the Greek Age* (Cambridge/London: Harvard University Press, 1988) 139.

[8] See Albert I. Baumgarten, with Jan Assmann and Guy G. Stroumsa (Eds.), *Self, Soul and Body in Religious Experience* (Leiden: E.J. Brill, 1998); Albert I. Baumgarten (Ed.), *Apocalyptic Time* (Leiden: E.J. Brill, 2000); Jan Assmann and Albert I. Baumgarten (Eds.), *Representation in Religion: Studies in Honor of Moshe Barasch* (Leiden: E.J. Brill, 2001).

PART ONE

SACRIFICE FROM A COMPARATIVE PERSPECTIVE

SACRIFICE IN AFRICAN TRADITIONAL RELIGIONS

Theo Sundermeier

In our tradition the interpretation of sacrifice is so strongly marked
by the Roman religion—which found its inculturized continuation
in the Roman-Catholic form of Christianity—and the miscompre-
hension of Greek philosophers, who no longer had a relationship
with the old religious rites of the archaic religion and did not understand its symbolism, that it seems impossible to escape from this
track of interpretation. Therefore one tends to rush to support any
new theory that seems to offer a way out of this dilemma. This
makes it understandable from the view of history of religion that the
different theories coming from other disciplines have enjoyed such
strong acceptance, although they give monocausal, almost monisti-
cally simplifying interpretations and attribute universal validity to
them. Three theories stand out in this context:

- the psychoanalytical theory, which starts from the death instinct
  (*"Todestrieb"*, S. Freud) of the human being and offers the model
  of sacrifice as an act of compensation;
- the cultural-anthropological theory, which attributes to hunting a
  central value of origin in the emergence of sacrificial customs—a
  theory that has gained weight again through Walter Burkert (see
  below);
- and at last the ethological theory, which understands sacrificing
  as a canalized aggressiveness and interprets the rites of sacrifice
  accordingly.

All that is known and does not have to be explained here. What is
solely interesting, is how these theories have recently been revitalised
in modern form. For this René Girard is the most renowned example. Certainly it is no coincidence that his radical scapegoat theory
is judged rather sceptically by scholars of comparative religions, but
scholars of humanities, particularly theologians, are especially fond
of referring to it. It seems to offer the possibility of giving the idea

of sacrifice, which is very central in Israelite and Christian belief, plausibility also in our times.[1]

I

W. Burkert gave new impetus to the cultural-anthropological theory of K. Meulis—who saw the origin of sacrifice in hunting and the restitution of life—by combining it with the theory of aggression of the ethology of Konrad Lorenz.[2] However, he continues to be influenced by the scepticism of Greek philosophers, who did not find direct access to the rites of sacrifice and hardly could conceive their sense, as the original symbolism was not accessible to them. From the point of view of history of religion, this is not an unusual process.

The original rites continue to be handed down and performed, but with the change of society or the superimposition of the native religion by an alien, immigrated one, the original symbolism is forgotten or is newly interpreted within the context of the secondary religion. The process of such "inculturation", as we would define it nowadays, is necessary and serves to facilitate both to preserve the given religion at least selectively and to give to the new religious practice the scope in which it re-orientates, colours and restructures the culture. If one looks at the result of such a fusion from outside as a rational theoretician—and that is what philosophers are—and if one does not take into account the mechanisms of superimposition and the resulting complexity of symbolism, deep misunderstandings arise. The idea of the "fraud of the gods" is one such misunderstanding. Any scholar who passes it on still today, shows that he does not try to understand the religion from within its own context.

I want to briefly demonstrate this by the example of Walter Burkert. A kind of ideal-type reconstruction of Greek sacrifice is shown in the following picture, according to Burkert. After the animal has

---

[1] The literature on René Girard goes on interminably. I refer to Norbert Lohfink (ed.), *Gewalt und Gewaltlosigkeit im Alten Testament* (*Quaestiones disputatae* 96; Freiburg/Basel/Wien: Herder, 1983) where most of the relevant titles are listed.

[2] Walter Burkert, *Homo Necans: Interpretationen altgriechischer Trauerriten und Mythen* (Berlin/NewYork: de Gruyter, 1972); *Wilder Ursprung. Opferritual und Mythos bei den Griechen* (Berlin: Wagenbach, 1990); *Griechische Religion der archaischen und der klassischen Epoche* (Stuttgart e.a.: Kohlhammer, 1977).

been prepared for the sacrifice, in the opening rite the priest cuts some of its forehead hair, which is thrown into the fire. According to Burkert, now the animal is regarded as irreversibly damaged. It is no longer unhurt and intact. "Then the deadly blow follows. The women there give a cry. Shrill and loud". The "Greek custom of sacrificial cry marks the emotional culmination of the action, concealing the death rattle of the animal".[3] Now the animal is cut up and taken apart. The ritual prescribes every detail. The entrails come "strange, bizarre and weird to the light" and are quickly roasted and eaten, with the exception of the inedible gall. The common consumption turns "the shudder into pleasure".[4] The bones and the gall, however, are put onto the altar in a natural order, so that they reflect the basic outline of the sacrificed animal and together with some pieces of meat symbolize the entirety of the killed animal. All those parts are then consumed by the fire or given to the gods, respectively. The skull of the animal, however, is preserved as a "permanent witness to the 'act' of 'sanctification'".[5] According to Burkert, a paradox results from this sacrificial practice, as the animal sacrifice that is made to the gods (the gall bladder and the bones are burnt on the altar) ultimately aims at eating! The good meat "is taken by the pious community in a festive meal. To sacrifice means to provide a banquet."[6] The fact that Hesiod regarded this as "fraud of the gods" is for Burkert very well comprehensible, because he too asks himself how and for what reasons a "fraud" can turn into a rite.

A more precise insight into the process of ritual formation of symbols, more exactly: the formation of symbols in primary religions, could have helped Burkert remove the inner contradictions by means of insights from the history of religion. To accomplish this, we have to follow the laws of analogy but also must have a knowledge of the practice of sacrifice itself.

A sheep or an ox, for example, never groans when its carotid artery is cut. Therefore the cries of the women do not drown out its groaning, but they are—if I see this right—the normal "hallel" shouts, which are made with a stroke of the tongue at the palate,

---

[3] Burkert, *Homo Necans*, op. cit., p. 12.
[4] Ibid. p. 13.
[5] Ibid. p. 14.
[6] Walter Burkert, *Anthropologie des religiösen Opfers: die Sakralisierung der Gewalt* (München: v. Siemens-Stiftung, 1983) 22.

as we know them from the Mediterranean up to the south of Africa. They are always given at special, festive occasions. They show and increase the joy. The slaughtering of an animal does not make the participants shudder, but it produces joy, as now they will have meat. Anyone who ever participated in a slaughtering in an archaic society knows that the entrails of the animals do not seem "bizarre and weird" to the participants. Instead, the slaughtering is a specially joyful action, because it opens the pleasant anticipation of the meal. In archaic societies meat is not an everyday food, but a feast! These were religious celebrations that provided the lower social level the opportunity to eat meat.

When we are dealing with the traditions of the early epoch, much could be said about the symbolical meaning of the bones and the gall bladder and why they are burnt. One thing however is certain, that in matters of sacrificing, the law "pars pro toto" is applied. It is a basic law of all rites, just as the dream imaging. Without this law no communication would be possible. Therefore "fraud" is out of the question.

II

In order to explain the inner coherence of my argumentation, we turn our attention to African religions, in which we still find traces of archaic culture and religion, as they were and still are to be found as basic religiosity in the primary religions in the whole world. To exemplify this, we turn to the Mbanderu in Namibia, among whom I worked and researched for many years.

The Mbanderu belong to the patri- and matrilineally orientated Bantu, who originally immigrated from East Africa to Namibia as acephalically organized heavy-livestock nomads. Although they had been christianized long ago, they retained, like all nomadic peoples, many of their old traditions. After a large number of them had separated from the Lutheran Mission Church, old traditions were revitalized, which the missionaries had thought to be extinct and forgotten. But exactly by the example of the burial rites and the national holidays one could have realised how strongly in particular mourning rites have persisted.

The Herero, who include the Mbanderu as a subtribe, have two herds of cattle. One of them belongs to the mother line and serves

The distribution of a Herero cow

for alimentation, and the other one belongs to the father line and may be slaughtered only for ritual purposes. When the master of the house is buried, traditionally all the cattle of this herd must be slaughtered. The cattle goes back to a cow that the master of the house received as a gift from his father when he was a boy. Multiplying it was not only a matter of prestige, but also served to visibly strengthen the religion, because those cows are directly under the blessing of the ancestors, whom the father of the house serves daily by taking the "okuruuo", ancestor fire from his fireplace outside and lighting it ritually and bringing it back into his house at night. The "holy herd" reminds him daily and directly of his father, who himself is only the last link in the ancestral line and as such the symbol of life in the tribe and the family.

Cattle nomads live in such a close symbiosis with the cattle that either one can become the symbol for the other. The society finds itself again in the cattle. The people are composed as a bull is composed, said a Dinka chief to Godfrey Lienhardt.[7] The same is true for the Mbanderu. Society is reflected in the cattle, and the distri-

---

[7] Godfrey Lienhardt, *Divinity and Experience: The Religion of the Dinka* (Oxford: Clarendon Press, 1961) 23.

bution of the meat "is fixed like on a map", an old Herero said to
me. What does that mean?

The left back leg (7), on which the cow stands, goes to the chief
of the kraal himself, on whom the familiy "stands", so to say. The
right back leg goes to the men of the surrounding dwellings, with
whom one keeps an especially close friendship, because co-operation
with those men guarantees the peace of the area. The back (3) goes
to the mother of the owner. The meat will strengthen her back, they
say, because she once carried the owner of the kraal. As the most
important representative of the mother line (eanda) she must be particularly generously taken into account. She is the "backbone" of the
eanda, and therefore has a determining influence on the life of the
Herero community. The flank and the filet (4), an especially popular piece of meat, are cut into four parts and given to the neighbours; attention is payed to change the distribution of this meat at
different occasions, so that everybody gets the best piece of meat
once in a while. Among the Kaokoveld-Herero the front legs (8) go
to the younger brothers of the owner, because they are the smaller
and weaker legs.[8] The meat around the genitals (6) may be eaten
only by the chief of the kraal and the men who were circumcised
with him in the same year. It strengthens their potency. For women
this meat is taboo. The sparerib (1) is at the uppermost place, it is
cut into three parts and sent to the adults of the neighbouring kraals.
The head (9) goes to the boys and girls; the children must not eat
the nose however, because then they will "raise their noses against
the women" like cows, i.e. they become impudent.

We abstain from giving further details.[9] What has been said,
sufficiently shows how the society of the Herero is fixed in the cow
regarding their familiar and neighbourly relations, and their matrilineal and patrilineal structures, which are renewed and reconfirmed
each time a cow is slaughtered. The body (man and cattle are inter-
changeable) becomes a symbol of society.

What does all this have to do with "sacrifice"? We remember: It
is about slaughtering the animals of the "holy herd" attributed to
ancestor veneration. At the same time it is a slaughtering on the

---

[8] Among the Sotho tribes in Northern Transvaal, one foreleg is allocated to the
older brother, as he is the "first", the "foremost".

[9] As to further details see Theo Sundermeier, *Die Mbanderu. Studien zu ihrer Kultur
und Geschichte*, St. Augustin, Anthropos, 1977.

occasion of a burial. All cattle "accompany", so to speak, the dead person to the next world. The cows are the link to the ancestors. Even if it is not explicitly said, it is self-evident that they are present. During the whole mourning period those cows of the holy herd are slaughtered and eaten. At the end of the mourning period, at the latest after one year, the skulls with the horns are piled up on the father's tomb, an obvious sign of the important man who is buried here. The skulls are a sign of remembrance, a "memorial".

The ritual and the social functions of sacrifice, which must not be separated one from the other—Walter Burkert is a victim of this error—are directly to be seen. Everything that belonged to the dead person is destroyed. At one time, at the end of the mourning period, the house of the master of the kraal was also demolished. Under the leadership of the new leader of the kraal the family's village had to be reconstructed at a place determined by the ancestors (mostly to the east(!) of the former kraal). So, it is evident that slaughter is an act of destruction. Everything, the cattle included, has to die just as the master died. Also the widows have to die ritually and have to be brought back to life, just as the deceased person is introduced to the new life with the ancestors by the burial rites.

At the same time the sacrifice serves life. The society reconstitutes itself. After the death of the master of the kraal everybody is given a new place in the hierarchical order and this place is confirmed by the distribution of the meat. The distribution of the meat publicly respects the value and the position of each family member and of the neighbours and strengthens the bonds within the community. As on the one hand the killing of animals emphasizes and intensifies the experience of death, so on the other hand it makes possible the new constitution of the community. This is the most important function of the sacrifice, as it helps to overcome the grief within the mourning ceremonies. Nothing will strengthen a community more than a common meal.

One thing must be emphasised here: The notion of a scapegoat is not to be found here. Nor should it be inserted. In every mourning process at a certain phase the feeling arises that one is guilty of the deceased person's death, and one blames oneself or other persons. Nowadays this is very well known due to the research of Elisabeth Kübler-Ross e.a. For this reason it is no surprise to see that those feelings are referred to ritually. Still today, the Herero living in the Kaokoveld look for the guilty person with the help of the dead body.[10] Ritually, however, this is another action, which must not be mistaken or mingled with the slaughtering of the cattle. Not every sacrifice has something to do with the thought of a scapegoat or has a representative function.

Also the linguistic background points to another direction. "Ozon-djoza" is the name for the cattle slaughtered at the burial and is in the first place a generic term for sacrificial cattle. The linguistic derivation, however, states more precisely: They are the cattle which "go ahead".[11] The cattle goes on ahead of the deceased person, namely into the reign of the forefathers.

Also other concepts like "ojambanga", a word that is used for all sacrifices that relate to a dead person, point to another direction: *Communio*. "Okupanga" means "to invoke the ancestors", but it derives from the root "-pang" = "to connect" and shows the original meaning of "invocation": to make a connection with the ancestors.

When sacrifices are offered, everything is important and full of symbolism: the place, the conditions, the person who has the right to sacrifice, the prayers etc. We have picked out only some aspects. It would also be important to ask, whether there is anything from the sacrificed cattle that is given directly to the ancestors but not eaten by the humans. For example, among all Bantu religions one has to mention the gall bladder. It is given directly to the ancestors, but not because it is inedible for humans. One has to understand the symbolism. As the ancestors live inversely to the humans[12] what is bitter for the humans is especially sweet there. The gall bladder is sweet "ambrosia"! "Deceiving" the ancestors is out of the question—this would be a real misinterpretation!

To sum up what has been said: The slaughtering of the cattle

---

[10] In his youth one of my students participated in such a search of the guilty person. The dead body is horizontally bound on a stick that is carried by at least four men. Now the dead is required to determine the guilty person. With an irresistible strength, which one cannot withstand, so the student said, you are now set in motion in the direction of a certain person. If he doesn't take to his heels on time the stick will run through him. About this see Theo Sundermeier, *The Individual and Community in African Traditional Religions*. Lit, Hamburg 1988, pp. 77 ff.

[11] Cf. H. Heinrich Brincker, *Wörterbuch und kurzgefaßte Grammatik des otji-Herero*, „ondjoza" Leipzig, 1886, p. 186.

[12] That means everything among them is inverted: black men have white ancestors; what is done here with the right hand, is done there with the left one. This is the reason why at the graves everything is done with the left hand, etc.

during the mourning period has a multiple meaning. Five meanings shall be given:

1. The cattle accompany the dead person into the next world. They are gifts to him. Or in other words: He takes with him what belongs to him.
2. The sacrifice sets up a connection to the ancestors.
3. It renews the community among the members of the community, which was injured by death. The community is strengthened and can then re-constitute itself.
4. The heir and new master of the kraal will do everything to ensure that the cattle that he has inherited from his father will reproduce at great numbers. The destruction of one herd gives space to another one. It will be under the blessing of the deceased person and will always be a reminder of him.
5. The erection of the funeral monument, the piling of the horns on the tomb becomes a sign of remembrance. The sacrifice, which at its core is a communio-sacrifice, becomes at the same time a sacrifice of remembrance.[13] Its purpose is to turn entirely to the dead person and commemorate him, but it also opens up the possibility of a later remembering. For example, if the son thinks the connection to the father as an ancestor is getting weaker and that his father's blessing is not felt anymore, then he will bring his herd to his father's grave and offer an "ondjambero" there, a libation which consists of "omaere", sour milk, and pieces of meat. The dead person is also supposed to enjoy the roaring of the cattle, which will increase his desire to give blessings, so that he will again and more strongly comply with his duty to grant good things to his descendants and to protect them against damages.[14]

We have compiled only a small spectrum of the rich practice of sacrificing of an African tribe. But one thing should have become clear: every reduction to *one* meaning is detrimental to the multidimensionality of every sacrificial practice. Every sacrifice is an aggregate of many symbols, a well from which one can draw new interpretations again and again, which do not exclude but comple-

---

[13] Cf. a similar expression in the Old Testament: "azkarah", Ps 38,70; Sir 39,11.
[14] Cf. Heinrich Brincker, *Wörterbuch*, ibid. p. 54 ref. „ondjambero".

ment one another. Depending on the participants' individual circumstances, their necessities and capacity of reception but also due to the superimposition by another religion, other and new aspects will come to the fore and replace older ones or re-interpret them. This reinterpretation is not violence to the sacrifice. Instead this is a sign of the liveliness of a given religion, since sacrifice is still a central part of every religion, whether it is really performed or whether it is transformed into thoughts and symbolically revaluated.

It is not necessary to finally make a close comparison with the representation of the Greek sacrificial practise by Walter Burkert. For this, a more detailed description would be necessary. But even a superficial phenomenological comparison can open our eyes to the fact that Burkert's ideal-typical summary is by no means objective but is charged emotionally and evidences the atmosphere of an "armchair culprit" who wants to prove his theory of the *homo necans* by all means. A comparison from the point of view of history of religion of those practices with the current sacrificial practices in archaic societies could have led Burkert closer to the reality of the sacrifice and its symbolism and the self-image of the person who makes the sacrifice.

TOWARDS A GENDERED TYPOLOGY OF SACRIFICE: WOMEN & FEASTING, MEN & DEATH IN AN OKINAWAN VILLAGE

SUSAN SERED

> To determine the status of women in matters of sacrifice is to enter by the back door into the system of ritual acts in which eating behaviors constantly intermingle with political practices.[1]

Introduction

In 1994–1995 I conducted fieldwork in Okinawa, the only extant society in which the official, mainstream, publicly funded religion is led by women. Women conduct almost all of the ritual sequences that comprise the Okinawan religious repertoire. Men, however, are the officiants at the small number of rituals that involve any sort of animal sacrifice.

Cross-culturally, animal sacrifice is one of the most dramatically and consistently gendered ritual constellations.[2] In order to begin to make gendered sense both of sacrifice in the Okinawan ritual map and of other instances of animal sacrifice described in historical and ethnographic literature (usually not from a gendered perspective), I have begun to develop a gendered typology of sacrifice. While I do not think that gender is the only useful lens through which to study sacrifice, the conspicuous gendering of almost all recorded sacrificial rituals makes it an unavoidable one. The typology, which I present in the first part of this paper, is neither an exhaustive nor a natural classificatory system, and many examples of sacrifice will fall between, encompass more than one category, or simply not fit any of

---

[1] Detienne, Marcel. "The Violence of Wellborn Ladies: Women in the Thesmophoria." Translated by Paula Wissing. In *The Cuisine of Sacrifice among the Greeks*, edited by Marcel Detienne and Jean-Pierre Vernant, 129–147. (Chicago and London: University of Chicago Press, 1989), p. 129.

[2] I find it significant that in the Catholic Church the last holdout for men is the Eucharist—a symbolic sacrifice. Women lay leaders are now permitted to perform almost all other priestly duties.

my proposed gendered sacrificial models.[3] Still, the typology hope-
fully will encourage the possibility of more conscious and subtle
understandings of why and how sacrifice is gendered in so many
different cultural contexts.

That sacrifice tends to be highly gendered is, perhaps, not entirely
surprising. Both gender and sacrifice are embodied cultural processes.
Gender is the mechanism through which social identities of 'woman'
or 'man' or 'other' are imprinted onto the bodies of individuals; the
culturally recognizable gendered body is the result of the process of
"doing gender."[4] Similarly, sacrificial rituals are processes in which
cultural meanings and symbols are imprinted onto the body of the
sacrificial victim. Moreover, both sacrifice and gender are matters
not only of embodiment, but also of disembodiment. In sacrificial
rites, the victim is dismembered via a variety of ritual procedures
such as cutting and burning. In a parallel manner, in many gendering procedures women (and men) are dismembered, as Mary Daly
has so persuasively argued, through circumcision, infibulation, foot
binding, or witch and widow burning.[5] Sacrifice, then, can be seen
to be analogous to gender; both are cultural processes of embodiment and disembodiment in which certain groups or individuals are
modified, marked, defined, set off, or classified.

Not infrequently, embodied discourses of gender are mapped onto,
appropriated by, or mystified via embodied sacrificial rituals; discourses of gender may include thoughts about who is expected to
sacrifice what for whom. We can ask how the embodying and disembodying of sacrificial victims constructs, confounds, or parallels
the gendering of human bodies in various cultural contexts. Are there
patterns, paradigms, or problems of gender that are solved by or
reflected in gendered sacrificial rites? How do the embodying and
disembodying practices of sacrifice tie into the embodying and disembodying practices of gender?

From a gendered perspective, perhaps the most striking observa-

---

[3] In order to avoid becoming overwhelmed by the material, I have chosen not
to address the myriad instances of sacrificial myths for which there is no solid ethnographic or historical evidence of accompanying ritual. I also have not looked at the
gender of the animal sacrificial victims in this typology. Again, this is a serious
omission, but one that was necessary given the huge amount of material that focuses
on the human participants.

[4] Lorber, Judith. *Paradoxes of Gender*. (New Haven: Yale University Press, 1994).

[5] Daly, Mary. *Gyn/Ecology: The Metaethics of Radical Feminism*. (Boston: Beacon,
1978).

tion that can be made about sacrifice, and especially animal sacrifice, is that it is almost always a male dominated and oriented ritual activity. Furthermore, in a surprisingly wide range of cultural contexts, men's involvement with sacrifice is—implicitly or explicitly—contrasted to women's involvement with childbirth. In other words, in many different cultures men and sacrifice stand in structural tension with, or opposition to, women and childbirth. Usually, this tension is expressed in terms of the opposition between life and death. However—and this "however" stands at the center of the typology that I am about to present—the meaning of that tension, or, more precisely, the way that tension is played out, is always linked to specific cosmologies, gender ideologies, and social structures. In other words, the differences in gendered constructions of sacrifice are probably more interesting than the similarities.

Men and sacrifice: questions of power, questions of death

The best-known analysis of sacrifice and gender has been developed by Nancy Jay.[6] Jay reviewed a number of African societies and concluded that there is an affinity between blood sacrificial religion and patrilineal social organization.[7] Sacrifice frequently serves as evidence of patrilineal descent and serves to constitute and maintain patrilineal descent systems.[8] Jay brings examples of societies such as the Nuer, Dahomey, and Tallensi among whom the word for patrilineage actually translates as "people who sacrifice together." Among the cases which Jay cites is the West African Yako who organize themselves into both patrilineal and matrilineal descent groups, yet only the patrilineages practice sacrifice. Other sacrificing societies, such as the Romans or the Nuer, distinguish between biological and jural paternity in their vocabulary, for example, the Latin distinction between *genitor* and *pater* respectively. In these cases it is typically the jural father who has sacrificial significance; in other words, sacrifice turns the jural father into the "true" father.[9]

---

[6] Jay, Nancy. *Throughout Your Generations Forever: Sacrifice, Religion and Paternity.* (Chicago: University of Chicago Press, 1992).

[7] More specifically, Jay links blood sacrificial religion with precapitalist societies in which there is some degree of technological development and in which rights in durable property are highly valued. See *Throughout Your Generations*, p. 289.

[8] *Throughout Your Generations*, 285.

[9] *Throughout Your Generations*, 290–291.

Jay asks why patrilineal societies need sacrifice. "Social structures idealizing 'eternal' male intergenerational continuity [i.e. patrilineages] meet a fundamental obstacle in their necessary dependence on women's reproductive powers."[10] Jay sees sacrifice as a means of establishing blood ties among men that supersede the "natural" blood ties produced through women's childbirth. In order to overcome the dissonance caused by women's empirical birthing of children, "What is needed to provide clear evidence of social and religious paternity is an act as definite and available to the senses as birth."[11] Sacrifice fits the bill especially well. In many male dominated religions, childbirth blood is the ultimate pollution which can only be removed by animal sacrifice. In this polarity, men religious leaders and killing receive a positive value, and women and childbirth a negative value. To phrase it differently, the blood of animal sacrifice purifies or neutralizes the blood of childbirth; kinship bonds are recreated through the blood of the sacrificial animal rather than through the blood of women.

Jay's approach has been criticized as a poor fit for certain examples of sacrifice, most specifically, for Eucharistic sacrifice performed by women priests today in the Episcopal church.[12] I would suggest that if Jay's schema is treated not as a universal theory of sacrifice but (as was her intention) as one of several gendered sacrificial models, her analysis can be appreciated as an excellent fit for a rather wide spectrum of cultural situations.[13]

A somewhat more nuanced exposition of the sacrifice and patrilineality model has been developed by M.E. Combs-Schilling in respect to the annual Islamic Great Sacrifice commemorating Ibrahim's willingness to sacrifice his son Isma'el. According to Combs-Schilling, "Islam's great sacrifice myth glorifies patrilineality for it depicts the most valuable of human ties as that which links father and son. . . . It is father and son who in combination achieve God's favor and

---

[10] *Throughout Your Generations*, 31.

[11] *Throughout Your Generations*, 36.

[12] Raab, Kelley Ann. "Nancy Jay and a Feminist Psychology of Sacrifice." *Journal of Feminist Studies in Religion* 13, no. 1 (1997): 75–89.

[13] Diane Jonte-Pace, correctly (to my mind) considers this to be a "minor variation in a very stable pattern"—a few women Episcopal priests are permitted to "act like men" as a result of the confluence of two symbol systems: one egalitarian and one matriphobic." See Jonte-Pace, Diane. "New Directions in the Feminist Psychology of Religion: An Introduction." *Journal of Feminist Studies in Religion* 13, no. 1 (1997): 63–74, esp. p. 68.

bring eternal hope to human life."[14] In the Moroccan version of the ritual each male head of household publicly kills a ram. The size and virility of the ram are symbolic of the man's own virility. The men of the household stand together during the ritual, while women are seated offstage. Combs-Schilling draws attention to the similarities between sacrifice and both the spilling of the bride's blood at the marriage ceremony (which verifies the male's domination of women's fertility and sexuality) and the spilling of blood at childbirth.[15] In the Great Sacrifice, which is always performed by men, a dramatic statement is made about men's control of cultural relations; the Islamic Great Sacrifice eliminates the female from the spiritual birth process.[16]

Another example of this model can be found in Valerio Valeri's brilliant exposition of kingship and sacrifice in ancient Hawaii. According to Valeri, through sacrifice a human is incorporated into, or establishes a spiritual association with, the god or goddess whose descendant he or she is. In fact, however, men dominate all sacrificial rituals, except those few that concern impure deities (that is, sacrifice in the context of sorcery). Thus, even though an individual sacrifices to a god or goddess analogous to his or her own gender, rank and class, "[Certain] pure goddesses often require male sacrificers as mediators between them and women, while [certain] impure gods may in certain cases be approached . . . through female mediators. This happens because purity is an essentially masculine property, while impurity is essentially feminine".[17] Valeri then goes on,

> The global inferiority of women relative to men in the sacrificial system contrasts sharply with their equality to men in the genealogically

[14] Combs-Schilling, M.E. *Sacred Performances: Islam, Sexuality, and Sacrifice*. (New York: Columbia University Press, 1989), p. 244.

[15] *Sacred Performances*, 242–243.

[16] *Sacred Performances*, 256. In a recent paper, John Bowen has shown that among the Gayo of highland Sumatra the Islamic Feast of Sacrifice has a rather different meaning. Gayo kinship is bilateral (not patrilineal like in Morocco), and the actual sacrifice at the Feast of Sacrifice receives relatively little notice. Smaller animals can be used, women are allowed to perform the sacrifice, and the killing takes place with hardly any ceremony. See Bowen, John R. "On Scriptural Essentialism and Ritual Variation: Muslim Sacrifice in Sumatra and Morocco." *American Ethnologist* 19, no. 4 (1992): 656–671. The point I wish to emphasize is that even within two Islamic societies—Moroccan and Gayo, the elaboration of sacrifice is correlated with patrilineality.

[17] Valeri, Valerio. *Kingship and Sacrifice: Ritual and Society in Ancient Hawaii*. Translated by Paula Wissing. (Chicago: University of Chicago Press, 1985), p. 112.

determined hierarchy.... Men's superiority to women expresses only
the superiority of a sacrificial relationship with the gods over a purely
genealogical relationship with them.... The superiority of sacrificial
links over genealogical ones is the superiority of action over passivity,
of direct relations over indirect ones, and ultimately, of political relationships over kinship.[18]

To summarize this first and particularly wide-spread model, patriarchy[19]
flip-flops nature, proclaiming that men are the life-givers; patrilineality defines the father as the relevant parent; and male creator
deities transpose birth into a male ability. In patriarchy, spiritual
birth—the birthing that is done by men and male gods, often via
sacrifice, becomes the true birth, the pure birth, the birth that saves
from feminine pollution and chaos.[20]

The next model that I shall present is one that deals with some
of the same issues: the construction and preservation of the male-
oriented or male-defined community. In this model, not only are
men the ritual officiants, but women are actually the sacrificial victims. The clearest example here, of course, is Indian suttee. In suttee—ritual immolation of widows, purity is a central theme. The
widow's sexual purity is "safeguarded;" in preparation for this ultimate purification she is ceremoniously bathed; and the suttee ritual
is not performed during times when the woman is impure from menstruation or childbirth.[21] Suttee—the sacrifice of women—serves to
preserve the patriline via the removal of marginal, foreign, extrane-
ous and dangerous women.

In the rituals of some cultures, only part of the woman's body is
sacrificed. Most commonly, those parts are associated with fertility
or sexuality. The examples that come to mind here include infibulation,
clitoridectomy, ritual defloration, or ritual rape of women accused
of actual, or suspected of potential, sexual misbehavior such as adul-

---

[18] *Kingship and Sacrifice*, 113–114.
[19] I use the word patriarchy to indicate societies in which men as a group are
systematically more powerful than women as a group. The manifestations of power
vary from society to society, as does the extent to which men as a group have
power over women as a group.
[20] For other examples of this model see Delaney, Carol. *The Seed and the Soil:
Gender and Cosmology in Turkish Village Society*. (Berkeley: University of California Press,
1991); Hauser-Schaublin, Brigitta. "Blood: Cultural Effectiveness of Biological
Conditions." In *Sex and Gender Hierarchies*, edited by Barbara Diane Miller, 83–107.
(Cambridge: Cambridge University Press, 1993), esp. p. 102.
[21] *Gyn/Ecology*, pp. 114–133.

tery or promiscuity. The "women as the sacrificial victim model" is particularly prominent in cultures in which male-oriented group identity and status is dependent upon women's sexual behavior—so called "honor and shame" cultures. Through sacrificing women, the male community can be kept pure. This sacrificial model often complements the first sacrificial model (Nancy Jay's analysis) presented earlier. In other words, the ritual embodiment of birth and community as male enterprises is sometimes accompanied by the ritual disembodiment of women, and especially of women's sexual and reproductive organs. This kind of ritual discourse emerges, I would argue, because the core meaning of patriarchy is that men procure actual and symbolic power over women's reproductive capabilities.

A third gendered model of sacrifice describes the variety of situations in which, through eating the sacrificial food provided by her husband's family or clan (or some other male-oriented institution), a woman becomes absorbed into (or—more accurately—absorbs into her body) some sort of male-defined or oriented group affiliation. As a result of eating the sacrifice, the woman becomes re-embodied as "good enough" for the male community.

A common variation of this model is a cultural rule that a married woman can no longer eat from the sacrifice of her natal family, but only from the sacrifice of her husband's family. In Levi-Strauss's terms,[22] this kind of ritual arrangement symbolizes women's transitional or transformative role in patrilineal societies, mediating between two male-defined groups. A less prevalent variation of this model is the cultural notion that a man cannot sacrifice without his wife's participation. This model has been eloquently developed by Stephanie Jamison in her study of gender, ritual and hospitality in ancient India. Interpreting a myth that is used in sacrificial contexts of the sort just mentioned (that is, the man is the ritual officiant but his wife must be present and perform certain secondary tasks), Jamison argues that,

> The wife is so prominent in the [ritual] story because she in some sense embodies exchange relations. She is a mediating figure between different realms, and whenever ancient Indian ritual or mythology requires or depicts the perilous contact between realms, a woman is often the central figure. This mediating quality is responsible both for

---

[22] Levi-Strauss, Claude. *The Elementary Structures of Kinship*. Translated by J. Bell and J. von Sturmer. (Boston: Beacon, 1969).

her power in the story and for her near sacrifice. And her role as mediator, as exchange *token*, allows her to be treated as an alienable chat-
tel, to be given at will.[23]

The sacrificial models that I have presented thus far have to do not
only with the cultural construction of gender, but also with the cultural construction of gender hierarchy—of patriarchy. This theme is
particularly clear in the next model. In a variety of contexts, men
perform sacrificial rituals as demonstrations of power, or as ritual
displays of the control of resources such as food or weapons or cattle or women. Through sacrificial rituals, certain men dramatize their
power over others, including women, who often are the required
audience to the sacrifice. Perhaps the most dramatic examples here
come from hierarchical societies in which kings are buried together
with their "possessions," including—sometimes—tens or hundreds of
women wives, slaves and kin.[24]

While women sometimes are allowed or required to serve as the
audience to the sacrificial ritual, menstruating women or post-partum
women may be forbidden to touch, consume or sometimes even look
at the sacrifice. Menstruating and post-partum women are too fully
embodied as female to be re-embodied as male-appropriate; they
are, perhaps, a physical reminder that men's sacrifice cannot fully
replace women's childbearing.[25] A slightly different model is what I
call "the absent audience." In some cultural situations women are
consistently defined as so thoroughly polluted, spiritually weak or
dangerous, that they are never allowed to be present at sacrificial
rituals. At the same time, however, they are required to actively
acknowledge the ritual, for instance, through refraining from certain
activities or through conspicuously avoiding the ritual site. In this
model, the absence of women should be regarded as a key ritual
element: Through their absence women contribute to the constitution of the all-male sacrificial community. Their absence acknowledges men's power and control of resources.

The models that I have presented until now have not especially
emphasized what seems to me to be a, if not the, primary element

---

[23] Jamison, Stephanie W. *Sacrificed Wife, Sacrificer's Wife: Women, Ritual, and Hospitality in Ancient India.* (New York: Oxford University Press, 1996), esp. p. 25.
[24] For example, on the Rajputs of northern India see Walker, Benjamin. *The Hindu World: An Encyclopedic Survey of Hinduism.* (New York: Praeger, 1968), esp. pp. 462–463.
[25] On the role of post-menopausal women in Greek sacrifice see "Violence," 142.

of sacrificial rituals—killing. Through killing the sacrificial victim, the sacrificer demonstrates his power to generate death. In the next model, men are dramatically and ritually gendered as empowered to kill. Whereas Nancy Jay's model (my first model) treats sacrifice as ritualizing men's control over life, this model highlights sacrifice as ritualizing men's control over death. Whereas the first model genders life-giving as a male enterprise, this model genders life-taking as a male enterprise. Both life-giving and life-taking, in these models, are, of course, embodiments of power.

Rosaldo and Atkinson have perceptively argued that,

> Killing, unlike childbirth, grants men wilful control over the processes of nature, and in particular, over the natural processes of life and death. Such an association is made explicit for cultural interpretations of forms of killing as distinct as warfare in New Guinea ... and live burial among certain African groups .... We would suggest, then, that the critical difference between giving and taking life is rooted in the fact that a man's killing is always an act of will, directed towards a body other than his own; giving life through childbirth, on the other hand, is a natural function of a woman's body, and usually is something over which she has little intentional control. Men's life-taking, because of its intentionality, becomes a means of culturally transcending the biological; whereas childbearing, despite values attached to it as the means of perpetuating a social group, remains grounded in the 'naturalness' of women's sexual constitution.[26]

To their analysis, I would add that sacrifice—completely intentional, ritualized, and "cultural" death, can be viewed as the most "perfect" form of life-taking, and as such, particularly valorizes men and men's roles.

The association between men and sacrifice is so strong that in certain cultures even when women are the leaders and officiants at sacrificial rituals, a man briefly enters the ritual arena in order to carry out the actual sacrificial killing. This model has been brilliantly explicated by Marcel Detienne in regard to the ancient Greek Thesmophoria. Through analyses of a wide range of literary and pictorial evidence, Detienne concludes that in the very few and clearly non-historical Greek stories in which women are depicted as holding

---

[26] Rosaldo, Michelle Zimbalist, and Jane Monnig Atkinson. "Man the Hunter and Woman: Metaphors for the Sexes in Ilongot Magical Spells." In *The Interpretation of Symbolism*, edited by Roy Willis, 43–76. (New York: John Wiley and Sons, 1975), esp. p. 70.

sacrificial weapons, the message seems to be that when women kill, they become dangerous to men. Thus, the fact that a man is needed to dart out into the ritual arena to perform the sacrifice indicates, "Nothing is at stake other than the maintenance of the male privilege to shed blood at a time that [this privilege] seems most threatened by a ritual order, that of the Thesmophoria, which calls both for the banishing of males, and the inauguration of a society of women having the high power to sacrifice animal victims."[27]

Whether killing or maleness are understood as superior or superordinate to life or femaleness depends upon specific cultural understandings of death and life. In some cultures, death is valorized, men associated with death are considered heroic, and sacrificial rituals dramatize men's control over death. It seems to me that this model tends to be found in militaristic cultures, and may be related to another form of male sacrifice—male self-sacrifice in times of war. In this model, the body of the self-sacrificial victim is reconstructed as a fully gendered, indeed a perfect male body—the military hero. Any androgynous elements are stripped away, leaving the essence, the ideal, of gendered masculinity. Through self-sacrificial rituals, the ambiguously natural human body is disembodied in order to be re-embodied in a more clearly and perfectly gendered manner. Just as Nancy Jay's model shows how sacrifice reconstitutes the community into a more perfect one that is born of men rather than women, heroic male self-sacrifice reconstitutes the individual body into a more perfect one—into one in which male-oriented culture rather than female-oriented birth has left its imprint.

Moreover, as Carolyn Marvin and David Ingle have argued in their analysis of the centrality of blood sacrifice in the establishment of both religious and national identity, heroic self-sacrifice distinguishes and reconstitutes not only the individual body but also the social body by setting off Us (those on whose behalf the sacrifice is made) from Them.[28] Marvin and Ingle do not specifically address questions of gender, yet it is implicit in their argument that the community typically is constructed out of the [male] bodies of those who are sacrificed, and by those [men] who exercise killing power. Self-

---

[27] "Violence," 143–144.
[28] Marvin, Carolyn, and David W. Ingle. "Blood Sacrifice and the Nation: Revisiting Civil Religion." *Journal of the American Academy of Religion* 64, no. 4 (1996): 767–780.

sacrifice defines the male-oriented community via the deaths of certain chosen men. The efficacy of the sacrifice is maximalized, it would seem, when the chosen victim is perceived as perfect (young, male and unblemished): In national contexts the self-sacrificial victims often are described as "the flower of our youth," "the best and the brightest," or "a few good men." In religious contexts the most perfect self-sacrifice may be the son of God himself.[29]

Self-sacrifice takes differently gendered forms among men and among women. Women's self-sacrifice has been extensively documented by Caroline Bynum in her studies of medieval Christian religious women.[30] I find it especially significant that one of the most prevalent forms of women's self-sacrifice—extreme fasting, can lead to singularly gendered manifestations—the sacrifice of female secondary sexual characteristics and fertility. When women's weight falls below a certain point, menstruation ceases. The self-sacrificial model described by Bynum may be particularly evident in religious systems in which it is believed that women can attain high spiritual powers or status, but the mainstream paths to spiritual power and status are dominated by men. I would suggest that unlike men's self-sacrifice that tends to reembody men as more perfectly male, women's self-sacrifice generally disembodies women as a means of making them less female. As Jesus declared in the *Gospel of Thomas*, "Every woman who will make herself male will enter the Kingdom of Heaven."

A rather different model that I wish to present focuses upon the gendering of death itself. Cross-culturally, we find in the ethnographic, literary and historical literature a rather widespread conceptual or symbolic association between women and death. According to psychologist of religion Diane Jonte-Pace, in patriarchal cultures "death, the unrepresentable, the ultimate absence, is symbolized as woman;

---

[29] Another well-known form of male self-sacrifice is sexual self-sacrifice. The clearest example would be ritual castration. Like in the heroic variation, the sexual self-sacrifice disembodies in order to construct a more perfect male body—in this case one that is exempt from the earthy and polluting processes of sexual reproduction. Similarly, in many cultural contexts circumcision both is understood to create a more perfect male, and serves as an initiation into the community of men that supersedes the domestic unit into which a boy was born and in which he was raised. In circumcision rituals, the mother may be required to physically or symbolically hand over HER son to the community of men, an act that could also be considered a form of women's self-sacrifice for the good of the male-constituted community. On Africa and New Guinea see "Blood," esp. p. 102.

[30] Bynum, Caroline Walker. *Holy Feast and Holy Fast*. (Berkeley: University of California Press, 1987).

woman becomes, through metonymy, death. Maternal absence, matricide, and castration (absence as female), are [then] negated in the
religious promise of presence through eternal life and paternal love
(presence as male)."[31] Jonte-Pace carefully traces the association of
women with death in western religious and psychoanalytic thinking,[32]
citing for example, the fourth century Church Father St. John Chrysostom who called the female body a "white sepulcher." In contrast,
Christians are truly born (or "born again") through the sacrificed male
body of Christ. In this kind of discourse, patriarchal religion is presented as the only means for conquering female-embodied death. In
sacrifice—a controlled and ritualized form of death-causing, men are
symbolically cast as able to control death, and by extension, death's
embodiment—that is, women. This model tends to be found in cultures characterized by dualistic thinking; that is, cultures in which
male and female are understood to be core dichotomous categories,
intrinsically linked to such other key dualisms as spirit and body.[33]

Gender and sacrifice in Okinawa

We turn now to the one clearly sacrificial ritual found in Okinawa's
rather vast ceremonial repertoire. My observations are drawn from
the fieldwork that I carried out in 1994–1995 on Henza, a small
one-village island located near the coast of Okinawa's main island.[34]

---

[31] Jonte-Pace, Diane. "Situating Kristeva Differently: Psychoanalytic Readings of
Women and Religion." In *Body/Text in Julia Kristeva: Religion, Woman, Psychoanalysis*,
edited by David Crownfield, 1–22. (Albany: State University of New York Press,
1992), esp. p. 21.

[32] An association of women and death or absence is also expressed in psychoanalytic theories. "Female genitals in Freud's analysis... are a gap, a lack, an
absence: the female acknowledges the fact of her castration, and with it, too, the
superiority of the male and her own inferiority" ("Situating Kristeva," 20). Winnicot,
according to Jonte-Pace, somewhat softens the equation of women and absence, yet
does not eliminate it: Winnicot writes that when the mother is away the child per-
ceives her as dead—the mother's absence is the very meaning of death. Julia Kristeva
maintains the homology of women and death: the feminine as the image of death
is a screen for both the fear of castration and for the matricide that is necessary
for the individual to become autonomous. Jonte-Pace clarifies that association between
women and death in western thinking is not always explicit or visible; to the contrary, the public discourse in the west tends to be that of "woman as life-bearer."
This discourse, however, is also used to restrict women's freedom and social power.

[33] Sacrifice also can be seen as a corrective for Death's non-cognizance of gender.

[34] For a more complete discussion of gender and Okinawan religion see Sered,
Susan. *Women of the Sacred Groves: Divine Priestesses of Okinawa*. (New York: Oxford
University Press, 1999).

Men's rituals

Susan: Are there any rituals that involve killing an animal?
Village man: *Ame tabore*, also *hama ogami*. Pig. Kill the pig, ask them to bring the bowl.
Susan: Is killing the pig a job for men?
Village man: Mr. Shiidu [a male ritual role] will cut the pig, and Mr. Tobaru [another male ritual role], all men.

Ame tabore—a rain ritual—is the only ritual that I have ever heard Okinawan villagers spontaneously categorize as a 'men only' ritual. It also is a flamboyantly blood-oriented ritual, incorporating actual animal sacrifice and a theme of symbolic human sacrifice.[35] *Ame tabore* centers upon the sacrifice of a goat. Men dance around the goat's head which is placed next to pots of water, a boy is dunked into the pot, and then the men eat soup made from the goat meat.

I never saw *ame tabore*, both because women do not attend, and because it is a ritual that is only performed in years of severe drought.[36] Here is how one village man describes *ame tabore*:

> We go to a place in the mountains and circle around it [the goat] seven times. We sing a song: *ame tabore, ame tabore* [please rain, please rain]. And then we come down from the mountain. We go to a river and pick up some water from there and carry it and go to the *nun-duruchi*'s [chief priestess's] place. And then all the important men of the village get together there and say to have rain. And then we grab a little boy, and there is a big bowl with water, and we push down the boy into the water to sit down in the water. If Henza does *ama goi* [*ame tabore*], strangely, it brings rain. Four years ago they did this and it rained.

Another village man, who has organized *ame tabore*, fills in a few more details:

> Up there [in the mountains] they kill the goat and bring it to the river and clean it and go someplace to cook it. The goat is usually male— there is more meat on male goats. They decorate the cooked food with the head. There is a big water bowl and a little bit of the juice of the goat is put in, and the boy is dumped in it in front of the

---

[35] The human sacrifice motif seems obvious to me, but I never heard a villager suggest that line of interpretation.
[36] One informant said it has been done four or five times in the past 65 years, but another informant said it is done far more often because droughts are frequent on the island.

kami-ya ["god house"]. The boy doesn't like to be the one who is dunked. Henza's *ame tabore* is very famous. [Neighboring] islands have their own ritual, but if Henza doesn't do it, it won't rain.

In light of the typology of gender and sacrifice introduced in the first part of this paper, the association between men and the one sacrificial ritual performed in Henza is rather predictable. As I have argued, sacrifice often has to do with the ritual construction, mystification and embodiment of gender and gender hierarchy. This ritual design makes sense in the many religious settings in which the idealization of patriarchy is a cosmological and ceremonial goal.

In Okinawa, however, women fill all other ritual roles, women serve as the clan and village priestesses, only women connect with the *kami-sama* (deities), and there is no ideology of male superiority or purity.[37] Moreover, villagers do not promote any sort of an ideology of gender difference: Men and women may carry out different tasks, but there are no traits, statuses, or roles that are inherently gender-linked.

If patriarchy is not part of the cosmological or ritual agenda in Okinawan religion, the specific models suggested earlier should not be expected to fit the Okinawan ritual reality. Thus, a last model that I wish to propose is one that flip-flops the previous models. We find that an association between men and death (as opposed to an association between men and the power to overcome or bring about death) is present in certain, although perhaps not many, cultural contexts. In some of these contexts, the association between men and death is treated as parallel to the association between women and life. In these societies, only men can conduct sacrificial rituals because women are so totally associated with life that they choose not to, or are not permitted to, participate in death or blood oriented rituals. Contact with blood or death rituals may be perceived as weakening the spiritual power that women need to create life. I would suggest that this model tends to be found in societies characterized by a strong matrifocal or matrilineal emphasis, and in which birth and menstruation are not considered polluting (although death

---

[37] For somewhat different interpretations of Okinawan religion and gender see Mabuchi, Toichi. "Spiritual Predominance of the Sister." In *Ryukyuan Culture and Society*, edited by Allan H. Smith, 79–91. (Honolulu: University of Hawaii Press, 1964); Kawahashi, Noriko. *Kaminchu: Divine Women of Okinawa*. Ph.D. diss. Princeton, New Jersey: Princeton University, 1992.

may be). Unlike in Nancy Jay's model, in this model men do not
co-opt or rectify women's association with life and birth. Instead, the
social ties that are generated through women's childbirth are acknowledged, institutionalized, and sacralized. Men's marginal role in con-
stituting the community is symbolized through their association with
that ultimate absence—death. This final model, perhaps the most
difficult to understand because the most foreign to the cultures most
scholars study, describes Okinawa's ritual configuration.

In Henza, men far more than women are responsible for death
related rituals. Since the official Okinawan kinship system is patrilineal, men are in charge of ancestor worship. The eldest son inher-
its the *butsudan* (household ancestral altar) and it lies on his shoulders
to take care of it, although the women of the household typically
see to it that the ancestors receive food offerings. Japanese anthropologist Teigo˘Yoshida has noted that in Okinawa men are far more
involved in rituals that take place soon after death; the more time
that elapses the more that women become involved.[38]

Nowadays bodies are cremated, thus many of the rituals dealing
with the actual corpse have disappeared. One or two days after a
death the remains are brought back from the crematorium on the
main island and a special, elaborate altar is set up in the deceased's
house. A (male) Buddhist priest, who comes to the village from the
city, chants and rings a bell inside the house. The mourners proceed to the cemetery where the priest conducts a prayer service. The
remains typically are carried to the tomb in an urn by the closest
male descendant.[39] Men of the family open the family's tomb and
one or two men go inside to rearrange the older urns in order to
make room for the newcomer. Although the entire family prays during the Buddhist service, men stand closer to the grave and take a
more prominent role even in such small things as giving out token
gifts to those who came to the funeral.

On the night after the funeral, three young male relatives gather
outside the deceased's house for a ritual called *hohai*. One young
man holds a stick, one holds a torch and one a bucket. The one
with the stick comes inside the house and hits three of the supporting poles of the house seven times each while saying *ane ane*.

---

[38] Personal communication, 1992.
[39] If there is no appropriate male descendant a female descendant carries the
remains.

The young men then light the torch and run down the street to the cemetery shouting *hohai hohai*. They leave the stick and other accoutrements at the cemetery and return by a different route in order to confound the spirit who might follow them home. It is suggestive that whereas women's elaborate food-oriented post-funeral rituals pull the dead spirit back into the domestic community, men's *hohai* and other post-funeral rituals dramatize the need to separate the dead spirit from his or her living kin group.

Susan: Are there any rituals only men do?
Village man: Only the ocean events. *Tairyo kiga*. To have a lot of fish to catch. Twice a year, February and August, *umi ogami* [ocean prayer]. Fishermen prepare *sake* and a fish meal and then go to the *noro* [chief priestess], and she prays for them.

Many men's rituals are related to fishing or the ocean. Some of these rituals have now disappeared because few local men are still fishermen; other rituals have been transformed from profound expressions of the dangers and unpredictability of fishing, to light-hearted village-wide festivals. Significantly, I was told on a number of occasions that although not many Henza men still go to sea, they continue to think of themselves as fishermen and sailors. In other words, the men's rituals are linked not only to their subsistence work, but also to their identity as seafarers and fishermen.

Hatsu-gyo was the first fishing of the new year. One villager explained, "And they would bring the fish to the house and invite relatives, and give away fish, and say that today we share so that throughout the year there should be a lot of fish." The (women) *noro* and *kaminchu* [priestesses] did not attend.

San gatsu [Third month] festival rituals incorporate a number of ocean themes and ceremonies. The exciting climax of *san gatsu* is a procession, mostly of men, to a small island off the coast of Henza. According to one elderly priestess,

> *San Gatsu* ritual is to catch the fish at the ocean and eat. There is no property, not much farmland in Henza, so the men go to the ocean to get fish. At *san gatsu* the fish is speared and there is a song: Poke and pull, poke and pull.

Haari boat racing is traditionally a men's ritual. According to another village woman,

> *Haari* boat races used to be for fishermen, to compete east and west [sides of the village]. In those days almost every house had someone

doing an ocean job. . . . There were no other jobs for men except at
sea. Women did farming. Men went to the mountains to bring wood
and sell it. They sold it in Naha or Itoman. There were many seamen.

Many local men seem intrigued both by competition and by fighting.
Bull fighting, *habu* snake fighting, chicken fighting, and dog fighting
are all popular in Okinawa (in Henza there is only chicken fighting
and dog fighting; bull fighting can be seen in a nearby village). An
elderly couple explained that, "Okinawan men will [watch] fight[s
of] anything that moves."[40]

Another ritual involving sacrifice (although in a less dramatic and
less exclusively male setting) is *shima kusara*, which used to be conducted on December 24 of the lunar calendar. *Shima kusara* centered
upon men killing a pig, after which bits were given out to families
as a kind of 'good luck' charm. A pig bone was hung in the entrance
to the house in order to keep out illness. *Shima kusara* was performed
during the coldest time of the year when, according to some of the
older villagers, certain diseases were prevalent.

And finally, at the traditional grave-making ritual (since graves
hold many bodies this long and elaborate ritual is not done very
often), the head of a pig—killed by a man—is put outside the new
grave. This ritual can be understood as bringing together two primary male ceremonial themes: killing and death.

In sum, although *ame tabore* is singled out by men and women in
Henza Village as the only ritual performed exclusively by men, there
are a number of rituals that are usually performed by men, although
villagers do not label them as "men's rituals" or suggest that women
are prohibited from attending. Like *ame tabore*, these rituals have to
do with danger, blood or death. Put differently, Henza's usually
unspoken and unacknowledged cultural association between men and
killing is dramatized and made explicit in a ritual in which men
gather and carry out a "perfect" killing—the ceremonial sacrifice of
a human (young, male) substitute during a time of communal danger.

Women's rituals

Ame tabore is the only ritual described by villagers as explicitly and
formally gender-linked. Empirically, however, just as certain rituals

---

[40] Still, Okinawa is a relatively non-violent society, and in Okinawan bull-fighting,
for example, there is no blood-shed. Two bulls try to push each other out of the
ring (like sumo wrestling), but no one is hurt.

are fairly consistently associated with men, many other rituals are fairly consistently associated with women. Rituals carried out by women tend to deal with themes of life, social integration and cosmic harmony. The ritual substance that symbolizes these themes is, in almost all women's rituals, food.

Food, in Henza, is women's business. Traditionally, men's fishing was a sporadic source of food; most food came from women's horticulture and shore foraging. The markets were and still are run by women. All food preparation is done by women; very few men cook at all. Almost all food is served by women. Food is a resource that women control, and food-oriented rituals sacralize women's everyday activities of cooking and serving. A *hinu-kan* (hearth deity) can be found in every Henza kitchen. The *hinu-kan* functions in a loose way as a sort of intermediary between the household and other *kami-sama*. Giving offerings to and praying at the *hinu-kan* are women's affairs.

In Okinawan culture there are no food taboos; food is considered to be an essentially *good* thing. Not only is it necessary for survival, it is also tasty. In public and semi-public contexts, villagers almost always seem to have something in their mouths. Any time a villager visits another house, something is served. Food is not only eaten with gusto, it is talked about with gusto.[41]

Eating is the most significant act of solidarity in Henza. Whom one eats with, who serves the food and who provides it, who is served and who is provided with food, are crucial social forces. Moreover, the "who" includes not only humans but also ancestors and *kami-sama*.[42]

Village ritual life revolves around food. Food is the most common ritual means used to relate to *kami-sama*, and food is regularly put out for ancestors and for *kami-sama*. After funerals, food and chopsticks are placed on the household altar. Food is offered on the *butsudan* (household ancestral altar), food is served at ceremonial occasions and informal gatherings, food is shared after or during almost every ritual whether at the household, clan or village level. During holi-

---

[41] For a Japanese parallel see Smith, Robert J., and Ella Lury Wiswell. *The Women of Suye Mura*. (Chicago: University of Chicago Press, 1982), p. 82.

[42] On Japanese food offerings see Befu, Harumi. "Gift-Giving in Modernizing Japan." In *Japanese Culture and Behavior: Selected Readings*, edited by Takie Sugiyama Lebra, 208–224. (Honolulu: University of Hawaii Press, 1974), esp. pp. 210–211. On food rituals on Hateruma Island see Ouwehand, C. *Hateruma: Socio-Religious Aspects of a South-Ryukyuan Island Culture*. (Leiden: E.J. Brill, 1985), pp. 132 ff.

days like *obon* and New Years the village is teaming with people (usually women) carrying plates of food to each other; men are more likely to be seen carrying wrapped, store-bought gifts.

Post-funeral rituals are composed almost entirely of eating. During the first days after a death the family stays home while friends, relatives and neighbors visit and bring food and eat. The deceased is also understood as needing food. Several times during the first week after the funeral, the family of the deceased gathers at the grave, prays, spreads out platters of food, and eats in the company of the deceased. The food eaten by the living participants and shared with the deceased consists of *sake*, sweets, tofu, squid, tempura, sea weed, and other popular food items. Villagers say that the purpose of these meals is to keep the deceased company, but I emphasize that the means by which the deceased is kept company is eating. Once each week for seven weeks following a death, and then once each year afterwards, plus on Dead People's New Year, *shiimi* (memorial days), and other special days, rituals are held in which incense is lit, short, informal prayers are quietly said, and large meals are served. On these occasions, food functions to maintain ties between the living and the dead, ties which are negotiated by women who prepare and serve food.

Something happens to the food when it is put on the altar. Not only do *kami-sama* or ancestors eat it (or suck out its essence), but they also put something into the food—something spiritual, something desired by villagers, something of the *kami* or ancestor's own essence. At rituals, food is placed on the altar not only to feed the *kami-sama* or ancestor but also to enable the embodied participants in the ritual to eat food that was "touched" by the disembodied participants. Through food being placed on the altar and then eaten by villagers, the ancestors or *kami-sama* and the villagers engage in an act of exchange that reinforces their association and identification with one another. By eating food put on the ancestor altar, villagers receive ancestor-essence; by eating food put on the *kami*'s altar, the priestesses receive *kami*-essence. In Henza households, live family members eat with their ancestors; in clan rituals, current clan members dine with other clan members and with clan ancestors (indeed, practically the only thing that clan members do together is eat).

In the chief priestess's rituals, she and her associates dine with the village *kami-sama*. During a ritual visit to the village sacred grove, I asked the priestesses, who had just eaten a large, leisurely meal at the village *kami-ya* ("god house") to explain to me why they were now eating again. They explained that this second meal consists of fish, and they eat fish in the ritual "because this [place] is the ocean *kami-sama*." At focal rituals, the priestesses embody clan or village *kami-sama*; while being *kami-sama*, the priestesses eat food offerings provided by the clan or village. Indeed, at many ceremonial occasions eating seems to be the entire point of the ritual.

For example, at *hama ogami* (a ritual in which the village is protected from "bad things" that come from outside the island) the priestesses begin at the *kami-ya* where they say a very short prayer, following which they chat with one another and eat large balls of rice. When they finish eating, they lie down to rest. One gets the feeling that the eating was strenuous—the eating constitutes the ritual work of the priestesses. During the next stage of *hama ogami*, the priestesses go to the sacred grove, pray briefly, chat some more, and are served cakes. They then make a round of the village ports, praying in front of trays of meat. Finally, they proceed to Town Hall where they are served large bowls of meat soup. In *hama ogami*, priestesses ritually protect their island by eating food provided by the village.

The ritual efforts of the priestesses do seem to have paid off. Okinawa has the longest life-expectancy of any society in the world today, and Henza villagers are especially healthy and long-lived, even for Okinawans. Significantly, the central theme in the prayer of priestesses is health. When priestesses are asked for what they pray, they answer, "Health, only health. That Henza should be healthy." Priestesses emphasize that they do not officiate at funerals; in fact, they prefer not to attend funerals at all. Priestesses deal with life and health, not with death and sickness.

Susan: Does the *noro* [chief priestess] pray at funerals or when someone is sick?
Noro: No! I don't take care of bad things, only good things.

Several themes emerge from this description of women's food rituals. First, the attention paid to the manner of preparing, serving and eating the food suggests that these acts are not auxiliary to Henza's rituals but actually constitute the rituals. Second, these food rituals sacralize women's everyday household tasks and demand cooperative efforts among women, and, in particular, the ability of women to meet together in some sort of public or semi-public context. Third, these rituals offer deities and ancestors foods which humans are known to especially like. Through the serving of delicious cooked food (as opposed to the offering of uncooked meat), deities and spirits are encouraged to become domesticated, to join the domestic community. Serving elaborate and cooked food pulls the deity into the circle of beings who receive life, health and nurture at the hands of women.

Gender, work and ritual work

One elderly village woman explained women's preeminent ritual role in Henza in this way:

> Women are always home and don't do the dangerous jobs. Women are home raising vegetables and taking care of the children and the house. Men go out of the house and go to the ocean and then die, sometimes, and typhoon and die, and war and die.

Ame tabore, shima kusara and other Okinawan men's rituals have a great deal in common. All are (were) men's rituals carried out at times of communal danger. All involve killing an animal and using parts of the animal for ritual purposes. Although women could cook the meat from the animals, killing was the job of men—all rituals involving killing an animal are conducted by men.

In a very broad sense, the ritual division of labor in Henza places men in the sphere of death-related rituals and women in the sphere of life-related (and especially food) rituals. We have seen that men have the key roles in burial rituals. According to one middle-aged village woman, death rituals are carried out at low tide, whereas birth occurs at high tide. "That is nature's way that birth occurs at high tide. In those days people lived according to nature." Traditionally (and still today) pregnant women and priestesses do not attend funerals. In the past men were not usually present at birth (although there was no actual prohibition involved). The chief priestess emphasizes that she only does "the good things" and not "the bad things" like rituals at times of death or disaster.

Unlike priestesses' rituals, *ame tabore* is performed in response to danger (drought)—a "bad thing." This pattern may also hold true for symbolic objects. I was told that the goat used in the men's *ame tabore* ritual is traditionally a male goat; in another context entirely, I was told that the goat eaten at housewarming rituals (a "good thing" attended by priestesses) is traditionally a female goat. (In both instances, villagers attributed the choice of the goat to which kind of goats have more and better meat.)

Henza women work in agriculture which is life-producing and a steady source of food. Men work in fishing which involves killing and which is an erratic source of food.[43] Women remain put doing land-based work in a culture in which the village and its environs are considered safe and healthy; men come and go doing sea-based work in a culture in which the ocean is considered dangerous, the source of disease and typhoons. Not only typhoons but also dynamite fishing injured and killed many fishermen in the past. According to one villager,

> The fishermen would dive . . . without any equipment, and sometimes they wouldn't make it up when they came up to breathe, and if no one went down to help them, they died. Before the War we took the boats all the way up to the northern point of Okinawa. Sometimes people got fish hooks stuck in them. And flying fish sometimes attacked.

This graphic account, I suggest, borders on the mythical: One wonders how many men truly were killed by flying fish! The point, of course, is the cultural perception of the sea as a source of multitudinous and aggressive dangers and death. Villagers constantly warned me to keep my children away from the beach "because so many people drown," although the water is actually very shallow for a long distance from Henza's shores.

I wish to emphasize that in Henza death is not understood to be an existentially bad state. Quite to the contrary, several villagers made a point of telling me that unlike people in other countries, Okinawans are not afraid of death because they know that when they die they stay in the family (on the household ancestral altar and in the communal family tomb). I was also told, on a number of occasions, that it is not always clear if someone is really dead: people assumed to be dead and placed in tombs "often" wake up and bang on the door of the tomb, and that people who have disappeared at sea for decades "maybe are dead, but I don't know for sure." The men/danger/absence/death complex that I have expli-

---

[43] Ito, Mikiharu. "Rice Rites in Japan Proper and the Ryukyus: A Comparative Study." In *Folk Cultures of Japan and East Asia*, 37–55. Monumenta Nipponica Monographs, no. 25. (Tokyo: Sophia University Press, 1966).

cated, then, is mitigated by a feeling that neither death nor life is an absolute condition.[44]

Unlike the ocean where the men do their work, the women's village is life-oriented. Violence and war are deplored, natality rates are high, virginity is not a cultural value, there are no birth or menstrual taboos, children are welcomed, life-expectancy is long, and long-life is celebrated at lavish rituals for people who reach their eighties and nineties. In Henza, women excel at creating the enduring social bonds that make life and culture possible. These social bonds are ritualized in complex and elaborate food rituals, rituals in which cooked and tasty foods are beautifully prepared and presented, served and shared, as the social bond par excellence. Men, however, leave the island and bring back with them disease, money, foreigners, competition, *sake*—all kinds of things that disrupt village harmony. Men's rituals are not existentially 'bad' rituals just as men are not existentially 'bad;' neither men nor women suggest that there is any kind of hierarchy or ideology involved in village ritual. Rather, men whose work is involved with outsiders and danger and killing carry out the very few rituals that deal with disruptions of the natural and normative state of social and bodily health. Moreover, it is crucial to understand that villagers do not make the categorical statement that only men kill animals, that men are associated with death and women with life, or that certain rituals are men's rituals and others are women's. The entire schema that I develop here rests upon my efforts to categorize and interpret village behavior; it does not reflect any sort of ideological or even perceptual schema advanced by villagers, and it does not lead to the development of rules or taboos.

Conclusion

Sacrifice, as I said earlier, is a rather common ritual means for thinking about embodiment and disembodiment. Cross-culturally, two especially mysterious and powerful kinds of embodiment and disembodiment often seem to elicit the bodily ritual attention that

---

[44] The ocean also is both dangerous and purifying. Things from the sea (salt, salt water, fish, stones from the sea) are used for *oharai* ("get out!" rituals) of various kinds.

sacrifice can so dramatically provide. On the most obvious level of meaning, animal sacrifice enacts, reenacts or plays around with themes of life and death, sometimes through inversion, sometimes through exaggeration, sometimes through mystification or any number of other ritual techniques. On an equally obvious empirical level, sacrificial rituals are highly gendered in terms of who actually performs the sacrificial rites. Specific rituals of animal sacrifice can be understood to construct gender and life and death as politically, cosmically and morally analogous phenomena of embodiment and disembodiment.

Henza's ritual arrangements do not fit the models of gendered sacrifice presented in the first part of this paper. In all but the Okinawan model, hierarchy is a crucial element of the constellation composed of sacrifice, gender, and life and death. Except in the Okinawan model, men's performance of sacrificial rituals seems to be a symbolic expression of men's moral superiority to women, and of life's moral superiority to death. By ritually overcoming death, men ritually overcome women. By inverting death, men become symbolically associated with life. In these models, men performing sacrifice can be seen to, in one way or another, create or preserve the male community, enhance male prestige or potency, allow men to co-opt women's reproductive power, valorize men's endeavors, and grant men the ability to control or overcome death.

Unlike most known societies, Okinawan society is not patriarchal. Power or hierarchy of any sort tend to be rejected and scorned by Henza villagers. The most salient community in the eyes of Henzans, is the village community—and that community is made up first and foremost by the women who stay put and farm, not by the men who go to sea—often never to return. Kinship is bilateral and household arrangements lean towards matrifocality. Death is not understood as frightening or evil, and killing is not understood to be valorous. Because death and life are not hierarchically construed, the gendering of sacrifice—of rituals of life and death—does not lend layers of power and prestige to gender arrangements. Men sacrificing a goat once every few years in *ame tabore* does not translate into notions of male dominance.

Still, despite the absence of a moral discourse of the superiority of men, even in Okinawa animal sacrifice enters the ritual repertoire at one of the very few points of culturally acknowledged gender difference—women farm and men go to sea. Animal sacrifice in Okinawa retains its power to express and encapsulate gender as a social process. Okinawans, like people in many other societies, construct sacrificial rituals as compelling expressions of concern with embodiment and disembodiment.

Contemporary anthropological understandings of gender as infinitely variable and dynamic social processes rather than as an inherent and biological endowment lifts from the scholar of religion the burden of expecting sacrificial rituals, even if they are highly gendered, to convey static meanings. Gender and animal sacrifice are often found to be reflectively good to think with, yet the thoughts that they elicit are as infinitely diverse as the ways in which human societies arrange and conceptualize social patterns. Animal sacrificial rituals, in this paradigm, can be seen as expressions of the mystification of gender processes. The analysis of animal sacrificial rituals can be seen as a means of revealing those processes.

Bibliography

Befu, Harumi. "Gift-Giving in Modernizing Japan." In *Japanese Culture and Behavior: Selected Readings*, edited by Takie Sugiyama Lebra, 208–224. (Honolulu: University of Hawaii Press, 1974).
Bowen, John R. "On Scriptural Essentialism and Ritual Variation: Muslim Sacrifice in Sumatra and Morocco." *American Ethnologist* 19, no. 4 (1992): 656–671.
Bynum, Caroline Walker. *Holy Feast and Holy Fast*. (Berkeley: University of California Press, 1987).
Combs-Schilling, M.E. *Sacred Performances: Islam, Sexuality, and Sacrifice*. (New York: Columbia University Press, 1989).
Daly, Mary. *Gyn/Ecology: The Metaethics of Radical Feminism*. (Boston: Beacon, 1978).
Delaney, Carol. *The Seed and the Soil: Gender and Cosmology in Turkish Village Society*. (Berkeley: University of California Press, 1991).
Detienne, Marcel. "The Violence of Wellborn Ladies: Women in the Thesmophoria." Translated by Paula Wissing. In *The Cuisine of Sacrifice among the Greeks*, edited by Marcel Detienne and Jean-Pierre Vernant, 129–147. (Chicago and London: University of Chicago Press, 1989).
Hauser-Schaublin, Brigitta. "Blood: Cultural Effectiveness of Biological Conditions." In *Sex and Gender Hierarchies*, edited by Barbara Diane Miller, 83–107. (Cambridge: Cambridge University Press, 1993).
Ito, Mikiharu. "Rice Rites in Japan Proper and the Ryukyus: A Comparative Study." In *Folk Cultures of Japan and East Asia*, 37–55. Monumenta Nipponica Monographs, no. 25. (Tokyo: Sophia University Press, 1966).
Jamison, Stephanie W. *Sacrificed Wife, Sacrificer's Wife: Women, Ritual, and Hospitality in Ancient India*. (New York: Oxford University Press, 1996).
Jay, Nancy. *Throughout Your Generations Forever: Sacrifice, Religion and Paternity*. (Chicago: University of Chicago Press, 1992).
Jonte-Pace, Diane. "New Directions in the Feminist Psychology of Religion: An Introduction." *Journal of Feminist Studies in Religion* 13, no. 1 (1997): 63–74.
———. "Situating Kristeva Differently: Psychoanalytic Readings of Women and Religion." *In Body/Text in Julia Kristeva: Religion, Woman, Psychoanalysis*, edited by David Crownfield, 1–22. (Albany: State University of New York Press, 1992).

Kawahashi, Noriko. *Kaminchu: Divine Women of Okinawa*. Ph.D. diss. Princeton, New Jersey: Princeton University, 1992.

Levi-Strauss, Claude. *The Elementary Structures of Kinship*. Translated by J. Bell and J. von Sturmer. (Boston: Beacon, 1969).

Lorber, Judith. *Paradoxes of Gender*. (New Haven: Yale University Press, 1994).

Mabuchi, Toichi. "Spiritual Predominance of the Sister." In *Ryukyuan Culture and Society*, edited by Allan H. Smith, 79–91. (Honolulu: University of Hawaii Press, 1964).

Marvin, Carolyn, and David W. Ingle. "Blood Sacrifice and the Nation: Revisiting Civil Religion." *Journal of the American Academy of Religion* 64, no. 4 (1996): 767–780.

Ouwehand, C. *Hateruma: Socio-Religious Aspects of a South-Ryukyuan Island Culture*. (Leiden: E.J. Brill, 1985).

Raab, Kelley Ann. "Nancy Jay and a Feminist Psychology of Sacrifice." *Journal of Feminist Studies in Religion* 13, no. 1 (1997): 75–89.

Rosaldo, Michelle Zimbalist, and Jane Monnig Atkinson. "Man the Hunter and Woman: Metaphors for the Sexes in Ilongot Magical Spells." In *The Interpretation of Symbolism*, edited by Roy Willis, 43–76. (New York: John Wiley and Sons, 1975).

Sered, Susan. *Women of the Sacred Groves: Divine Priestesses of Okinawa*. (New York: Oxford University Press, 1999).

Smith, Robert J., and Ella Lury Wiswell. *The Women of Suye Mura*. (Chicago: University of Chicago Press, 1982).

Valeri, Valerio. *Kingship and Sacrifice: Ritual and Society in Ancient Hawaii*. Translated by Paula Wissing. (Chicago: University of Chicago Press, 1985).

Walker, Benjamin. *The Hindu World: An Encyclopedic Survey of Hinduism*. (New York: Praeger, 1968).

SACRIFICE IN MESOPOTAMIA

Tzvi Abusch

This paper treats the topic of sacrifice in Mesopotamia. It focuses on sacrifice as it was performed in the public or temple realm and places the topic in a broad Mesopotamian context. The paper is divided into two sections—one informational, the other argumentative. In the informational section, I have presented a synthesis of our general understanding of the topic. In the argumentative, I take up one theme and develop it.[1]

I

When we think of sacrifice we tend to think of slaughtering animals or consuming an offering by means of fire. But we must imagine sacrifice a bit differently when we approach the topic in Mesopotamia. For our Mesopotamian religious sources emphasize neither the slaughter of animals nor the process of consumption. Rather, they usually focus on presentation. To understand the Mesopotamian view of sacrifice, it is important that we constantly keep this perspective in mind.

Before approaching the topic of sacrifice, however, we do well to understand the Mesopotamian and, in particular, the Sumerian view of human life, the gods, and the city.[2]

---

[1] This essay is a slightly revised version of the first part of the presentation on Sacrifice in Mesopotamia that I delivered in Israel in February, 1998 at the conference "Sacrifice: A Comparative Inquiry" sponsored by the Jacob Taubes Minerva Center of Bar Ilan University. (The second part dealt with sacrifice in the private realm.) I am grateful to the Center and its director Prof. A.I. Baumgarten for the invitation and for their kind hospitality on that occasion. The explanation of the difference between Israel and Mesopotamia as regards the use of blood in the sacrificial cult, subsequently, also formed part of an invited address "Blood in Mesopotamia and Israel" delivered later that spring at the session "Cult in the Temple: Blood" of a conference sponsored by the Center for Judaic Studies of the University of Pennsylvania; that paper will be published in the proceedings of the Philadelphia conference. I wish to thank Kathryn Kravitz for her helpful comments on this paper and to express my gratitude to Lucio Milano and Marcel Sigrist, with whom I enjoyed conversations on the topic of sacrifice in Mesopotamia while preparing the conference version of this paper.

[2] In this context, I should mention that my understanding of early Mesopotamian

The purpose of human life, the purpose of the community, was to serve the gods, to provide them with whatever care a powerful ruling class, a landed aristocracy, would require. Paramount among these are shelter and food. But this represents the developed or classical form of theology and was probably not the original ideology or theology of god and temple. For in the earliest periods, the divine powers were forces of nature, powers experienced in those natural phenomena that were of importance for the survival and growth of the settlers and settlements. In the main, in these early periods, the gods were not human in form.

Gods were linked to specific settlements, and the two, god and settlement, developed together. During the Ubaid period, that is down till the end of the fifth millennium, we have indications of cult places evolving in the midst of developing villages and towns. It is probable that these cult places served as store-houses for the community and focal points for rituals directed to the afore-mentioned powers of nature, rituals of thanks and rituals of revitalization.

As noted, the gods in this period probably had not yet attained a predominantly human physical and social form. Upon these forces of nature, the original settlements had depended for their sustenance. The goal of the earlier ritual was to keep these forces present, vital, and productive. And the cult place would have served as the place where the rites centering upon these forces were carried out. Some of these rites involved the bringing of offerings by the community as expressions of thanks, and perhaps even to allay communal guilt; others took the form of agricultural, magical rituals and served to revitalize nature. Here I have in mind rites that later became rites of offering and rites of the *hieros-gamos*.

But eventually, the powers in natural phenomena were anthropomorphized as the masters of the city, the ones who gave sustenance and care to the city and upon whom the city depended. The form of their presence was that of a lord in his home. Certainly by

---

religious history follows in the tradition of several scholars, most notably that of my late teacher Thorkild Jacobsen; see especially *The Treasures of Darkness: A History of Mesopotamian Religion* (New Haven/London, 1976). On the topic of temple and sacrifice in Mesopotamia, see, e.g., W.G. Lambert, "Donations of Food and Drink to the Gods in Ancient Mesopotamia," in J. Quaegebeur, ed., *Ritual and Sacrifice in the Ancient Near East* (Leuven, 1993), 191–201; M. Roaf, "Palaces and Temples in Ancient Mesopotamia," in J.M. Sasson, et al., eds., *Civilizations of the Ancient Near East* (4 vols; New York, 1995), vol. 1, 423–441; F.A.M. Wiggermann, "Theologies, Priests, and Worship in Ancient Mesopotamia," in ibid., vol. 3, 1857–1870.

the beginning of the third millennium, the characteristic and defining forms of classical Mesopotamian theology had emerged. This new ideology was part of the evolution of early civilization and of the development of hierarchical structures within the cities. Naturalistic gods were now seen as manorial lords, as the divine equivalents to the newly emerging human chieftains and kings.[3] Along with a human form, the gods were given families and households. Most important, their homes were now seen as manors or palaces, that is, the temples were now treated as the divine equivalent of the human ruler's abode. Hence, older cultic centers now became the classic Mesopotamian temples in which the god and his family were treated by his subjects as the ruling class of the city.

In Mesopotamia, then, by the third millennium the temple had evolved into the god's home. It was believed that the god had built the city for his or her own residence and sustenance. The god was now regarded as the primary owner of the city, and the city existed in order to support his or her needs. Thus, the temple was not simply a dwelling place to which a god repaired occasionally, but rather a permanent home in which the god and his family lived continually.

For its part, the city was required to care for these anthropomorphized deities. A classical expression of this human responsibility to the gods is found in the myth of "Atrahasis." The myth is made up of two originally separate parts; each part was an independent solution to the problem of the role of humans in the world. Originally, the gods created cities and lived there by themselves. Because humans had not yet been created, the gods themselves were required to do all the work necessary for their own survival. Not suprisingly, they found the labor of maintaining the cities and of producing and preparing food wearisome and burdensome. The worker gods rebelled and threw down their tools. As a solution, humanity was created from clay mixed with the blood and flesh of the leader of the rebellion in order to work and care for the gods. Man now produced food for the gods, but, as we learn in the second

---

[3] We imagine that this development took place in the early third millennium partly because this is the time when a prominent human ruling class with its own special domiciles emerges, and partly because the evidence suggests that it was only then that the gods attained full human form. Prior to the Early Dynastic II period, there seem to be no unambiguous anthropomorphic representations of deities. It is from this period onward that deities in human form were distinguished from mortals by being shown wearing special head-gear with horns.

part, humans also reproduced and created a disturbance in the world. After trying unsuccessfully to decimate humanity, the great god Enlil finally decided to exterminate them by means of a flood. As a consequence, the gods suffered from starvation, for there was no one to provide food for them. One man, Atrahasis by name, was saved. After the flood he sacrificed food to the gods on the mountain on which his ark had landed. This mountain becomes a new exemplar of the temple.[4] The gods were delighted with the offering, and their hunger was sated. Now, a new cosmic order was permanently instituted. The gods realized their folly and recognized their need for human beings. Humanity would never again be destroyed and would permanently provide food for the gods in the form of offerings.

In the course of time, then, the nature of the temple and cult changed. There was a shift of emphasis from storage to presentation. The original temples may have served as communal storehouses. The economic function was never lost and temples developed many rooms and buildings that served for production, storage, and distribution. But the central rooms of the temple were the god's cella, and the development that we have noted of the temple from a locus for natural power to an abode for a divine ruler is evident, for example, in the addition of a reception room to the cella.

The earlier communal festivals which derive from magical rites for prosperity remain important for the cult. But here I shall take further note only of the daily service of the god. The god sat in his cella in the form of a divine statue made of wood overlaid with precious materials and valuable garments. The statue was both alive and holy, having attained identity with a god by means of the ritual of the washing of the mouth. Each day the god and his family were awakened, bathed, clothed, fed, and entertained. We learn from temple ritual texts[5] that there were two main meals during the day, one in the morning and one in the evening, and each of these meals was divided into a lesser and greater course. These meals included beer, wine, cereals, loaves of bread, cakes, meat, etc.

Libations seem to have been poured out. Food was treated differently; after being placed on the god's table and somehow magically

---

[4] So I understand *ziqqurrat shadê* in the "Epic of Gilgamesh," XI 156.
[5] This regime is nicely illustrated by first millennium ritual texts from Uruk; see, e.g., A. Sachs, "Daily Sacrifices to the Gods of the City of Uruk," in J.B. Pritchard, *Ancient Near Eastern Texts Relating to the Old Testament*[3] (Princeton, 1969), 343–345.

eaten by the god, it was distributed to the temple personnel and to the king. This was not the only food slaughtered and prepared in the temple. The temple was a major storehouse and economic center, and therein took place the secular preparation and butchering of food for distribution to those who were temple dependents.[6]

The central act of the daily cult is not sacrifice in the sense of giving the food over to a fire which consumes it, nor is it acts of slaughter and the pouring out of blood. Food was placed before the god and consumed by him through that mysterious act that characterizes Babylonian religiosity. As A. Leo Oppenheim noted,

> Looking at the sacrifice from the religious point of view, we find coming into focus another critical point in that circulatory system, the consumption of the sacrificial repast by the deity, the transubstantiation of the physical offerings into that source of strength and power the deity was thought to need for effective functioning. Exactly as, in the existence of the image, the critical point was its physical manufacture, so was the act of food in the sacrificial repast. It represents the central *mysterium* that provided the effective *ratio essendi* for the cult practice of the daily meals and all that it entailed in economic, social, and political respects.[7]

The act of killing the animal is almost hidden behind the construct of feeding the god, a construct which emerges out of a combination of the earlier offering and storage and the later image of feeding a divine king in his palace.

The temple is the center of an urban world. The temple and the feeding and care of its gods define the primary community of the dwellers in the land between the two rivers. To serve the god by supporting and participating in the economy of the temple constitutes the mark of membership in the urban community, a community which thus replaces or, at least, overshadows membership in one or another kinship community such as the family or clan.

---

[6] Animals were slaughtered also for other reasons. Here mention should be made, for example, of extispicy; in this classical form of Babylonian divination, sheep were slaughtered so that their innards could be inspected in order to determine the will of the gods.

[7] A.L. Oppenheim, *Ancient Mesopotamia: Portrait of a Dead Civilization*, rev. edit. (Chicago/London, 1977), 191.

II

I turn now to a phenomenon that has been previously noticed but not explained. It is not my intention to propose definitive answers, but, rather, to suggest a tentative hypothesis that will surely require further testing and modification. It has been noted, again by Oppenheim, that a "difference that separates the sacrificial rituals in the two cultures [scil. Mesopotamia and the West, "represented best by the Old Testament"] is the 'blood consciousness' of the West, its awareness of the magic power of blood, which is not paralleled in Mesopotamia."[8]

This observation seems to be correct so far as the major urban temples are concerned. And yet one can find an important place where blood does play a role in Mesopotamia, and this place may provide a clue to the significance of the emphasis on blood in the Semitic West and its apparent absence in Mesopotamia. Actually, this can be found, I think, in texts that tell the story of the creation of man for the service of the gods. For example, in the myth of *Atrahasis*, discussed earlier, the god who led the rebellion was slaughtered and his flesh and blood mixed together with clay in order to create the human creature necessary for the welfare of the gods. The use of flesh and blood in addition to clay in the formation of humanity represents a *novum*. The flesh and blood are actually unnecessary, for the original model for the creation of humanity in this mythological tradition is that of a potter who creates statues by forming them out of wet clay. In fact, we even possess a Sumerian myth, "Enki and Ninmah," which describes the discontent of the divine

---

[8] Oppenheim, *Ancient Mesopotamia*, 192. In his discussion of the "deep-seated differences between the West—represented best by the Old Testament—and Mesopotamia with regard to the concept of the sacrifice," Oppenheim notes that in addition to blood, "The Old Testament concept is best expressed by the burning of the offered food, a practice which had the purpose of transforming it from one dimension—that of physical existence—into another, in which the food became assimilable by the deity through its scent" (ibid., 192). Oppenheim also notes that, "There is no trace in Mesopotamia of that *communio* between the deity and its worshippers that finds expression in the several forms of commensality observed in the sacrificial practices of circum-Mediterranean civilizations, as shown by the Old Testament in certain early instances and observed in Hittite and Greek customs" (ibid., 191). These observations support the explanation presented in this paper for the presence of blood-consciousness in the West and its general absence in the Mesopotamian temple cult.

workers and the subsequent creation of human beings from clay.[9] The killing of the god and the use of his flesh and blood to create humanity are an intrusion into the Mesopotamian system of thought, an intrusion which affects two major early Mesopotamian mythological traditions, those of Eridu and Nippur. Hence, gods are killed in order to create human beings not only in "Atrahasis" and texts related to it, like "Enuma Elish," but also in the Nippur text *Keilschrifttexte aus Assur religiösen Inhalts*, no. 4.

In the new construct, the clay still serves to form the physical person, while the flesh and blood of the slaughtered god add qualities to the clay and to the human that is created therefrom. The addition of the flesh and blood reflects a new point of view. While the flesh is the source of the human ghost, the blood, as I have argued elsewhere,[10] is the origin of an ability to plan, that is, of human intelligence, and is, ultimately, the source and etiology of the personal god or, rather, the family god who is passed down from generation to generation by the male progenitor. The personal god is not simply the god of an isolated individual; rather, he is the god of the individual as a social being. He is both the divine personification of individual procreation and achievement and the god of the family or tribal group.[11] It is the god of the family who finds expression first of all in the act of reproduction, an act basic to the continuation of the god's group. The god is the blood, or is in the blood, and his transmission from father to son creates a relationship

[9] But see now W.G. Lambert, "The Relationship of Sumerian and Babylonian Myth as Seen in Accounts of Creation," in D. Charpin and F. Joannès, eds., *La circulation des biens, des personnes et des idées dans le Proche-Orient ancien, XXXVIIIᵉ R.A.I* (Paris, 1992), 129–135. Basing himself upon a bilingual version of "Enki and Ninmah," Lambert argues that Enki created man by mixing clay and blood. If Lambert's understanding also applied to the original Sumerian text, the episode in "Enki and Ninmah" might then represent an earlier example of the mixing of blood and clay; however, if "Enki and Ninmah" is dependent upon "Atrahasis," as has also been suggested, the occurrence of blood in "Enki and Ninmah" may be no more than a carryover from "Atrahasis."

[10] Abusch, "Ghost and God: Some Observations on a Babylonian Understanding of Human Nature," in A.I. Baumgarten, et al., eds., *Self, Soul and Body in Religious Experience*, SHR 78 (Leiden, 1998), 363–383.

[11] For my understanding of the personal god, see Abusch, "Ghost and God," 378–383 and "Witchcraft and the Anger of the Personal God," in T. Abusch and K. van der Toorn, eds., *Mesopotamian Magic: Textual, Historical, and Interpretive Perspectives*, Ancient Magic and Divination 1 (Groningen, 1999), 105–107, 109–110 and the literature cited in "Ghost and God," 379, n. 35, and "Witchcraft and Anger," 106, n. 62.

of kinship between generations of men by the emphasis on the tie of blood.

This intrusion into the Mesopotamian mythological tradition and into its understanding of the nature of humanity is probably due to Western Semitic influences.[12] The killing of a god seems to be depicted already on seals dating to the Old Akkadian period;[13] but it entered the literary tradition in the Old Babylonian Period possibly as a consequence of the settlement of the tribal Amorites in Mesopotamia. Certainly, the family god, a god represented by blood, was important for the Western Semites; it is they who created and cemented alliances by means of the bloody splitting of animals and to whom we owe the image of divine blood in the *Atrahasis* epic.

Turning back to sacrifice, let me generalize in an attempt to formulate a possible solution to our problem. Sacrifice may serve to maintain a group that is drawn together by, or whose identity is based on, some common characteristic. One may consider the possibility that those systems of sacrifice that emphasize blood serve to maintain family groups, groups which are organized along common blood lines that are usually, though not necessarily, tribal and patrilinear. That is, blood sacrifice maintains a relationship of kinship between men by the emphasis on a tie of blood and would agree with the emphasis on blood in a clan context.[14]

---

[12] Cf. also T. Frymer-Kensky, "The Atrahasis Epic and its Significance for our Understanding of Genesis 1–9," *Biblical Archeologist* 40 (1977), 155, where Frymer-Kensky suggests that "Considering the special notion of blood that we find in the Bible, it seems likely that the blood motif in Atrahasis and in Enuma Elish may be a West Semitic idea, and may have entered Mesopotamian mythology with the coming of the West Semites."

[13] See F.A.M. Wiggermann, "Discussion" in E. Porada, *Man and Images in the Ancient Near East* (Wakefield, RI/London, 1995), 78–79.

[14] I owe some of my understanding of blood sacrifice to the recent work of Nancy Jay (*Throughout Your Generations Forever: Sacrifice, Religion, and Paternity* [Chicago/London, 1992]). Among other things, she develops and modifies some of the insights of Robertson Smith along lines suggested by modern gender studies. According to Jay, "sacrifice is at home in societies where families are integrated into extended kin groups of various kinds" (so K.E. Fields in her Foreword to Jay, ibid., p. xxiv). Jay notes that while sacrifice may serve to define both matrilineal and patrilineal descent systems, it is especially prevalent and significant in patrilineal societies, where "sacrificing orders relations within and between lines of human fathers and sons, between men and men, at least as effectively as it does relations between men and their divinities" (ibid., 34). Sacrifice establishes blood ties among men that supersede the natural blood ties produced through women's childbirth (cf. ibid., 30–40). Jay does not distinguish between animal sacrifice that emphasizes blood and animal sacrifice that does not; that distinction is mine, as are my application of some

This function of sacrifice surely applies to the tribal shepherds and herdsmen who spread out over the ancient Near East and entered Palestine and Mesopotamia during the middle and late Bronze Age and who were primarily organized according to family and clan. Accordingly, we may suggest that the importance of blood in the West reflects the fact that an important element in Israelite (as well as in Hittite and Greek) society derived from a semi-nomadic element which defined itself in tribal terms. And it is significant, moreover, that the livelihood of this group was involved in the flesh and blood of animals of the herd. Moreover, at least in the case of the Israelites, this semi-nomadic element saw itself as different from the indigenous, auto-chthonic element of the population and tried to maintain that separateness by means of blood rituals.

For the Semites, then, it was the family, the tribe, and the wider tribal territory that defined identity and power. This remained true even of the Semites of northern Babylonia and northeastern Syria. For while they absorbed the culture of the urban Mesopotamians of the South, they did not fully give up their own identities; rather, they transformed the culture that they had assimilated, introducing new images into it that were consonant with their own background and social situation—images such as the image of blood that they introduced into the Mesopotamian mythological tradition of the creation of man.

But the image of blood could not dominate the Mesopotamian cultic landscape whose form was and remained fundamentally urban. For the classical Mesopotamian city defined itself not as a community of kinsmen, but rather as a community of service which had grown out of and around a female center, the fertility of the earth. Its admission rules were based on a willingness to serve the city god, not on family ties. In Mesopotamia, the basic form was created in Sumer: that society seems to have descended directly from the Neolithic villages of the same area where the Sumerians lived in historical times, and saw itself as indigenous to the land. Hence, the central forms of the Mesopotamian temple had little use for blood.[15]

---

of her gender based insights to the tribal Semites (but not to the urban Mesopotamians) and my attempt to explain Western blood consciousness thereby.

[15] The fact that, in contrast to the tribal world, the distribution and consumption of meat in these cities were several steps removed from the process of slaughter undoubtedly contributed to the relative unimportance of blood in the Mesopotamian sacrificial cult.

Its form of sacrifice emphasized offerings, first to natural forces and then to divine owners of the city.

It is in the context then, of a contrast between kin-based and temple-based communities that we should view the blood-consciousness in the Israelite cult and its apparent absence in the Mesopotamian temple.

WERE THE FIRSTBORN SACRIFICED TO YHWH?
TO MOLEK? POPULAR PRACTICE OR
DIVINE DEMAND?

Jacob Milgrom

Many scholars have conjectured that originally Israel sacrificed its firstborn males to YHWH (literature cited in de Vaux 1964: 70, n. 69). Its purpose would be akin to that of the firstfruits of the field, namely, to induce greater fertility (cf. Morgenstern 1966: 63–64). However, one can only side with de Vaux's categorical rejection: "It would indeed be absurd to suppose that there could have been in Israel or among any other people, at any moment of their history, a constant general law, compelling the suppression of the firstborn, who are the hope of the race" (1964: 71). And if one would point to the plethora of child burials in the Punic colonies as possible evidence of sacrifice, the paucity of infant jar burials in ancient Israel would provide evidence to the contrary. Besides, as demonstrated by the excavations at Carthage, children found in a single tomb probably came from the same family (Stager and Wolff 1984: 47–49).

Most of those who maintain the sacrifice theory turn to purported textual sources, particularly to Exod 22:28–29:

> *mělēatěka wědim'ākā lōʾ těʾaḥēr běkôr bānêkā titten-lî kēn-taʿăśeh lěśōrěkā lěṣōʾněkā šibʿat yāmím yihyeh ʿim-ʾimmô bayyôm haššěmínî tittěnô-lî*

> [28]You shall not delay the first (processed) fruits of your vat and granary. You shall give me the firstborn among your sons. [29]You shall do the same with your cattle and your flocks: Seven days it shall remain with its mother; on the eighth day you shall give it to me.

Since the most recent and comprehensive advocacy of this position has been advanced by Fishbane (1985: 181–87), I shall deal with his arguments seriatim:

1. The phrase "You shall do the same with your cattle and your flocks" (v. 29a) does not, as Fishbane claims, disrupt the syntax linking vv. 28b and 29b. If v. 29b were the continuation of v. 28b, one would have expected the legist to have added v. 29a at the end, yielding: "You shall give me the firstborn among your sons: Seven days it shall remain with its mother; on the eighth day you shall

give it to me. You shall do the same with your cattle and your flocks." On the contrary, the fact that v. 29b follows v. 29a shows that the two phrases are connected, that is, the injunction to give "it" to God after the eighth day refers only to the animal but not the human firstborn. Moreover, the very examples of the *kēn-taʿăśeh* formula adduced by Fishbane (1985: 177–81): Deut 22:1–3 (cf. Exod 23:4) and Exod 23:10–11 (cf. Lev 25:47) as well as its other attestations. Exod 26:4, 17; Deut 20:15; Exek 45:20, demonstrate that it applies only to the cases that follow. Thus v. 29 is a unity, and if there is an addition in Exod 22:28–29 it is all of v. 29.

2. The syntax of v. 29 (MT) is not "grammatically awkward." The lack of a *waw* connecting *lĕšōrĕka lĕṣōʾnĕkā* indicates that each noun is to be treated separately so that the following sg. verbs are correct. (Indeed, even if a *waw* were present it could mean "or," e.g., Exod 21:15).

3. The attempt to interpret Num 18:15a as connoting the sacrifice of firstborn human males is misbegotten. The verb *yaqrîbû* here does not mean "will sacrifice" but "will contribute, donate" (e.g., Num 7:2, 10–12, etc.).

4. Ezek 16:21 and 23:39 do not speak of the firstborn; Ezek 20:25–26 is discussed below.

It is crucial to keep in mind that the verb *nātan* "give" in sacrificial contexts (occurring twice in Exod 22:28–29) is neutral. In no way does it imply that the "given" object need be sacrificed. The three occurrences of this verb in Lev 18:20, 21, 23 certainly do not mean "sacrifice." Indeed, in the Molek prohibition (v. 21) which clearly refers to a sacrifice, an additional verb *lĕhaʿăbîr* has to be added to denote a sacrifice (cf. also Ezek 16:21). The same holds true for *nātan* in many other sacrificial contexts (e.g., Exod 30:12, 13; Num 18:12). And of course, the Levites who are "given" to the priests (Num 3:9; 8:19) are not sacrificed; neither is Samuel who is "given" to God (1 Sam 1:11). That *mattānâ* 'gift' can refer to firstborn sacrifice (Ezek 20:31; cf. Levenson 1993: 31) is countered by Num 18:6, 7 where it refers to the dedication of the Levites and priests to the sanctuary (cf. also Exod 28:38; Deut 16:17 and see now Brin 1994: 215–17). Moreover, the ambiguous term *titten* (Exod 22:28b) is rendered *tipdeh* 'you shall redeem' in the reworked passage, Exod 34:20—an inner biblical halakhic midrash (Bar-On 1998: 166–67). Finally, just as the "first (processed) fruits of your vat and granary" (for the rendering of *mĕlĕʾātĕkā* and *dimʿăkā*, see Milgrom 1976: 61, n. 216) are "given", i.e., dedicated to the priests but not to the altar, so also are the firstborn. How the firstborn is "given," whether as human or animal, is not stated. Thus the meaning of *nātan* in Exod 22:28–29 is equivalent to *qaddēš* 'dedicate' in Exod 13:2 (see below).

Jon Levenson's thesis (1993: 3–31) that before the advent of the seventh-century prophets. Jeremiah and Ezekiel, YHWH not only approved but also demanded the sacrifice of the firstborn is subject to question. He adduces as evidence the following four cases: the binding of Isaac (*ʿăqēdâ*, Gen 22), the vow of Jephthah (Judg 11:29–40), the sacrifice of Mesha (2 Kgs 3:26–27) and the accusations of the prophets (Ezek 20:25–26; Mic 6:6–8).

To start with, the basic fact must be set forth: But for the case of the *ʿăqēdâ*, God does not demand the sacrifice of the firstborn. Jephthah's vow is no different than the war *ḥērem* (e.g., Num 21:1–3): Both are conditioned by *do ut des*, a bargain with God, repaying God for granting victory over the enemy. Mesha pays his god in advance. His act is not unique. Classical sources report the frequent sacrifice of children in cities under siege in Phoenicia and its north African colonies (cf. Weinfeld 1972: 133–40 for a survey of the evidence). To be sure, these sacrifices are premised on the widespread belief that human sacrifice, especially of one's own child, is the most efficacious gift of all and, as evidenced by the narratives about Jephthah and Mesha, that it works. This fact stands out in the case of Mesha since the lifting of the siege effected by his sacrifice totally cancels Elisha's victory prophecy to the forces of Israel and their Edomite ally (2 Kgs 3:18). Again, these narratives only reflect popular belief. Indeed, even the great prophets in their opposition to this practice never deny that it could be efficacious.

Certainly, Abraham's sacrifice of Isaac is explicitly demanded by God. Levenson, correctly in my view, citing archaeological evidence from Punic tophet urns of animal bones that were found alongside urns of children's bones, concludes that "the lamb or kid *could* take the place of the child, but at no period was the parent *obligated* to make the substitution. This strikes me as essentially the situation in Genesis 22, where Abraham is *allowed* to sacrifice the ram instead of Isaac but never *commanded* to do so" (1993: 21).

As a result of this statement, Levenson is forced to conclude that the firstborn "given" to God in Exod 22:28 is commutable to an animal. In effect, Levenson is admitting that the verb *nätan* means

"dedicate," cf. Num 18:6; Speiser, 1963. To be sure, *in theory*, the
father has the option to sacrifice his firstborn. But is that what God
wants? The only such example is the story of the ʿăqēdâ. Abraham
could not have been shocked—in fact he did not demur—when commanded by God to sacrifice Isaac, since child sacrifice occurred in
his contemporary world, if not frequently, certainly *in extremis*. Abraham,
however, could not exercise this option. He could not take along a
substitute animal (note Isaac's question and Abraham's reply, Gen
22:7–8). Isaac may have intuited that he was the intended victim,
but in effect he asked his father: don't you have a substitute animal? And Abraham, in replying that God will provide the animal,
was actually hoping that at the last minute God would change his
mind and allow for an animal. By this reading, the suppressed prayer
of the two protagonists surfaces into view and the tension mounts.
God *demanded* the sacrifice of Isaac and Abraham complied. Thus
he passed the test of faith. Why, then, does the story not continue
(and end) with the divine blessing (vv. 15–19); why the intervening
story of the ram (vv. 12–14)? The key is that God, *not Abraham*, provided the animal. It was an indication that, henceforth, the option
of animal or child, as practiced by Israel's neighbors, remains theoretical for Israel. God, however, prefers the sacrifice of an animal.

Another point: Abraham's test was not that Isaac's death would
have been a violation of the divine promise of progeny. According
to the epic (JE) tradition no such promise had been given to Abraham.
Gen 17 is H, and God's intention in Gen 18:18 is undisclosed. As
for the vague promise of Gen 12:2, it could have been and was
fulfilled through Ishmael (note the common expression gòy gādôl, Gen
12:2; 21:18). The promise of progeny is bestowed on Abraham as
a reward for his unflinching faith (Gen 22:16–18).

"I gave them laws that were not good and rules by which they
could not live" (Ezek 20:25–26; cf. also v. 31). Rather than denying that God ever sanctioned human sacrifice as does his older contemporary Jeremiah (Jer 7:31; 19:5; 32:35). Ezekiel uniquely takes
the tack that God deliberately gave such a law in order to desolate
them. The only way to justify Ezekiel's theodicy is that the people
misinterpreted either Exod 22:28b (de Vaux 1964: 72) or Exod 13:1–2
(see below), or that God deliberately misled them to punish them
(Greenberg 1983, 368–70; Hals 1989: 141), on the analogy of God
hardening Pharaoh's heart or Israel's heart (Isa 6:9–10; 63:17), but

not that "YHWH once commanded the sacrifice of the first-born but now opposes it" (Levenson 1993: 8). If that were the case, the prophet would have said so, as he did whenever a person radically altered his behavior (cf. Ezek chap. 18).

Thus, Ezekiel does not contradict Jeremiah's view that the people were mistaken in believing that God demanded human sacrifice; he supports it by the example of the firstborn males, whom the people sacrifice because they erroneously assumed it was God's will (or because they did not realize it was God's condign punishment).

Mic 6:7b: "Shall I give my firstborn for my transgression, the fruit of my body for my sin?" This verse unambigously states that the practice of sacrificing the firstborn was known and commonly thought to be desired by God. Its function is piacular, i.e., in a time of crisis (*pace* Ackerman 1992: 140), but not for fertility. Diana Ackerman's citation of votive sacrifices of children as indicated in Phoenician and Punic stelae cannot be used as evidence to the contrary. First, it is methodologically unsound to base an argument (in our case for biblical Israel) from another culture without additional supporting evidence. Then, one might ask: Are not all vows responses to crises, which must be exceptionally great if the sacrifice is one's own child? Finally, Ackerman's only textual support that child sacrifice was a frequent occurrence in Israel is plural *bannĕḥālim* (Isa 57:5), a reference to many wadis where child sacrifice took place. Assuming that this difficult verse and its equally difficult context speak of child sacrifice, it is still precarious to draw any conclusion from a single verse, much less a single word. In my opinion (equally conjectural) the plural form *bannĕḥālîm* 'in the wadis' suggests that with the official (under Manasseh) Molek site in the Valley of Hinnom permanently defiled by Josiah (2 Kgs 23:10), postexilic Israelites were forced to continue their *private* Molek worship in other wadis. This does not imply, however, that child sacrifice occurred frequently.

Ackerman (1992: 161) categorically states that Exod 13:1–2, 13, 15; 22:28; 34:19–20; Num 3:13; 8:17–18; 18:15 refer to child sacrifice, all without substantiation. Exod 13:2; 22–28: Num 18:15 have been refuted above. Exod 13:13, 15; 34:19–20 call for redemption not sacrifice, and Num 13:13; 8:17–18 deal with the substitution of the first-born by Levites (Milgrom 1990a: 17–18). In all these cases redemption is for service not sacrifice. It therefore was optional and rare, not mandatory and frequent, and it is categorically rejected by God. In any event, Micah's question reflects popular belief not divine law.

Michael Fishbane (1985: 181–82, n. 90) also adduces Exod 13:2 "Consecrate to me every firstborn: man and beast, the first issue of every womb among the Israelites is mine." As shown by Brin (1971: 148, n. 22), what man and beast have in common is the sanctification of their firstborn, which is explicated by the second statement that they must be transferred to the domain of God. But nothing is said concerning the *method* of sanctification (on which see Exod 13:12–13). Although Exod 13:2 can be interpreted as referring to an earlier practice of dedicating the firstborn to lifelong service in the sanctuary (cf. Rashbam, *ad loc.*)—an interpretation grounded in the priestly texts and in ancient Near Eastern parallels—it in no way allows for or alludes to the sacrifice of the firstborn. All that can be said is that the verb *pâdâ* 'ransom' used in connection with the firstborn (Exod 13:13, 15; 34:20; Num 18:15–17) implies that *in theory* the firstborn should be sacrificed. Israel's God, however, has decreed that they should be ransomed.

Furthermore, it is significant that the priestly laws exclusively use the verb *pādâ* rather than its near synonym *gā'al* for the redemption of the firstborn (Exod 13:13; Num 3:46–51; 18:15–17); *gā'al* signifies that the dedicated object originally belonged to the donor, whereas *pâdâ* implies that, from the outset, it was the property of the sanctuary, i.e., of YHWH (see Milgrom 1990: 152). Such is the case in Num 18:15. The first half *kol-peṭer reḥem . . . bā'ādām ubabbĕhēmâ yihyeh-lak*. "The first issue of the womb . . . human or animal shall be yours" is a general law. It stipulates that *theoretically* the firstborn belongs to the priest. That is, the meat of the sacrificial firstling is a priestly prebend, and the firstborn is a servant of the sanctuary (cf. Milgrom on Num 3:1990: 17–18, 22–24). The second half of the verse *'ak pādōh tipdeh 'ēt bĕkôr hā'ādām* is a (later?) qualification. *In practice* the priest shall see to it that the human firstborn is redeemed.

Finally, the suggestion that the Molek cult was dedicated to the sacrifice of the male firstborn must be dismissed out of hand. As recognized by Mosca (1975: 236–37; cf. Heider 1985: 254), daughters as well as sons were sacrificed to Molek (Deut 18:10; 2 Kgs 23:10; Jer 7:31; 32:35), and if 2 Chr 28:3; 33:6 are credible witnesses, in addition to the firstborn, children of the same family were sacrificed (Day 1989: 67). Moreover, Stager's excavations at Carthage (1980: 4–5) show that in earlier centuries only single-child urns are in evidence, but in the fourth century, one out of three burial urns contained two or three children from the same family! Ackerman's proposal (1992: 138–39) of an evolution from firstborn to multiple child sacrifice, based on this Carthagenian evidence is unwarranted. First, there is no evidence that the single-child urns were only of firstborn. Nor can any support be mustered for her thesis from biblical or ancient Near Eastern texts.

In sum, there is no evidence that the firstborn, except in crisis situations (e.g., 2 Kgs 3:27), were sacrificed; there is no indication that Israel's God ever demanded or even sanctioned this practice (except in popular belief); and there is no connection between the firstborn and the Molek.

BIBLIOGRAPHY

Ackerman, S. 1992. *Under Every Green Tree*. Atlanta: Scholars Press.
Bar-On, Sh. 1998. The Festive Calendars in Exod xiii 14–19 and xxxiv 18–26 *VT* 48:161–95.
Brin, G. 1971. The First Born in Israel in the Biblical Period. Univ. of Tel Aviv dissertation (Hebrew).
———— 1994. *Studies in Biblical Law*. Sheffield: JSOT Press.
Day, J. 1989. *Molech: A God of Human Sacrifice in the Old Testament*. Cambridge: Univ. of Cambridge Press.
Fishbane, M. 1985. *Biblical Interpretation in Ancient Israel*. Oxford: Clarendon.
Greenberg, M. 1983. *Ezekiel 1–20*. Garden City, NY: Doubleday.
Halls, R.M. 1989. *Ezekiel*. Grand Rapids, MI: Eerdmans.
Heider, G.C. 1985. *The Cult of Molek*. Sheffield: JSOT Press.
Levenson, J.D. 1993. *The Death and Resurrection of the Beloved Son*. New Haven, CT: Yale Univ. Press.
Milgrom, J. 1976. *Cult and Conscience*. Leiden: Brill.
———— 1990. *Numbers*. Philadelphia: Jewish Publication Society.
Morgenstern, J. 1966. *Rites of Birth, Marriage, Death and Kindred Occasions Among the Semites*. Cincinnati: Hebrew Union College Press.
Mosca, P.G. 1975. Child Sacrifice in Canaanite and Israelite Religion. A Study in Mulk and Molech. Harvard University dissertation.
Stager, L.E. 1980. The Rite of Child Sacrifice at Carthage. Pp. 1–12 in *New Light on Ancient Carthage*. Ed. J.G. Pedley. Ann Arbor, MI: Univ. of Michigan Press.
Stager, L.E. and S.R. Wolff 1984. Child Sacrifice at Carthage: Religious Rite or Population Control? *BAR* 10.1:30–51.
de Vaux, R. 1964. *Studies in Old Testament Sacrifice*. Cardiff: Univ. of Wales Press.
Weinfeld, M. 1972. The Worship of Molech and of the Queen of Heaven and its Background. *UF* 4:133–54.

THE SEMIOTICS OF THE PRIESTLY VESTMENTS IN ANCIENT JUDAISM

Michael D. Swartz

> Once upon a time, the ruler of a vast empire
> wanted to prepare for a great procession by com-
> missioning an exquisite new garment to wear. He
> enlisted his best tailors, who made a great fuss of
> fitting him and flattering him on how splendid he
> looked. The day came and the great procession
> began. Then all of a sudden, a child exclaimed,
> "But the emperor isn't wearing any clothes!"
>   So the adults said to the child, "Silly child! Don't
> you know that clothes are culturally constructed
> anyway? Go home and read your Foucault!"

The Emperor's New Clothes is a story about what happens when a
player in a ritual reveals the rules of the game. This type of self-
consciousness is one factor that allows for ritual discourse—the systematic thinking about ritual that characterizes modern anthropology
and religious studies, and that we find in different manifestations in
some forms of Neoplatonism, early Christianity, Mīmāṃsā Hinduism,
and, it can be argued, Hellenistic and Rabbinic Judaism.[1] This discussion will explore one example of ancient ritual discourse: the
significance of the vestments in Jewish sources on sacrifice in the
Hellenistic and Roman periods.[2] Sources for this study will include

---

[1] The most thorough recent account of the enterprise of ritual theory is Catherine
Bell, *Ritual Theory, Ritual Practice* (New York and Oxford: Oxford University Press,
1992). Although there is much literature on ritual theory, there is less on how pre-
modern or non-Western religious communities engage in ritual theory or comparable forms of discourse. See for example, Francis X. Clooney, *Thinking Ritually:
Rediscovering the Pūrva Mīmāṃsā of Jaimini* (Vienna: Sammlung De Nobili, 1990) and
Veena Das, "The Language of Sacrifice," *Man* (n.s.) 18 (1983), 445–62.

[2] This topic is occasioned by two related concerns in my current research. The
first is a study in progress of concepts of sacrifice in post-biblical Judaism, focusing
particularly on depictions of the Yom Kippur sacrifice from the second-temple period
to the late Talmudic era. This study will deal with the question of whether we can
discern systems of ritual theory in antiquity; see also Michael D. Swartz, "Sage,
Priest, and Poet: Typologies of Leadership in the Ancient Synagogue," in Steven
Fine (ed.), *Jews, Christians and Polytheists in the Ancient Synagogue: Cultural Interaction During*

Hellenistic writers such as Philo and Josephus as well as the Talmuds and midrashim of Late Antiquity. Another important source will be the genre of synagogue poetry (*piyyut*), written in the fourth through seventh centuries, that depict the Yom Kippur service. These poems, known as the *Avodah* piyyutim, are striking for their extensive preambles surveying the mythic history of the world in such a way that it leads to the description of the cult and their minute poetic descriptions of the sacrificial procedure. But they are also striking in their inclusion of long excursuses on the vestments of the high priest as he performs the morning sacrifice. The length and richness of this description deserve to be accounted for.

Why focus on the priestly vestments in a volume on sacrifice? First of all, it will be shown here that the vestments served as a significant component in how ancient Jews saw biblical sacrifice. Moreover, the case of the vestments illustrates an important set of dynamics in the way we study sacrifice and ritual in general: the relationship between the instrumental and the expressive as indicators of meaning in ritual.

I. *Method*

The subject of the vestments of the priest brings us to a nexus of dress and ritual, both popular subjects for systems of signification. In his book *The Fashion System*, Roland Barthes lays down a basic principle for understanding discourse about the most well-developed system of discourse about dress, "fashion:"

> A Fashion Utterance involves at least two systems of information: a specifically linguistic system, which is a language (such as French or English), and a "vestimentary" system according to which the garment (*prints, accessories, a pleated skirt, a halter top*, etc.) signifies either the world (the races, springtime, maturity) or Fashion.[3]

───────────

the Greco-Roman Period, (London: Routledge, 1999), 101–17; and "Ritual about Myth about Ritual: Toward an Understanding of the *Avodah* in the Rabbinic Period," *JJTP* 6 (1997), 135–55. The second concern is an interest in non-textual systems of meaning in Rabbinic civilization, in which the topic of exegesis of material details in the cult plays a role. I wish to thank Professors Joseph Yahalom, Emily Sokoloff, Itzik Gottesman, and Uri Ehrlich for their suggestions on matters relating to this article.

[3] Roland Barthes, *The Fashion System* (trans. Matthew Ward and Richard Howard; New York: Hill and Wang, 1983), 27. Italics in the original.

Substitute the world *ritual* for fashion and you have an account of some of the factors involved in analyzing ancient ritual theory. First, there is the language of our sources—not only Hebrew and Greek but the exegetical, historical, and legal nuances carried by them. Beyond this, we have a system of utterances about ritual by which ritual details, ostensibly opaque in themselves, can represent either cosmic, mythic, or moral elements or the world of ritual behavior— such as the world of the Patriarchs, Temple or city cult—that such utterances are meant to evoke. The self-consciousness that ritual is in need of decoding in such a way and that there are methods by which we can do so constitutes ancient ritual theory and corresponds nicely with the semiotic analysis of clothing.

Of course, the garments of the priest in the ancient Temple are the very opposite of fashion. The priestly vestments are presumably eternal, and they are meant for one person on earth at a time. Indeed, an important feature of ritual is its repeatability, as against the presumed newness of fashion. But we can still learn much that is relevant to the study of ritual from the ability of clothes to signal identity, convey power, and confer on the wearer new properties.

In fact, analysis of clothing has one important sphere of affinity with the analysis of ritual. Students of the social roles of clothing stress that we can parse its function into instrumental, that is, active or performative, and representational, that is, symbolic or expressive purposes.[4] For example, the instrumental function of a coat is to

---

[4] On the idea of performative speech, a concept developed by James L. Austin, *How to Do Things With Words* (2nd ed. Cambridge: Harvard University Press, 1975) and incorporated into ritual studies, see Stanley J. Tambiah, "The Magical Power of Words," *Man* n.s. 3 (1968), 175–208. Cf. Stuart Clark's account of the semiotics of early-modern demonology, "The Magical Power of Signs," in *Thinking with Demons: The Idea of Witchcraft in Early Modern Europe* (Oxford: Clarendon, 1997), 281–93. One of the earliest analyses of the semiotics of clothing is Petr Bogatyrev, *The Functions of Folk Costume in Moravian Slovakia* (The Hague and Paris: Mouton, 1971); two more recent works that stress the communicative function of clothing are Ruth P. Rubinstein, *Dress Codes: Meanings and Messages in American Culture* (Boulder: Westview, 1995) and Nathan Joseph, *Uniforms and Non-Uniforms: Communication Through Clothing* New York: Greenwood Press, 1986. For a critique of linguistic models for understanding dress see Grant McCracken, "Clothing as Language: An Object Lesson in the Study of the Expressive Properties of Material Culture," in Barrie Reynolds and Margaret A. Stott, *Material Anthropology: Contemporary Approaches to Material Culture* (Lanham, MD: University Press of America, 1987), 103–28. An excellent analysis of the significance of dress for Jewish prayer in the Rabbinic period that takes theories of nonverbal communication into account is Uri Ehrlich, *"Kol ʿAṣmotai Tomarnah: Ha-Safah ha-lo*

keep the wearer warm, and the representative function of the same
coat is to signal the wearer's social status, youth or maturity (or aspi-
rations to youth or maturity), and even his or her religious or political affiliation. Indeed, one can look to any highly factionalized
religious environment, such as eighteenth-century Philadelphia or
twentieth-century Jerusalem, for some fine examples of the political
nuances of coats and headgear. A system of discourse about clothing—
say, fashion magazines or dress codes—wraps around these functions
a vocabulary imparting them immediacy, significance, and value.
Likewise, a system of discourse about ritual—be it Victor Turner,
the Sutra of Jaimini, Philo of Alexandria, or the Mishnah—creates
criteria by which the material details of a procedure are meant to
say more. It will be argued here that the distinction between instrumental and representational or expressive notions of interpretation
helps us understand ancient readings of these particular ritual garments.

The potency of the vestments as indicators of status and cultic
objects can be illustrated by observing how they served as a source
of contention in Palestine during Roman rule. According to Josephus,
the sacred garments were a subject of an ongoing custody battle
between the Roman authorities and the priestly administration of
the Temple. In his *Jewish Antiquities*,[5] the historian relates that the
robe of the High Priest was kept in the Antonia fortress, under state
control, for safe keeping under Herod and was only relinquished for
festivals and Yom Kippur under an elaborate protocol. The Roman
governor Vitellus returned them to the custody of the priests, but
when Fadus later took them back, according to Josephus, the Jews
protested and the Emperor Claudius feared that the protest would
fan into rebellion.[6]

When the Temple was destroyed in 70 CE, the vestments, like all
the accouterments of the cult, became of necessity not a physical
object but an object of discourse only. In response to the loss of the
cult, the Rabbis continued to describe it and speculate about its regulations, yet held that the study of sacrifice was a worthy equivalent

Milulit shel ha-Tefila" (Jerusalem: Magnes, 1999) 128–147. For a survey of studies
on Jewish dress, see Yedida K. Stillman, "Jewish Costume and Textile Studies: The
State of the Art," *Jewish Folklore and Ethnology Review* 10 (1988), 5–9.
    [5] Josephus *Ant.* 15.403–8, 20.6–16, and 19.93; See also *Bell.* 6.389.
    [6] See Gedalyahu Alon, *Jews, Judaism, and the Classical World* (Jerusalem: Magnes,
1977), 85–88, and Seth Schwartz, *Josephus and Judean Politics* (Leiden: Brill, 1990),
154–6.

of the act itself. At the same time, the poets of the synagogue constructed elaborate recreations of the central annual sacrifice, the
Avodah of the Day of Atonement, in which they tried to render the
cult as vivid as possible.[7] An examination of how each of these groups
interpreted the vestments can serve as a model for understanding
the changing attitudes of generations of Jews to the sacrificial system.

II. *The components of the Priestly vestments*

The fundamental biblical sources for the vestments of the priesthood
are Exodus chapters 28 and 39, from the Priestly code (P) of the
Pentateuch. Leviticus 8:6–9 also contains a brief narrative description.[8]
The Mishnah, compiled at the beginning of the third century CE,
classifies the vestments by distinguishing between the four garments
of the ordinary priests and the four additional components added to
those of the High Priest. *M. Yoma* 7:5 lists them in this way:[9]

> The High Priest serves in eight garments (Heb. *kelim*) and the com-
> mon priest in four.
> 1. a fringed linen tunic (*kutonet*);
> 2. breeches (*mikhnasayim*);
> 3. a royal headdress (*misnefet*);
> 4. and a sash (*avnet*).
>
> The High Priest adds to this:
>
> 1. the breastpiece (*hošen*, also known as breastpiece of judgment);
> 2. the ephod (a richly ornamented garment);
> 3. a robe (*me'il*, the hem of which was lined with cloth pomegranates
>   and bells, apparently in an alternating pattern).
> 4. The frontlet (*sis*, also translated as diadem).

---

[7] On early Rabbinic attitudes to sacrifice see Jacob Neusner, "Map Without
Territory: The Mishnah's System of Sacrifice." *History of Religions* 19 (1979), 103–27.
On theories of sacrifice in liturgical poetry see Swartz, "Ritual about Myth about
Ritual;" on the contrast between the two approaches, see Swartz, "Sage, Priest, and
Poet."

[8] For an analysis of the biblical sources on the vestments see Menahem Haran,
*Temples and Temple Service in Ancient Israel: An Inquiry into the Character of Cult Phenomena
and the Historical Setting of the Priestly School* (Oxford: Clarendon, 1978), 165–74. For
commentaries to Exodus 28 and 39 see also Nahum Sarna's commentary to those
chapters in *Exodus: The Traditional Hebrew Text with the New JPS Translation: Commentary
by Nahum M. Sarna* (Philadelphia: Jewish Publication Society, 1991).

[9] This translation of terms for the vestments is based on the NJV, slightly modified.
Explanatory notes are placed in parentheses.

Here the Mishnah adds, referring to the divinitory instruments attested in Exod 28:30 and elsewhere:

> In these [garments] he would inquire of the Urim and Thumim.

The breastpiece contained twelve precious stones, the exact identity of which is still in doubt, engraved with the names of the twelve tribes. Two shoulder straps on the ephod contained stones, which are designated as "stones of remembrance of the children of Israel." In addition, according to Leviticus 16:4, the High Priest changed from the golden garments of the daily service (the *Tamid*) to fine white garments (*bad*) when he entered the Holy of Holies once a year in his encounter with the Divine Presence.[10] Rabbinic classifications distinguished between those white garments and the gold garments of the rest of the year.[11]

More informally, it is possible to divide the garments according to materials and functions:

1. cloth garments for covering: breeches, robe, tunic, and sash;
2. headgear: *miṣnefet*, perhaps the diadem (cf. below), and, according to Josephus and Ben Sira, a crown;[12]
3. ornamental or cultic objects: The breastpiece and the precious stones, and perhaps the diadem, which functions more as a cultic object than headgear. It is possible that the ephod fits into this category as well. Here can also be added the bells and pomegranates on the robe, which are the object of some speculation in interpretations.

These latter categories are not exact. It is unwise to divide too sharply between utilitarian objects, such as the robe, and ornamental objects, such as the breastpiece. All of these garments had cultic value and were revered by interpreters both for their ritually instrumental and

---

[10] On second-temple depictions of the vestments see Douglas R. Edwards, "The Social, Religious, and Political Aspects of Costume in Josephus," in Judith Lynn Sebesta and Larissa Bonfante, *The World of Roman Costume* (Madson: University of Wisconsin Press, 1994), 156–57; and Alfred Rubens, *History of Jewish Costume* (2nd ed. London: Peter Owens, 1981). On Jewish dress in general in late antiquity see Lucille A. Roussin, "Costume in Roman Palestine: Archaeological Remains and the Evidence from the Mishnah," in Sebesta and Bonafante, *World of Roman Costume*, 182–90.

[11] See *m. Yoma* 7:3–4 and *y. Yoma* 7:3 (44b).

[12] See Sir 45:12 and Josephus *Ant.* 3.172–78; see especially Ralph Marcus's commentary in LCL ad loc.

symbolic properties. At the same time, the terms for some of these objects could be used for non-cultic purposes and go back to secular functions. To give an example from Rabbinic civilization, the term *avnet*, which designates the sash worn by priests, is used in the Talmud and medieval sources to designate an ordinary sash or belt worn by Jews.[13] Josephus uses both culturally specific terminology, such as the transliterated term *essén* for the *ḥošen* or breastpiece, and common Greek terms, such as *chiton*, for the robe or *me'il*. Nevertheless, most of the more ornamental objects such as the stones and the frontlet serve as objects of special attention by interpreters.

In the second-Temple period, much effort went into describing this apparatus, particularly in Greek-Jewish sources. Josephus, Philo, the Letter of Aristeas, and Pseudo-Philo all describe it in lavish detail.[14] Josephus in particular adds many details we would not have known otherwise, and some details that only emerge later in the Avodah piyyutim.[15] Rabbinic literature contains a good deal of material on the subject, although it is difficult to gauge whether the amount of material is disproportionate in comparison to its interest in other subjects. One basic exegetical discussion, which appears in Palestinian sources as well as the Babylonian Talmud, will be analyzed below. In addition, the extensive excursuses on the vestments in the Avodah piyyutim deserve special attention because of their aesthetic properties and because they form a systematic statement.[16]

---

[13] See, for example, *b. BK* 94b; cf. Yeruham b. Meshulam's 14th-century code *Toledot Adam ve-Ḥavah* (Venice, 1553), fol. 26b, in which the *avnet* has the ancillary function of preventing lewd thoughts during prayer. See Ehrlich, "*Darkhe ha-Tefillah*," 149.

[14] Josephus, *Ant.* 3.151–78 and *Bell.* 5.227–36; *Ep. Arist.* 96–99; Philo, *Vita Mosis* 2.109–35; *Spec. Leg.* 1.82–97.

[15] See, for example, Aaron Mirsky, *Piyyute Yose ben Yose* (2nd ed. Jerusalem: Mossad Bialik, 1991), 160 and Joseph Yahalom, *Az be-'En Kol: Seder ha-'Avodah ha-'Eres-Yisra'eli ha-Qadum le-Yom ha-Qippurim* (Jerusalem: Magnes, 1996), 126.

[16] Two iconographic sources from these periods should be mentioned here. The mosaic from the synagogue in Sepphoris does depict a sacrificing priest; however, most of the figure of the priest has been destroyed. Only a small fragment of the garment remains; it is bluish with yellow dots. A bell on the hem of the robe is also visible; on this detail of the vestments, which is significant in several interpretative schemes, see below. The figure of Abraham at Mt. Moriah is also mostly destroyed, although his shoes are off; this may reinforce the Rabbinic assertion that the High Priest officiated barefoot in the Temple. See Ze'ev Weiss and Ehud Netzer, *Promise and Redemption: A Synagogue Mosaic from Sepphoris* (Jerusalem: The Israel Museum, 1996), 20. In the Dura paintings, Aaron wears a vestment rich in details based on the biblical descriptions but at the same time indebted to Persian styles. His robe is, however, blue with yellow dots as in the Sepphoris mosaic. See C.H. Kraeling,

III. *Elements of interpretation*

Interpretations of the vestments fall into several motifs, some more pronounced in some sources than others:

1. Midrashic and esoteric traditions (such as magical and divination texts) contain stories of the miraculous origin and properties of the vestments.
2. One of the most widely attested motifs sees the priest as a symbol of Israel and its representative in the sacred realm.
3. Another, found mainly in Philo, Josephus, and the Wisdom of Solomon, sees in the priestly vestments a model of the cosmos.
4. A type of interpretation, found especially in late antique and early medieval sources, focuses on the active capacity of the garments to procure atonement or perform some metaphysical or material task.
5. There are also intriguing hints at a type of interpretation that sees the vestments as conferring upon the High Priest aspects of divinity, or at least significations of divine authority.

A. *The miraculous origin of the vestments*

Second-temple and Rabbinic sources hint at the supernatural origin of the priestly vestments.[17] According to several midrashim, the priestly vestments were the very same garments that God had provided for Adam in Eden. C.T.R. Hayward argues that this idea may go back to the Second-Temple era.[18] In Jubillees, Adam offers an incense offering immediately after he dons his garments.[19] Furthermore, Jerome and Syriac exegetes explicitly link the priestly vestments with the garments of Adam, suggesting that they were familiar with the idea from earlier sources.[20]

This notion is fully developed in several Rabbinic midrashim. In Genesis 2:21, following Adam and Eve's expulsion from the garden,

---

The Excavations at Dura Europos: The Synagogue (Final Report vol. 8 Part 1) (New Haven: Yale University Press, 1956; repr. New York: Ktav, 1979), 126–28.

[17] For the example of the gems on the breastpiece in second-Temple sources, see Robert Hayward, "Pseudo-Philo and the Priestly Oracle," *JJS* 46 (1995), 48–54.

[18] See C.T.R. Hayward, *The Jewish Temple: A Non-Biblical Sourcebook* (London and New York: Routledge, 1996), 45–47.

[19] Jub 3:26–27. See Hayward, *The Jewish Temple*, 90.

[20] Ibid., p. 45.

God makes skin tunics (*kotenot ʿor*) for them. The Rabbis find in this phrase occasion to make two wordplays: One, between the word for skin—*ʿor*, written with the letter *ʿayin*—and light—*ʾor*, written with the letter *ʾalef*. The other wordplay concerns the occurrence of the word *kotenot*, which is also used to describe the priest's tunic. Genesis Rabbah states:

> In the Torah of Rabbi Meir they found written robes of *light*. These were the garments of the first Adam that were like a lantern, wide at the bottom and narrow at the top. R. Revayah said: they were as smooth as a fingernail and as lovely as a jewel. R. Yoḥanan said: They were like the delicate linen garments that come from Bet She'an. Resh Lakish said: It was milk-white[21] and the first-born used to use it.[22]

In this midrash, most of the interpreters describe the lumnious beauty of the garment. But Resh Lakish adds that the first-born of each family used the cloak to officiate as family priest. Tanḥuma Buber expands this idea, although it does not emend "skin" to "light" as Genesis Rabbah did:

> How does Israel honor the Sabbath? With eating and drinking and clean clothes, for that is what the Holy One, Blessed Be He did from the beginning, as it is said: "And the Lord God made for the man and his wife tunics of skin and clothed them." [Gen 3:21]. What is a tunic (*ketonet*) of skin? High-Priestly garments in which the Holy One, Blessed be He dressed them, as he was the first-born of the world.
>
> And further our Rabbis taught:[23] Until the tabernacle was erected high-places[24] were permitted and sacrifice[25] was performed by the first-born. Therefore the Holy One, Blessed be He dressed Adam in garments of the High Priesthood, for he was the first-born of the world. Noah came and handed it down to Shem, and Shem to Abraham and Abraham to Isaac and Isaac to Esau, who was the first-born. But Esau saw his wives practicing idolatry and gave it to his mother for safe-keeping. When Jacob took the birthright from Esau, Rebecca said, "since Jacob took the birthright from Esau, it is only right that he should wear those garments," as it is said: "and Rebecca took Esau's best garments that were with her in the house and put them on Jacob her younger son" (Gen 27:15).[26]

---

[21] Gk. *galaktinon*.

[22] *Bereshit Rabbah* (ed. Theodor-Albeck) 20:12, pp. 196–97.

[23] See *Tanḥ. Buber. Toledot* 4.

[24] Heb. *bamot*. On the permitting of the high-places cf. b. *Zeb.* 112b and b. *Meg.* 10a.

[25] Heb. *ʿAvodah*.

[26] *Tanḥ. Buber Toledot* 12.

This brief but complex tale weaves together several exegetical and literary motifs. Although its initial premise is the idea that Israel honors the Sabbath by wearing clean clothes,[27] its principal subject is the origin of the garments of the patriarchal priesthood. The beginning and end points are exegeses of two verses from Genesis that relate the garments mentioned in both scriptural verses to a single garment, a skin tunic, which is handed down from generation to generation. This tunic is identified both as the first clothing of Adam and as the garment of Esau in which Rebecca dressed Jacob to deceive Isaac. That garment is none other than the primordial garment of the high priesthood of the pre-tabernacle family cult—the antecedent of Aaron's vestments. As the garment was passed down from father to son, Isaac was deceived not simply because Rebecca had disguised Jacob as Esau, but because Isaac would presume that Esau not Jacob would be wearing the ancestral vestment.[28]

The structure of the midrash is a folkloric and literary motif common to the Hellenistic world, identified by Henry Fischel as the *sorites* or chain of tradition,[29] in which an object or tradition is passed down through a succession of ideal figures. The most famous example of the sorites in Rabbinic literature is the opening Mishnah of the tractate *Avot*, or Sayings of the Fathers, by which Torah is transmitted from God to Moses through generations of disciples, and eventually to the Rabbis. In this alternative sorites, the lineage is a priestly one and garment serves as the potent instrument of authority. Indeed, when Fischel first explored the idea of the sorites comparatively, his primary example from classical literature was Agamemnon's scepter in the Iliad (2.100–109), which was the signal of kingship deriving from the gods.[30] The primordial cloak functions much the same way, acting as the authorizing agent by which the chief priesthood is conferred on each successive heir.[31] The midrash thus gives the

---

[27] As with many such midrashim belonging to the *Tanḥuma-yelamdenu* genre, a question on a legal or ritual matter serves as an introduction to a discourse on a rather different subject.

[28] The detail about Esau depositing it with his mother serves to explain why it was "with her in the house" according to Gen 27:15.

[29] Henry Fischel, "The Use of Sorites (*Climax, Gradatio*) in the Tannaitic Period, *HUCA* 44 (1973), 119–51; on its uses in the literature of early Jewish mysticism and magic see Michael D. Swartz, *Scholastic Magic: Ritual and Revelation in Early Jewish Mysticism.* (Princeton: Princeton University Press, 1996), 173–205.

[30] Fischel, "Sorites" 124–26. Cf. Isaac Heinemann, *Darkhe ha-ʾAggadah* (Jerusalem: Magnes and Masada, 1970), 30; and Swartz, *Scholastic Magic*, pp. 197–98

[31] In another midrash (*Bereshit Rabbah* 63:13, ed. Theodor-Albeck, p. 697), the

vestment an instrumental role in validating the priesthood. More strikingly, it traces the origin of that instrument to God Himself, who first made it for Adam, the first-born of the world.

Another midrash reinforces the idea of the divine derivation of the priestly vestments by associating them with a miracle. In the tractate *Mekhilta de-Millu'im*, an early Rabbinic commentary to Leviticus chapter 8,[32] God Himself is said to provide the priests with garments. When Aaron is about to die, God commands Moses to take off Aaron's garments and put them on his son Eleazar. The midrash asks how he could put them on Eleazar in correct order, for if he did so he would have to take off Aaron's undergarments before dressing Eleazar, thus leaving him standing nude in front of everyone.[33] The answer is that a miracle happened. When Aaron took off his priestly garments, he was wearing "the garments of the *Shekhinah*" (the divine presence) under them. Thus God honored him "more in his death than in his life."

Other accounts of the miraculous qualities of the vestments focus particularly on the stones of the shoulders and the breastpiece and the Urim and Thumim, said to be worn in the ephod. These often focus on their divinitory powers. According to Josephus, the stones on the shoulders flashed the appropriate message.[34] In the middle ages, these traditions are related to esoteric gemology.[35] Some traditions about those gems attested in the piyyut only crop up again in medieval and Renaissance interpreters like Baḥya ben Asher and Abraham Portaleone.[36]

---

cloak has the power to attract animals, and is stolen by Nimrod and passed down to Esau. See Heinemann, *Darkhe ha-'Aggadah*, 30.

[32] *Sifra Mekhilta de-Millu'im* 1:11 (ed. I.H. Weiss, Vienna, 1962), fols. 41a–b, to Lev 8:1–13: 1:6: *Mekhilta de-Millu'im* is a fragment of a composition related to *Sifra*, which was inserted into some *Sifra* manuscripts and editions. See H.L. Strack and G. Stemberger, *Introduction to the Talmud and Midrash* (Edinburgh: T&T Clark, 1991), 259–66. Cf. also the text in *Sifra or Torat Kohanim according to Codex Assemani LXVI with a Hebrew Introduction by Louis Finkelstein* (New York: Jewish Theological Seminary of America, 1956), pp. 179–98.

[33] See the commentary of Ra'abad ad loc.

[34] Josephus, *Ant.* 2.215–17; see Edwards, "Costume in Josephus," 156.

[35] On the gemological tradition see Joshua Trachtenberg, *Jewish Magic and Superstition: A Study in Folk Religion* (New York: Atheneum, 1939), 136–38 and the excerpt from *Sefer Gematriot* printed on pp. 165–68; and Moritz Steinschneider, "Lapidarien, ein culturgeschichtlicher Versuch," in George Alexander Kohut (ed.), *Semitic Studies in Memory of Rev. Dr. Alexander Kohut* (Berlin: S. Calvary, 1897), 42–72.

[36] See Bahya b. Asher, commentary to Exodus 28:15–20 and Gen. 49 (Shimon Shevel [ed.], *Rabbenu Bahyah: Bi'ur 'al ha-Torah* [Jerusalem: Mosad ha-Rav Kook, 1966–67] 1:378–95 and 2:296–302; and Abraham Portaleone, *Šilṭe ha-Gibborim*,

B. *Model of Cosmos: Philo and Josephus*

One pattern of interpretation that seems to be characteristic to Jewish-Greek literature of the second-Temple era is the idea that the vestments are a model of the cosmos. Philo is the most celebrated and systematic advocate of that idea. For example, according to his *Life of Moses*,[37] the robe, by virtue of its color and span, is "an image of the air." The pomegranates and flowers on the robe represent earth and water respectively, and the bells represent the harmony of the two. The ephod represents heaven, and the two stones represent either the hemispheres or the sun and the moon. The twelve stones on the breastpiece represent the signs of the zodiac. Josephus, who is somewhat more interested in describing the physical details of the vestments clearly, uses a very similar symbolic system, with a few variations in particulars. Recently C.T.R. Hayward has suggested the idea that the Temple and its accouterments serve for interpreters as a model of the cosmos. This idea is the centerpiece of Hayward's account of second-temple notions of the Temple.[38]

A succinct representation of that view appears in the Wisdom of Solomon. In Numbers 17:11–13, Moses and Aaron avert God's intention to annihilate the Israelites after a rebellion by offering incense. The Wisdom of Solomon describes the expiation as Aaron's action, achieved "not by bodily strength, nor by force of arms, but by word he subdued the chastiser, by recalling the oaths and covenants of the fathers." (18:22)[39] At that point it describes his vestments:

> On his full-length robe there was a representation of the entire cosmos, and the glories of the fathers upon his four rows of carved stones, and your splendor on the diadem of his head. (18:24)

The author has thus shifted our attention from a narrative that would seem to support an extreme instrumental view of ritual—that the incense itself as a material affects expiation—to a more purely representational view—that the priest represents the cosmos and Israel, and thus appeases God by persuasion.

(Mantua; repr. Jerusalem, 1970), chs. 46–50 (fols. 44a–51a). My thanks to Adam Shear for the latter reference.

[37] Philo, *Vita Mosis* 2.23–26.

[38] Hayward, *The Jewish Temple*.

[39] The translation used here is that of David Winston, *The Wisdom of Solomon: A New Translation with Introduction and Commentary* (Anchor Bible vol. 43; Garden City: Doubleday, 1979), p. 314. Cf. Yahalom, *Az be-'En Kol*, 32.

Another type of allegorical interpretation relates details of the vestments to moral qualities. In his *Questions on Exodus*, Philo relates the four rows of stones to the four virtues of knowledge, moderation, courage, and justice.[40] Naomi Cohen has shown how Philo's terminology in these sections informs his moral language as well.[41] A moral interpretation of the meaning of the vestments also appears in the Testament of Levi, in which the patriarch is instructed to don the vestments:

> And I saw seven men in white clothing who were saying to me, "Arise put on the vestments of the priesthood, the crown of righteousness, the oracle of understanding, the robe of truth, the breastplate of faith, the miter for the head, and the apron for prophetic power." (8:1–2)[42]

This variation on the purely expressive interpretation of the vestments provides an interesting contrast to Philo's. Whereas Philo's interpretation is allegorical, each row of stones *representing* a virtue, the Testament of Levi attributes to each vestment the *power* to impart a specific quality to the priest.

IV. *Representative of Israel: Rabbinic literature*

The mode of interpretation by which the priest wears a model of the cosmos seems to have been abandoned after the destruction of the Temple in 70 CE. In Rabbinic literature, the most common system of interpretation of the vestments is the idea that the priest carries signifiers of Israel with him into the sanctuary. This notion is grounded in the Torah's statement that the stones on the High Priest's shoulder straps are engraved with the names of the tribes: "And Aaron shall carry the names before the Lord on his two shoulders for remembrance" (Exod 28:12). This verse makes explicit what is also implied by the placing of the names of the tribes on the stones of the breastpiece. Ben Sira also makes poetic use of this notion in his panegyric to Aaron:

---

[40] *Quaest. in Ex.* 2.112.

[41] Naomi G. Cohen, "The Elucidation of Philo's *Spec. Leg.* 4.137–8: 'Stamped Too with Genuine Seals," in Ranon Katzoff, Yaakov Petroff, and David Schaps (eds.), *Classical Studies in Honor of David Sohlberg* (Ramat Gan: Bar-Ilan University Press, 1996), 153–66.

[42] H.C. Kee, "Testaments of the Twelve Patriarchs, in James H. Charlesworth, *The Old Testament Pseudepigrapha* 1:790–91.

Precious stones with seal engravings
in golden settings, the work of a jeweler
To commemorate in incised letters
each of the tribes of Israel. (45:11)[43]

In rabbinic literature, the idea of the priest as representative of Israel
is most clearly articulated in an exegetical essay on the significance
of the basic elements of the costume that appears in the Palestinian
Talmud, *Yoma* 7:3 (fol. 44b), in several Palestinian Midrashim, especially Leviticus Rabbah 10:6 and a Tanhuma-like fragment published
by Jacob Mann;[44] and, more extensively, in two places in the
Babylonian Talmud.[45] These passages represent an interesting dialec-
tic between representational and instrumental conceptions of the function of the garments.

The exegetical occasion for the discussion differs among the texts.
In the Talmuds the occasion is the Mishnah's list of priestly garments mentioned above, and in Leviticus Rabbah it is the preparation for the installation ceremony (*millu'im*) that Moses and Aaron
perform in Leviticus Chapter 8. The Palestinian Talmud asks why
the High Priest serves in eight garments. The answer given by Ḥanna-
niah, Associate of the Rabbis,[46] is that the number eight corresponds
to circumcision, which takes place after eight days. The text then
quotes Malachi 2:5: "My covenant was with him [Levi]." In the
Babylonian Talmud it is made clear that the exegetical occasion for
the midrash is the proximity of Chapter 7 of Levitivcus, which details
various classes of sacrifices, to the discussion of Aaron's vestments
in Leviticus 8:6–9:

> R. 'Anani bar Sasson said: Why is the passage about the sacrifices
> placed next to the passage about the priestly vestments? To tell you
> that just as the sacrifices atone so do the vestments atone. (*b. Ẓeb.* 88b)

This conclusion is presented in the Palestinian Talmud and Midrashim as a separate statement independent of the exegetical question.

---

[43] The translation is that of Patrick W. Shekhan and Alexander A. Di Lella, *The
Wisdom of Ben Sira* (New York: The Anchor Bible, Doubleday, 1987), 507.

[44] See Mordecai Margulies (ed.), *Midrash Vayikra Rabbah* (New York: Jewish
Theological Seminary of America, 1993), 210–12; Jacob Mann, *The Bible as Read
and Preached in the Old Synagogue* (1940; repr. New York: Ktav, 1971) vol. 1, p. 258
in the Hebrew section.; see also *Cant. Rabbah* 4:5.

[45] *B. Ẓeb.* 88b; *b. Arak.* 16a.

[46] Hannaniah, *Ḥaverehon de-Rabbaban*, one of two lay brothers who made their living as shoemakers and studied with R. Yoḥanan in Tiberius.

The focus of the passage is the power of the vestments to atone for Israel's sins. At this point the midrashic pattern proper begins. The Palestinian Talmud's version is quoted here:

> 1st. R. Simon said: Just as the sacrifices atone so do the garments atone.
> 2nd. "In the tunic, breeches, headdress and sash:" [m. Yoma 7:5]
>> 1. [The tunic would atone for those who wore mixed fabric (kilayim):[47] And there are those who said:][48] for those who shed blood, as it is said: [referring to Joseph's tunic (ketonet passim) in Gen 37:31]: "And they dipped the tunic in blood."
>> 2. The breeches would atone for incest, as it is said: "make for them linen breeches to cover their private parts" (Ex 28:42).
>> 3. The headdress would atone for the arrogant, as it is said: "And you shall place the headdress on top of his head" (Ex 29:6).
>> 4. The sash would atone for [the thieves and some say for][49] the devious. R. Levi said: It was 32 cubits long and he wound it this way and that.[50]
>> 5. The breastpiece would atone for perverters of justice: and you shall make a breastpiece of judgment. (Ex 28:30)
>> 6. The ephod would atone for idolaters, as it is said, "without ephod and teraphim." (Hos 3:4)[51]
>> 7. The robe: R. Simon in the name of R. Jonathan of Bet Guvrin said: Two things were not atoned for and the Torah set a means of atonement for them, and they are these: One who speaks maliciously (lešon ha-raʿ) and inadvertent manslaughter. For the one who says speaks maliciously the Torah has set a means of atonement in the bells of the robe: "And they will be on Aaron when he serves and its voice will be heard." (Exod 28:35): Let the voice [of the bells] atone for the voice [of the one who speaks maliciously]. . . .

At this point there is an excursus on the types of atonement for bloodshed. Finally:

---

[47] The idea here seems to be that Joseph's tunic was made from a mix of wool and flax, forbidden according to Dt 22:11. See Margulies, Vayiqra Rabbah, p. 210 and the sources cited in his commentary.

[48] This passage appears in a gloss in MS. Leiden and was incorporated into Venice and the other editions.

[49] This phrase appears in a gloss in MS. Leiden.

[50] So Jastrow, Dictionary, s.v. ʿqm.

[51] See Rashi's comment to Zeb. 88b ad loc., which he cites as a tradition regarding b. Arak. 16a: "The sin of teraphim is revealed; if there is an ephod there are no teraphim."

8. Diadem: Some say blasphemers; some say the insolent. Those who
say blasphemy can justly claim [that it derives from the verses] "the
stone struck [Goliath's] forehead" (1 Sam 17:49) and the verse "on
his forehead" (Exod 28:38). Those who say insolence [derive it from
the verse] "You have a harlot's brow" (Jer 3:3).

(*y. Yoma* 7:3 [44b–c])

The climax of the ceremony is the encounter between the priest and
God. He thus, as we have seen, brings Israel in with him into the
sanctuary. But if the stones of the ephod and breastpiece constitute
a map of Israel on the body of the priest, the garments according
to this interpretation present the deity with a map of Israel's sins.
The purpose of the sacrifice, according to the garments, as it were,
is atonement for moral transgressions. This is not a self-evident idea;
it could be argued that purification of the cultic space is no less a
function of the biblical Yom Kippur. Furthermore, the representational nature of the garments—that is, their ability to tell the history
and constitution of the people—is at the same time their instru-
mentality. Each separate garment has a distinct role in the active
affecting of atonement.

V. *The representational and the instrumental in the Avodah*

By far the most extensive and systematic consideration of the meaning of the priestly vestments in the Rabbinic era is found in one of
the most important sources for the study of sacrifice in post-exilic
Judaism: The elaborate Avodah piyyutim, a set of liturgical poems
that recount, in epic fashion the Yom Kippur ceremony. These compositions contain valuable evidence for the way sacrifice and the
priesthood were perceived by circles that lay within the sphere of
Rabbinic influence, but were independent of the Rabbinic estate.[52]

The Avodah piyyutim developed out of a custom to recite a version of the Mishnah tractate Yoma in the ancient synagogue. The
greatest of these compositions were written between the fourth and

---

[52] For summaries of the history of the Avodah, see Ismar Elbogen, *Jewish Liturgy:
A Comprehensive History* (trans. Raymond P. Scheindlin; Philadelphia: Jewish Publication
Society and New York: Jewish Theological Seminary of America, 1993), 174, 217,
238–39, and 249–50; Daniel Goldschmidt (ed.), *Maḥazor le-Yamim Nora'im* vol. 2
(Ashkenaz) (Jerusalem: Mosad Bialik, 1970), 18–25; and Ezra Fleischer, *Širat ha-
Qodeš Ha-'Ivrit Bi-Yeme ha-Benayim* (Jerusalem: Keter, 1975), 173–77. A comprehen-
sive study of the Avodah service and piyyutim from the perspective of the history

seventh centuries. Particularly important are an anonymous composition called *Az be-'En Kol*, "when all was not in existence," which
has recently been published by Josef Yahalom; and several compositions by the pioneering fifth-century poet Yose ben Yose, notably
Azkir Gevurot, "I will declare the mighty deeds of God," which were
published by Aaron Mirsky.[53] It is in the nature of this highly allusive
and ornate literature to ornament every detail of the mythic history
of Israel and the sacrificial procedure. These particular compositions
are remarkable for their epic sweep, extending from the story of creation to the political history of the Second Temple.

They are remarkable in another way as well. The Avodah piyyutim, unlike the Mishnah, engage in an unusually elaborate glorification
of the High Priest. Whereas the Mishnah is likely to depict the
(Sadducean) priest of the second-temple period as an ignoramus or
heretic, the Avodah depicts him as pious and devoted. Moreover,
the priest is himself an object of splendor. Based on a literal interpretation of Leviticus 21:10 that the priest must be "greater than
his brothers" (*gadol me-'ehav*), the poems depict him as exceptionally
big and strong. As Yose ben Yose's *Azkir Gevurot* puts it:

> His strong body
> fills his tunic,
> doubled and woven[54]
> as far as the sleeves.

It is in this context that we can understand the depiction of the
priestly garments in these compositions. For example, *Az be-'En Kol*
marvels how

> his stature
> rose to the height of a cedar

---

of Hebrew literature is Zvi Malachi, "*Ha-'Avodah' le-Yom ha-Kippurim—'Ofiyah, Toledoteha
ve-Hitpathuta ba-Širah ha-'Ivrit*" (Ph.D. diss., Hebrew University, 1974). See also idem,
Be-Noʿam Siaḥ: Peraqim mi-Toledot Sifrutenu (Lod: Haberman Institute for Literary Research,
1983), 46–113. An important early discussion is found in J. Elbogen, *Studien zur
Geschichte des jüdischen Gottesdienstes* (Berlin: Mayer & Müller, 1907); cf. also A. Zeidman,
"*Matbeaʿ Seder ha-'Avodah Le-Yom ha-Kippurim*," *Sinai* 13 (1944), 173–82, 255–62.

[53] See note 15 above.

[54] Heb., *kefulah mešubeṣet*. According to some sources, such as y. *Yoma* 3:6 (40c)
and Ben Sira 45:12–13, it was a double garment. On the other hand, according
to *Sifra Ṣav* ch. 2, and b. *Yoma* 72b; the term *šeš*, translated here as fine linen,
means that it was made of six-fold thread. On the possible interpretations of this
line see Mirsky's commentary ad loc., *Yose ben Yose*, p. 155.

when he was fit with embroidered garments
to ornament his body. (lines 551–52)

Both poems contain extensive descriptions of the vestments. These
excursuses lavish detail on the exact design of the clothes, the breastpiece and the ephod and the rings and cords that connect them. In
fact, some of these details are found nowhere in Rabbinic literature,
but are related by Josephus. This is probably a sign that the poets
had access to independent priestly traditions. More important, the
extravagant poetic descriptions of the royal garments of the priest
serve to make the magnificence of the ancient Temple vivid to lis-
teners in the synagogue, bereft of the Temple.

The midrashic pattern that we have just seen, which seeks to
demonstrate how each garment atones for specific sins, is also well
represented in the piyyutim. Thus, following the description of the
tunic quoted above, Yose ben Yose states:

> The sin of the house of Jacob
> is atoned by this—
> those who sold the righteous one[55]
> over a sleeved tunic. (lines 159–60)

Here the poet has made more explicit what the Talmud implies:
that Israel atones for its sins against Joseph when the priest's tunic—
the antithesis of Joseph's blood-stained tunic—enters the Temple.
Yose ben Yose also adds an original touch to the midrash we have
just seen equating the voice of the bells of the robe with the voice
of malicious gossips:

> When they (the bells) strike each other
> the voice of one with the other,
> they atone for the voice
> of one who strikes his neighbor in secret.[56]

Az be-ʾEn Kol, an anonymous composition which Yahalom argues is
earlier than Yose's, adds another dimension to this idea of the active
role of the garments in expiation. The representative role of the vestments is articulated in a passage relating each of the gems on the
breastpiece to one of the tribes as described in Jacob's blessing in
Genesis 49. But according to this poet, it is the duty of the gar-

---

[55] That is, Joseph.
[56] Verbally, through slander.

ments not just to represent Israel, but to arouse God's compassion for his people on the day of judgment and to dispel the malevolent forces. Thus he says of the bells:

> He set golden bells
> and wove them into his hem
> to recall [God's] love
> of [Israel, of whom it is said]: "How beautiful are your steps." (SoS 7:2)
> (559)

Here the word *pa'amon*, "bell," hints at the word *pe'amayikh*, "steps," in the Song of Songs. In fact, the idea behind this seems to be the Rabbinic concept of "the merit of the fathers" (*zekhut avot*), according to which God is importuned to save Israel not because of its contemporary virtue, but because of its ancestors' righteous deeds.[57] This is a frequent device in the rhetoric of prayer and is thus appropriate to the conventional function of Yom Kippur. Indeed, several centuries earlier, Ben Sira interpreted the bells in a similar way as arousing God's remembrance of his people:

> and a rustle of bells round about
> through whose pleasing sound at each step
> he would be heard in the sanctuary
> and the families of his people would be remembered. (45:9)[58]

But in *Az be-'En Kol*, the active properties of the vestments extend to their role in dispelling the hostile forces preventing purification. Returning to the bells on the robe, the poem makes it clear that their function is not only atonement but to announce, noisily, the presence of the priest to all present. As he steps into the sanctuary,

> When his soles move
> they give voice
> like that which calls in the wilderness
> to make a path straight.[59]

> The servants of the Divine Presence[60]
> are fearful of him

---

[57] On this idea see the classic essay of Solomon Schechter, "The *Zachuth* of the Fathers," in *Aspects of Rabbinic Theology* (2nd ed. New York: Schocken, 1961), 170–98.

[58] Shekhan and Di Lella, *Ben Sira*, 506–7.

[59] Although this is a reference to Isa 40:3, Yahalom (*Az be-'En Kol*, 32) also suggests a relationship to Aaron's intervention in Num 17.

[60] Heb. *Šekhinah*.

for the robe is named
after the One who wears justice.[61] (lines 567–70)

That is, the hostile angels in the sanctuary—who are essentially body-guards fending off intruders in the sacred precinct—are frightened by the sound of the bells, which carry with it divine authorization. This notion is close to that found in the literature of early Jewish mysticism, which depicts the ascent of Rabbis into the heavenly realm, in which they must ward off angelic guards using the authorization of esoteric divine names.[62]

VI. *Priest as representative of the Divine world*

This function of the robe hints at another aspect of the vestments according to the Avodah piyyutim and a few midrashim: the idea that the priest is not only a representative of Israel but of the divine world as well. This motif can be traced back to Malachi 2:7, in which the priest is called a messenger, *mal'akh*, a word that can also mean angel.

An intriguing midrash plays on this dual nature of the priest. The midrash is based on an apparent contradiction in Leviticus 16. Verse 17 states that "no man shall be in the tent of meeting." But what about the priest himself? Leviticus Rabbah addresses this question:

> "And no man shall be in the tent of meeting" (Lev 16:17): R. Pinhas and R. Hilqiah in the name of R. Abbahu: Even those [angels] about whom are written "Their faces were the faces of men" [Ezek 1:10] were not in the tent of meeting when he entered it. On the year in which Shimon the Just died he said to them, "this year I [will] die." They said to him, "How do you know?" He said to them, "every year an old man dressed in white and wrapped in white would go in with me and go out. This year he went in with me and did not go out with me."

---

[61] Isa 59:17.

[62] See Gershom Scholem, *Major Trends in Jewish Mysticism* (2nd ed. New York: Schocken, 1954), 40–79; David Halperin, *The Faces of the Chariot: Early Jewish Responses to Ezekiel's Vision* (Tübingen: Mohr, 1988), and Peter Schäfer, *The Hidden and Manifest God: Some Major Themes in Early Jewish Mysticism* (Albany: SUNY Press, 1992); on affinities to Temple literature see Johann Meier, *Vom Kultus zum Gnosis* (Salzburg: Otto Müller, 1964); Martha Himmelfarb, *Ascent to Heaven in Jewish and Christian Apocalypses* (Oxford: Oxford University Press, 1993); Swartz, *Scholastic Magic*, 169–72; and Rachel Elior, "Mysticism, Magic, and Angelology—The Perception of Angels in Hekhalot Literature," *JSQ* 1 (1993/94), 3–53.

R. Abbahu said: and was not the High Priest a man? Rather, it is like what R. Pinhas said: when the Holy Spirit was resting on him his face shone like torches. About him it is written: "The lips of the priest will preserve knowledge..[for he is a messenger (mal'akh) of the Lord of hosts]" (Mal 2:7).[63]

Shimon knew who this man was because of his white clothes, like the linens of the priest himself.[64] The shining face of the priest is also described in ecstatic terms in a popular hymn in Ben Sira 50:1–24, which found its way into the Yom Kippur liturgy.[65]

Yose's ben Yose's Avodah poem *Atah Konanta 'Olam me-Rosh* describes the priest in heavenly terms:

His likeness is like Tarshish,
like the look of the firmament
when he puts on the blue robe,
woven like a honeycomb. (line 103)[66]

Here we can hear echoes of Philo's use of the blue of the robe to represent the sublunar air. Lacking the specific physics of Philo, however, Yose clearly wishes his listener to think of heaven.

Az be-'En Kol describes the headdress in this way:

Sparks of the seraphim
clambered out from it
for its image
is like that of a helmet of redemption. (lines 645–46)
. . . . .

And[67] he placed on his forehead
the frontlet, the holy diadem
and his eyes
shone like the heavens.

---

[63] Lev. R. 21:12. Cf. *y. Yoma* 5:2, *t. Sota* 13:5, *b. Yoma* 39b, and *b. Men* 109b. The idea that the priest is a visitor in the divine abode who effectively impersonates angels recalls similar ideas in Hekhalot litearture; cf. Swartz, *Scholastic Magic*, 168.

[64] That in the ancient Near East supernatural beings were said to be distinguished by their dress, and that their dress can be emulated by the priesthood can be seen from A. Leo Oppenheim, "Golden Garments of the Gods," *JNES* 8 (1949), 172–93.

[65] See M.H. Segal, *Sefer Ben Sira ha-Šalem* (Jerusalem: Mosad Bialik, 1972), 240–46; on the hymn *'Emet Mah Nehedar*, (Truly, How Glorious"), a version of which is published in Goldschmidt, *Mahazor* 2:483–84, see Cecil Roth, "Ecclesiasticus in the Synagogue Service," *JBL* 71 (1952), 171–78.

[66] Mirsky, *Yose ben Yose*, 192.

[67] The conjunction *vav* is used here for the acrostic.

And on it was written
the letters of the Great Name
"*YY*"[68] above
and "Holy" below.

And the supernal demigods
made room for him
lest their eyes be filled with [the sight of him]
and grow dim. (lines 651–56)

Here the last two themes we have seen are combined. Not only does the priest evoke the heavenly world, but he does it so successfully that the creatures in the sanctuary make way for him as he enters. Thus he becomes not only a representative of Israel, but the divine world.

VII. *Conclusions*

We have seen a wide range of methods and conclusions in interpretations of the significance and function of the priestly vestments. It is now possible to reflect on what we can learn about sacrifice not only from the individual interpretations in the sources we have surveyed today, but from the very act of constructing systems of meaning based on the vestments of the priest.

The systems of interpretation developed by thinkers and poets in the second-temple and rabbinic eras had their origin in the nature of the vestments themselves. Visually striking yet mysterious, they called out for analysis as sources of signification and as ritual objects. Whereas all clothing signals information about such issues as the status of the wearer and his or her ideology and stance vis á vis society, the vestments gained additional layers of hermenuetical possibilities because their fabric, form, and order were commanded by God to be used in the cult. At the same time, it was presumed that the vestments had an active role to play in representing Israel before its God. This led the way to a rich semiotic system in which each detail of the vestments could stand for something greater or perform a significant function in the cult, depending on the sensibilities of the interpreter. Philo, for example granted the expressive function of the vestments a pedagogic role and a moral purpose as well, by main-

---

[68] That is, the Tetragrammaton, for which *YY* is a common scribal circumlocution.

taining that the priest, representing the world on his body, sought redemption for all nations.[69] Other second-temple Palestinian authors stressed the miraculous functions and the physical splendor of the vestments.

The need to develop criteria by which the community could understand the recondite details of Exodus 28 and 39 predated the loss of the Temple in 70, but those criteria were made more complicated by that loss. The Rabbis sought to diminish the prestige of the priesthood—who were, after all, competitors for authority with the sages at one point—but still had to account for the reasons for God's laws. The liturgical poets of the ancient synagogue were under no such strictures.[70] In fact, several of them seem to have been of priestly descent themselves.[71] Moreover, by recalling sacrifice in such a way on Yom Kippur, those poets brought a host of enhanced functions to their prayers. Not only were their prayers means of importuning God for forgiveness and blessing, but they could convey some of the benefits of the sacrificial system. These benefits included not only atonement, but a much more intimate encounter with God. By presenting the priest both as representative of Israel and an active instrument in its entrance to the divine world, these compositions reassured their audience that the sacrificial system was not only about morality and expiation, but the presence of God.

Their descriptions of the vestments served this purpose by making the priest himself the vehicle of that encounter. It is interesting to think that by clothing the priest in a dense symbolism—of the cosmos, of Israel's sins and the merit of its fathers—the interpreters were in fact emptying him of his own personality. This reminds us of those schemes of sacrifice, such as that of Edmund Leach, that see the sacrificer entering a liminal world which is something of heaven and something of earth, bearing something of the community to the deity, and something of the divine back with him.[72]

---

[69] See for example *Vita Mosis* 2.133–35.

[70] On the differing models of leadership among the two sectors of the community see Swartz, "Sage, Priest, and Poet."

[71] See Yahalom, *Az Be-ʾEn Kol*, 56–57, and Baron, *A Social and Religious History of the Jews* 7 (New York: Columbia University Press, 1958), 90–92 and the references cited there.

[72] Edmund Leach, "The Logic of Sacrifice," in *Culture and Communication* (Cambridge: Cambridge University Press, 1976), 81–93; and H. Hubert and M. Mauss, *Sacrifice: Its Nature and Function* (Chicago: University of Chicago Press, 1964).

The poets and scholars we have studied here, like ourselves, were participants in discourse on ritual. Their participation required the self-consciousness to understand that ritual, like sacral clothing, was a system of communication whose channels could extend vertically, to the deity, or laterally, to the community. Their efforts to understand that system therefore found an appropriate focus in the dazzling, mysterious details of the vestments of the High Priest. At the same time, their audiences could be forgiven for forgetting that they were listening not to the bells of the High Priest's robe but to the teaching of the Rabbi or the song of the prayer-leader, clad in the garments of rhetoric and poetry.

SACRIFICE AND SACRIFICIAL CEREMONIES OF THE ROMAN IMPERIAL ARMY*

Peter Herz

In theory the Roman army under the empire still pretended to be a national army, the *exercitus populi Romani*, with a national religion and a very special relation to the emperor. Needless to say, the reality was different. During the early years of the empire at least the soldiers who served in the legions were Roman citizens (*cives Romani*), which means they were soldiers who shared a certain common base in their religious traditions. With the beginning of the second century CE even most soldiers within the legions came from a provincial background. From a legal perspective that means they were Roman citizens, but their religious tradition reflected a least partially local traditions, e.g. of Spain or the Balkans.

Inscriptions prove that many cults that had only a very local tradition traveled with the soldiers to the different parts of the empire.[1] Thus we find Arabic gods along the *limes* in Upper Germany, Celtic and Germanic gods in Rome. Certainly those religious changes were noted by the Roman authorities, but how did they react? As far as we can see, the general reaction was positive. In some cases we can even suppose that the authorities encouraged the soldiers to maintain their national cults, because those religious activities endangered neither the character nor the duties of the Roman army. Besides the ordinary set of military duties, each soldier as a member of the army was requested to participate in the religion of the army that followed strict rules.

* I would like to thank my student Florian Himmler, who undertook the task of removing some of the extreme Germanic expressions from my text.

[1] For general information concerning Roman military religion cp. Arthur D. Nock, "The Roman Army and the Roman Religious Year", *HTR* 45 (1952) 187–252; H. Ankersdorfer, *Studien zur Religion des römischen Heeres von Augustus bis Diokletian* (Diss. Konstanz, 1973); John Helgeland, "Roman Army Religion", *Aufstieg und Niedergang der römischen Welt* II 16,2 (Berlin: De Gruyter, 1978) 1470–1505; Eric Birley, "The Religion of the Roman Army: 1895–1977", *Aufstieg und Niedergang der römischen Welt* II 16,2 (Berlin: De Gruyter, 1978) 1506–1541; Manfred Clauss, "Heerwesen/Heeresreligion", *RAC* XIII (1986) 1094 ff.

We are quite fortunate to have an excellent set of sources from the old Roman camp of Dura-Europos in the *provincia Mesopotamia* on the banks of the river Euphrates.[2] The most important part is a papyrus, the so-called *Feriale Duranum*, a copy of the official *calendarium* of the Severan Dynasty, that registers all official festivities of the unit and specifies at the same time the necessary sacrificies and ceremonies for about two thirds of the year (January to the end of September).[3] (Cp. the appendix)

The unit that was supposed to arrange its religious life according to that *feriale* was the *cohors XX Palmyrenorum*, a unit with Arabian or at least Syrian soldiers. Beside the *feriale* we have the chance to adduce some so-called 'morning-reports' and a fresco from the camp picturing the commanding officer, conducting an official sacrifice.

If we take a closer look on the *feriale*, we find three quite different sets of festivities. 1. Beside the actual festivities of the reigning emperor Severus Alexander (*dies imperii, dies Caesaris*) and his immediate family we find a second group of dates that are important for the history of the Severan dynasty or the empire in general. To this group belong the *dies natales* and *dies imperii* of the divinised predecessors and their wives. The catalogue is nearly complete for the emperors of the Severan and Antonine dynasties, while the Flavians and the Julio-Claudians are only represented by a reduced program. We have the birthdays of 14 *divi* or *divae* and the *dies imperii* of 6 emperors and are entitled to suppose that about 8 more dates were registered in the missing parts of the *feriale*. The fact that the birthday of Germanicus on May 24th is still celebrated more than 200 years after his death is quite enigmatic and not yet properly explained, since Germanicus never officially joined the ranks of the *divi*.

Not very surprising is the second group, that includes dates of special importance for the military. It includes festivities to honour the *signa* of the unit (*rosaliae signorum*), the official date for retirement (7 January) or the days for payment.

Until now all festivities could be easily explained as a result of the special circumstances of military life that demanded a perma-

---

[2] C. Hopkins, *The Discovery of Dura-Europos*, ed. by B. Goldman (New Haven/London: Yale University Press, 1979) 101 ff.

[3] The most convenient edition is by R.O. Fink, *Roman Military Records on Papyrus* (Case Western Reserve University Press: Ann Arbor, 1971). Cp. Peter Herz, "Feriale Duranum", *Der Neue Pauly* IV (1998) 480–481. Still of fundamental importance: R.O. Fink, A.S. Hoey, and W.F. Snyder, "The Feriale Duranum", *YCS* 7 (1940) 1–221; J.F. Gilliam, "The Roman Military Feriale", *HTR* 47 (1954) 183–196.

nent show of loyalty towards the emperor. But in the third group things are very different. Here we have at least 7 festivities that fall in the category of 'national Roman religion'. For example we have festivities for Mars, Minerva, Vesta, Salus, Neptunus and even the city of Rome (*Mars Pater, Quinquatria, dies natalis urbis Romae, circenses Martiales, Vestalia, Neptunalia, circenses Salutares*). Besides that we can add the official Roman New Years Day on 1 January and the Day of Vows (*nuncupatio votorum*) on 3 January. All in all the *Feriale Duranum* provides us with a very precious set of information that allows us an unparalleled view of religious every-day life within the army. To sum up some of the facts: according to the *feriale* every soldier had to participate each year in about 40 or 50 sacrifices. In some years this number could be significantly raised if political circumstances demanded that the unit perform additional sacrifices. To this special category belong festivities to celebrate an imperial victory (*laetitia publica*), imperial jubilees (*decennalia* or *vicennalia*) or the nomination of a new emperor.

Within the *feriale* we can detect a clear ranking of sacrifices, the *immolatio* of animals and the lower-ranking *supplicatio* without the sacrifice of animals, but with the presentation of incense and wine (*thure ac vino*).[4] The *immolatio* was reserved for the emperor himself and his mother, the *divi*, but only for a selection of the *divae*. I can give no reasonable explanation, why the *dies natalis divae Iuliae Maesae* was only celebrated by a *supplicatio*, while the mother of the emperor was entitled to receive an animal. On the other hand we may suppose that the combination of an *immolatio* with a *supplicatio* [e.g. the double *dies imperii* of Severus Alexander: 13/14 March] was caused by religious motives and was not the result of a spontaneous decision. Our main problem is the lack of any information to elucidate the theological reasoning behind such a combination of sacrifices.

Some of the more technical details of the sacrifice are known from the usually hostile comments of the Christian sources, from papyri, but also from archaeological sources. Sacrifices were performed according to the rules and the tradition of the Roman religion, even in cases when nearly all soldiers came from a different ethnic or religious

---

[4] The old book by Georg Wissowa, *Religion und Kultus der Römer* (München: Beck, 1912) 412 (*immolatio*) and 423–426 (*supplicatio*) is still valuable for technical details. For the *supplicatio* cp. also Gérard Freyburger, "La *supplication* d'action de grâces sous le Haut-Empire", *Aufstieg und Niedergang der römischen Welt* II 16,2 (Berlin: De Gruyter, 1978) 1418–1439.

background. Responsible for performing the sacrifice was the commanding officer of the unit, who combined in his person the highest
military and religious authority. The analysis of a fresco from Dura-
Europos provides some additional information. We see the commander of the unit, the *tribunus* Terentius, during a sacrifice. On the
left hand we can recognize three life-size statues of Roman emperors
with military dress and nimbus. In the center we have one of the
flags of the unit, a so-called *vexillum*, in the forefront we see Terentius
clad in white clothes (*veste candida*) who has just started the ceremony
on a small portable altar. The altar is a *thymiaterion* or *foculus* that
was usually used for sacrifices of incense and wine (*thure ac vino*).

The most convincing interpretation of this sacrifice was offered by
Thomas Pekàry, who combined the fresco with information culled
from the so-called morning- reports from the unit's archive.[5]

> Morning report (P. Dura 82 = Fink Nr. 47)
> Text: [ca. 8] *ti[miniu]s pa[u]linus dec. admissa pron[u]nt[iavit ca. 23]*
> *iiii kal. april. expungentur suplicatio immolatio et ad omnem tesseram parati erimus*
> *excuba[nt] ad signa d.n. alexandri aug. dec(urio) [timinius paul]i[nus] sesq(uipli-*
> *carius) aurel. absas aedit(uus) aurel. silvanus sig(nifer) cl. natalius lib(rarius) aurel.*
> *capiton ci. anton. val. opt[io]n ii ogelus malchi ...*
>
> There follows a additional group of ordinary soldiers
>
> Timinius Paulinus, decurion, announced the order of the day.
> [... because] on 29 March (soldiers) will be checked off, a *supplicatio*
> and *immolatio* and at every order we will be ready. These are stand-
> ing watch at the standards of our Lord Alexander Augustus: decurion,
> Timinius Paulinus; sesquiplicarius, Aurelius Absas; shrine-keeper, Aurelius
> Silvanus; signifer, Claudius Natalius; clerk, Aurelius Capito; inspector
> of sentries, Anton() Val(); lieutenant, Ogelus son of Malchus ...[6]

Each morning all soldiers of the unit who were present in the camp
gathered in front of the unit's *signa* (and the images of the emperors)
to receive the watch-word of the day and reinforce their loyalty to
the emperor. All circumstances indicate that the fresco shows this
peculiar ceremony that was connected with a regular morning sacrifice
with wine and incense. The soldiers on the right side of the fresco
are presumably those assigned for the honour-guard of that day.

---

[5] Thomas Pekàry, "Das Opfer vor dem Kaiserbild", *Bonner Jahrbücher für Alter-
tumswissenschaft* 186 (1986) 91–103.
[6] The interpretation of some parts of the papyrus is open for discussion. The
name of the 'inspector of sentries' (a probable solution for *ci(rcitor)*) should be read
as Anton(ius) Val(ens). The two vertical strokes before 'Ogelus son of Malchus' could
be read as an H and interpreted as part of a personal name, Hogelus.

These collective acts of sacrifice were not the result of a personal religious decision of e.g. the commanding officer or the soldiers of the unit. They were the result of orders or decisions made by the emperor himself or central institutions of the empire. This means not only the festivities directly connected with the cult of the emperor, but also such festivities as *Quinquatria, Vestalia* or *Neptunalia* that were genuine parts of the religious tradition of Rome or Italy performed because they were part of the official *calendarium*. The Roman emperor or the Roman high command were not concerned that the religious traditions of most soldiers had no connection at all to Italy and the national religion of the Romans. The soldiers were members of the Roman army and as a consequence they were supposed to act like Roman soldiers originating from Italy. It would not be appropriate to say that it was the emperors' main intention to achieve a religious Romanization of all soldiers without any regard to their origin or personal beliefs. Such an intention would be contrary to all our information about the religious practice under the Roman empire. But certain circumstances of military life led to that result. Especially the long time of military service (as an average a soldier serving in the *legio* spent more than 20 years with the military, *auxiliares* or soldiers from the fleet were usually released after 25 years) and the regularity of these ceremonies were very helpful to achieve such a result.

It is a legitimate assumption that the way those festivities and sacrifices were performed was pretty uniform throughout the Roman empire. There were different ways to achieve such a goal. First of all there were official orders from Rome that prescribed which festivity had to be included in the *calendarium* or the other way round should be eliminated. The use of the chain of command by the Roman authorities to regulate the religious life of the army has been proved by a recently found inscription, that was published in 1996.[7] The great *senatus consultum de Gnaeo Pisone patre*, registers decisions of the Roman senate from 10 December, 20 CE, and gives at the same time very detailed instructions how the *senatus consultum* should be brought to the attention of the public everywhere in the empire.

---

[7] Werner Eck, Antonio Caballos and Fernando Fernàndez, *Das Senatus consultum de Gnaeo Pisone patre* (München: Beck, 1997) 51 line 172: 'also that this decree of the senate should be fixed (to the wall) near the *signa* in the winter-camp of each legion (. . . *itemq(ue) hoc s(enatus) c(onsultum) in hibernis cuiusq(ue) legionis at signa figeretur*).

The governors of the Roman provinces were ordererd to publish a
bronze copy of the *senatus consultum* in the most frequented places of
the main cities, and, this came as a real surprise, the commanders
of the legions were ordered to place their copy in the chapel of their
unit, where usually only the *signa* and the imperial pictures were
stored. Until the discovery of this inscription the transmission of such
orders via the chain of command had never been explicitly proved.
If it was possible to transmit a *senatus consultum* dealing with important political news it should not have been very difficult to transmit
the order to perform a sacrifice for a certain member of the imperial family.

But the information from this new inscription can also help to
clarify another urgent problem. The existence of an official *calendarium* was never in doubt, but we were not sure which Roman emperor
was responsible for the first regulations of the military *calendarium*.
The *senatus consultum de Gnaeo Pisone patre* was published during the reign
of Tiberius, the second emperor (14–37 CE). As we know, Tiberius
was very conservative in religious matters and is therefore a very
unlikely candidate for such a far-reaching decision. Therefore everything points to Augustus, the first emperor, as the man responsible
for the first regulations of the military religion, and Augustus was a
very innovative person in the field of religious organisation and propaganda. The fact that the *ludi Martiales* on 12 May are a part of
the *feriale* seems to corroborate the fact that Augustus was indeed
the creator of the first *calendarium*. As has been proved the *ludi Martiales*
were established in memory of the dedication of the *templum Martis
Ultoris* in Rome, one of the most prestigious buildings of the whole
Augustan period.[8]

It would be very one-sided to presume that only official orders
were necessary to obtain the desired uniformity of military religion.
At least as important as the official policy was the military itself. To
order the performance of sacrifices is one facet of the problem, to
maintain the religious tradition within the military is another. In this
case the willing cooperation of the military leadership on all levels
was necessary. The officers and the NCOs, to employ a modern
word for the Roman *centuriones*, were the people who took the respon-

---

[8] Cf. Peter Herz, "Zum Tempel des Mars Ultor", in Joachim Ganzert, *Der Tempel
des Mars Ultor auf dem Forum Augusti* (Mainz: Zabern, 1996) 265–281 for the historical background.

sibility to enforce the official orders and guarantee at the same time that sacrifices and ceremonies were correctly performed everywhere. On the other hand this special group of military personnel was regularly transferred between units everywhere in the empire. A second-century *centurio*, whose military career is known by his tombstone from North Africa, changed his assignment every third year.[9] After nearly 50 years active service as a *centurio* and after 15 different legions he had traveled the Roman empire from North England and North Spain to the lower Danube, the Euphrates, Egypt and North Africa. Such a system of permanent transfers did not only ensure the high technical standards of the military profession but also the uniformity of the religious traditions within the military.[10]

A very special part of the religious life was concentrated on the cult of the *signa militaria*. While our knowledge of the religious importance for the *signa* within the sub-units is very limited, the cult of the *aquila*, the eagle-standard of the legion, is quite well documented.[11]

First of all, the *aquila* was treated like a divine being. The day when the *aquila* was first presented to the newly raised unit was at the same time the birthday of the *aquila* and the unit. To lose the *aquila* during battle meant the ritual death of the unit. The best example is the history of the three legions of Varus who lost their *aquilae* during the *bellum Varianum*. Even after the *aquilae* had been recovered by the Romans the units were dead, their names and their numbers vanished. Within the everyday life of the unit the *aquila* was under the special surveillance of the first *centurio* or captain of the legion, the *centurio primi pili*, who was also responsible for the sacrifices concentrating on the *aquila*. In camp the *aquila* stayed together with the pictures of the emperors in a special chapel, and it was regularly treated with fragrant oils and received sacrifices.

Compare the text of an inscription from the Roman camp of Novae on the lower Danube.

Corpus Inscriptionum Latinarum III 6224 = Dessau, Inscriptiones Latinae Selectae 2295

---

[9] Dessau, Inscriptiones Latinae Selectae 2658.

[10] Corpus Inscriptionum Latinarum VIII 217 = Dessau, Inscriptiones Latinae Selectae 2658.

[11] Oliver Stoll, "Die Fahnenwache in der römischen Armee", *Zeitschrift für Papyrologie und Epigraphik* 108 (1995) 107–118. Oliver Stoll, *Excubatio ad signa. Fahnenwache, militärische Symbolik und Kulturgeschichte* (St. Katharinen: Scripta Mercaturae, 1995).

(Novae/Moesia inferior)
*Dis militaribus/Genio, Virtuti, A/quilae sanc(tae) signis/que leg(ionis) I Ital(icae)
Seve/rianae.*
*M. Aurel(ius)/Iustus domo Hor/rei Margensis m(unicipii) Moesiae superio/ris,
ex CCC (trecenario) p(rimus) p(ilus) d(ono) d(edit).*
In latere: *XII kal(endas) Oct(obres) Iuliano/II et Crispino/co(n)s(ulibus)/[pe]r
Annium Italicum/leg(atum) Aug(usti) pr(o) pr(aetore)*

To the gods of the military, the genius, the courage, the holy eagle
and the *signa* of the *legio I Italica Severiana.* Marcus Aurelius Iustus, from
Horreum Margum, a city of Moesia superior, a former *trecenarius,* the
primus pilus gave as a present.
On the flank: (Dedicated) on 20 September under the *consules* Iulianus
II and Crispinus by Annius Italicus, the *legatus Augusti pro praetore.*

In this case the *aquila* and the other *signa* of the legion are part of
a whole series of divinities, the *dei militares,* that were honoured with
a sacrifice. Each *primus pilus* who retired was expected to pay for an
altar and a sacrifice to honour the *aquila.* I suppose that in this case
no ordinary sacrifice with wine and incense was expected but an
animal. The importance of this ceremony is revealed by the identity of the priest who conducted the sacrifice: it is the provincial governor himself, the *legatus Augusti pro praetore.* Therefore the different
parts of the ceremony are clearly differentiated. The *primus pilus* pays
for the altar and the sacrifice (*dono dedit*), the governor acts as a priest
[*per . . .* or *dedicante*]. The day of the ceremony is probably identical
with the birthday of the unit.[12]

The second inscription from Roman North Africa shows a very
special part of this ceremony. By the way this text is our only information explicitly mentioning this peculiar part.

Corpus Inscriptionum Latinarum VIII 2634 = Dessau, Inscriptiones
Latinae Selectae 2296 (Lambaesis/Numidia)
*Deo/Marti militiae/potenti statuam/in honorem leg(ionis)/III Aug(ustae)
Valerianae/Gallienae Valerianae/Sattonius Iu/cundus p(rimus) p(ilus), qui/primus
leg(ione) reno/vata aput aquilam vitem posu/it, votum dedit/dedicante/Veturio
Vetu/riano v(iro) c(larissimo), leg(ato)/Auggg(ustorum) pr(o) pr(aetore).*

---

[12] The Late Roman *calendarium* of Silvius (Inscriptiones Italiae. Volumen XIII—
Fasti et elogia. Fasciculus II—Fasti anni Numani et Iuliani curavit Attilius Degrassi
(Roma: Istituto poligrafico dello stato, 1963) 263–276) registers for this day *ludi tri-
umphales.* As I hope to show in a forthcoming paper dealing with the *calendaria* of
late antique festivities this day was connected with the posthumous triumph of
Trajan in 118 CE.

To the god Mars strong at military things, in fulfillment of a vow, the *primus pilus* Sattonius Iucundus gave a statue in honour of the *legio III Augusta Valeriana Galliena Valeriana*, who as the first after the reconstitution of the *legio* deposed his stick in front of the *aquila*. The dedication was conducted by Veturius Veturianus the *vir clarissimus*, the *legatus Augustorum pro praetore*.

The inscription registers that the *primus pilus* deposed his *vitis*, the stick that was the official sign of his rank as a *centurio* and his undisputed right to punish the soldiers. The last official act of his life as an active soldier was to depose his *vitis* in front of the *aquila*, the divinity he had to protect and to honour during the period of his active service: *aput aquilam vitem posuit*. It is quite legitimate to suppose that such a ceremony was performed by each *primus pilus*, while the evidence for comparable ceremonies on lower levels of the military, e.g. for the *signa* of smaller units, is still lacking. But I would not be surprised if some day we would find the relevant information to fill this void.

Until now I have concentrated my efforts on the ceremonies of the greater units, legions or *cohortes*, but they represent only a small part of the evidence. Below the ceremonial level of those units there was a whole set of smaller ceremonies or cults concentrating on sub-units (e.g. *centuriae* or *vexillationes*), groups of soldiers performing special duties (*officiales, signiferi*) or on special assignment (*beneficiarii*). It is difficult to give an opinion about the underlying religious beliefs of the common soldiers, but I suppose the most important fact was feeling to be part of a close interdependent community, that gave security in a dangerous world.

If we try to evaluate to what extent religion permeated the life even of a common Roman soldier we are surprised.

First of all, the religious demands for the common soldier were not very specific. The decisive point was not to prove one's personal religious belief, but to participate in the official ceremonies (*ceremoniis interesse*). To participate was one way to prove one's loyalty to the emperor and the empire in general. Under those circumstances even a Christian could do service as a common soldier, since nobody expected him to take an active part in the performance of sacrifices.

Ceremonies that were performed by the unit as a collective were an important tool to create something like a corporate identity of the unit.

1. Sacrifices were usually performed in the presence of the *signa*.
2. An integral part of the sacrifices (*immolationes*) was a meal in which all soldiers were supposed to participate. The meat that had not been deposed on the altar was served to the soldiers, a part of the ceremony that was very repellent for Christian soldiers.[13]
3. Even every-day business of military life was accompanied by religious ceremonies.
   a) Thus it is no special surprise that the first entrance into military life was accompanied by an oath of loyalty (*sacramentum*). The *sacramentum* established for the young soldier a special personal relation to the emperor. The real surprise is the regular renewal of this ceremony by the whole unit. In most cases, this renewal took place on the first day of the year, sometimes on the anniversary of the *dies imperii*.[14] Needless to say that this ceremony was accompanied by a sacrifice. The same ritual regularity can be detected in the annual ritual vow for the well-being of the emperor (*nuncupatio votorum*) on 3 January.[15] The *nuncupatio* was a ceremony combining fulfilling the vows from the last year by sacrificing the promised animals and the delivering of promises for the new year. In this case we have the chance to use the files of a brotherhood of priests, the *fratres Arvales*, from Rome to corroborate our findings. The *acta* of the *fratres* are very helpful to follow the regular textual adoption of the *vota* and to show the huge amount of animals for

---

[13] Georg Schöllgen, *Ecclesia sordida? Zur Frage der sozialen Schichtung frühchristlicher Gemeinden am Beispiel Karthagos zur Zeit Tertullians* (Münster: Aschendorffsche Verlagsbuchhandlung, 1984).

[14] The Roman governor Plinius reports to emperor Trajan (Plin. ep. 10, 100–101): 'The vows that we made last year we have eagerly and happily fulfilled, and we offered new vows while the devotion of our fellow-soldiers and the inhabitants of the province was striving (to be first)' (*Vota . . . priore anno nuncupata alacres laetique persolvimus novaque rursus certante commilitonum et provincialibus pietate suscepimus*). The traditional Roman New Year's Day on 1 January was generally observed in the Roman army, even if the units were stationed in regions with a different New Year's Day, e.g. 29 August (Thoth 1) in Egypt or 23 September in many parts of Asia, where the birthday of emperor Augustus was identical with the new year's day. This underlines the way that the tradition of the Roman army helped to establish a certain uniformity in religious matters.

[15] This act is based on the assumption that the well-being of the emperor (and his family) is instrumental to preserve the security and the peace of the whole empire. Cp. Hans Ulrich Instinsky, "Kaiser und Ewigkeit", *Hermes* 77 (1942) 313–355, reprinted in Hans Kloft, ed., *Ideologie und Herrschaft in der Antike* (Darmstadt: Wissenschaftliche Buchgesellschaft, 1979) 416–472.

the sacrifices. In the *Feriale Duranum* we can establish that a least 8 animals were sacrificed on that day. On the other hand the text of the *vota* shows that the number of deities that were asked to maintain the security of the emperor and the empire changed from reign to reign, sometimes even from year to year. It is very difficult to decide whether the texts of the *vota* were prescribed by the high-command or were selected by the commanding officer of the unit. In any case the inclusion of other members of the reigning family in the formula had to approved by the emperor himself.

b) The ceremonial dismissal of veterans was celebrated by a collective sacrifice on an altar registering the names of all soldiers. The sacrifice was performed by the commanding officer of the unit, in some cases even by the governor of the province, who was at the same time the commander of the provincial army.

c) The successful fulfillment of a special assignment was celebrated by sacrifices, too. Especially revealing are the *beneficiarii* or soldiers for special services.[16] When they had spent their time on an outpost somewhere in the province and were ready to return to their camp, the leading *beneficiarius* dedicated an altar registering their time on duty. We have some stations (Osterburken behind the Limes in Upper Germany or Sirmium near Belgrade) with up to 60 altars that were dedicated within a few years. We can be sure, that those altars are indeed proof of religious ceremonies and that they were quite uniform throughout the empire. The inscriptions show a quite regular formula including the notice '*pro se et suis votum solvit libens merito*', he fulfilled the vow for himself and his men, that indicated that a sacrifice had been delivered. Usually the supreme god of the empire, Iuppiter Optimus Maximus, was the main recipient of the sacrifice. In many cases the invocation of Iuppiter was combined with a collective invocation of all other gods and goddesses (*dis deabusque omnibus*) as well as of the divine power thought to possess special protective strength for the place where the soldiers had spent their time (*genius loci*).

---

[16] Most of the material has been conveniently collected by Egon Schallmayer et al., *Der römische Weihebezirk von Osterburken I. Corpus der griechischen und lateinischen Beneficiarier-Inschriften des römischen Reiches* (Stuttgart: Theiss, 1990).

The Roman army was an integrated part of the Roman state, therefore all our evidence indicates that all official sacrifices within the
Roman army were conducted in a prescribed way, like civil sacrifices
according to the religious rules of the *ritus Romanus*: of course the
animals had to be flawless, the sacrifice was accompanied by a flute-
player (*tibicen*) who had to assure that no disturbing sounds interrupted the ceremony, a *victimarius* killed the animal and took the
parts that belonged to the god and then the *haruspex* had to inspect
the entrails of the animal. Other soldiers connected with sacrifices
are the *pullarius*, who had to look after the holy chicken, the *t(h)urarius*
had to care for incense and the *cereus* had the responsibility to provide candles.[17]

We have some so-called *laterculi* registering the names of all soldiers serving in a unit at the same time, for example all one thousand soldiers of a *cohors praetoria* or a *cohors urbana*. If the soldier had
a special assignment within the unit, for example if he was a clerk
of the staff or assigned to a certain officer, this fact was carefully
registered after his name. Thus we can prove that at least the units
of the imperial capital had regular *victimarii* and *haruspices* on their
rosters. If by chance we should find comparable *laterculi* for the fron-
tier units I am convinced the picture would not change.

Of course, many questions remain. It is not difficult to learn how
to properly slaughter an animal during a sacrifice and to remove
the parts that were destined for the altar. A *victimarius* did not need
special training, but what about the *haruspices* who needed profound
knowledge of the *disciplina Etrusca* in order to perform their task correctly.[18] Was there a regular distribution of trained *haruspices* within
the army or were they trained on the job? I must confess my complete ignorance. The casual way those people were registered side
by side with soldiers responsible for weaponry, food or the salary
seems to prove that the religious part of a soldier's life was as much
part of the military routine as the training with his weapons or the
assignment as a guard.

Our technical knowledge about Roman sacrifices in general is very
limited and the field of military sacrificial ceremonies is even more
hampered by a great scarcity of detailed information. Nevertheless,

---

[17] Cp. O. Stoll, "Fahnenwache", 115.
[18] Ambros Josef Pfiffig, *Die etruskische Religion. Sakrale Stätten, Götter, Kulte, Rituale*
(Wiesbaden: VMA-Verlag, 1998) 115–127.

it seems to be quite legitimate to outline the necessary conditions that have to be expected within the framework of the military. First of all the animals destined to be sacrificed had to be flawless. How the outer quality of the animals was guaranteed and what institution or person decided in those cases is completely unknown.

At the beginning of each sacrifice or each public ceremony in general the leading magistrate or officer had to confirm the ritual consensus between man and deity by the old ceremony of *augurium*. It meant inspection of the sky to detect any indications of unfavorable circumstances. Any celestial sign such as thunder, a flash of light or even a sudden rain-shower could indicate that the deity that should be the recipient of the sacrifice was indignant and not likely to accept the sacrifice. Such a sign invalidated the whole sacrificial ceremony, which had to be repeated all over again.[19] It is completely unknown how these problems were dealt with by the military, or to say it in a slightly different way the level of religious training for the Roman officers or commanders is completely unknown.

Romans took a very formalistic approach to all religious acts that reminds me sometimes more of the legal niceties of Roman law than of religion. Each step of a sacrificial ceremony, each prayer was meticulously prescribed and had to be performed exactly. Certainly, the prayers or songs that are likely to be used by the Roman military are not of that old-fashioned type as the *carmen arvale*, whose text has by a mere chance been handed down to us in a inscription from the 3rd century CE. In this case the brotherhood of the *fratres Arvales* used old prayer-books, because they no longer understood the archaic Latin text. They tried to perform their song in a way that was as phonetically correct as possible. After their performance, that combined the song with an archaic three-step-dance (*tripodaverunt*), a *servus publicus* collected the prayer-books.[20] If the Roman army did not create its own set of religious rules from scratch, something that seems very unlikely and very un-Roman to me, we have to expect that there existed a kind of military prayer-book or at least

---

[19] Jerzy Linderski, "Römischer Staat und Götterzeichen. Zum Problem der obnuntatio", *Jahrbuch der Universität Düsseldorf* (1969/70 [1971]) 309–322, reprinted in Jerzy Linderski, *Roman Questions. Selected Papers* (Stuttgart: Steiner, 1995) 444–457.

[20] In this case I am more sceptical than John Scheid, *Romulus et ses frères. Le collège des frères Arvales. Modèle du culte public dans la Rome des empereurs* (Rome: École française de Rome, 1990) 617–622.

a collection of religious formulas covering the common types of sacrifices the Roman officer had to perform during his time of duty.

To establish the ritual purity of the sacrificant before the beginning of a sacrifice or even before entering a building or an open space that was not *profanum* constituted a very important problem for most religions in antiquity. The *leges sacrae* of the Greek world have preserved a rich collection of material dealing with those problems.[21] It is only by chance that we learn that the Roman army also had a problem with ritual purity.[22] When in 15 CE Germanicus reached the *saltus Teutoburgensis* and buried the remains of the Roman soldiers who had died there in battle, Tiberius rebuked him afterwards.[23] One of Tiberius's arguments is quite revealing: 'it was not right for a commander belonging to the old and venerable priesthood of the augurs to have handled objects belonging to the dead (*neque imperatorem auguratu et vetustissimis caerimoniis praeditum adtrectare feralia debuisse*). As Germanicus was an *augur* he was subject to an additional set of religious limitations, it is difficult for us to decide which limitation was caused by the *auguratus* and which was the result of the religious rules of the army.

---

[21] Cp. in general Robert Parker, *Miasma. Pollution and Purification in Early Greek Religion* (Oxford: Clarendon Press, 1983). The Jewish and Egyptian material shows how detailed the prescriptions could be. The Christian tradition took a lot of material from the Jewish or more generally from the Oriental tradition that led to the first schism in the Western church. The African church of the Donatists adhered to the tradition that the ritual purity of the priest was all-important (*opere operandi*), while the Church of Rome, influenced by the Roman tradition, maintained that the correctness of the ceremony was the important point not the person of the priest (*opere operando*). I hesitate to jump to premature conclusions but it seems to me that we can find a certain indication how the Roman military probably dealt with those problems. For the Romans we know only the basic condition, that sacrifices had to be offered with clean hands (*manibus puris*). The custom to cover one's hands with a cloth (*manibus velatis*) before touching anything sacred seems to have been introduced in late antiquity.

[22] The question of special sacrifices to purify oneself from defilement has to best of my knowledge never been adequately treated for the Roman religion. We only know that after touching a corpse, opening a grave or tampering with anything that belonged to the category *sacrum* it was necessary to offer a special sacrifice, a so-called *piaculum*. Most revealing is the case of the imperial freedman M. Ulpius Phaedimus (Corpus Inscriptionum Latinarum VI 1884 = Dessau, Inscriptiones Latinae Selectae 1792), whose mortal remains were first buried in Asia Minor and then brought to Rome, after the permission of the pontifices, the highest authority for all questions of Roman sacral law, had been obtained and a special sacrifice had been offered (*ex permissu collegii pontific(um) piaculo facto*).

[23] Tac. *Ann.* 1.62.2.

The legal fiction that the imperial army was still the *exercitus populi Romani* has already been mentioned. Now we have to cope with a set of questions that are a direct result of this legal construction. The commander in chief of the whole Roman army was of course the emperor himself. Most provincial governors who were at the same time commanders of a provincial army were not autonomous commanders with an *imperium* of their own, they were only representatives of the imperial commander in chief who just happened not to be present. The official title of those officers was *legatus Augusti pro praetore* [then followed the name of the province or army they commanded], while their reduced rank was indicated by the number of *lictores*, who accompanied them during their public appearance. While a *praetorius* with an *imperium* of his own was entitled to parade six *fasces* in public, these *legati* had only five *fasces* (*legati quinquefascales*).

It is not difficult for us to imagine how the legal niceties of such a political construction worked in reality, but the field of religion is much more problematic. As those officers had no *imperium* of their own they also lacked the religious component of each regular commanding competence, the *auspicia*. To have the right of *auspicia* meant that the person endowed with that right had e.g. the right to deliver in the name of the *res publica Romana* binding vows towards the gods that had to be fulfilled after the return to Rome. To possess the unlimited *auspicia* for a command (*auspiciis suis*) was identical with the right to celebrate a triumph after a victorious return to Rome. As the emperors beginning with Augustus were the only persons to have *auspicia* of their own all the commanders of provincial armies under the *imperium* of the emperor could no longer obtain the coveted title of *imperator* (in this case with the original meaning 'victorious commander') or have a triumph, because the possession of the *auspicia* was much more important than the fact that the leading officer (the emperor) was not present on the battlefield.[24] The emperor was not even obliged to leave Rome in order to take the *acclamatio imperatoria* from a victorious army far away, because the *auspicia* mattered, not the actual command.

Now to the problems that evolve if we try to take this information down to the field of military sacrifices. Within the world of the

---

[24] Leonard Schumacher, "Die imperatorischen Akklamationen der Triumvirn und die Auspicia des Augustus," *Historia* 34 (1985) 191–222.

military there existed a certain set of ceremonies connected with
sacrifices that had to performed by the commander in chief. To
name only one important occasion, the ritual purification of the army
at the beginning or the ending of the campaign (*lustratio exercitus*), a
ceremony that was usually accompanied by the sacrifice of the so-
called *suovetaurilia* (*sus, ovis, taurus*).[25] Of course the emperor could not
be present and the local commander had to act in his place. But
how were the resulting religious questions dealt with? Can we imagine that the emperor endowed his *legatus* with a limited set of religious rights to act as his representative?[26]

I must admit that these problems have not been properly dealt
with before. But I want to give some information that may serve as
an incentive for further research in this field. I have already mentioned that in many cases the sacrifices of the *primi pili* and the *veterani*, that marked the end of their professional involvement with the
army, were conducted by the provincial governor himself. I suppose
that in theory those sacrifices were expected to be performed by the
emperor himself with the governor only acting as his local representative. Such a solution seems especially attractive in the case of
the *veterani* because they swore their *sacramentum* not to the *res publica
Romana* but to the emperor. In some cases the ceremony of the *missio
veteranorum* is even described as *sacramento solutus*, the freeing from the
religious obligations of the oath.[27] In theory, the very personal bond
between soldier and emperor required the personal presence of the
emperor since he was the only person that could properly free the
soldier.[28] In this case we have probably to imagine a regulation that
transmitted this exclusive right of the emperor to his *legatus*.

There seems to be a certain possibility to bridge the gap between
the religious demands of the army and the necessity to do without

---

[25] Jörg Rüpke, *Domi militiae. Die religiöse Konstruktion des Krieges in Rom* (Stuttgart:
Steiner, 1990) 144–151.
[26] Tac. *Ann.* 15.26.3 seems to prove that Roman commanders without the full
imperium could perform the *lustratio: . . . tum lustratum rite exercitum ad contionem vocat. . . .*
[27] Interesting is the formula 'honeste sacramento solutus', that we find in the juristic
literature to characterize the veteran. 'Solutus' moves the whole ceremony in the
same religious sphere as the ritual fulfillment of vows (*votum solvit*). Cf. *Dig.* 49.18.2:
Honeste sacramento solutis; C. Just. 4.21.7: *si solemnibus stipendiis et honeste sacramento solutus.*
[28] At least for the units that had Rome as their permanent garrison (*praetoriani,
urbani, vigiles, equites singulares*) we can expect that the *missio* was regularly performed
in the presence of the emperor. That seems to be indicated by the proud title *vete-
ranus Augusti* transmitted by many *veterani* of the urban troops: the emperor himself
freed them and dismissed them to their life as civilians.

the emperor and his priestly competence. In my opinion, the presence of the imperial images within the army offer an attractive solution.[29] Imperial images, usually life-size statues made of bronze, could
be found in the camp of almost any unit. Smaller images, usually
busts, were certainly to be found in the chapel where the *signa* of
the unit were kept. Bronze or silver portraits of the emperor were
attached to the military *signa* and marched together with the soldiers
into battle. The soldier who carried the imperial image, the *imag-
inifer*, held a regular position in each unit. The existence of portable
images within the army is amply documented and shows a broad
spectrum of possibilities. Therefore we know of the existence of
wooden pictures with a painted portrait of the emperor on stucco,
other portraits (usually life-size busts) were produced from metal.[30]

Usually those images are dealt with under artistic or archaeological aspects while the religious function of those objects remains very
vague. In our modern conception of pictures we have usually lost
the ability to understand the importance of images properly; for us
they are usually part of the decoration and nothing else. In the religious thinking of the Roman army the imperial images not only gave
a vivid impression of what the emperor looked like, but also were
able to establish a bodily presence of the emperor. There is not
enough room to deal with such a complex problem in all details.
Therefore I limit myself to some significant facts that seem to be
useful for further discussion.

In 38 CE Vitellius, the Roman governor of Syria, met the Parthian
king Artabanos on the banks of the Euphrates, and forced him to
sacrifice to the imperial images of Augustus and Caligula, in order
to confirm the peace with Rome.[31] A comparable ceremony took
place in 63 CE when the Armenian king Tiridates deposed his diadem in front of the image of emperor Nero.[32] A famous inscription

---

[29] For the imperial images in general cp. Thomas Pekàry, *Das römische Kaiserbildnis
in Staat, Kult und Gesellschaft dargestellt anhand der Schriftquellen* (Berlin: Gebrüder Mann,
1985). Still useful Helmut Kruse, *Studien zur offiziellen Geltung des Kaiserbildes im römischen Reiche* (Paderborn: Schönigh, 1934).

[30] Very important: Heinz Heinen, "Herrscherkult im römischen Ägypten und
damnatio memoriae Getas. Überlegungen zum Berliner Severertondo und zu Papyrus
Oxyrhynchys XII 1449," *Mitteilungen des Deutschen Archäologischen Instituts Römische
Abteilung* 98 (1991) 263–298.

[31] Cassius Dio 59.27.4.

[32] Tac. *Ann.* 15.29.2–3: "... On the dais in the middle was a Roman official

from Ponte Luciano near Rome informs us about the career of the great Roman senator Tiberius Plautius Silvanus Aelianus, who spent several turbulent years under the reign of Nero as governor of the province of Lower Moesia.[33] One of the highlights of his period of service was the reception of several barbarian *reges* into the Roman domination. In the words of the inscription 'he guided kings, who were unknown until that time or angry with the Roman people, to the banks (of the Danube) that he was used to guard in order that they should adore the Roman images' (*ignotos ante aut infensos p.R. reges signa Romana adoraturos in ripam, quam tuebatur, perduxit*).[34] As the text of the inscription seems to transmit at least part of an official speech by the emperor Vespasian to the Roman senate we seem to be quite close to the official view of the function of imperial images.

People whose personal experience is shaped by the history of the 20th century and a strict separation of church and state will be surprised at the influence of religion on the life of the Roman soldier. But this holds true only if we limit our investigation to the surface of modern armies. If we take a closer look we can see that even the armies of today have many ritualized ceremonies which in Roman times were surely accompanied by sacrifices. It seems as if armies cannot do without them!

APPENDIX

Festivities of the *Feriale Duranum*

1 January   New years day [lacuna in text, may be sacrifice of 3
            animals to the Capitoline trias]

---

chair, bearing Nero's effigy. To this Tiridates advanced. When the customary sacrifices had been made, he took the diadem from his head and laid it at the feet of the statue" (*. . . medio tribunal sedem curulem et sedes effigiem Neronis sustinebat. ad quam progressus Tiridates, caesis ex more victimis, sublatum capiti diadema imagini subiecit . . .*). The English translation was taken from Tacitus, *The Annals of Imperial Rome* ed. Michael Grant (Harmondsworth: Penguin, 1956).

[33] Corpus Inscriptionum Latinarum XIV 3608 = Dessau, Inscriptiones Latinae Selectae 986.

[34] The Latin word *signum* covers a very broad field. It can mean the insignia of a military unit, but in many cases it has the meaning of a 'small portable picture'. In this special case I am convinced that portable images of the emperor were meant.

3 January	*nuncupatio votorum* [up to 8 animals]
7 January	*dies missionis* [at least 5 animals]
8 January	*dies natalis divae* [*supplicatio*]
9/23 January	*dies natalis Lucii Sei Caesaris* [1 animal ?]
24 January	*dies natalis divi Hadriani* [1 animal]
28 January	*dies imperii Traiani, Victoria Parthica* [2 animals]
4 February	*dies imperii Aurelii Antonini Magni Pii* [*supplicatio*, 1 animal]
1 March	*Mars Pater* [1 animal]
7 March	*dies imperii Marci Aurelii et Lucii Veri* [2 animals]
13 March	*Severus Alexander imperator apellatus* [4 animals, *supplicatio*]
14 March	*Severus Alexander Augustus, pater patriae, pontifex appellatus* [*supplicatio*, 1 animal]
19–23 March	*Quinquatria* [*supplicationes* for each day]
4 April	*dies natalis divi Marci Aurelii Antonini* [1 animal]
9 April	*dies imperii divi Septimii Severi* [1 animal]
11 April	*dies natalis divi Septimii Severi* [1 animal]
21 April	*dies natalis urbis Romae* [1 animal]
26 April	*dies natalis divi Marci Aurelii* [1 animal]
7 May	*dies natalis divae Iuliae Maesae* [*supplicatio*]
9/11 May	*rosaliae signorum* [*supplicatio*]
12 May	*circenses Martiales* [1 animal]
21 May	*acclamatio imperatoria divi Severi* [1 animal]
24 May	*dies natalis Germanici* [*supplicatio*]
31 May	*rosaliae signorum* [*supplicatio*]
9 June	*Vestalia* [*supplicatio*]
26 June	*dies Caesaris, toga virilis Severi Alexandri* [1 animal]
1 July	*Severus Alexander consul designatus* [*supplicatio*]
2/5 July	*dies natalis divae Matidiae* [*supplicatio*]
10 July	*dies imperii divi Antonini Pii* [1 animal]
12 July	*dies natalis divi Iulii* [1 animal]
23 July	*Neptunalia* [*immolatio, supplicatio*]
1 August	*dies natalis divi Claudii et divi Pertinacis* [2 animals]
5 August	*circenses Salutares* [1 animal]
14/29 August	*dies natalis Mamaeae Augustae, matris Augusti* [1 animal]
15/30 August	*dies natalis divae Marcianae* [*supplicatio*]
31 August	*dies natalis divi Commodi* [1 animal]
7 September	*ludi Romani* (?) [*supplicatio* ?]
18 September	*dies natalis divi Traiani, dies imperii divi Nervae* [2 animals]
19 September	*dies natalis divi Antonini Pii* [1 animal]

20/22 September   *dies natalis divae Faustinae* ? [*supplicatio*]
23 September   *dies natalis divi Augusti* [1 animal]

Additional Festivities were included in the lost part of the *Feriale Duranum*. The *dies natales* and the *dies imperii* are certain candidates. *Augustalia* and *Saturnalia* are probable.

1 October   *dies natalis imperatoris Severi Alexandri* [at least 4 animals]
12 October   *Augustalia* (?) [*supplicatio* ?][35]
8 November   *dies natalis divi Nervae* [1 animal]
17 November   *dies natalis divi Vespasiani* [1 animal]
27 November   *dies imperii divi Commodi* [1 animal][36]
15 December   *dies natalis divi Lucii Veri* [1 animal]
17/20 December   *Saturnalia* (?) [*supplicatio* ?]
30 December   *dies natalis divi Titi* [1 animal]

---

[35] I am very confident, that the *Augustalia* became part of the military *feriale*, because the festivity was established after Augustus' triumphant return from the East in 19 BCE when he had compelled the Parthian king to return the Roman *signa*, lost since Crassus' defeat near Carrhai.

[36] This *dies imperii* marks the beginning of the joint rule of Marcus Aurelius and Commodus in the year 176 CE. By assuming such a solution we can solve the old problem why 19 March, the day when Commodus became sole emperor after the death of his father in 180 CE, was not registered by the *Feriale Duranum*.

SACRIFICE AND THEORY OF SACRIFICE
DURING THE 'PAGAN REACTION':
JULIAN THE EMPEROR

NICOLE BELAYCHE

"In my opinion, it is worth while ("Άξιον δέ) to add some short remarks (βραχέα προσθεῖναι) about sacrifices", said the neoplatonist philosopher Saloustios as if he invited us to this colloquium. Iamblichus also, in his own way, legitimates our studies when he declares that there is "a problem which is shared, we could say by everybody, by those who practise *artes liberalia* as much as by those who do not have any experience of philosophy, that is . . . the issue of sacrifices".[1]

The choice of these patrons for an analysis of the sacrifices of Julian the Emperor is natural, for two reasons at least. First, the cultural links[2] of these two thinkers with the "crowned philosopher"[3] are well known[4] and their systematic explanations will confirm, together with other testimonies, the information given by Julian himself.[5] Second, whether bloody or not, sacrifice is the central rite in every religious culture because it defines hierarchies between men and gods in the *ordo rerum*. In Graeco-Roman paganism, it makes possible to consecrate something to the divinity that is a partner in the city even if he is superior by nature, in the form of homage, vow or appeasement. Through *consecratio*, the city "is allowed to share

---

[1] Saloustius *De mundo* 16.1 and Iamblichus *De mysteriis* 5.1.

My warm thanks to Frédérique Lachaud and Monica Brain who amicably helped me to give an English form to my paper. Julian's writings are cited by the title of work only, omitting the author. *Ep.* are cited with Budé's letter-number (in brackets Hertlein). The French version of this paper appeared in *RHR* 218, 4 (2001) 455–486.

[2] For Julian, they weaved stronger links than those of hospitality, *Ep.* 35(39).416a.

[3] Cf. Mamertinus *Panegyr.* 11.23.4; Libanius *Orat.* 12.33–34, 13.1 and 13. For "philosophy" as an *"exercice spirituel"*, cf. the perfect definition in Pierre Hadot, *Qu'est-ce que la philosophie antique?* (Paris: Gallimard, 1995) and Bouffartigue [1992] 633–40.

[4] Cf. J.Ch. Balty, "Julien et Apamée. Aspects de la restauration de l'hellénisme et de la politique antichrétienne de l'Empereur", *Dialogues d'Histoire Ancienne* 1 (1974) 267–303; Athanassiadi-F. [1981] and Smith [1995] 23–48.

[5] It has been said that the Saloustius' treatise is a *"catéchisme de la religion païenne renouvelée par l'apport des croyances platoniciennes"*, G. Rochefort, "Le Περὶ θεῶν καὶ κοσμοῦ de Saloustios et l'influence de l'Empereur Julien", *REG* 69 (1956) 50–66. Cf. Bowersock [1978] 86 and Athanassiadi-F. [1981] 154.

the table of the gods (κοινωνεῖν ἄξιον καὶ τραπεζοῦν θεοῖς)".[6] Despite this central place in the Roman religious conception, Julian's sacrificial practices have spoiled his *memoria* in the historiography. I shall try to demonstrate that on the contrary, they are a good indication of a fourth century's mentality built on the cultures of his time.

At first sight, and after reading the numerous and good studies devoted to Julian,[7] one would think that the question of his attitude towards sacrifice cannot be the subject of further study. Julian's sacrificial acts are unanimously rejected by his contemporaries, either followers or opponents. Even Ammianus Marcellinus, a fascinated witness to the Emperor's epopee,[8] describes Julian's sacrificial mania as superstitious and prodigal. He repeats with good will the hard criticisms broadcast by the Antiocheans: "that if he had returned from the Parthians, there would soon have been a scarcity of cattle (*boves iam defuturos*)".[9] He echoes the violent finale of Gregorius Nazianzen applauding the death of the impious: "Where are the sacrifices (αἱ θυσίαι) . . .? Where are the immolations, the public ones as well as the clandestine ones (σφάγια φανερά τε καὶ ἀφανῆ)? Where is this much-boasted art, the cutting up of victims (τέχνη κατὰ τῶν ἐντόμων ἐπαινουμένη)? . . . Where is this whole world whose meanings became clear by virtue of the drop of a cursed blood (ἐναγοῦς αἵματος)?".[10] The historiographical tradition since Voltaire and Edward Gibbon has not spared the Apostate either.[11] Julian's apparent ritualistic "hysteria" fitted so well the supposed unbalance of the man, "*d'une bigoterie abusive*" to use the expression coined by Jean Fontaine,[12] that its motivations have been very rarely looked into, even in the rehabilitations of the Emperor's mental state.[13] Glen Bowersock's biog-

---

[6] Julien *Mother of the Gods* 17 [176d].

[7] Cf. recent bibliographical lists at the end of the paper.

[8] Cf. Fontaine [1978] 31 ff.

[9] 25.4.17. He never abandoned his "amulets and talismans", *Ep.* 80(1*) page 88 l. 6.

[10] *Orat.* 5.25. Libanius draws an exact reversed portrait, *Orat.* 17.4 and 18.281.

[11] Voltaire, *Discours de l'empereur Julien contre les chrétiens*, J.-M. Moureaux, ed., (Oxford, 1994) 199–200; Edward Gibbon, *The History of the Decline and Fall of the Roman Empire*, vol. 2 (London: Bell and Daldy, 1867) 510–7. *Contra*, the portrait by Lenain de Tillemont of the "*malheureux apostat*" (*Mémoires pour servir à l'Histoire ecclésiastique des six premiers siècles*, VII [Paris: Ch. Robustel, 1700] 322–7) avoids, for the main, judgements of value.

[12] Fontaine [1978] 55 and 60.

[13] "*la dévotion excessive de l'empereur, autre aspect anormal de son comportement*", Bouffartigue [1989] 532 and 534.

raphy was the first work that started giving him his due but the message has not been widely heard.[14] If the *innumeras sine parsimonia pecudes mactans*[15] of the Emperor is not included in his heavy psychological file, one makes use of his sacrifices in a purely informative way, like J. Bidez, in order to date the beginning of the "pagan reaction" during the reign[16] or to study the various measures of the so-called "restoration" of paganism. These views are naturally useful; even combined, however, they do not explain, in my opinion, what Iamblichus called "the mystery of sacrifices",[17] as long as one accepts the authenticity of Julian's words and acts. "One must avoid the crowd and act discretely ... when he presents to the gods the right victims and homages".[18]

Any historian intending to study this very complex personality is lucky in having, for a figure as controversial as Julian, a rich documentary corpus made up of very different sources: stories by fond admirers or implacable enemies, legal decisions, vitriolic pamphlets from opposing sides, confessions and conceptual or mystical treatises by the Emperor's own hand.[19] Julian's exceptional life has been served by a number of good biographies,[20] enough for me to pass rapidly over it. For the question that I want to examine here, I just have to remind you that Julian's ritual behaviour is inspired by the three traditions which formed his cultural and ideological personality.[21] As he confesses himself, the Graeco-Roman intellectual tradition turns a Thracian into a Greek.[22] His Hellenism goes hand in hand with the Roman tradition, since he belongs to an imperial family. When he was a child enclosed in Macellum, he was first brought up in

---

[14] Bowersock [1978] 86 and 89.

[15] Ammianus 25.4.17: "he sacrificed innumerable victims without regard to cost".

[16] Cf. Bidez [1914] 406–61.

[17] Iamblichus *De mysteriis* 5.26.

[18] *Ep.* 98 [400d].

[19] Cf. Bowersock [1978] 1–11.

[20] Besides those already mentioned, cf. the still fundamental J. Bidez, *La vie de l'Empereur Julien* (Paris: Les Belles Lettres, 1965); E. v. Borries, "Iulianos (Apostata)", *RE* 10 (1917) 26–91; G. Ricciotti, *Julien l'Apostat* (French translation, Paris, 1959).

[21] Cf. his *paideia* in Athanassiadi-F. [1981] 131–60 and Smith [1995] 23–48. Scott [1987] 345–62 studied his "*syncrétique*" mind; Gauthier [1987] 227–35 stresses the psychological reasons to separate the three traditions.

[22] *Misop.* 367c and Libanius *Orat.* 15.25–27. Athanassiadi-F. [1981] stressed the Roman aspect of his Hellenism, 1–12, 121 ff (= ch. IV) and 229–31. Cf. also Huart [1978] and Alan Cameron, "Julian and Hellenism", *The Ancient* World 24 (1993) 25–9.

the Christian tradition since, paradoxically, the "Apostate" was the
first Emperor to have been already baptised when he donned the
purple.[23] Growing up, he chose another way, the neoplatonist tradition that he learnt first from Maximus of Ephesus. "He used to teach
me to practise virtue before all else and to regard the gods as my
guides to all that is good (θεοὺς ἁπάντων τῶν καλῶν [. . .] ἡγεμόνας)".[24]
Later on, courses that he followed in Aedesius' and Chrysanthius'
schools definitely oriented his positions.[25] In following Julian's sacrifices,
we shall notice that his ritual attitude is rooted in these three traditions, despite the strains that appear as contradictory.

   "He [Julian] it was who divided up his life into preoccupation
for the state and devotion to the altars (ὁ μερίσας αὑτοῦ τὸν βίον
εἴς τε τὰς ὑπὲρ τῶν ὅλων βουλὰς εἴς τε τὰς περὶ τοὺς βωμοὺς δια-
τριβάς)".[26] As soon as Julian marched against Constantius during the
summer of 361, he broadcast himself as *cultor deorum*[27] and encouraged sacrificial rituals' celebration that he must himself have practised secretly for the past ten years.[28] Libanios glorifies him for having
performed more sacrifices in ten years than all the Greeks united![29]
Hence, these sacrificial orgies which actually give off a sour smell.
In Antioch as elsewhere, he regularly honours the local gods. "The
Emperor sacrificed (ἔθυσεν) once in the temple of Zeus, then in the
temple of Fortune (Tyche); he visited the temple of Demeter three
times in succession. (I have in fact forgotten how many times I
entered the shrine (τέμενος) of Daphne) [. . .] The Syrian New Year
arrived, and again the Emperor went to the temple of Zeus Philios.
Then came the general festival, and the Emperor went to the shrine
of Fortune. Then, after refraining on the forbidden day (τὴν ἀποφράδα),
again he goes to the temple of Zeus Philios, and offers up prayers

---

   [23] Cf. André-J. Festugière, "Julien à Macellum", *JRS* 47 (1957) 53–8; Athanassiadi-
Fowden [1981] 25–7.
   [24] *Heracl.* 235b.
   [25] Eunapius, *Lives of the Sophists* 473–5. Cf. H.-Adrien Naville, *Julien l'Apostat et sa
philosophie du polythéisme* (Paris-Neuchatel: Sandoz, 1877) 24–6; Hans Raeder, "Kaiser
Julian als Philosoph und religiöser Reformator", *Classica et Mediaevalia* 6 (1944) 179–93
repr. in R. Klein, ed., *Julian Apostata* (Darmstadt, 1978) 206–21; Athanassiadi-Fowden
[1981] 30–41.
   [26] Libanios, *Or.* 24, 35.
   [27] *Ep.* 26(38).415c. Cf. Ammianus 22.5.1–2 and Libanius *Orat.* 13.14 and 18.121.
   [28] Ammianus 21.1.4–5 and Libanius *Orat.* 12.69. Cf. DiMaio [1989].
   [29] *Orat.* 24.35. Cf. Petit [1978] 75–8.

(τὰς εὐχάς) according to the custom of our ancestors (κατὰ τὰ πάτρια)".[30] Ammianus' testimony confirms the Emperor's one and denounces the sacrificial meals that were transformed into orgies by the soldiers. "He drenched the altars with the blood of an excessive number of victims (*Hostiarum tamen sanguine plurimo aras crebritate nimia perfundebat*), sometimes offering up (*immolando*) a hundred oxen at once, with countless flocks of various other animals . . . So that, almost every-day, the soldiers, *carnis distentiore sagina victitantes*, acted without the slightest discipline. They became brute from their drunkness and were carried . . . from the public temples (*ex publicis aedibus*) where they held their *convivia*".[31] The emperor behaved himself in a more modest manner. Fashioning himself as another Marcus Aurelius, his official imperial model, he "nourished [his] body because [he] believed, though perhaps falsely, that even gods' bodies require to be nourished by the fumes of sacrifice (τὰ ὑμέτερα σώματα δεῖται τῆς ἐκ τῶν ἀναθυμιάσεων τροφῆς)".[32] The reserve that we read here prefigures his spiritualistic question on sacrifice that we shall consider later.

On becoming Augustus, Julian also became *pontifex maximus*,[33] in the line of all his predecessors to the imperial seat. Consequently, he was the supreme religious manager of the Roman state cult, he was the guardian, the guarantor and the interpreter of its rules, as explained in his defence of the edict on funerals.[34] The great religious accomplishment of the reign of one Libanios called ὁ βασιλεύς ἄριστος[35] was the restoration of the forms of the pagan cult.[36] Inscriptions celebrate him as *templorum restaurator* or ἀνανεωτὴς τῶν ἱερῶν.[37] But, we must keep in mind that, since Constantine, the official cult had been put aside and opposed to by laws forbidding

---

[30] *Misop.* 346bc. Cf. Libanius *Orat.* 15.79 and 17.18.
[31] Ammianus 22.12.6; 22.14.4 (at Mount Casios).
[32] *Caes.* 333d.
[33] *Ep.* 88(62).451b.
[34] *Ep.* 136b(77).
[35] *Orat.* 17.31.
[36] *Misop.* 361c. Cf. his prayer in form of hymn to the Mother of gods, *Orat.* 8[5] 180a and the two famous letters to Arsacius (*Ep.* 84(49).429c–432a) and Theodorus (89a and b(63).452a–454b and 288a–305d). Cf. Libanius *Orat.* 18.126 and 24.35.
[37] Cf. Bowersock [1978] 123–4; Al.N. Oikonomides, "Ancient Inscriptions Recording the Restoration of Greco-Roman Shrines by the Emperor Flavius Claudius Julianus (361–363 AD)", *The Ancient World* 15 (1987) 37–42; A. Negev, "The Inscription of the Emperor Julian at Ma'ayan Baruch", *IEJ* 19 (1969) 170–3; DiMaio [1989] 101–6.

sacrifices and divination as "*contagiosa superstitiosa*", even in the imperial cult as in Hispellum in Ombria.[38] "*Sacrificiorum aboleatur insania . . .*", as Constantius' law had decreed.[39] Hence, great public sacrifices listed in the Roman calendar were almost never performed. They were still known only through the reliefs. We can understand, then, the horrified surprise of Julian's contemporaries who saw the Emperor performing sacrifices two times a day[40] and establishing the same rule for the pagan "clergy".[41] In Constantinople, the imperial city, the Bishop Maris tried to stop him on his way to Fortune's altar.[42]

The main religious aim of the reign was the restoration of the cultic forms. Following Diocletian and many other Emperors, Julian was convinced that restoration of the public cult was the condition for the restoration of the Empire and the definition of the State. The new *pontifex maximus* might perform sacrifices at the great public festivals, when the city defines its identity before the god through *consecratio*[43] and "when on the altars fire surges up (ὅτε πῦρ μὲν ἐπὶ βωμῶν αἴρεται) and the smoke of sacrifice purges the air (καπνῷ δὲ ἀὴρ ἱερῷ καθαίρεται), when men feast with gods and gods consort with them (ἐστιῶσι δὲ ἄνθρωποι δαίμονας καὶ δαίμονες ἀνθρώποις ὁμιλοῦσι)".[44] For Julian then, sacrifice is the means to participate in the divine order and to make real the hierarchy between gods and Emperors. "I sacrifice oxen in public (ἡμεῖς φανερῶς βουθυτοῦμεν). I have offered to the gods many hecatombs as thanks-offerings (ἀπεδώκαμεν τοῖς θεοῖς χαριστήρια περὶ ἡμῶν ἑκατόμβας πολλάς). The

---

[38] The imperial rescript from Hispellum (*ILS* 705.46–47) establishes a cult for the *gens Flavia* but forbids bloody sacrifices. See *Heracl.* 228b, for the inspired description that Julian gives of the policies of the repression of the cult since Constantine. About the anti-pagan policies since Constantine, cf. Pierre de Labriolle, "Christianisme et paganisme au milieu du IV᷎ siècle", Auguste Fliche & Victor Martin, *Histoire de l'Église*, vol. 3, *De la paix constantinienne à la mort de Théodose* (Paris: Bloud & Gay, 1936) 177–183 and J.-M. Mayeur—Ch. & L. Piétri et al., *Histoire du christianisme*, vol. 2: *Naissance d'une chrétienté (250– 430)* (Paris: Desclée, 1995), 210-2 and 289–291.

[39] *CTh.* 16.10.2. Cf. *Ep.* 61(42).423c; Mamertinus *Panegyr.* 11.23.5; Libanius *Orat.* 18.23.

[40] *Ep.* 98(27).401b.

[41] *Ep.* 89b.302ab; Sozomen 5.16.2. Cf. Libanius *Orat.* 12.80–81 and 18.127.

[42] Socrates 3.11.3 ff and Sozomen 5.4.8 ff.

[43] *Ep.* 114(52).438a. Cf. Jean-Pierre Vernant, "Théorie générale du sacrifice et mise à mort dans la ΘΥΣΙΑ grecque", *Le sacrifice dans l'Antiquité* (Entretiens Fondation Hardt 27, Vandoeuvres-Genève, 1981) 1–39; Bouffartigue [1978] 19–21; Georges Dumézil, *La religion romaine archaïque* (2d ed.: Paris: Payot, 1987) 545–66; John Scheid, *La religion des Romains* (Paris: A. Colin, 1998) 72–84.

[44] Libanios, *Or.* 13, 47; cf. also 17.9.

gods command me to restore their worship in its utmost purity (ἀγνεύειν)".[45] In consequence, Julian considered that the gods themselves are the very authors of the religious restoration.[46]

Julian was deeply convinced of his responsibility towards the *res publica*. Considering that the care of the relation to the gods is the responsibility of the political structure, "it befits the city, I think, to offer both private and public sacrifice (θύειν ἰδίᾳ καὶ δημοσίᾳ)"[47] and "the civil magistrates . . ., as guardians of the laws, act as a kind of priest for the gods".[48] Even more, the Emperor is invested with a sacerdotal mission which goes beyond a simple institutional direction of the cult and which drove him to transform his palace into a temple.[49] "It is only proper, in my opinion, that a general or king should always serve the god with the appointed ritual (θεραπεύειν ἀεὶ ξὺν κόσμῳ τὸν θεὸν), like a priest or prophet (καθάπερ ἱερέα καὶ προφήτην), and not neglect this duty".[50] We better understand then his bitter anger against Antioch that did not offer even "a bird in the name of the city" for the civic festival.[51] In Julian's mind, this attitude came close to the crime of *maiestas*. Even the most hostile sources agree to recognise his concern. This helps to explain why this man, careful with public money, frugal and ascetic, could have spent so generously as soon as the happiness of his subjects was concerned, either for social purposes[52] or to bring the city in line with the gods, consequently with sacrifices.[53]

Thus, Julian sacrificed on each public occasion, according to Numa's laws, in which he recognised "true perfection (ὁ καλὸς καὶ ἀγαθὸς ὁ Νουμᾶς)".[54] In the midst of battles, he sought the gods'

---

[45] *Ep.* 26(38).415c.
[46] *Ep.* 61(42).423c.
[47] *Misop.* 363a.
[48] *Ep.* 89b.296c.
[49] Libanius *Orat.* 12.81. Cf. the description of the Julian's "*zèle idolâtre*" by Lenain de Tillemont, *Mémoires* . . . VII. 325–6.
[50] *Basileia* 68b. Cf. Libanius *Orat.* 12.80, who compares Julian with a Pythia (*Orat.* 13.48). Hence a clear hierarchy between gods and emperors, *Ep.* 176(64) page 217 ll. 6–9; cf. Arthur Darby Nock, "Deification and Julian", *JRS* 47 (1957), 115–23.
[51] *Misop.* 362cd and 363b.
[52] Cf. Mamertinus *Panegyr.* 11.10.3, 11 and 13.1–3. Cf. Athanassiadi-Fowden [1981] 97–109.
[53] Ammianus 22.12.7 and Libanius *Orat.* 18.170. Hence the rhetor's revolt when he met death, *Orat.* 17.6. *Contra* Greg. Naz. (*Orat.* 4.117): "impiety combined with expenditure".
[54] *C. Galileos* 193d (last ed.: Emmanuele Masaracchia, Rome, 1990). On the sacrosanctity of tradition for Julian, Weiss [1978], 128–30 and Scott [1987] 345–6.

support, like so many *imperatores* before him.[55] Hence, for Libanios, "the many sacrifices (αἱ πυκναὶ θυσίαι), the frequent blood-offerings (τὸ αἷμα τὸ πολύ), the clouds of incense (οἱ τῶν ἀρωμάτων ἀτμοί)", let us say his piety only, succeeded in forcing the Parthians to ask for peace.[56] When the *consules* took up their functions, he would perform the usual sacrifices of January calends.[57] His work, *The Caesares*, began with the sacrifice of the *Saturnalia* presided over by Romulus.[58] Distributions to soldiers were organised under the aegis of the gods: "Gold was exposed, incense also; not far, the fire".[59] On his way east, when he is received by the governor of Cilicia and a sacrifice,[60] Julian did not forget to deliver a religious and cultural homage at the great pagan sanctuaries of Asia Minor. He turns "sacred tourism" into "a pretext to enter into the temples".[61] During his Parthian campaign also, he was careful to celebrate Cybele's annual feast and stopped to sacrifice to the departed soul of Gordian III.[62] Gregorius Nazianzen even suggests that Julian had planned to make the burning of incense on the altars compulsory before any public act.[63] In short, Julian respected scrupulously the ritual of secular ceremonies. "I imagined in my own mind the sort of procession (πομπήν) it would be [. . .], beasts for sacrifice (ἱερεῖα), libations (σπονδάς), choruses (χορούς) in honour of the god, incense (θυμιάματα) and the youths of your city down there surrounding the shrine, their souls adorned with all holiness and themselves attired in white and splendid raiment".[64] We could believe we are attending an average feast of the most classical period of pagan state religion. Julian did not use sacrifice, however, as a theme of ideological propaganda for his reign. His coinage exalts the traditional Roman values but does not make use of any ritual object or of sacrificial type. This is in spite of the

---

[55] Cf. Libanius *Orat.* 12.88–90 and 18.169.

[56] *Or.* 12, 79.

[57] Cf. *Misop.* 339c; *Ep.* 41(20).388b; Ammianus 22.7.1–2.

[58] 307b. Cf. also *Helios* 131d and 155b.

[59] For Greg. Naz. (*Orat.* 4.83), this proves the "Apostate"'s satanic nature. Cf. Libanius *Orat.* 18.168.

[60] Libanios, *Or.* 18, 159.

[61] *Ep.* 79(78) p. 85, ll. 17–18. Cf. Ammianus 22.9.5 and 8 ("*hostiisque litato votis* (after Julian had propitiated [the deity] with victims and vows") and Libanius *Orat.* 12.87, 17.17 and 18.161–162.

[62] Ammianus 23.3.7 and 5.8.

[63] *Orat.* 4.96.

[64] *Misop.* 362a.

coin type of the bull, most probably the Apis bull, that the Antiocheans and some Christian historians misinterpreted maliciously as a representation of a sacrifice.[65]

There is no need yet to mention the transfiguring experience that announced his mission.[66] His Roman vision of the world explains sufficiently why Julian wished to be in conformity with the will of the gods before any action. And he did this according to a traditional pantheon—Zeus, Helios, Ares, Athena and all the gods—[67] and in following the Roman ritual rules so religiously that he considered his—eventual—death in the shape of an antique *devotio*.[68] The formula of the prayer that he addressed to Zeus was, hence, traditional: "Father Zeus, or whatever name thou dost please that men should call thee by (ὅτι σοι φίλον ὄνομα καὶ ὅπως ὀνομάζεσθαι), show me the way that leads upwards to thee".[69] But Julian differed greatly from the pure Roman tradition in the role that he gave himself during the ceremonies. In Roman tradition, the priest or the magistrate performing the sacrifice is the master and supervisor of the legality of ritual operations. He accomplishes himself the noble and fundamental gesture of the *immolatio*. Then he spells out the words of the prayer and orders the gestures of the sacrificial sequence. He collects

---

[65] Ammianus 22.12.16, Socrates 3.17 and Sozomen 5.19. Cf. *RIC* VIII (1981) 46–7 and Pierre Bastien, *Le monnayage de l'atelier de Lyon de la mort de Constantin à la mort de Julien (337–363)* (Numismatique romaine 15; Wetteren: Éditions Numismatique Romaine, 1985) n° 284–9 et pl. XXVI. The signification of the type, commonly interpreted as the Apis bull, raised a large debate. Frank D. Gilliard ("Notes on the Coinage of Iulian the Apostate", *JRS* 54 (1964) 138–41 et pl. X n° 13) has found a zodiacal representation of Julian. J.J. Arce ("Algunas problemas de la numismatica del emperador Fl. Cl. Iulianus", *Archivo espanol de Arqueologia* 45–47 (1972–1974), 477–96) follows the sources quoted (a sacrificial bull), without convincing us, since we do not find the usual ornaments of sacred animals (e.g. *dorsuale*, garments) or an altar. More generally, Jean-Luc Desnier ("Renaissance taurine", *Latomus* 44 (1985) 402–9), recognizes the victorious Augustean bull, that would mean an emphasis on the Julianic policy of *renovatio*. This explanation does not convince either: despite his high concern with religious matters, Augustus was never a positive imperial model for Julian, as we know from the portrait that he has drawn of him in the *Caesares* 33 (*contra* Desnier 407).

[66] Julian told it disguised in form of a myth in his Antiochean treatise *Heracl.* 227c–234c.

[67] In 361 at Lutetia during his acclamation by the army: "I call to witness . . ." (*Ad Athen.* 284bc); the same list in *Ep.* 26(38).415a; cf. Libanius *Orat.* 15.79 and 17.4. Cf. Bouffartigue [1992] 646–51.

[68] Ammianus 23.5.19: "*vovisse sufficiet* (I shall be content with having sacrificed myself")".

[69] *Heracl.* 231b. Cf. *Misop.* 357d and *Ep.* 98(27).399d. By the way, Julian is here consistent with the Platonist tradition about the name of the gods, Plato *Cratyl* 400e.

the information given by the examination of the entrails in order to translate it into a public and political meaning. Finally he checks the respective parts of gods and men.[70] Instead, Julian set himself as the *victimarius*, "*victimarius pro sacricola dicebatur*" to quote a well-known Antiochean satire.[71] "He performs the sacrifice in person (αὐτουργεῖ); he busies himself with the preparations (περιτρέχει), gets the wood (σχίζης ἅπτεται), wields the knife (μάχαιραν δέχεται), opens the birds (ὄρνις ἀνέρρηξε) and inspects their entrails (τὰ ἔνδον οὐκ ἠγνόησε)".[72] Considering that political and ritual responsibilities should be kept in the same hands, he assumed the charges normally accomplished by cultic auxiliaries, who were slaves or manumitted, as it is documented.[73] This confusion of roles, proper to bad Emperors like Caligula and Commodus,[74] probably did much to spoil his image.[75] It draws this now legendary portrait of a superstitious man, in the Roman sense of the word, if we accept his portrait by the Christian poet Prudentius.[76]

Is there any way for us to reconcile the high idea Julian had of the imperial function and this lowering of himself into "butchery"?[77] His anxious psychology, even neurotic according to some,[78] provides us with a solution that is unsatisfactory if we remind ourselves that Julian had a very high conception of sacrifice. The idea that this very pious man had of his relation to the divinity offers a first answer. Whatever the priestly mission belonging to the manager of *politeia*, Julian considered priesthood to be superior because it is τὸ τιμιώτατον τῶν θεῶν κτῆμα.[79] Here, Julian appears as the heir of Elagabalus—

---

[70] Th. Mommsen et J. Marquardt, *Manuel des Antiquités romaines*, vol. 12.1: *Le culte chez les Romains* (Paris, 1889) 201–27.

[71] Ammianus 22.14.3.

[72] Libanius *Orat.* 12.82 et 18.114 ("αὐτοῦ τε θύοντος making sacrifice in person"), even before Constantius' death.

[73] Cf. Robert Turcan, *Religion romaine* (vol. 2: Iconography of Religions 17.1; Leiden, 1988).

[74] Suetonius *Caligula* 32; *SHA Comm.* 5, 5.

[75] "*Vehens licenter pro sacerdotibus sacra* (carrying in the priests' place the sacred objects without any shame)", Ammianus 22.14.3.

[76] Prudentius *Apotheosis* 460–502.

[77] Cf. Marcel Detienne et Jean-Pierre Vernant, *La cuisine du sacrifice en pays grec* (Paris: Gallimard, 1979).

[78] J. Geffcken, *Kaiser Julianus* (Leipzig, 1914) VIII, was already upset by an approach so far from methodical rules. The medical research of Bouffartigue ([1989] 529–39) reaches the conclusion of the Julian's mental health: "*on n'a pas affaire à un exalté superstitieux*" (538).

[79] *Ep.* 89b.297a.

the priest-king[80] more than that of Augustus or of his model Marcus Aurelius. The superiority that he attributed to priesthood drove him irresistibly towards the altars and his conception of the relation to the divinity explains why he cannot stand any mediator in the communication with the gods.[81] His conception of the dedicated priest—ἀνὴρ καθοσιωμένος τοῖς θεοῖς—, chosen for his love of gods and men, justifies the strict rules that he set for himself as ἀρχιερεὺς μέγιστος[82] and for the pagan clergy in the reform he planned.[83] Despite the strict moral rules he decreed for the pagan priests, he did not transform them into consecrated *sacerdotes* of a Christian type. The function lasted only during the rituals, the priest falling back into an average noble status once the duties of his ministry were over.[84] Thus, the anti-Christian challenge cannot explain by itself Julian's position. We must consider his spiritual involvement to appreciate the necessity for these ethical rules—*excellere . . . moribus primum*[85]—, as is done when one studies his school law.

Julian was convinced that "everything is full of gods", an expression attributed to Thales that Julian made his own, following Cicero in old times and Iamblichus much closer to him.[86] The gods "are here and see him",[87] they direct his destiny and surround him with their *pronoia*.[88] This legitimises the thanksgiving sacrifices.[89] He never ceases to proclaim his faithfulness to the gods in a way that is Roman and yet, at the same time, struck by a less juridical and more personalised relation to the divinity.[90] "Yet for all that I feel awe of

---

[80] Cf. Francis Dvornik, "The Emperor's Julian "Reactionary" Ideas on Kingship", *Late Classical and Medieval Studies in Honor of Albert M. Frend Jr.* (Princeton, 1955) 71–8; Armstrong [1984] 5; Mario Mazza, "Filosofia religiosa ed "imperium" in Giuliano", B. Gentili, ed., *Giuliano Imperatore* (Urbino, 1986), 39–108. On the conception of the sacred sovereignty, L. Warren-Bonfante, "Emperor, God and Man in the IVth century: Julian the Apostate and Ammianus Marcellinus", *La Parola del Passato* 19 (1964) 401–27; Athanassiadi-Fowden [1981] 161–81; Scott [1987] 350–2.

[81] Cf. Gauthier [1992] 89–104.

[82] *Ep.* 89b.297b and d.

[83] *Ep.* 89b.301b and 84(49).431d.

[84] *Ep.* 89b.302c–303b. Cf. W. Koch, "Comment l'Empereur Julien tâcha de fonder une église païenne", *RBPh* 6 (1927) 123–46, 7 (1928) 49–82, 511–50 and 1363–85.

[85] *Ep.* 61b = *CTh.* 13, 3, 5.

[86] Cicero *Leg.* 2.11; Iamblichus *De mysteriis* 1.9.

[87] *Ep.* 89b.299b–300a.

[88] *Ad Athen.* 275b, 280b, 282c. Cf. *C. Galileos* 171d and Libanius *Orat.* 13.16, 15.30, 18.29–30 and 192. Thus the comparisons used by Julian are often inspired by divine imagery, *C. Galileos* 285c. Cf. Bowersock [1978], 17–20.

[89] Cf. Saloustius *De mundo* 16.1.

[90] In consequence, Libanius (*Orat.* 15.29 ff) grants him an intimacy (ἑταιρία καὶ συνουσία) with the gods that goes further than his ritual piety.

the gods (τοὺς θεοὺς πέφρικα), I love (φιλῶ), I revere (σέβω), I venerate them (ἄζομαι) and in short have precisely the same feelings towards them as one would have towards kind masters (ἀγαθοὺς δεσπότας) or teachers (διδασκάλους) or fathers (πατέρας) or guardians (κηδεμόνας)".[91]

Among the main types of sacrifices performed by Julian, divinatory sacrifices were the most frequent.[92] And in the tradition fixed on him, these sacrificial divinatory rituals are the most fiercely attacked. These operations were not limited, naturally, to sacrificial rituals. They could also be oracles[93] or other moments of privileged communication with the divinity, mainly during his frequent dreams or waking visions. His public life is opened and closed by two visions of the *Genius publicus*.[94] In every occasion, even a trivial one like a magistrate's reappointment,[95] he prays for divine inspiration and "takes counsel with the gods" through divinatory rites. *A fortiori* on perilous ones. This explains why he took away with him to Persia some *haruspices*, theurgian philosophers and other specialists in omens who, of course, could not agree in their interpretation of the *signa*.[96] As soon as he began the war against Constantius, he performed divinatory sacrifices, *placata ritu secretiore Bellona*.[97] Once his *conversio* was proclaimed, he "imparted it to the gods who see and hear all things. Then when I had offered sacrifices (θυσάμενος) for my departure, the omens were favourable (γενομένων καλῶν τῶν ἱερῶν)".[98]

This did not prevent Julian from allowing himself a certain freedom concerning the answers received in the course of divinatory sacrifices, and this not only during his last expedition. "We built

---

[91] The authenticity of this confession arouses emotion, *Heracl.* 212a.

[92] "*Praesagiorum <in> sciscitatione nimia deditus* (too much given to the consideration of omens and portents)", Ammianus 25.4.17; cf. *Ep.* 87(6*).

[93] Cf. Julian's interest in Apollinic oracles, Timothy E. Gregory, "Julian and the Last Oracle at Delphi", *GRBS* 24 (1983) 355–66.

[94] Ammianus 20.5.10 and 25.2.3. Cf. Iamblicus *De mysteriis* 3.1–2 and Zosimus 3.9.5–6.

[95] *Ep.* 88(62).451c. Cf. Libanius *Orat.* 18.172 and 15.31: "οἷς συμβουλεύῃ περὶ τῶν πραγμάτων ([the gods] close by you as counsellors on matters of state)".

[96] Ammianus 23.5.10–14. Weiss [1978] 137–9.

[97] Ammianus 21.5.1. During the intentional burning of his fleet on the river Euphrates, Julian is for the second time possessed by Bellona (24.7.4). Cf. 22.1.1: "*exta rimabatur adsidue avesque suspiciens* (constantly prying into the entrails of victims and watching the flight of the birds)". He was moved by the injunction of the gods to challenge his cousin, *Ep.* 28(13).382b.

[98] *Ad Athen.* 286d. Cf. immediately after Constantius' death, *Ep.* 26(38).415a and 415b. In Antioch, combination of sacrifice with favourable omen, Libanius *Orat.* 15.80–81. Negative picture at Greg. Naz. *Orat.* IV.92.

altars and slew victims (*exstructis aris caesisque hostiis*), in order to learn
the purpose of the gods [. . .]; but on inspection of the organs, it
was announced that neither course would suit the signs (*quorum neu-
trum, extis inspectis, confore dicebatur*)".[99] His strong and energetic personality and a life driven with the urgency of a new Alexander may
help to explain that he observed the will of the gods only when it
fitted the plan of action on which he had decided. Here also Julian
is truly Roman. Indeed all the Roman divinatory system aims at
preserving the freedom of man and his capacity of action in the
world, while, at the same time, giving the gods their due place.[100]
Practice of the *religio* liberates the human capacity of action through
a strict respect for the rights of the two parties, much more than it
subjects the man to the all-powerful good will of an all-present divinity.[101] From the ritual point of view, in fact, Julian is far less slav-
ishly subjected to the gods than on the spiritual level, in his religious
declarations of faith.[102] He is not so far from the Varronic tradition
of the three forms of theology that we know through Augustine.[103]
The means he employed in order to keep his freedom were traditional, even if this was in vain, as indeed the clear-sighted Julian
realised himself.[104] "He did not comply with the dictates of conven-
tion and offer sacrifices on some occasions (νῦν μὲν ἔθυσε) and refrain
on others (νῦν δὲ ἔληξεν)".[105] According to the various cases, he performed apotropaic rituals[106] or, "*indignatus acriter*", he felt himself free
to ignore the gods who have disdained his piety.[107] Sometimes, he
took into account only the sacrifices that had turned out to be
favourable.[108] Like Caesar landing in Africa, he turned upside-down
the meaning of the *signa*,[109] for instance in the episode of the "horse

---

[99] Ammianus 24.8.4.
[100] Cf. Raymond Bloch, *Les prodiges dans l'Antiquité classique* (Paris: Presses Universitaires
de France, 1963) 77–86.
[101] Cf. Michel Meslin, *L'homme romain* (Paris: Hachette, 1978) 197–200.
[102] Cf. e.g. *Ep.* 86(2*) page 149 ll. 1–10 and Ammianus 23.2.6–8.
[103] Varro *ap.* Augustine *Civ. D.* 4.27.
[104] "*fide fatidica praecinente* (through the words of a trustworthy prophecy)", Ammianus
25.3.19; cf. 23.5.4. Among unfavourable omens, Ammianus 23.1.5–7, 5.6 and 12.
[105] Libanios, *Or.* 12, 80.
[106] Ammianus 25.2.4.
[107] When Mars Ultor refuses the bulls "prepared *ad hoc*", Ammianus 24.6.17. Paul
Veyne ("Une évolution du paganisme gréco-romain: injustice et piété des dieux,
leurs ordres et leurs oracles", *Latomus* 45 [1986] 279) connects this attitude with
superstitio.
[108] *Ep.* 98(27).399d.
[109] Ammianus 21.2.1.

called Babylonian" and then he confirmed the omen by a sacrifice.[110]
In yet another case, in face of the inherent equivocalness of divine
signs, he chose the interpretation he was looking for,[111] without always
fooling himself.[112] We see him repeating the consultation as often as
necessary until he obtained the favourable answer, considering—even
if the sources do not say so clearly—that a mistake during the ritual had corrupted the result.[113] This disengagement, difficult to understand of a devotee like Julian, choked his fellows. Zosimus thus
imagined a possible mysterious reason to discharge him of having
neglected the numerous fatal omens at the beginning of his Persian
expedition in the spring of 363.[114] Or again, he refused to perform
the consultation[115] or modified the question *a posteriori*, after it had
been answered.[116]

Indeed Julian is deeply, from the ritual point of view, the heir of
the old Roman tradition of relation to the divinity.[117] These ceremonies demonstrate, if need be, that Roman religious traditions, even
if they had stood on the defensive for a quarter of a century,[118] had
in no way disappeared by the beginning of the 360s. This is true
even in Syria where Christianization and the power of the local bishops so much upset Julian. When he arrived in Ilion, Julian visited
"the altars still alight, I might almost say still blazing", guided by
the "bishop" Pegasius named as a priest.[119] Even Gregorius Nazianzen knows quite well the main rules of the sacrifice: "show us
which victims we must offer and to which wicked god (τὸ θύειν ἔστιν
ἅ καὶ οἷς τῶν δαιμόνων). Because it is not allowed to offer the same
victims to any wicked god (οὔτε γὰρ πᾶσι τὰ αὐτὰ), nor to offer all

---

[110] "*ut omen per hostias litando firmaret* (in order to confirm the omen by favourable
signs from victims)", Ammianus 23.3.7.
[111] Ammianus 23.5.8 (the lion episode). Cf. the cross which appeared during a
sacrifice, Greg. Naz. *Orat.* 4.54.
[112] Ammianus 22.1.3. Cf. Scott [1987] 354–355.
[113] Zosimus 3.12.1: "he left Antioch despite the unfavourable result of the rites
(οὐδὲ τῶν ἱερείων αἰσίων αὐτῷ γενομένων)".
[114] Cf. François Paschoud (Paris: CUF. Les Belles Lettres, II.1, 1979), pages 103–4
n. 31. Maximus of Ephesus acted in the same way with the unfavourable predic-
tions at the beginning of the reign, Eunapius *Lives of the Sophists* 477.
[115] Ammianus 25.2.7.
[116] E.g. for his Parthian expedition according to Libanius *Orat.* 18.306.
[117] Cf. his recurrent professions of traditionalism, *Ep.* 89a(63).453b.
[118] Cf. Libanius *Orat.* 30.6.
[119] *Ep.* 79(78). Id. the *Adonea* at Antioch (Ammianus 22.9.15); at Bathnae (*Ep.*
98(27).400c); at Apamea (Libanius *Ep.* 1351).

of them to the same one (οὔτε ἑνὶ τὰ πάντα), nor to sacrifice them with the same *ritus* (οὔτε τὸν αὐτὸν τρόπον), according to your hiero-phantes (ἱεροφάνταις) and specialists in sacrifices (τοῖς τῶν θυσιῶν τεχνολόγοις)".[120] In Julian's time, these rules were not much prac-ticed or taught and Julian is complaining about the fact. "For I observe that, as yet, some refuse to sacrifice (τοὺς μὲν οὐ βουλομένους) and that, though some few are zealous (ὀλίγους δέ τινας ἐθέλοντας μέν), they lack knowledge (οὐκ εἰδότας δὲ θύειν ὁρῶ)".[121]

According to Roman tradition strengthened by Julian's neo-platonist "conversion",[122] sacrifice involves prayer that states the re-lation to the divinity on the objective level, through a ritualised enunciation.[123] Prayer, naturally, cannot be conceived without the sacrifice that gives reality to the enunciation. "Αἱ μὲν χωρὶς θυσιῶν εὐχαὶ λόγοι μόνον εἰσίν (Prayers without sacrifice are only words)".[124] Julian does not always betray such a Roman religious inspiration. For prayer is not for him the strict application of a *ius*. It placates oneself through the intimate relationship it thus creates with the divinity and leads the soul to rest with the divinity.[125] "Prayer inter-weaves into an indestructible fabric the sacred communion with the gods", as Iamblichus said.[126] The divinatory sacrifices that the Emperor asked for so often were thus not rooted exclusively in his Graeco-Roman education. Their justification borrows a lot, if not more, from the mystical experience learned from Maximus of Ephesus.[127] His theurgical engagement—this "holy *mystagogia*" that perpetuates

---

[120] Greg. Naz., *Orat.* 4.103.

[121] *Ep.* 78(4).375c. Cf. Libanius *Orat.* 15.53 and 17.22 who contradicts *Misop.* 361a. The question is delicate. For Bidez [1914] 456, his followers have exagger-ated the demonstrations of the pagan cult.

[122] Cf. the solar picture that Julian draws of the Roman pantheon and of the origins of Rome, Helios 153d–154a. Cf. Robert Turcan, *Mithras Platonicus. Recherches sur l'hellénisation philosophique de Mithra* (EPRO 47; Leiden: Brill, 1975) 105–28 and Huart [1978] 131–2.

[123] Iamblichus *De mysteriis* 5.26: "no rite exists without the supplication of the prayer".

[124] Saloustius, *De mundo* 16.1.

[125] *Ep.* 80(1*) page 88 ll. 8–10: "I do not even offer up many prayers (εὔχομαι), though naturally I need now more than ever to pray very often and very long (εὐχῶν πολλῶν πάνυ καὶ μεγάλων)".

[126] Iamblichus *De mysteriis* 5.26.

[127] Cf. Gauthier [1992] 94–104. He received the mithraic initiation in Constan-tinopolis, *Helios* 130b: "εἰμι τοῦ βασιλέως ὀπαδὸς Ἡλίου (I am the devotee of King Helios)"; cf. Libanius *Orat.* 18.127. Cf. Smith [1995] 124–138.

the communion with the gods[128]—strengthened his concern for divination.[129] The "truly divine Iamblichus"[130] dedicated the whole third book of his *Mysteries of Egypt* to questions relating to divination and Julian was his worthy pupil.[131] It is obvious that, in his ritualistic attitude to divination, Julian was at no risk to seek inspiration in his first, Christian, education. We shall see, however, that his conception of sacrifice may partly have been strengthened by it.

The Emperor's appetite for ritualistic forms of religion according to his religious conceptions is the key to his attitude towards Judaism. As soon as the beginning of the Vth century, three Christian historians have already noticed it.[132] Among modern studies, before Glen Bowersock reasserted it twenty-two years ago,[133] Yohanan Lewy and Marcel Simon had already put forward the hypothesis.[134] Beyond the legendary resentment of the "Apostate" against Christianity, exaggerated by the two fiery speeches of Gregorius Nazianzen and the subsequent Christian tradition,[135] his pamphlet *Against the Galileans* shows plainly that his respect for Judaism—although he does not spare it[136]—is derived from its sacrificial form, itself borrowed from the Chaldeans, "the holy race of theurgians (γένους ἱεροῦ καὶ θεουργικοῦ)".[137] "Hebrews have precise laws concerning religious worship (ἀκριβῆ τὰ περὶ θρησκείαν ἐστὶ νομίμα) and countless sacred things and observances which demand the priestly life and profession (δεόμενα

---

[128] *C. Galileos* 198cd. Cf. Iamblichus *De mysteriis* 1.11 and 2.11.

[129] Cf. *Mother of the Gods* 180b. In consequence, Julian considers Abraham as a religious model, *C. Galileos* 358d. Cf. the adverse picture of Greg. Naz. *Orat.* 4.55–56.

[130] *Ep.* 98(27).401b et 12 [4*].

[131] Cf. the rich study of Bouffartigue [1992] 331–58.

[132] Socrates *PG* 66.429–430, Sozomen *PG* 67.1284 and Theodoret *HE* 3.19.20.

[133] Bowersock [1978] 89.

[134] un "*mobile très vraisemblable . . . le goût amplement attesté de Julien pour le culte sacrificiel*", Simon [1964] 142–3. Later studies on the decision of the rebuilding of the Temple did not pay enough attention to this, except Ricciotti, *Julien* 264 and Aziza [1978] 152 but without carrying on the search. Edward Gibbon (*Decline and fall* II,535) was a precursor for the understanding of "the appetite of Julian for bloody sacrifice": "his emulation might be excited by the piety of Salomon, who had offered, at the feast of the dedication, twenty-two thousand oxen and one hundred and twenty thousand sheep. These considerations might influence his designs".

[135] Cf. Bouffartigue [1978] 25–8 and Braun [1978] 169–75. Robert J. Penella [1993] studied his figure as a persecutor in the *Hist. eccl.* of the Vth century.

[136] "These masters in theology are far from worthy of our poets", *Ep.* 89b.296b. Cf. Meredith [1980] 1142–5. Julian's ambivalency towards Judaism has already been noticed by Jean Juster, *Les Juifs dans l'Empire romain*, vol. I (Paris, 1914) 38 and Marcel Simon [1964] 140–1.

[137] *C. Galileos* 354b.

βίου καὶ προαιρέσεως ἱερατικῆς)".[138] The pamphlet is organised around
a comparison between Hellenism, Judaism and Christianism.[139] Sacrifice holds such a central place in the Roman and the Jewish religious conception as well that he nearly merges the two religious
systems, the only difference left being the unique God. "All the rest
we have in a manner in common with them (ἐπεὶ τά γε ἄλλα κοινά
πως ἡμῖν ἐστι)—temples, sanctuaries, altars, purifications, and certain
precepts. For as to these we differ from one another either not at
all or in trivial matters".[140] Thus, the Emperor may profess: "I revere
always (ἀεὶ δὲ προσκυνῶν) the God of Abraham, Isaac and Jacob".[141]
Like Numenius of Apamea for whom Plato was an ἀττικίζων Moses,[142]
"Abraham used to sacrifice even as we Hellenes do, always and continually ("Εθυε μὲν γὰρ 'Αβραάμ, ὥσπερ καὶ ἡμεῖς, ἀεὶ καὶ συνεχῶς)".[143]
Therefore, the Apostate worked to the same extent at the reestab-
lishment of the Temple of Jerusalem[144] as at the restoration of the
cult in pagan temples, as he granted privileges to Pessinons, the city
of the Mother of the gods.[145] But I would not go as far as Yohanan
Lewy (followed by Michael Avi Yonah)[146] who thought that Julian
had put the Jewish God on the same level as Helios and wanted
mainly to benefit from Jewish prayers during his Parthian campaign.
It is a fact that, in his letter to the Jewish ambassadors, he asked

---

[138] C. Galileos 238c.

[139] C. Galileos 42e and 57e. Cf. Pierre de Labriolle, La réaction païenne. Étude sur la
polémique antichrétienne du Ier au VIe siècle (Paris: L'artisan du livre, 1942), 391–418;
Bernardi [1978] 89–98; Demarolle [1986] 39–47; Aziza [1978] 148–50.

[140] C. Galileos 306b.

[141] C. Galileos 354b.

[142] Ap. Clement Alex. Strom. 4.150. Numenius is a step in the neoplatonist tradition; cf. Bouffartigue [1992] 264; Louis H. Feldman, Jew and Gentile in the Ancient
World (Princeton: Princeton University Press, 1993) 241–2.

[143] C. Galileos 356c. For once, Greg. Naz. (Orat. 4.109) agrees with Julian about
the Chaldean origin of the sacrifices. Cf. Adler [1893] 602–3.

[144] It is not necessary for the argument to deal specifically with this question, cf.,
after the basic study by Adler [1893], among recent researches: Sebastian P. Brock,
"The Rebuilding of the Temple under Julian: A New Source", PEQ 108 (1976)
103 ff; James Seaver, "Julian the Apostate and the Attempted Rebuilding of the
Temple of Jerusalem", Res Publica Litterarum 1 (1978) 273–84; Joshua Schwartz,
"Gallus, Julian and Anti-Christian Polemic in Pesikta Rabbati", ThZ 46 (1990) 11–9.

[145] Ammianus 23.1.1–3. Greg. Naz. Orat. 5.3–4. Cf. J.J. Arce, "Reconstrucciones
de templos paganos en epoca del Emperador Juliano (361–363 d.C.)", Rivista storica
dell' Antichita 5 (1975) 201–15; DiMaio [1989] 107–8.

[146] Y. Lewy, "Julian the Apostate and the Building of the Temple", Zion 6 (1941)
[Hebrew] translated in The Jerusalem Cathedra 3 (1983) 70–96; Michael Avi-Yonah,
The Jews under Roman and Byzantine Rule (Jerusalem, 1984) 185–207.

them to "address still more fervent prayers for my empire to the Almighty Creator of the Universe, who has deigned to crown me with his own undefiled right hand".[147] But, since Augustus, Jews prayed to their God for the Emperors.[148] In Julian's religious system, the Jewish God was a local god, an *ethnarchos*,[149] unlike Helios, "ὅς ἐπιτροπεύει τὸν αἰσθητὸν κόσμον (a god who governs this world of sense)",[150] and he felt concerned with the Jewish God insofar as He demands worship like any other god.

In parallel with theological attacks, Julian aims at proving that the greatest fault of Christians is to have dropped the traditions of their ancestors, whether Jewish or Gentile, both of them being ritualistic.[151] This *negligentia* of the *pietas erga parentes*, to speak like Julian[152] or any traditional Roman is a clear enough demonstration of Christian impiety. As a proof of their ungratefulness, Julian draws a lot on the sacrificial ritual, and probably even more than the remaining text testifies, since it ends precisely in the course of the argument over sacrifices. Moreover, Christians had two arguments to refuse sacrifices.[153] First, Jesus has accomplished once and for all the perfect sacrifice and the second argument was the Old Testament interdiction to sacrifice outside Jerusalem.[154] By ordering the restoration of the altar on the Temple Mount, Julian took away from the Christians a solid pillar of their identity[155] and, in his mind, he was thus revealing their felony.

The sacrificial frenzy of the Emperor, so much decried,[156] could look like what the Romans defined as *superstitio*: "superstitious rather than truly religious (*superstitiosus magis quam sacrorum legitimus observator*)".[157]

---

[147] Cf. *Ep.* 204(25).397c. The debate on the authenticity of the letter is now over.
[148] Josephus *Bell.* 2.410.
[149] The conception of national gods is not new, cf. Maximus Tyr. 17.5.
[150] Cf. *Ep.* 89a(63).454a.
[151] *C. Galileos* 238b & d and 343c. Cf. Simon [1964] 141–2; Meredith [1980] 1145–7; Braun [1978] 176–7.
[152] *Basileia* 86a.
[153] *Ep.* 61c(42).423d: "ἱερείων ὑμεῖς ἀπέχεσθαι νομοθεῖτε (when you ordain that men shall refrain from temple worship)".
[154] *C. Galileos* 305d. Julian contradicts Rom 18:19, *C. Galileos* 324cd.
[155] Cf. Bidez [1914] 447 and Bowersock [1978] 89.
[156] Cf. *Misop.* 344b.
[157] Cf. H. Fugier, *Recherches sur l'expression du sacré dans la langue latine* (Strasbourg: Presses Universitaires, 1963); Émile Benveniste, *Le vocabulaire des institutions indo-européennes*, vol. 2: *Pouvoir, droit, religion* (Paris: Éd. de Minuit, 1969) 265–79; S. Calderone, "*Superstitio*", *ANRW* I.2 (1972) 377–396.

However the basis of his behaviour is not a mishaped sense of *religio*[158] but rather a mind extremely concerned with *eusebeia* and purity.[159] "He never allowed his intellect to be diverted from his consideration of the gods (οὗτος ὁ μηδαμοῦ τὴν διάνοιαν ἀποστήσας τῆς περὶ θεῶν ἐννοίας)".[160] Without forcing them to a pagan "conversion",[161] he asked the apostates to purify themselves from Christian baptism,[162] to "purify [their] souls by supplications to the gods and [their] bodies by purifications that are customary (τὸ δὲ σῶμα τοῖς νομίμοις καθαρσίοις καθήρασθαι)".[163] According to the Nazianzen bishop, he purified himself when he performed his *metanoia*: "to purify by means of impious blood the bath that he had received (αἵματι μὲν οὐχ ὁσίῳ τὸ λουτρὸν ἀπορρύπτεται)".[164] In the cities where he settled such as Antioch and Daphne, he also ordered the purification of different places like fountains.[165]

Naturally, Julian was aware of the philosophical and religious debates around the bloody sacrifice and the eating of meat which had run through paganism since at least Porphyry, without mentioning a debate as old as Pythagoras.[166] He dealt with this question in his treatise *On the Mother of the Gods*: "the eating of meat involves the sacrifice and slaughter of animals who naturally suffer pain and torment (τὸ καταθύεσθαι καὶ κατασφάττεσθαι τὰ ζῷα ἀλγοῦντά γε ... καὶ τρυχόμενα)".[167] But, as he explains by using an argument taken from the Old Testament—the sacrifice of Cain and Abel[168]—, "things that have life are more precious than those that are lifeless to the living God who is also the cause of life (τιμιώτερα δὲ τῶν ἀψύχων ἐστὶ τὰ

---

[158] He is accused of "disturbing the gods (ἐνοχλεῖν τοῖς θεοῖς)", *Misop.* 346c.

[159] *Basileia* 70d.

[160] Libanius *Orat.* 24.35. Cf. Scott [1987] 355–7.

[161] Cf. A.H. Armstrong, "The Way and the Ways: Religious Tolerance and Intolerance in the Fourth Century AD", *VC* 38 (1984), 4–11; Robert J. Panella [1993] 31–43. On Julian's Policy on Schools, cf. B. Carmon Hardy, "The Emperor Julian and his School Law", *Church History* 37 (1968) 131–43; Thomas M. Banchich, "Julian's School Laws: *Cod. Theod.* 13.3.5 and *Ep.* 42", *The Ancient World* 24 (1993) 5–14.

[162] For purity is *the* condition for the divine to be able to spread in the material world.

[163] *Ep.* 114(52).436cd.

[164] *Orat.* 4.52. Cf. Gauthier [1992] 91.

[165] Theodoret 3.15.1.

[166] Cf. Porphyrus *De abstinentia* 2.34.

[167] *Orat.* 8 [5] 174b.

[168] Gen 4:3–4. Greg. Naz. (*Orat.* 4.25) stresses Abel's pious share.

ἔμψυχα τῷ ζῶντι καὶ ζωῆς αἰτίῳ θεῷ), inasmuch as they also have a
share of life".[169] Consequently the perfect sacrifice, τελεία θυσία, is
the bloody one. But the ritual treatment of the offerings is subjected
to justice and virtue of the heart. "Without piety, I will not say
hecatombs but, by the gods, even the Olympian sacrifice of a thousand oxen is merely empty expenditure and nothing else".[170] This
spiritualised conception of the intercourse with the divinity—the
offering of the heart—puts on the same level praise of the gods and
sacrifice. "The saying "To the extent of your powers offer sacrifice
to the immortal gods" [Hesiod *Works and Days* 336], I apply not to
sacrifice only, but also to the praises that we offer to the gods (οὐκ
ἐπὶ τῶν θυσιῶν μόνον, ἀλλὰ καὶ τῶν εὐφημιῶν τῶν εἰς τοὺς θεοὺς
ἀποδεχόμενος)".[171] This conception is completely consistent with the
conception that he holds up for the priest: "to do [the gods] honour by their nobility of character and by the practise of virtue and
also to perform to them the service that is due (λειτουργεῖν σφίσι
τὰ εἰκότα)".[172] Therefore Julian prefers "in devotions [. . .] sanctity
(τὴν ὁσίαν) to expenditure".[173] This preference is less in contradiction to his maniac ritualism than it seems at first sight, and it is not
new. Cicero already in the *De divinatione* has combined an exegetical scepticism with a ritualistic position. Julian himself replied in
advance, as it were, to the objection when praising the non-ritual-
istic piety of the great Diogenes: "But if anyone supposes that because
he did not visit the temples or worship statues or altars, this is a
sign of impiety, he does not think rightly. For Diogenes possessed
nothing that is usually offered, incense or libations or money to buy
them with. But he held right opinions about the gods, that in itself
was enough. For he worshipped them with his whole soul through
his thoughts".[174]

In his two treatises against the Cynics, Julian stresses the significance
of sanctity, which to him is justice (δικαιοσύνη) and pious virtue
(ἀρετὴ ὁσία). "The wicked gain nothing by penetrating within the

---

[169] *C. Galileos* 347c.
[170] *Heracl.* 213d–214a.
[171] *Helios* 158ab.
[172] *Misop.* 363a. Cf. *Ep.* 89b.296bc. Cf. Athanassiadi-F. [1981] 187–8.
[173] *Heracl.* 214a.
[174] *Cynics* 199b. Greg. Naz. (*Orat.* 4. 29) does say the same. Cf. Georg Mau, *Die
Religionsphilosophie Kaiser Julians* (Leipzig-Berlin: Teubner, 1907) 109–111; Smith [1995]
52–5.

sacred precincts".[175] Indeed, writes Julian with an inspiration that is both Roman and philosophical, "piety is the child of justice (τῆς δικαιοσύνης ἔκγονος) and justice is a characteristic of the more divine type of soul (τοῦ θειοτέρου ψυχῆς εἴδους)".[176] As a worthy heir to Platonist tradition,[177] on the speculative as well as on the spiritual level, Julian knows that the First Principle, the transcendental god of philosophers, does not need ritual in any way.[178] Μηδενὸς ὁ θεὸς δεῖται. His whole religious conception is based on the affinity and connection of man with the gods,—μίμησις καὶ ὁμοιότης—, and the participation into this world of divine ideas;[179] hence the providence of the gods for the *piissimi*.[180] "The Providence of the gods spreads everywhere and we need only adjustment to welcome it; every adjustment is based on imitation and similitude (μιμήσει καὶ ὁμοιότητι), therefore sanctuaries imitate the sky, altars the earth (οἱ δὲ βωμοὶ μιμοῦνται τὴν γῆν) [...] and animal sacrifices the irrational life that is inside us (τὰ δὲ θυόμενα ζῷα τὴν ἐν ἡμῖν ἄλογον ζωήν)".[181] This is why acts of piety (τὰ τῆς εὐσεβείας ἔργα) come first and put man on a familiar standing with the gods. Ritual is a safeguard created by the gods "to prevent the souls from failing", says Saloustios.[182]

The cult is nothing else than a free homage of men to their "invisible essence (τῆς ἀφανοῦς αὐτῶν οὐσίας)".[183] But, adds Julian, "as we live, however, within a body (Ἐπειδὴ γὰρ ἡμᾶς, ὄντας ἐν σώματι), so the cult of the gods must be corporal (σωματικὰς ἔδει ποιεῖσθαι τοῖς

---

[175] Cf. *Cynics* 239c; cf. also 199d–200a and 213d.

[176] *Basileia* 70d.

[177] Cf. Plato *Timae* 29E.

[178] *Ep.* 176(64) frgt. page 217.

[179] Theurgy is precisely the hieratical art that operates the appropriate connections between the inferior forms and the superior beings, cf. Erwin R. Dodds, "Theurgy and its Relationship to Neoplatonism", *JRS* 37 (1947) 55 ff and *The Greeks and the Irrational* (Berkeley: University of California Press, 1959); Smith [1995] 104–13.

[180] *Ep.* 89b.301a.

[181] Saloustius *De mundo* 15.2. Cf. Iamblichus *De mysteriis* 1.19 and 5.12. In his *ultima verba*, Julian rejoiced that his soul was on its way to liberate itself from its low part, Ammianus 25.3.19.

[182] *De mundo* 12.6: "prayers, sacrifices and initiation rites (εὐχαί τε καὶ θυσίαι καὶ τελεταί), laws and civic institutions (νόμοι τε καὶ πολιτεῖαι) [...] have been created to avoid falling to the souls".

[183] *Ep.* 89b.293d and 295a. Id. in Saloustius *De mundo* 15.1 (and 3): "By himself, the divine has no need (ἀνενδεές) and devotions are offered for our own need (αἱ δὲ τιμαὶ τῆς ἡμετέρας ὠφελείας ἕνεκα γίνονται)".

θεοῖς καὶ τὰς λατρείας)".[184] Saloustios has developed the same idea in his work, which has been considered as a kind of catechism of the reign: "There lies the reason why men are used to sacrifice living beings (διὰ τοῦτο ζῷα θύουσιν ἄνθρωποι) [. . .] offering to each god the appropriate victims (ἑκάστῳ θεῷ τὰ πρέποντα)".[185] Both think according to the neoplatonist definition of the theological triad, related to a hierarchical and analogical conception of the universe, from the intelligible god to the visible gods.[186] Ritual must be adapted to the hierarchy of divine orders and "offer to them a type of cult of the same nature as theirs. Therefore it is inconsistent to offer material things to the immaterial gods, but they are very consistent for the material gods".[187] Bloody sacrifices fit the gods of the sublunar world, the gods who preside over matter, that is to say the gods of the official pantheon, who have been nominated by the immaterial "God of sacrifices", in order to protect the men of various nations.[188] It is now clearer how Julian succeeded in integrating the Jewish God among the material gods in charge of a nation or a sanctuary. This is why there is no contradiction nor disturbed mind, no mania in the fact that Julian was able both to exhaust his entourage in endless hecatombs and to fall, by the means of theurgy, into the deepest contemplative mystical experience of the unique God.[189] Even more, both modalities are necessary, because "the inferior is a stepping stone towards the most precious"[190] as Iamblichus explains. Accomplishment of sacrifices provides the means of expressing one's gratitude to the Creator and to elevate oneself towards the ἄρρητος θεός.[191] In fact, sacrifices are beneficial to men, insofar as they attract upon them the well-intentioned solicitude of providence.[192] The soul

---

[184] *Ep.* 89b.293b.

[185] *De mundo* 16.2.

[186] Cf. his truly Plotinian definition of the behaviour of man towards the divine, *Heracl.* 209c. Cf. Saloustius *De mundo* 16.2. Cf. Foussard [1978] 189–212; A.H. Armstrong [1984] 6.

[187] Iamblichus *De mysteriis* 5.14; cf. also 5.22.

[188] Iamblichus *De mysteriis* 5.25.

[189] Cf. Foussard [1978] 206: "*Monothéisme philosophique et polythéisme religieux se conjuguent à chaque niveau grâce à la distinction de l'essence et des puissances*".

[190] "The cause (of sacrifices) is to be found in a friendship, a relation, an intercourse that links the workers to their works and the genitors to those who have engendered them", Iamblichus *De mysteriis* 5.9. For the two kinds of sacrifices, 5.15 and 18. Cf. Scott [1987] 352.

[191] Cf. Bowersock [1978] 86: "Sacrifice was an essential component of the ritual observances by which one approached the gods".

[192] Cf. Saloustius *De mundo* 16.3: "If through prayers and sacrifices (εὐχαῖς καὶ

is, thus, lifted towards the divinity through ritualistic piety, thanks to the intimacy created by offerings.[193] Therefore, we can say that the politico-religious attitudes of Julian are based on his philosophical engagement, which necessitates the materiality of the cult. Rituals, sacrifices mainly, the ceremonial of which he found in the Roman tradition, help to welcome the divine light that is already in us.

As we can see from his confession of his mystical experience,[194] his neoplatonist education did not prepare him to be content with ritualistic techniques.[195] Furthermore, although he was an apostate, Julian did not entirely forget the Christian teaching,[196] which itself had inherited the spiritualisation of the cult present in the Old Testament post-exilic conception.[197] Even Gregorius Nazianzen stresses the identity of attitudes, as far as faith is concerned, between Julian's habit of referring to the divine philosophers and the "creed" of the Christian faith.[198] Without spending too long recalling these well-known facts, let us remember here the point that Judaism had gradually substituted the offering of the heart for sacrifice,[199] opening thus the way for the synagogue cult. Christianity, which took so much inspiration from the *Prophets*, had inherited this approach and in a spiritualist like Julian, this conception met with his philosophical interests.

It would be pretentious to conclude, like Saloustios, that "these remarks solve the two problems, one of the sacrifices and the other one concerning honours given to gods (καὶ ἡ περὶ θυσιῶν καὶ τῶν ἄλλων τῶν εἰς θεοὺς γινομένων τιμῶν λέλυται ζήτησις)".[200] They necessarily lead, however, to abandoning definitely the caricatural image

---

θυσίαις) we found absolution for our sins (λύσιν τῶν ἁμαρτημάτων εὑρίσκομεν), if we worship the gods (τοὺς θεοὺς θεραπεύομεν) [. . .] through the conversion towards the divine (τῆς πρὸς τὸ θεῖον ἐπιστροφῆς), we feel again the gods' benevolence". Cf. also Iamblichus *De mysteriis* 1.13.

[193] Iamblichus *De mysteriis* 1.16.

[194] Cf. *Heracl.* 234b: "steadfastly obeying our laws (ἀμετακινήτως τοῖς ἡμετέροις πειθόμενος νόμοις); [. . .] and let no man [. . .] persuade thee to neglect our commands (ἀναπείσῃ τῶν ἐντολῶν ἐκλαθέσθαι τῶν ἡμετέρων)". We could recognize Deut 4:2 quoted by Julian, *C. Galileos* 320b.

[195] Cf. Athanassiadi-Fowden [1978] 13–51.

[196] Cf. G.J.M. Bartelink, "L'Empereur Julien et le vocabulaire chrétien", *VC* 11 (1957) 37–48.

[197] Cf. "*La Bible de Julien*", *index* of the 180 quotations (which were more numerous since the second book is lost) in Demarolle [1986] 47.

[198] *Orat.* 4. 102.

[199] E.g. Isa 1:11 ff.

[200] *De mundo* 15.1.

attached to Julian's sacrifices. He had made his own the beautiful
sentence of Iamblichus: "we lift ourselves, by sacrifices and the fire
of victims, to the fire of the gods".[201] This demonstration, naturally,
implies that one recognises a genuine authenticity to the spiritual life
of Julian.[202] It shows how well the Emperor had realised, in his conscience as well as in his religious behaviour, a synthesis of the spiritual trends of his time.

BIBLIOGRAPHY

Sources:
Julian's works:
– L'empereur Julien, *Discours de Julien César*, J. Bidez ed., Paris, CUF-Les Belles
   Lettres, 1972, *Au sénat et au peuple d'Athènes*, Discours V.
– L'empereur Julien, *Discours de Julien empereur*, I, G. Rochefort ed., Paris, CUF-Les
   Belles Lettres, 1963, *Contre Héracleios le Cynique*, Discours VII;
       Sur la Mère des dieux, Discours VIII[V];
       Contre les Cyniques ignorants, Discours IX[VI].
– L'empereur Julien, *Discours de Julien empereur*, II, C. Lacombrade ed., Paris, CUF-
   Les Belles Lettres, 1964, *Le banquet ou les Césars*, Discours X;
       Sur Hélios-roi, Discours XI[IV];
       Le Misopogon, Discours VII.
– *Epistulae, leges, poematia, fragmenta varia*, J. Bidez et Fr. Cumont ed., Paris, CUF-
   Les Belles Lettres, 1922 (rééd. 1960).
– *Iuliani imperatoris Contra Galilaeos quae supersunt*, K.J. Neumann ed., Leipzig, 1880;
   L'empereur
– Julien, *Contre les Galiléens*, trad. C. Gérard, Bruxelles, 1995.

Other authors:
   Ammien Marcellin, *Histoire*, E. Galletier, J. Fontaine et M.-A. Marié. ed., Paris,
       CUF-Les Belles Lettres, 1968–1984.
   The Theodosian code, Th. Mommsen ed., Berlin, 1905 (reimpr. 1963).
   Grégoire de Nazianze, *Discours* 4 et 5 (*In Iulianum* I–II), J. Bernardi ed., Paris,
       Sources chrétiennes, 1983.
   H. Dessau, *Inscriptiones Latinae Selectae*, Berlin, 1892–1916.
   Jamblique, *Les mystères d'Égypte*, E. Des Places ed., Paris, CUF-Les Belles Lettres,
       1966.
   Libanios, *Orationes*, R. Foerster ed., Leipzig, 1903–1908.
   Saloustios, *Des dieux et du monde*, G. Rochefort ed., Paris, CUF-Les Belles Lettres,
       1969.
   Zosime, *Histoire nouvelle*, F. Paschoud ed., Paris, CUF-Les Belles Lettres, 1971–1989.

---

[201] *De mysteriis* 5.11.
[202] "For things that are sacred to the gods and holy ought to be away from the
beaten track and performed in peace and quiet", *Ep.* 98(27).400d.

Recent bibliographical lists:
Kaegi, W.E., 1965. "Research on Julien the Apostate, 1945–1964", *CW* 58, 229–238.
Caltabiano, M., 1983–1984. "Un quindicennio di studi sull' imperatore Giuliano (1965–1980)", *Koinonia* 7, 15–30 & 113–132 and 8, 17–31.
Bouffartigue, J., 1981. "Julien dans la littérature savante des XIXᵉ et XXᵉ siècles", *L'Empereur Julien*, Paris, 2, 83–111.

Studies:
Adler, M., 1893. "The Emperor Julian and the Jews", *JQR* 5, 591–651.
Arce, J., 1972–1974. "Algunos problemas de la numismatica del Emperador Fl. Cl. Iulianus", *Archivo Espanol de Arqueologia* 45–47, 477–496.
————, 1975. "Reconstrucciones de templos paganos en epoca del Emperador Juliano (361–363 d.C.)", *Rivista Storica dell'Antichita*, 5, 201–215.
Armstrong, A.H., 1984. "The Way and the Ways: Religious Tolerance and Intolerance in the Fourth Century AD", *Vigiliae Christianae* 38, 1–17.
Athanassiadi-Fowden, P., 1992. *Julian: An Intellectual Biography*, London.
Aziza, C., 1978. "Julien et le judaïsme", *L'Empereur Julien*, Paris, 1, 142–158.
Balty, J.-C., 1974. "Julien et Apamée. Aspects de la restauration de l'hellénisme et de la politique antichrétienne de l'empereur", *DHA* 1, 267–304.
Bernardi, J., 1978. "Un réquisitoire: les *Invectives contre Julien* de Grégoire de Nazianze", *L'Empereur Julien*, Paris, 1, 89–98.
Bidez, J., 1914. "L'évolution de la politique de l'empereur Julien en matière religieuse", *Bulletin de l'Académie Royale de Belg.ique Cl. Lettres* 7, 406–461.
————, 1965². *La vie de l'Empereur Julien*, Paris.
Bouffartigue, J., 1978. "Julien par Julien", *L'Empereur Julien*, Paris, 1, 15–30.
————, 1989. "L'état mental de l'empereur Julien", *REG* 102, 529–539.
————, 1992. *L'empereur Julien et la culture de son temps*, Paris.
Bowersock, G.W., 1978. *Julian the Apostate*, London.
Braun, R., 1978. "Julien et le christianisme", *L'Empereur Julien*, Paris, 1, 159–187.
Cameron, A., 1993. "Julian and Hellenism", *The Ancient World* 24, 25–29.
Demarolle, J.-M., 1986. "Le *Contre les Galiléens*: continuité et rupture dans la démarche polémique de l'Empereur Julien", *Klèma* 11, 39–47.
DiMaio, M., 1989. "The Emperor Julian's Edicts of Religious Toleration", *The Ancient World* 20, 99–109.
Dodds, E.R., 1947. "Theurgy and its Relationship to Neoplatonism", *JRS* 37, 55–69.
Dvornik, F., 1955. "The Emperor's Julian Reactionary Ideas on Kingship", *Late Classical and Medieval Studies . . . A.M. Frend*, Princeton, 71–78.
Dumézil, G., 1987². *La religion romaine archaïque*, Paris.
(L')Empereur Julien. De l'histoire à la légende (331–1715), 1978–1981. R. Braun et J. Richer ed., Paris, 2 vol.
Festugière, A.-J., 1957. "Julien à Macellum", *JRS* 47, 53–58.
Fontaine, J., 1978. "Le Julien d'Ammien Marcellin", *L'Empereur Julien*, Paris, 1, 31–65.
Foussard, J.-C., 1978. "Julien philosophe", *L'Empereur Julien*, Paris, 1, 189–212.
Gauthier, N., 1987. "L'expérience religieuse de Julien dit l'Apostat", *Augustinianum* 27, 227–235.
————, 1992. "Les initiations mystériques de l'empereur Julien", *Mélanges P. Lévêque* 6, Besançon-Paris, 89–104.
Gibbon, E., 1867. *The History of the Decline and Fall of the Roman Empire*, Londres (Bell and Daldy), I.
Hadot, P., 1995. *Qu'est-ce que la philosophie antique?*, Paris.
Huart, P., 1978. "Julien et l'hellénisme. Idées morales et politiques", *L'Empereur Julien*, Paris, 1, 99–123.

Koch, W., 1927–1928. "Comment l'empereur Julien tâcha de fonder une église païenne", *RBPh* 6, 123–146 and 7, 49–82, 511–550 & 1363–1385.

Labriolle, P. de, 1942. *La réaction païenne. Étude sur la polémique antichrétienne du Ier au VIe siècle*, Paris.

Lewy, Y., 1983. "Julian the Apostate and the Building of the Temple", *Zion* 6, 1941 (hébr.), trad. *The Jerusalem Cathedra* 3, 70–96.

Mazza, M., 1986. "Filosofia religiosa ed "imperium" in Giuliano", *Giuliano Imperatore*, B. Gentili ed., Urbino, 39–108.

Meredith, A., 1980. "Porphyry and Julian against the Christians", *ANRW* II, 23, 2, 1120–1149.

Naville, H.A., 1877. *Julien l'Apostat et sa philosophie du polythéisme*, Paris-Neuchâtel.

Negev, A., 1969. "The Inscription of the Emperor Julian at Ma'ayan Baruch", *IEJ* 19, 170–173.

Oikonomides, Al.N., 1987. "Ancient Inscriptions Recording the Restoration of Greco-Roman Shrines by the Emperor Flavius Claudius Julianus (361–363 AD)", *The Ancient World* 15, 37–42.

Penella, R.J., 1993. "Julian the Persecutor in Fifth Century Church Historians", *The Ancient World* 24, 31–43.

Petit, P., 1978. "L'Empereur Julien vu par le sophiste Libanios", *L'Empereur Julien*, Paris, 1, 67–87.

Raeder, H., 1944. "Kaiser Julian als Philosoph und religiöser Reformator", *Classica et Mediaevalia* 6, 179–193 (repr. *Julian Apostata*, R. Klein ed., Darmstadt, 1978, 206–221).

Ricciotti, G., 1959. *Julien l'Apostat*, French transl., Paris.

Rochefort, G., 1956. "Le Περὶ θεῶν καὶ κοσμοῦ de Saloustios et l'influence de l'empereur Julien", *REG* 69, 50–66.

Scheid, J., 1979–1980. "La théorie romaine du sacrifice", *Annuaire EPHE Section Sciences religieuses* 88, 327–333.

———, 1985. "Sacrifice et banquet à Rome. Quelques problèmes", *MEFRA* 97, 193–206.

———, 1985. *Religion et piété à Rome*, Paris.

———, 1985. "Numa et Jupiter ou les dieux citoyens de Rome", *Archives de Sc. Soc. des Religions* 59, 41–53.

Scott, S., 1987. "L'empereur Julien: transcendance et subjectivité", *RHPhR* 76, 345–362.

Simon, M., 1974. *Verus Israel. Étude sur les relations entre chrétiens et juifs dans l'Empire romain (135–425)*, Paris.

Smith, R., 1995. *Julian's Gods. Religion and Philosophy in the Thought and Action of Julian the Apostate*, London-New York.

Thélamon, F., 1981. *Païens et chrétiens au IVe siècle. L'apport de l' Histoire ecclésiastique de Rufin d'Aquilée*, Paris.

Vernant, J.-P., 1981. "Théorie générale du sacrifice et mise à mort dans la ΘΥΣΙΑ grecque", *Le sacrifice dans l'Antiquité*, Entretiens Hardt 27, Vandoeuvres-Genève, 1–39.

Voltaire, 1994. *Discours de l'empereur Julien contre les chrétiens*, J.-M. Moureaux ed., Oxford.

Warren-Bonfante, L., 1964. "Emperor, God and Man in the IVth Century: Julian the Apostate and Ammianus Marcellinus", *La Parola del Passato* 19, 401–427.

Weiss, J.-P., 1978. "Julien, Rome et les Romains", *L'Empereur Julien*, Paris, 1, 125–140.

ANIMAL SACRIFICE IN ANCIENT ZOROASTRIANISM: A RITUAL AND ITS INTERPRETATIONS[1]

Albert de Jong

The subject of the present article are the rites of animal sacrifice in ancient Zoroastrianism, that is to say rituals in which the life of an animal is taken and its meat handled in the history of Zoroastrianism up to the tenth century CE. These rituals have been studied in depth by other scholars and have been a prominent aspect in debates on the original intentions of Zarathustra and the development of the Zoroastrian tradition. Animal sacrifice has been a controversial subject in the study of Zoroastrianism for a long time, both because of Western notions of the spirituality of "true" Zoroastrianism and because of the fact that the ritual has been abandoned by the best known and most self-conscious modern Zoroastrian community, the Parsi community of India. Whereas modern developments are not our concern here, it should be noted that animal sacrifice is a living ritual in modern Irani Zoroastrianism and is known to have been practised by the Parsis up to the late nineteenth century. It was one of the vital rituals of Zoroastrianism in the ancient, pre-Islamic, period. Modern observers have frequently expressed difficulties in connecting the ritual with ideas surrounding death and killing in Zoroastrian literature. This has led to a larger emphasis being placed on theological interpretations of animal sacrifice than on the meaning of the ritual for lay Zoroastrians. It is always difficult to extract lay religiosity from the priestly Zoroastrian writings, but we shall see two very different appreciations of animal sacrifice reflected in Zoroastrian literature which in all likelihood correspond to priestly speculations and more generally held views on the subject.

We shall begin with a quick overview of the history of the study of animal sacrifice in Zoroastrianism and then depart from the earliest almost complete description of the ritual in the writings of the Pontic

---

[1] The following abbreviations are used to refer to Iranian texts: *Dk.* = *Dēnkard; GBd.* = *Greater Bundahišn; N.* = *Nērangestān; PhlRDd.* = *Pahlavi Riwāyat accompanying the Dādestān ī dēnīg; SDN* = *Ṣad dar-e naṣr; ŠnŠ* = *Šāyest nē-šāyest; SupplTxtŠnŠ* = *Supplementary Texts to the Šāyest ne-šāyest; Vd.* = *Vendīdād; Y.* = *Yasna; Yt.* = *Yašt.*

Greek geographer Strabo of Amaseia. Then, we shall reconstruct the phases of the ritual itself and try to unravel the various interpretations of the ritual as they (seem to) have existed from the early days up to the early Islamic period.

1. *Studying animal sacrifice in Zoroastrian history*

Zoroastrian rituals to the present day require the presence of a representative of animal life in the ritual offering and tasting of a cake and its complements, as part of the celebration of the *drōn*-ritual, either incorporated into the *Yasna*, the daily high ritual, or as a separate rite.[2] This representative of the animal kingdom is called in Middle Persian *gōšūdāg*, a word derived from Avestan *geuš hudå*, "beneficent cow." In modern rituals, the *gōšūdāg* most often is a piece of ghee or butter, but from Irani Zoroastrian rituals and ritual texts concerning pre-modern Zoroastrianism, it is clear that a piece of meat from a sacrificial animal was a common (though not the only) source of the *gōšūdāg*. One of the distinctive differences between the modern Irani and Parsi Zoroastrian communities, based in the Islamic Republic of Iran and India respectively, is the fact that Irani Zoroastrians have preserved the rites of animal sacrifice, whereas Parsi Zoroastrians have abandoned them, probably under pressure of the local Hindu population. Animal sacrifices in Irani Zoroastrian traditions, however, are not very frequent;[3] the comparative rarity of the rite in modern Zoroastrianism should not blind us to the fact that in ancient Zoroastrianism, animal sacrifice was a normal and regular part of religious life.[4]

---

[2] Cf. M. Boyce & F.M. Kotwal, "Zoroastrian *Bāj* and *Drōn* I," *BSOAS* 34 (1971) 56–73; K.M. Jamasp-Asa, "On the *drōn* in Zoroastrianism," in *Papers in Honour of Professor Mary Boyce* (Acta Iranica 24; Leiden: Brill, 1985) 335–356; F.M. Kotwal and J.W. Boyd, *A Persian Offering. The Yasna: A Zoroastrian High Liturgy* (Studia Iranica Cahier 8; Paris: Association pour l'avancement des études iraniennes 1991) 94–97 with n. 89; J.J. Modi, *The Religious Ceremonies and Customs of the Parsees* (Bombay: British India Press, 1922) 281–282.

[3] For these rituals, cf. M. Boyce, *A History of Zoroastrianism I: The Early Period* (Handbuch der Orientalistik 1.8.1.2.2.1; Leiden: Brill, 1975) 149–157; ead., *A Persian Stronghold of Zoroastrianism* (Oxford: Oxford University Press, 1977) 157–158; 244–246; ead., "Ātaš-zōhr and Āb-zōhr", *JRAS* (1966) 100–118; ead., 'Mihragān among the Irani Zoroastrians', in J.R. Hinnells, ed., *Mithraic Studies* (Manchester: Manchester University Press, 1971) 106–118.

[4] For which, cf. A. de Jong, *Traditions of the Magi. Zoroastrianism in Greek and Latin Literature* (Religions in the Graeco-Roman World 133; Leiden: Brill 1997) 357–362.

Although there is a broad scholarly consensus on this issue nowadays, the status of animal sacrifice in Zoroastrianism has been hotly debated in the first half of the twentieth century. Certain passages in the Gāthās, the earliest Zoroastrian texts, ascribed to Zarathustra himself, had suggested to some that the prophet was opposed to the rite of animal sacrifice and had attempted to abolish it.[5] This interpretation of the Gāthās, in fact, was instrumental in the creation of an image of ancient Zoroastrianism as a wholly spiritual ethical religion.[6] Zarathustra was seen as an anti-ritualistic theologian, who opposed the rites of animal sacrifice and the pressing of Haoma (a plant pressed to produce an intoxicating substance) and replaced them by rituals consisting of prayers, contemplation and the feeding of the sacred flame.[7] Since it is undisputed that animal sacrifice and the pressing of Haoma were among the core rituals of Zoroastrianism shortly after the days of the prophet,[8] scholars believed that he was unsuccessful in his ritual reforms; this produced the image of Zoroastrianism as the product of the reintroduction of pagan practices into the reformed tradition. The immediate followers of Zarathustra could not meet the stern ethical and spiritual demands he had made of them, but quickly lapsed into their half-pagan customs.

Modern scholarship has not left much of these reconstructions uncontested.[9] The "spiritual" focus of earlier scholarship (warmly embraced by leading Parsi intellectuals) was very much a product of its age, but has by now been abandoned by all but a few.[10] Subsequent

---

[5] Cf., for instance, H. Lommel, "War Zarathustra ein Bauer?," *Zeitschrift für vergleichende Sprachforschung* 58 (1931) 248–265; an overview of early interpretations of Zarathustra's life and message is given by K. Rudolph, "Zarathuštra—Priester und Prophet," *Numen* 8 (1961) 81–116.

[6] Critically discussed in the first part of M. Molé, *Culte, mythe et cosmologie dans l'Iran ancien. Le problème zoroastrien et la tradition mazdéenne* (Annales du Musée Guimet, Bibliothèque d'études 69; Paris: Presses universitaires de France, 1963).

[7] Most brilliantly reconstructed by H. Lommel, *Die Religion Zarathustras nach dem Awesta dargestellt* (Tübingen: Mohr, 1930).

[8] Evidence for this comes mainly from the *Yašts*, traditional hymns to individual deities, which will be discussed briefly below.

[9] Cf. particularly the works by Boyce and Molé mentioned above and the overview in H. Humbach, "Zarathustra und die Rinderschlachtung," in: B. Benzing, O. Böcher and G. Mayer, eds., *Wort und Wirklichkeit. Studien zur Afrikanistik und Orientalistik* (Meisenheim am Glan: Anton Haim, 1977) vol. 2, 17–29.

[10] The main exception being Gh. Gnoli, *Zoroaster's Time and Homeland. A Study on the Origins of Mazdeism and Related Problems* (Istituto Universitario Orientale. Seminario di studi asiatici. Series Minor 7; Naples: Istituto Universitario Orientale, 1980) 150–152 et passim.

scholarship has both uncovered the ideological (liberal Western European) nature of this approach and improved greatly on the understanding of the actual texts. The earliest Zoroastrian texts are so difficult to interpret that there can be no certainty in this field, but most specialists currently believe that the Gāthās are, first and foremost, ritual texts and that ritual (including animal sacrifice) was one of the main triggers for Zarathustra's novel views on religious truth.[11] However one interprets the difficult Gathic passages, there is no reason to interpret the existence of the rite of animal sacrifice in Zoroastrianism as a betrayal of the message of the prophet, if message there was.

If we leave aside the problematic Gāthās, the situation becomes much clearer: the sacrifice of animals is presented and, so one is led to believe, experienced as a normal part of religious life. It is likely, in view of the great historical depth of Zoroastrian texts, that the meaning and interpretation of the rite of animal sacrifice changed with the development of the Zoroastrian tradition, but such changes are difficult to document. In the case of Zoroastrianism, the difficulties in tracing such developments are greater than in the case of other ancient religions, because of the significant lacunae in documentation. This also holds for synchronic layerings: priestly, royal and lay perceptions of rituals and doctrines,[12] and for internal variations in, for instance, Sasanian Zoroastrianism. To take an example, there are some traces of the advocacy of vegetarianism in certain Zoroastrian traditions and, consequently, there must have been Zoroastrians in the Sasanian period who rejected the tradition of animal sacrifice altogether, but we cannot grasp them historically.[13]

To remedy the many uncertainties in the field, two strategies have been commonly adopted. Some scholars, particularly those working on the earlier layers of Zoroastrianism, view the Zoroastrian practice in comparison with the rich materials from Vedic India, with

---

[11] Boyce, *History* I, 214–216; J. Kellens & E. Pirart, *Les textes vieil-avestiques* I (Wiesbaden: Reichert, 1988), 32–36; H. Humbach, *The Gāthās of Zarathuštra and the Other Old Avestan Texts* (Heidelberg: Winter, 1991) 67–94.

[12] For the diachronic and synchronic layerings of Zoroastrian traditions, cf. A. de Jong, "Purification *in absentia*: On the Development of Zoroastrian Ritual Practice," in J. Assmann and G.G. Stroumsa, eds., *Transformations of the Inner Self in Ancient Religions* (Leiden: Brill, 1999) 301–329.

[13] Cf. S. Shaked, *Dualism in Transformation. Varieties of Religion in Sasanian Iran* (London: School of Oriental and African Studies, 1994) 43–44.

which Zoroastrianism shares a common ancestry.[14] Both on a lexical and grammatical level and, it seems, with regard to certain basic conceptions of animal sacrifice, the two traditions show remarkable similarities.[15] Such a comparison can therefore yield important information on possible meanings of the rite in either tradition. There are also significant and undeniable differences: Vedic religion is, in all senses of the expression, a sacrificial religion: sacrifice is at the core of the tradition and forms the basis of virtually all speculation.[16] This does not apply to Zoroastrianism in any of its expressions, with the possible but inconclusive exception of the Gāthās.

The alternative to this comparative approach is the study of Zoroastrian traditions as they unfold on the basis of the earlier texts. This approach is mainly productive for those working on the later periods of Zoroastrian history, for it presupposes the existence of an early layer of tradition (laid down in the Gāthās and the Younger Avesta), beyond which historical research cannot reach.[17] Ideally, the two approaches are used in combination, but for the specific subject of animal sacrifice this has proven to be extremely difficult.[18] In the present contribution, we shall limit ourselves to the second approach to explore the meanings of sacrifice in the development of the Zoroastrian tradition.

2. *Early outside witnesses*

The earliest datable references to sacrifice in Iranian religious traditions come from two sources: Greek descriptions of the religion of

---

[14] For an introduction, cf. J.C. Heesterman, *The Broken World of Sacrifice. An Essay in Ancient Indian Ritual* (Chicago: University of Chicago Press, 1993).

[15] Elaborated by Kellens and Pirart, *Les textes vieil-avestiques* I, 3–36.

[16] For recent careful explorations of the subject, cf. Heesterman, *Broken World* and S.W. Jamison, *The Ravenous Hyenas and the Wounded Sun. Myth and Ritual in Ancient India* (Ithaca: Cornell University Press, 1991). The rituals associated with animal sacrifice (*paśubandha*) are amply described in R.N. Dandekar (ed.), *Śrautakośa* English Section I (Poona: Vaidika Samsodhana Mandala, 1962) 770–876; for quick reference, consult A.B. Keith, *The Religion and Philosophy of the Veda and Upanishads* (Cambridge, MA: Harvard University Press, 1925) 324–326.

[17] Good recent examples of such an approach are G. Kreyenbroek, *Sraoša in the Zoroastrian Tradition* (Orientalia Rheno-Traiectina 28; Leiden: Brill, 1985); A. Hintze, "The Rise of the Saviour in the Avesta," in C. Reck and P. Zieme, eds., *Iran und Turfan. Beiträge Berliner Wissenschaftler, Werner Sundermann zum 60. Geburtstag gewidmet* (Wiesbaden: Harrassowitz, 1995), 77–97.

[18] The best attempt is Boyce, *History of Zoroastrianism* I, 149–157.

the Persians and Elamite tablets from the Achaemenian administration in Persepolis in the period of Darius I. The evidence from the latter, however, tends to be inconclusive. The tablets mainly mention rations apportioned to priests and others for the performance of certain rituals; the rituals themselves are often named but it has not yet been possible to identify or interpret these terms with any confidence.[19] In Greek descriptions of (mainly) royal Persian rituals, animal sacrifice is especially prominent, but this may have been conditioned by the interests of the Greek observers themselves.[20]

Two texts stand out in importance: Herodotus, *Histories* 1.132 and Strabo, *Geography* 15.3.13.–15.[21] Herodotus, our earliest witness, describes a lay sacrifice, initiated and performed by a Persian on his own wish, in order to honour the god of his liking. A priest (a Magus) is present, but only to sing an invocation to the gods. Herodotus' description of the sacrifice shows so many lacunae that it is difficult to evaluate accurately. The opposite is true of Strabo's account, which is highly detailed and of the greatest importance for the history of Zoroastrian rituals.

Strabo was born in Amaseia around 63 BCE and died around 23 CE. His family had lived in Pontus for several generations and had entertained close contacts with the Graeco-Iranian Mithradatic dynasty. These contacts were severed for reasons of political expediency when the family established relations with the Romans in the person of Lucullus. When Lucullus was ousted by Pompey, the family's prestige and influence suffered accordingly. Strabo, who had been educated in Nyssa, travelled through large parts of the ancient world, from Armenia to the West and from Pontus to Ethiopia. He never went to Persia proper, but he had intimate knowledge of Iranian culture in the diaspora, and of the mix of Greek, Armenian and Iranian cultures that dominated the Eastern half of Anatolia for several centuries. He is one of the few Greek authors to transmit first-hand information on Zoroastrianism as a living faith, among the diaspora communities of Cappadocia and Eastern Anatolia. In his

---

[19] H. Koch, *Die religiösen Verhältnisse der Dareios-Zeit. Untersuchungen an Hand der elamischen Persepolistäfelchen* (Göttinger Orientforschungen, Rh. 3, Bd. 4; Wiesbaden: Harrassowitz, 1977) 120–153. Cf. also M. Boyce, *A History of Zoroastrianism II: Under the Achaemenians* (Handbuch der Orientalistik 1.8.2.2.2A.2; Leiden: Brill, 1982) 132–149.

[20] A brilliant *vue d'ensemble* is given by P. Briant, *Histoire de l'empire Perse. De Cyrus à Alexandre* (Paris: Fayard, 1996) 252–260.

[21] For these texts, cf. De Jong, *Traditions of the Magi*, 76–156.

description of Zoroastrian rituals (*Geography* 15.3.13–15; he hardly mentions the beliefs of the Persians), Strabo writes the following:

13. [. . .] And they perform sacrifices after dedicatory prayers in a purified place, presenting the victim wreathed. And when the Magus, who directs the ceremony, has cut the meat to pieces, the people take them away and depart, leaving no portion for the gods. For they say that the god needs the soul of the victim and nothing else. And yet, according to some, they put a small piece of the omentum on the fire.

14. They bring sacrifices to fire and water in a different way. For fire, they place upon it dry pieces of wood without the bark and place soft fat upon it; then, they pour oil upon it and light it below, not blowing but fanning; they even kill those who do blow or put a corpse or filth upon the fire. But for water, they go to a lake or a river or a spring, dig a trench and sacrifice (the victim) over it, taking care that nothing of the water near by is soiled with the blood, because thus they will defile it. Then they arrange the pieces of meat on myrtle or laurel, the Magi touch it with slender wands and sing invocations, while pouring out a libation of oil with milk and honey, not into fire or water, but upon the ground. And they sing invocations for a long time, holding the bundle of slender tamarisk wands in their hand.

15. But in Cappadocia-for there the tribe of the Magi is large; they are also called fire-kindlers, and there are many sanctuaries of the Persian gods-they do not even sacrifice with a knife, but they beat (the animal to death) with a piece of wood as with a cudgel. [. . .]

Some details in this description are obscure. This is particurly true of the libation poured on the earth. The main elements of the ritual, however, are clearly recognizable and are important for filling some gaps in our documentation in the Iranian texts. It is to these that we turn now.

3. The ritual as described in Zoroastrian texts

With some notable exceptions, most animals could be offered in sacrifice. The most important exceptions are animals that were held to have been created by the Evil Spirit (the so-called *xrafstras*) and certain animals that were particularly sacred because of their great use in the battle against evil: the cockerel, the dog, the beaver and the hedgehog, for instance. The evil animals are a separate section of the animal kingdom created by the evil spirit in order to harm the good creation. Mainstream Zoroastrian ideas on cosmogony and cosmology involve a double creation in the second stage of creative activity. First, Ahura Mazdā created the universe and what is in it in a perfect, spiritual (*mēnōg*) state. This creation could not be attacked by the Evil Spirit (Angra Mainyu/Ahreman), but in order to make it possible to solve the conflict between the two spirits-the main reason for this creation to exist-Ahura Mazdā transferred his initial creation into a material (*gētīg*) state, vulnerable to the activities of the Evil Spirit. Angra Mainyu immediately rushed to that creation and counter-created various sections in this universe, in order to make it more accessible to his destructive purposes. These creations include salt water, smoke, diseases and death, deserts, mountains and the evil animals (*xrafstra*). The *xrafstra*-category includes reptiles and insects, felines, wolves and other predators. Since these animals belong to Angra Mainyu, killing them is one of the greatest virtues anyone can perform; in expiation of sins, certain numbers of *xrafstras* must be killed and people were supposed to have with them a whip-like instrument, called *xrafstrayna-*, "*xrafstra*-killer" in order to do so. Such animals, however, were not suitable to be offered in sacrifice to Ahura Mazdā or any of the yazatas. They do have a "soul", but in this case that soul is not held to be released or saved by killing the animal in a sacrificial setting, as is the case with the "good" animals.[22] Offering such an animal in sacrifice is considered to be "devil-worship", the opposite of what is required of man. Descriptions of such devilish rites usually focus on the wolf as the animal to be sacrificed, just as descriptions of good sacrifices usually mention the cow as the sacrificial animal *par excellence*.[23]

Among the beneficent animals, the cockerel is often explicitly excluded from sacrifice.[24] The bird is sacred to the god Sraoša and its call in the morning chases the demons away. Likewise, sacrificing a dog seems to have been unimaginable: the animal was considered particularly holy and indispensable in the battle against pollution. It

---

[22] For the soul of the *xrafstras*, cf. *Andarz ī wehdēnān ō māzdēsnān* in J.M. Jamasp-Asana, *Pahlavi Texts* (Bombay, 1897) 123.3 ff: "Who created the soul (*gyān*) in the *xrafstars*? He said: 'Ōhrmazd.'"

[23] Cf. *Nērangestān* 59 (in A. Waag, *Nirangistan. Der Awestatraktat über die rituellen Vorschriften* (Iranische Forschungen 2; Leipzig: Hinrichs, 1941): "One satisfies the *Ratus* with the body of a she-wolf and her milk among all the devil-worshippers and those whose bodies are forfeit [. . .]." This *topos* probably led to the description of actual sacrifices of a wolf in Plutarch, *De Iside et Osiride* 46; cf. De Jong, *Traditions of the Magi*, 177–180.

[24] Cf. in particular *PhlRDd.* 58.81.

shares its anti-demonic qualities with the beaver and the hedgehog, all animals that were not eaten and not sacrificed.

Theoretically, at least, all other animals could be offered in sacrifice. Some, of course, never were because they were not caught to be eaten. In some texts, the range of animals suitable for sacrifice is restricted to domesticated animals and all fish and birds (with the exception of the cockerel and birds not eaten, such as vultures). Wild animals, that is to say those animals caught in the hunt, are a problematic category. Since all sacrificial rites we hear of in the texts mention the killing of the animal (with a cudgel and a knife), whether as part of the ritual or preceding it (both varieties are attested),[25] it is unclear how wild animals would qualify for the ritual. In *PhlRDd*. 58.78–80,[26] a distinction is made between tame animals (killed with cudgel and knife) and wild animals (killed with bow and arrow). The latter (the example given is the "mountain cow" (*gāw ī kōfig*)[27] can also be captured and domesticated; if they are, the rules that apply to them are identical to the rules applying to tame animals. This suggests that the meat of animals killed during the hunt had a separate status, because it did not derive from animals killed in a ritual setting.[28]

A further problem arises with several lists of animals that should not be killed or eaten that appear in Pahlavi texts.[29] These have sometimes been interpreted as giving rules on animals not suitable for

[25] M. Boyce, "Haoma, Priest of the Sacrifice," in M. Boyce and I. Gershevitch, eds., *W.B. Henning Memorial Volume* (London: Lund Humphries, 1970) 62–80, p. 68.

[26] For this text, cf. A.V. Williams, *The Pahlavi Rivāyat Accompanying the Dādestān ī Dēnīg* (Det Kongelige Danske Videnskabernes Selskab, Historisk-Filosofiske Meddelelser 60; København: Munksgaard, 1989) ad loc. Cf. also K.M. Jamasp-Asa, 'On the *drōn* in Zoroastrianism' in *Papers in Honour of Professor Mary Boyce* (Acta Iranica 24; Leiden: Brill, 1985) 335–356.

[27] According to Ph. Gignoux, "Dietary Laws in Pre-Islamic and Post-Sasanian Iran," *Jerusalem Studies in Arabic and Islam* 17 (1994) 16–42, a mouflon.

[28] For hunting and its benefits according to Iranian traditions, cf. Ph. Gignoux, "La chasse dans l'Iran sasanide," in Gh. Gnoli, ed., *Orientalia Romana 5. Iranian Studies* (Serie Orientale Roma 52; Roma: Istituto Italiano per il medio ed estremo Oriente, 1983) 101–118.

[29] An overview is given by Gignoux, "Dietary Laws." J.C. Tavadia announced in *Šāyest-nē-šāyest. A Pahlavi Text on Religious Customs* (Alt- und Neu-Indische Studien 3; Hamburg: Friedrichsen, De Gruyter, 1930) 130 an article on "Lawful and Unlawful Animal Food According to Iranian Writers," but this unfortunately did not appear as announced in the Pavry *Festschrift*.

sacrificial rituals, but their exact status is unclear. They proscribe, for instance, the killing of the pig and the eating of pork under certain conditions.[30] An Avestan fragment in the *Nērangestān*, however, seems to indicate precisely the opposite, by listing the pig (strangely enough along with various young animals) as an animal "to be sacrificed during the ritual for the gods" (*pad yazišn ī yazadān kušišn*).[31] Similarly, various forbidden animals listed in *ŠnŠ* 10.9 appear as choice meats in the description of royal cuisine in the court romance *King Khusraw and his Page*.[32]

If the animal species suitable for sacrifice are not unequivocally specified, other rules are clear. Both male and female animals could be offered in sacrifice.[33] Young animals were not suitable. This rule, one of the most often repeated prescriptions, is in accordance with similar rules concerning fruits and vegetables: these could only be picked or harvested when they were ripe.[34] Lambs, kids, calves and colts were, consequently, not considered admissible sacrificial animals. At the other end of the age spectre, animals that were too old were not admissible either.[35]

If female, the animal should not be with young and should not be suckling its young. All animals should be intact (i.e. not missing certain body parts), healthy and strong. Lean, sickly and wounded animals were not suitable.[36] The animal obviously also had to be alive at the moment of sacrifice. A final restriction appears to have been one of quantity: it was considered best to kill as small a number of animals as possible in order to feed the congregation.[37]

---

[30] Gignoux, "Dietary Laws," 20; 29.

[31] H. Hoffmann, "Drei indogermanische Tiernamen in einem Avesta-Fragment," *Münchener Studien zur Sprachwissenschaft* 22 (1967) 29–38. The fragment occurs in *N.* 58 (Waag) with a parallel in *PhlRDd.* 58.83.

[32] For which, cf. D. Monchi-Zadeh, "Xusrōv i Kavātān ut rētak. Pahlavi Text, Transcription and Translation," in *Monumentum Georg Morgenstierne II* (Acta Iranica 22; Leiden: Brill, 1983) 47–91.

[33] Gignoux, "Dietary Laws," 17, suggests that only male animals were suitable, but this is flatly contradicted by certain rules applying only to female animals (e.g. those proscribing the slaughter of animals with young) and by the fact that the Avestan parts of the *Nērangestān* refer to the sacrificial animals with feminine forms only.

[34] Evident, for instance, from the *Irani Patita*, a late confession of sins, which includes the confession that "I have cut down young wood and trees and picked unripe fruits and vegetables." For the text, cf. E.K. Antiâ, *Pâzend Texts* (Bombay: Trustees of the Parsee Punchâyet, 1909) 139.5–6.

[35] *N.* 54 (Waag) appears to proscribe the use of an animal that no longer has milk to give.

[36] *N.* 56.

[37] *PhlRDd.* 58.71, discussed by Boyce, "Haoma," 69–70 (and cf. below).

In certain cases, rules applied to the food the animal could have eaten. If one wanted to sacrifice a pig, which was thought to feed on *xrafstras*, it should have been fed on grass and vegetables for a year in order to qualify.[38] In the case of cows, neither their meat nor their milk could be used for ritual purposes if the owner found out that the animal had accidentally consumed carrion.[39]

Some rules also applied to whoever provided the animal. The *Nērangestān* 54 (Waag) says that the animal should come from the personal possessions of the dedicant and his family, but may also be procured (by confiscation) from devil-worshippers and mortal sinners. In that case, the confiscation was only allowed, it seems, if the animal was indeed sacrificed.

After the selection and inspection of the animal, a priest dug a trench or a pit over which the animal was to be killed and constructed a separate mound of grass on which the pieces of meat were supposed to be placed. Both elements are mentioned by Strabo and the mound of grass also figures prominently in the oldest description of Persian animal sacrifice in Greek literature, Herodotus' *Histories* 1.132.[40] Both elements are also known from the *Nērangestān*: "[Placing] the rump toward the *zōt*, breast to the fire, dig a hole, put down a cushion without recitation. If no hole is dug the cushion will be damaged."[41] This is the only passage in Zoroastrian literature to confirm the digging of a pit before the sacrifice and give its reason: to prevent the blood from defiling a sacred space; such is the case with the water in Strabo's description and with the "cushion" (*bāliš*) in the *Nērangestān*.

The pit presumably was dug to collect the waste products of the sacrifice: the inedible intestines of the animal and, possibly, its blood.[42] The practice is well known from other Zoroastrian rules with regard

---

[38] Gignoux, "Dietary Laws," 20.

[39] *Vd.* 7.77 with commentary.

[40] For which, cf. De Jong, *Traditions of the Magi*, 110–119.

[41] Pahlavi *Nērangestān* f. 128v, in: D.S. Flattery & M. Schwartz, *Haoma and Harmaline. The Botanical Identity of the Indo-Iranian Sacred Hallucinogen "Soma" and its Legacy in Religion, Language, and Middle Eastern Folklore* (University of California Publications: Near Eastern Studies 21; Berkeley and Los Angeles: University of California Press, 1989) 83, n. 14.

[42] The status of the blood of the sacrifical animal is uncertain: in modern Irani Zoroastrian usage, the blood is collected in a bowl and prepared to be eaten (as a form of black pudding); since Islamic observance forbids the eating of blood, this is unlikely to be a recent innovation. The observance itself, however, is not known from any literary source. Cf. Boyce, "Mihragān," 111.

to impure substances. More than most other religions, Zoroastrianism has difficulties with the ways by which to dispose of impure substances (i.e. everything that leaves the body).[43] Since earth, water and fire are all sacred and polluting these elements must be avoided, simply throwing them on the earth, throwing them in water or burning them are no viable solutions. The solution prescribed throughout Zoroastrian literature is that of digging a hole and protecting the earth from being polluted by certain formulae, before and after the "burying" of the impure substances. This rule applies to the disposal of nail-clippings and hair as well as to urinating and defecating.[44] The hole that is dug is marked off by the drawing of furrows which prevent the impurity from spreading; the recitation of texts neutralizes the evil that attaches to the impure substances.

The animal was made to face the fire.[45] Its legs were bound together, a dedication was recited, dedicating the animal to Vohu Manah, Lord of Cattle, and the neck of the animal was broken with a log of wood, or at least the animal was stunned. Then, it was killed by slitting its throat with a knife. The sequence of activities at this stage of the sacrifice is perhaps best illustrated by a passage from the short poetic text *Draxt ī Asūrīg* 14–17. In this text, a Parthian-Middle Persian dispute between a Babylonian tree and a goat on the question who is the best, the tree addresses the goat thus:

> They make ropes of me   which bind your legs.
> They make clubs of me   which break your neck.
> They make pegs of me   which hang you upside down.
> I am fuel for the fires   which roast you terribly.[46]

The question of stunning the animal before killing it with a knife has attracted a lot of attention, both among non-Zoroastrians in antiquity and in modern scholarly literature.[47] In the *Questions of Bōxt-*

---

[43] For an introduction to the subject, cf. A.V. Williams, "Zoroastrian and Judaic Purity Laws. Reflections on the Viability of a Sociological Interpretation" in S. Shaked and A. Netzer, eds., *Irano-Judaica III* (Jerusalem: Ben Zvi Institute, 1994) 72–89; further materials in J.K. Choksy, *Purity and Pollution in Zoroastrianism. Triumph over Evil* (Austin: University of Texas Press, 1989).

[44] Cf. also De Jong, "Purification *in absentia*."

[45] Boyce, "Haoma," 68 with n. 57.

[46] Translated by C.J. Brunner, "The Fable of *The Babylonian Tree*," *JNES* 39 (1980), 191–202; 291–302, ad loc.

[47] The fundamental study is E. Benveniste, "Sur la terminologie iranienne du sacrifice," *JA* 252 (1964) 45–58.

Mahrē, part of the fifth book of the *Dēnkard*, we find this aspect of the ritual as one of the items in the discussion between a Christian and a Zoroastrian high priest.[48] The question asked is: "What is the reason that the sacrificial animal is struck with the wood before the knife?" (*gōspand pad kuštan pēš az kārd cōb zadan cim*) and this is the answer:

> The reason for striking cattle with a log before (applying) the knife, together with the other things which are to be done in that matter, apart from the ritual efficacy of cleansing the body from a number of demons, especially the portion of excrement and bad taste, and (apart from) preventing the unjust and ill-considered slaughter of cattle, is first pity for the beast and on this account the lessening of its fear and pain when the knife is applied to it, and its prevention of the slaughter of cattle in an ill-considered manner, impulsively and at any time when one's desire is urgent.[49]

This particular aspect of the Zoroastrian ritual is also known to us from two unexpected traditions. The Mandaeans, who sacrifice animals with a knife, do so only while holding a piece of wood, undoubtedly under the influence of Zoroastrian practices.[50] It has long been known that Mandaean ritual terminology and practice was heavily influenced by Zoroastrianism.[51] The piece of wood, incidentally, is *not* used in the sacrifice, but it is mandatory that it be held.

The practice of stunning the animal before killing it is also known from Armenian literature, where the Iranian loan-word *yaz-el* (from the root *yaz-*, "to sacrifice") came to be used to indicate precisely this way of sacrificing. Eating meat from an animal killed in the Zoroastrian way was considered proof of (re-)conversion.[52] In Syriac,

---

[48] For the background of these questions, cf. A. de Jong, "Zoroastrian Self-Definition in Contact with Other Faiths," in S. Shaked and A. Netzer, eds., *Irano-Judaica* 5 [forthc.]. For a translation of the text, cf. M.F. Kanga, "Pursišnīhā ī Bōxt-Mārā ut-šān passoxˈīhā. A Pahlavi Text," *Indian Linguistics* 25 (1964–1965; *Baburam Saksena Felicitation Volume*) 3–20.

[49] Translated by R.C. Zaehner, *Zurvan. A Zoroastrian Dilemma* (Oxford: Oxford University Press, 1955) 52.

[50] K. Rudolph, *Die Mandäer II. Der Kult* (FRLANT NF 57; Göttingen: Vandenhoeck & Ruprecht, 1961) 297; E.S. Drower, *The Mandaeans of Iraq and Iran* (Oxford: Oxford University Press, 1937) 49–50.

[51] Cf. Ş. Gündüz, *The Knowledge of Life. The Origins and Early History of the Mandaeans and their Relation to the Sabians of the Qur'ān and to the Harranians* (JSS Supplement 3; Oxford: Oxford University Press, 1994) 79–83.

[52] Benveniste, "Terminologie," 51–53; J.R. Russell, *Zoroastrianism in Armenia* (Harvard Iranian Series 5; Cambridge, MA: Harvard University, Department of Near Eastern

too, the practice has been recorded.[53] The controversy over the eating of meat from sacrificial animals will be discussed below.

The description in the *Draxt ī Asūrīg* also omits some essential elements: the animal was bound and stunned and hung from wooden pegs, after which it was flayed and dissected.[54] The roasting of the animal could also be replaced by cooking the meat in a cauldron, as witnessed by Herodotus and observed among modern Irani Zoroastrians.[55] Raw meat, at any rate, was not allowed (*N.* 57). The inedible innards were probably buried in the pit and the skins were prepared and could be offered (separately) as part of the ritual. We do not know much about the treatment of the meat, apart from the fact that it was cut to pieces and roasted or cooked. One thing, however, is essential: some parts of the head (or the entire head) were kept aside, because they were consecrated to the god Haoma. We find this prescription already in the Avesta: the two jaw-bones, the tongue and the left eye are the share of Haoma (Y. 11.4–7). Apart from being the god of the plant Haoma (one of the essential elements of Zoroastrian ritual), Haoma is also known as the divine priest and, as such, receives a fixed portion.[56]

The consecration of the head, and more particularly of the tongue, of the animal is one of the very few elements of the ritual that have been attested throughout the history of Zoroastrianism. A special ritual, in which a flat cake (*drōn*) was offered with the tongue was part of the sacrificial rites. The only exception occurs when birds or fish are offered as sacrificial animals; these animals were not dedicated to Haoma but to the god Gōš, the "soul of the bull," who looks after animal welfare.

In all Zoroastrian rituals, the dedication takes place by reciting the appropriate words and by a ritual tasting (*cāšnī*) by the priest. Generally, there are the *drōn*, prepared Haoma and representations of vegetal and animal life (the latter known as *gōšūdāg*, cf. above). During the ritual, the priest tastes some of it and afterwards the rest

---

Languages and Civilizations; National Association for Armenian Studies and Research, 1987) 491–494.

[53] Cf. the evidence from Mār Barhad-bešabba in J. Bidez & F. Cumont, *Les mages hellénisés* (Paris: Les Belles Lettres, 1937) vol. 2, 100–101.

[54] *SupplTxtŠnŠ* 11.4–11.6.

[55] Boyce, *Stronghold*, 246.

[56] Brilliantly studied by Boyce, "Haoma," passim.

of the *gōšūdāg* as well as the share of Haoma (the consecrated tongue, which the priest may not taste) is given to a dog, one of the most sacred animals in Zoroastrianism.

What is striking in Zoroastrian rites of animal sacrifice is the fact that almost all of the meat is of no consequence to the ritual. Apart from the tongue, some of the fat, which is given to the fire, and the piece of meat near the *drōn*, the meat is of no consequence.[57] The priest gets his share and the rest is either consumed by those present or is shared and taken away. The sharing of the meat was considered a sacred duty, and failing to comply with it is condemned in strong terms in Y. 11.1.

4. *Controversies over Zoroastrian sacrifices*

Like systems of purity and pollution, the rites of sacrifice can produce and uphold boundaries between religious groups. In the cultural mix of Sasanian Babylonia and Iran, virtually all religious communities banned the eating of meat from animals killed by "others." This is true of Jews, Zoroastrians, Mandaeans and Christians in various degrees of rigidity. The Zoroastrian legislation on the subject, however, is not very clear. One often finds bans on killing animals "not in accordance with the law" (*adādīhā*), something which Jews and Christians were said to do, but the laws in question are rarely specified. One can reasonably guess that the fact that Jews were thought to kill young animals constituted illegal ways of taking animal life.[58]

Zoroastrian sources frequently mention the fact that it is not allowed to buy meat from non-Zoroastrians, or to sell meat to them, but such a prescription is part of a larger set of rules against exchanging food commodities of various types and the ban on buying them from unbelievers is connected with their failure to observe the purity

---

[57] On the *omentum*-offering mentioned by Strabo, cf. De Jong, *Traditions of the Magi*, 132–133, with references to parallels in Indian and Zoroastrian literature and in modern practice.

[58] Cf. *Dk.* 3.288.9: "One, <against that which Yima> counselled not to kill cattle before they reach maturity, Dahāg taught to kill cattle freely, according to the custom of the Jews." Translated and discussed by S. Shaked, "Zoroastrian Polemics against Jews in the Sasanian and Early Islamic Period," in S. Shaked and A. Netzer, eds., *Irano-Judaica* II (Jerusalem: Ben Zvi Institute, 1990) 85–104.

rules and not specifically related to sensitivities in the area of animal sacrifice.

Such sensitivities are known, however, from the opposing sides: the best known and most interesting case is the charge, brought forward in martyrologies, that Christians were required by their Zoroastrian persecutors to "eat blood."[59] The most likely interpretation of these charges is connected with the Zoroastrian practice of sacrifice, which seems to be designed to keep the blood in the animal for as long as possible; animals were bled, eventually, but no particular importance attached to the bleeding of the animal, which must have been unacceptable to Jews, but here appears to have been unacceptable to Christians, too. From Armenian literature we also find reports on the fact that re-converted Zoroastrians were required to eat meat from a sacrificed animal, which apparently constituted proof of true (re-)conversion.[60]

5. *Interpretations of sacrifice: the sacrifice as a gift to the gods*

To the question why the ritual of animal sacrifice is important or necessary, the obvious answer in the texts would be: "for the sake of the soul."[61] But the meaning or interpretation of the sacrifice has taken different directions, stressing either the nature of the ritual as a pleasing gift to the gods or as the only legitimate way of procuring meat. It is to these interpretations that we must turn now.

The first interpretation, which focuses on the commerce between mortals and gods, is in all likelihood the oldest tradition. It is similar to ideas on sacrifice in the religion of Vedic India, which shares a common ancestry with Zoroastrianism. It is also most explicitly present in the Avesta, the oldest layer of Zoroastrian literature, and more particularly in the *Yašts*, hymns to the individual divinities.[62] In these hymns, the gods are praised and invoked. One often finds

---

[59] Some texts have been collected and discussed by Gignoux, "Dietary Laws," 21–22.

[60] Benveniste, "Terminologie," 53.

[61] Cf. S. Shaked, "'For the Sake of the Soul': A Zoroastrian Idea in Transmission to Islam," *Jerusalem Studies in Arabic and Islam* 13 (1990) 15–32.

[62] For the *Yašts*, cf. H. Lommel, *Die Yašts des Awesta* (Quellen der Religionsgeschichte 15: Göttingen: Vandenhoeck & Ruprecht; Leipzig: Hinrichs, 1927); P.O. Skjaervø, "Hymnic Composition in the Avesta," *Die Sprache* 36.2 (1994) 199–243.

in them a catalogue of divine and heroic worshippers, describing sacrifices performed in honour of the deity to whom the hymn is addressed. These passages are highly formulaic. A typical example from the hymn to Anahita, a popular river goddess and goddess of fertility, is:

> The brave, powerful Kavi Usan sacrificed to her (Anāhitā) on Mount Erezifya a hundred stallions, a thousand cows and ten-thousand sheep. Then he asked her: 'Good strong Aredvī Sūrā Anāhitā, grant me this favour, that I may become the supreme ruler over all lands, over *daēvas* and men, over sorcerers and witches, over petty rulers, *kavis* and *kara-pans*. Aredvī Sūrā Anāhitā granted him that favour, to him who brought her libations, who worshipped her and brought her sacrifices. (Yt. 5.45–47)

The majority of passages in which sacrifices are performed follow this pattern. A markedly different formula is used in the case of priestly and divine worshippers, Zarathustra and Ahura Mazdā, for instance, who do not take animal life, but engage in the typically priestly Haoma-libations and sacred words.[63] A further difference can be observed in those passages where evil mythical persons perform the sacrifice: they can kill as many animals as the good persons do, but their wishes are never granted.

The incredible number of animals killed in these texts are due, no doubt, to epic exaggeration, but the species offered (horses, cows and sheep) were certainly all offered once, even though there does not seem to be direct evidence for horse sacrifice.[64]

The ideas underlying this interpretation of sacrifice are reasonably clear: an individual turns to a specific deity in order to please him or her and obtain merit or a specific favour in return. The deity is offered the sacrifice, invited to partake of it and is supposed to do something in return. This is also very much the interpretation suggested by Herodotus and other Greek authors.

There are some traces of an even older conception of sacrifice in the Avesta: that according to which the gods were actually in need

---

[63] Yt. 5.17–19; 5.104–106, for example. Cf. also A. Panaino, "An Aspect of Sacrifice in the Avesta," *East and West* 36 (1986) 271–274.

[64] It is mentioned in several places in Greek literature, but there it may owe more than a little to Greek ideas on sacrifice. Cf. in particular Appian, *Mithridateia* 70, with De Jong, *Traditions of the Magi*, 361–362.

of those sacrifices. This is a well known idea from Vedic India, but only poorly attested in the Avesta. The only straightforward example is from the hymn to Tištrya (Yt. 8), the star Sirius, bringer of rain, with a parallel passage in the hymn to Verethraghna (Yt. 14), the god of victory.[65] In the hymn to Tištrya, we read that the calamities coming over the Aryan nations (the "we" of these texts) are due to the fact that Tištrya did not receive enough sacrifices. The solution to these problems is given by Ahura Mazdā himself: "Then Ahura Mazdā answered: 'Let the Aryan nations bring libations unto him; let the Aryan nations spread the *baresman* for him; let the Aryan nations cook a sheep for him, either white or black or of any colour, but of one colour'." (Yt. 8.58). Ahura Mazdā adds that if a wicked, non-Iranian person is allowed to partake of this sacrifice, it is void and the calamities will not be averted (Yt. 8.59–61).

In this passage, the idea is clearly expressed that the gods were thought to be strengthened by the sacrifice. This conception, however, is rare because in Zoroastrian literature, the main idea has always been that prayer, worship and belief strengthen the good gods in their fight against evil.

These are some early examples of the understanding of sacrifice as a commerce between mortals and gods, the typical expression of which is the invitation to a meal. A significant aspect for the development of Zoroastrianism seems to be the stress on the morality of the dedicant, upon which (and not upon the correct procedure) the acceptability of the offering depends.

Although it is not commonly found in Zoroastrian literature, there can be little doubt that this continued to be the way in which most Zoroastrians understood the rites of animal sacrifice: as a personal gift to a divinity in order to acquire spiritual merit or to obtain a certain goal. As such it is usually presented in Greek literature on the religion of the Persians, where we find many descriptions of (mainly) royal sacrifices, carefully chosen and dedicated to specific divinities by the Magi, the Zoroastrian priests.[66]

Further confirmation of the continuing prominence of this interpretation of sacrifice comes from the inscriptions of the Sasanian king Šāpūr I (r. 242–272 CE). In his monumental trilingual inscrip-

---

[65] Cf. A. Panaino, *Tištrya. Part I: The Avestan Hymn to Sirius* (Serie Orientale Roma 8.1; Roma: Istituto Italiano per il Medio ed Estremo Oriente, 1990).
[66] De Jong, *Traditions of the Magi*, 357–362.

tion on the Kaʿbeh-ye Zartušt (ŠKZ),[67] this Sasanian monarch specifies the number of sheep to be killed on a daily basis for the sake of his soul and for the sake of the souls of various relatives.[68] There is no reason to doubt that these sacrifices were actually performed and they entailed the killing of thousands of sheep on a yearly basis.

6. *Animal sacrifice from a priestly perspective*

This conception of sacrifice is rarely attested in the priestly Pahlavi writings (to be dated collectively in the ninth and tenth centuries CE, but containing materials that are much older). These writings often focus more on the technicalities of the sacrifice, describing with great care which texts are to be recited when. Some of these texts, in particular the *Nērangestān*, a treatise on ritual, were used more or less as manuals for practising priests.[69] Wherever we find something about the underlying ideas, the focus is more on compassion with the animal and the deeply felt theological problem of taking life, in a tradition where this is an action usually ascribed to the Evil Spirit.[70]

Before evil entered the world, there was no death. The first animal to be killed was the Uniquely Created Bull (*gāw ī ēk-dād*) and it was killed by Ahreman, the Evil Spirit, in his attempt to destroy the good creation. As an unexpected salutary effect of this first act of violence, a variety of plant and animal life came into being and the progression of life began. This progression of life is a vital part of the struggle against evil, which is the only reason for this world to exist.[71] Death, in other words, is what Ahreman does to people, animals and plants. It is one of his countercreations to the life created by Ahura Mazdā. There is no escaping the reality that in order to

---

[67] For the text, cf. M. Back, *Die sassanidischen Staatsinschriften* (Acta Iranica 18; Leiden: Brill, 1978) 284–371.

[68] The passages in question are to be found in Back, *Sassanidischen Staatsinschriften*, 336–368.

[69] For the nature of the *Nērangestān*, cf. F.M. Kotwal & Ph.G. Kreyenbroek, *The Hērbedestān and Nērangestān II: Nērangestān. Fragard I* (Studia Iranica Cahier 16; Paris: Association pour l'avancement des études iraniennes, 1995) 13–14.

[70] This interpretation of the ritual has been carefully explored in the works by Mary Boyce referred to above.

[71] The most extensive version of this aspect of the cosmogony is found in *Greater Bundahišn* 4.21–4A6, for which cf. B.T. Anklesaria, *Zand-ākāsīh. Iranian or Greater Bundahišn* (Bombay: Rahnumae Mazdayasnan Sabha, 1956) ad loc.

sacrifice an animal, or in order to eat meat, one has to kill it. In a sense, this act imitates the behaviour of the Evil Spirit and is, therefore, potentially harmful to the good creation. Much of the priestly speculations is connected with this theological problem.

There are several aspects that are important here. First of all, there are priestly, divine and heroic examples of sacrifices offered to further the cause of good. The renovation of the world, which will bring about the final defeat of the powers of evil and the cleansing of creation, will be inaugurated by the performance of several rituals by Ahura Mazdā himself, and by the Redeemer (Saošyant) and his associates; one of these rituals will be the killing of a bull, the fat of which mixed with White Hom will produce the draught of immortality for the resurrection of the dead.[72] A famous first sacrifice is also attributed to the first human couple, Mašyā and Mašyāna, but this sacrifice was not performed according to any acceptable rule (it included tossing meat into the fire and into the air) and they were severely punished for it.[73] These examples do show, however, that the concept of animal sacrifice could be construed in terms of the emulation of divine or heroic examples, rather than an imitation of the activities of the Evil Spirit.

At an unknown point in time, but presumably quite early, the taking of animal life came to be restricted to a sacrificial context. The only permissible way to kill beneficent animals was to offer them up in sacrifice. Any other way of killing them was equated with a sin known as *būdyōzadīh*, "destroying existence/conscience." The basic idea is that killing the animal in the course of sacrifice releases its consciousness, soul, or spirit, which can then rise up to be collected and taken care of by the god "Soul of the Bull" (Geuš Urvan, Gōš). Killing it any other way equals destroying the animal, which is a serious sin.

We have seen above that this rule does not apply to "evil creatures" (*xrafstra*), the killing of which is instantly meritorious, and may not have applied to wild animals either. For the latter subject, the evidence is too limited to decide either way, but it is true to say

---

[72] *Greater Bundahišn* 34.22–23.
[73] *GBd.* 14.21–22. This is a very difficult passage. For an interpretation, cf. A. de Jong, "Shadow and Resurrection," *Bulletin of the Asia Institute*, N.S. 9 (1995) 215–224, pp. 216–217 with references.

that most of the rules given for sacrifice seem to presuppose domesticated animals and, therefore, exclude discussions of exceptional
cases, such as animals caught during the hunt.

The interpretation of sacrifice as the legal way to obtain meat
gives the impression of a secondary rationalisation, mainly because
of its absence in the early layers of the tradition. The idea of releasing the animal's soul, however, is known from early texts. In an
Avestan fragment preserved in the late catechetical text *Pursišnīhā*
("Questions") we find the following ritual exclamation: "We send
forth, O beneficent, good-giving bull, thy conscience and soul among
the nearest created lights, the sight of the eyes of men."[74]

Later texts not only stress the fact that killing animals in sacrifice
saves their souls, but also limits their suffering to the required min-
imum. This, too, is based on earlier ideas, for instance on the prescription that the killing is done quickly.[75] The number of animals
killed should be limited as much as possible[76] and the stunning of
the animal was considered an act of compassion. Sacrificers, moreover, should be fully aware of what they were going to do and of
the necessity of killing the animal, both features that are stressed in
the discussion of the clubbing of the animal. A philosophical adap-
tation of these rules is found in *Dk.* 3.388, where a distinction is
made between "killing without consciousness" (*a-bōy zadan*) and "perfect killing" (*bowandag zadan*). The former amounts to killing at ran-
dom and is found among sinners and demons, whereas in the case
of the latter, the acceptance of the prescriptions of the religion leads
to a way of taking life that does not endanger the soul.[77] The necessity of sharing the meat procured from the sacrificial animal is also
evident from a number of texts. The cow, the prototype of the
sacrificial animal, pronounces the following curse in *Y.* 11.1: "May
you be without offspring and accompanied by disgrace, (you) who
do not share me when I am cooked, but you, you fatten me for

---

[74] K.M. JamaspAsa and H. Humbach, *Pursišnīhā. A Zoroastrian Catechism* (Wiesbaden: Harrassowitz, 1971) 52–53; cf. also J. Kellens, "Die Religion der Achämeniden," *Altorientalische Forschungen* 10 (1983) 107–123, p. 118.

[75] Boyce, "Haoma," 69–70, discussing the Avestan word *āsu.yasna-*, "swiftly sacrificing."

[76] *PhlRDd.* 58.71, discussed by Boyce, "Haoma," 71–72.

[77] Translation in P.J. de Menasce, *Le troisième livre du Denkart* (Paris: Klincksieck, 1973) ad loc.

your wife, your son or your own belly."[78] The sharing of the meat was also commented upon by various Greek observers (see above).

Several limitations on sacrifice were also introduced on religious grounds: on days under the tutelage of Vohu Manah, lord of cattle, no sacrifices could be performed. The best known prescription in this context is the ban on eating meat during the first three days after the death of a relative. If this rule was not observed, it was feared that another member of the family would die soon.[79] Eating meat at any rate was an activity fraught with danger and, therefore, awareness of its consequences was always required. *Ṣad Dar-e Naṣr* 23, for instance, warns its readers to abstain from sin after the eating of meat: if one sins after having eaten meat, the sins of the animal (which are unknown, but can be serious) are added to the stock of the eater.

Meat is a normal part of the human diet. According to the *Bundahišn*, mankind originally only took water, then plants, then milk and then, finally, meat and will give up consuming these in reversed order at the end of time (*GBd*. 34.1–2).[80] Their final consumption, however, the draught of immortality, will be made of all these substances. This perhaps illustrates the ambiguities inherent in the notion of sacrifice in Zoroastrianism: it is, in general, a joyful occasion, taking place in communal gatherings, accompanied by a shared meal, but it is at the same time a situation that instills a deep sense of distress, perhaps even guilt, in the minds of those willing to ponder its theological resonances.

---

[78] Most recently discussed by J. Josephson, *The Pahlavi Translation Technique as Illustrated by Hōm Yašt* (Studia Iranica Upsaliensia 2; Uppsala: Uppsala University Library, 1997) ad loc.

[79] *SDN* 78.

[80] Discussed in De Jong, "Shadow and Resurrection," 216–218.

PART TWO

ALTERNATIVES TO SACRIFICE

FORGIVENESS OF SINS WITHOUT A VICTIM: JESUS AND THE LEVITICAL JUBILEE

ADRIANA DESTRO and MAURO PESCE

Introduction

The concept of sacrifice current "in the nineteenth century and the first half of the twentieth" has been criticized by scholars in the comparative study of religions for quite some time.[1] What in the past was defined as sacrifice is present in various cultures in a great variety of forms. The features of sacrifice and the reasons why it was used vary widely from one culture and religion to another. To speak of sacrifice therefore means to single out an individual cultural context and one specific way of conceptualizing society and the cosmic order, without renouncing a comparative perspective and a general concept. From this point of view, Claude Rivière argues that: "à defaut d'éléments absolument universels et constants, l'idéaltype se construira à partir des frequences majeures de traits observés et d'interpretations attestées".[2] Cristiano Grottanelli also reaches similar conclusions. He believes it both possible, and necessary, to arrive at a "descriptive generalization" of what had once gone under the name of "sacrifice". A new definition, however, must be based "on some empirically verifiable features" present "(even if in not necessarily identical ways) in all human cultures that have been studied".[3]

According to Rivière's definition,

> Le sacrifice est une action symbolique de séparation, de détachment et d'offrande d'un bien ou de soi même, en signe de soumission, d'obéissance, de repentir ou d'amour, qui noue de manière dynamique des rapports asymétriques entre des instances surnaturelles sollicitées et la communauté humaine par l'intermédiaire d'un sacrifiant et d'une victime.

---

[1] C. Grottanelli, "Uccidere, donare, mangiare: problematiche attuali del sacrificio antico", in C. Grottanelli—N.F. Parise (Eds.), *Sacrificio e società nel mondo antico* (Roma/Bari, Laterza, 1988), 3.
[2] C. Rivière, "Approches Comparatives du sacrifice", in F. Boespflug—F. Dunad, *Le comparatisme en histoire des religions* (Paris, Cerf, 1997), 288.
[3] Grottanelli, "Uccidere, donare, mangiare", 15.

Il suppose un acte coûteux, une privation en hommage à une entité spirituelle, donc désir de communication, et se traduit par l'offrande abandonnée, par la mortification personelle et fréquemment par l'immolation d'une victime animale suivie d'un repas communiel comme conclusion des procédures rituelles comprenant des purifications et des prières, et comme acte unificateur, l'homme étant dans le repas l'hôte invité de son dieu.[4]

Grottanelli argues for a different definition, taking into account the findings of French historical anthropology (J.-P. Vernant, M. Detienne, and J.-L. Durand). His definition is mainly oriented towards the "eating of meat". The basic characteristics of sacrifice would therefore be: "the ritualized killing", the "giving of (parts) of the victim to supernatural beings", and the meal of meat with the distribution of parts of the animal to the various participants in the ritual.[5]

In our study of early Christianity we shall be concentrating on one particular problem: the forgiveness of sins. We shall be considering sacrifice only from this limited perspective, the link between sacrifice and expiation or forgiveness of sins. We are therefore aware that this aspect by no means exhausts the subject of the nature of sacrifice.

In a 1995 article we argued that John's Gospel excludes and criticizes the cult of sacrifice and yet retains certain basic features of the sacrificial system of the Temple of Jerusalem, above all the necessity of the expiation of sins through a victim (Jesus): the sacrificial pattern that requires a victim is still there.[6] Here we shall be examining a different process, which emerges in the Synoptic Gospels.

Three different conceptions of the forgiveness of sins in the New Testament

In the present canon of early Christian writings that goes under the name of New Testament, three different conceptions of the forgiveness of sins can be found.

---

[4] Rivière, "Approches Comparatives du sacrifice", 288.
[5] Grottanelli, "Uccidere, donare, mangiare", 17. See now, however, C. Grottanelli, *Il sacrificio*, Bari-Roma, Laterza, 1999, 31–33.
[6] A. Destro—M. Pesce, "Lo spirito e il mondo vuoto. Prospettive esegetiche e antropologiche su Gv 4,21–24", *Annali di Storia dell'esegesi* 12 (1995), 9–32. See also A. Destro—M. Pesce, "Identità collettiva e identità personale nel cristianesimo paolino e giovaneo", in *I quaderni del ramo d'oro*. Università di Siena. Centro Interdipartimentale di Studi Antropologici sulla Cultura Antica 2 (1998), 33–63; "Self, Identity, and Body in Paul and John", in: A.I. Baumgarten, J. Assmann, G.G. Stroumsa (Eds.), *Self, Soul and Body in Religious Experience* (Leiden, Brill, 1998), 184–197.

(1) A first group of texts connects the forgiveness of sins by God to the death of Jesus Christ. G. Barth has classified the various conceptions through which, in the New Testament, an attempt is made to explain the way the death of Jesus Christ leads to the forgiveness of sins. In some texts it is thought of as a substitutive expiation, i.e. as a death which substitutes the one the sinners would have deserved; in others it is considered as a redemption, and still others insist on the participation of the believers in the death of Christ. Finally, certain others see the death of Christ as a victory over the supernatural "powers" of death.[7]

We are not interested here in defining the differences between each of these conceptions, but wish rather to bring out the feature they have in common: in each of them, a decisive function in the forgiveness of sins is attributed to the death of Jesus Christ. It is this conception, indeed, that has allowed later Christian theology to define the death of Jesus as a *sacrificium*.

The theory according to which the death of Jesus is a *sacrificium*, that takes the place of the *sacrificia* of the Temple of Jerusalem, is already present in Tertullian:

> Hunc enim oportebat pro omnibus gentibus fieri sacrificium (*Adv.Iudaeos* 12, 122);

> Haec est enim hostia spiritalis, quae pristina sacrificia delevit (*De Oratione* 28,1).

This theory presupposes a definition of sacrifice in which the death of the victim is the essential element. From Rivière's definition, however, it can be seen that immolation is only one of various possible kinds of sacrifice. From Grottanelli's definition it turns out that ritualized killing is only one aspect, and by no means exhausts the range of central features of sacrificial rituals.

In the early Christian texts we find just one aspect of biblical sacrificial rituals underlined: that of the killing of a victim. And it is starting from this feature that the concept of sacrifice is defined. This happens because it is supposed that the key to the reading of biblical sacrifices lies in Jesus' death. We are not faced here with a concept found ethnographically in the biblical texts and then applied to Jesus, but with an exactly opposite procedure.

---

[7] Cf. G. Barth, *Der Tod Jesu Christi im Verständnis des Neuen Testaments* (Neukirchen, Neukirchener Verlag, 1992), at pages 37–71; 71–75; 75–85; 85–97 respectively.

(2) Yet on other occasions in the writings of the New Testament, forgiveness is the result of a simple declaration made by Jesus, without any reference to his death. For example, Mark, Luke and Matthew narrate the way in which Jesus communicates forgiveness of sins to a paralytic:

> When Jesus saw their faith, he said to the paralytic, 'Son, your sins are forgiven (*afientai*)' (Mk 2:5 // Lk 5:20 // Mt 9:5).

The theory that attributes this power to Jesus is made clearly explicit at the end of the episode:

> the Son of Man has authority on earth to forgive (*afienai*) sins (Mk 2:10 // Lk 5:24 // Mt 9:6).

(3) There is, however, a third series of texts, in the gospel tradition, in which the forgiveness of sins is not obtained either through the death of Jesus, or through faith in him, and is not even conceded by the authority of Jesus, but only directly by God's intervention, without Jesus' mediation. In these cases, forgiveness depends simply on the relationship between the sinner, God, and the sinner's fellows.

It is with this third series of texts that we shall be dealing.

Jesus' conception of the forgiveness of sins without expiation, i.e. without sacrifice[8]

1. In Matthew's Gospel one of the invocations of the Lord's Prayer states

> forgive (*afes*) us our debts as we also have forgiven (*afekamen*) our debtors (Mt 6:12).[9]

---

[8] Cf. Schnackenburg 1971, 84–92; 120. See also I. Broer, "Jesus und das Gestetz. Anmerkungen zur Geschichte des Problems und zur Frage der Sündenvergebung durch den historischen Jesus", in Id., (Hrsg.), *Jesus und das jüdische Gesetz* (Stuttgart/Berlin/Köln, Kohlhammer, 1992), 61–104; P. Fiedler, *Jesus und die Sünder* (Frankfurt a.M., Peter Lang, 1976).

[9] D.J. Harrington, *The Gospel of Matthew* (Collegeville Minnesota, The Liturgical Press, 1991), 95: «The Idea of granting a release of debts appears in Deut 15:1–2», that is to say in the context of the laws on the sabbatical year. For the translation, cf. Jeremias 1993, 48. The term "debt" used by Matthew is nearer to the original than the term "sin" used by Luke 11:4, and is confirmed also by the *Didache* (8:2) "and forgive us our debt as we also forgive our debtors". Yet Lk 11:4 keeps the word debtors in the second part of the verse ("for we too forgive every one in debt to us"). This leads us to think that Matthew's version is nearer the original, and that Luke corrected only one part of the invocation, without managing to eliminate entirely the metaphor debt/sin which structured it. Probably the problem arose

Jesus himself, according to Matthew's Gospel, comments on this invocation in the following words (which are probably an independent saying going back to Jesus,[10] which nonetheless fits fully into the same conception):

> If you forgive (*afete*) others their trespasses, your heavenly Father also will forgive (*afesei*) you. But if you do not forgive (*afete*) others, neither will your Father forgive (*afesei*) your trespasses (Mt 6:14–15).[11]

This explanation, absent in Luke's Gospel, can be found in a different form in Mark's Gospel:

> Whenever you stand praying, forgive (*afete*), if you have anything against anyone; so that (*ina*) your father in heaven may also forgive you your trespasses (Mk 11:25).

---

in the passage from Aramaic to Greek. The term "debt" in Aramaic, besides its socio-economic meaning, had taken on the meaning of religious sin for some time past. In Greek, on the other hand, the word "debts" could not be the vehicle for this complexity of very closely connected religious and social meanings, and the choice was therefore made to use the term "sins", more clearly embodying a religious sense. Cf. J. Jeremias, *Das Vater-Unser im Lichte der neueren Forschung* (Calwer Verlag, Stuttgart, 1965³), 13–14; J. Gnilka, *Das Matthäusevangelium I.Teil. Kommentar zu Kap. 1,1–13,58* (Freiburg, Herder, 1986), 224–226; 232–234. Unlike Matthew the *Didache* does not have the aorist tense "we have forgiven", but like Luke uses the present "we forgive". Gnilka attributes some significance to Matthew's use of the aorist tense. According to him, it is "an act that occurs once only, as if to say the final cancellation man must make, cancelling his debtors' debts before arriving at God's [eschatological] judgment". Lk 11:4b would have eliminated this eschatological perspective (*Das Matthäusevangelium I*, 225).

[10] Gnilka, *Das Matthäusevangelium I*, 234 correctly recognizes that Matthew here depends on an "archetype, and that Mk 11:25 is a parallel to this saying; above all he remains strictly in line with the invocation of pardon in the Lord's Prayer". Gnilka concludes "the logion fits Jesus' message, and in its original version can be attributed to him".

[11] Cf. Gnilka, *Das Matthäusevangelium I*, 232–234. For the social background cf. B.J. Malina—R.L. Rohrbaugh, *Social Science Commentary on the Synoptic Gospels* (Minneapolis, Fortress Press, 1992), 63–64: «in an honor-shame society, sin is a breach of interpersonal relations. In the Gospels the closest analogy to the forgiveness of sins is the forgiveness of debts (Matt 6:12; see Luke 11:4), an analogy drawn from pervasive peasant experience. Debt threatened loss of land, livelihood, family. It made persons poor, that is, unable to maintain their social position. Forgiveness would thus have had the character of restoration, a return to both self-sufficiency and one's place in the community. Since the introspective, guilt-oriented outlook of industrialized societies did not exist, it is unlikely that forgiveness meant psychological healing. Instead, forgiveness by God meant being divinely restored to one's position and therefore being freed from fear of loss at the hands of God. Forgiveness by others meant restoration to the community. Given the anti-introspective attitude of Mediterranean people, "conscience" was not so much an interior voice of accusation as an external one—what the neighbors said, hence blame from friends, neighbors, or authorities (cf. 1 Cor 4:4 [. . .])». The commentators rightly underline Mt 6:14's affinities with Sir 28:2.

The absolutely essential condition for obtaining the forgiveness of sins by God, is therefore the prior forgiveness of one's fellows. Here the conception of forgiveness by God does not seem to require an expiation either on the part of the sinner or on the part of a savior who substitutes himself for him/her. The death of Jesus has no function in the forgiveness of sins. The person of Jesus has no mediatory function at all. Forgiveness depends exclusively on the direct relationship between God, the individual and other people.[12]

The overall picture of this conception of the forgiveness of sins without expiation would not be complete without light being shed on the conditions necessary to gain forgiveness.[13] In Matthew's Gospel, Peter asks Jesus:

> Lord, if my brother sins against me, how often should I forgive (*afeso*)? As many as seven times? Jesus said to him 'Not seven times, but, I tell you, seventy-seven times' (Mt 18:21–22 // Lk 17:4).

Luke indeed makes it clear that repentance by the sinner is necessary:

> If your brother sins, you must rebuke him; and if he repents, forgive (*afes*) him. If he sins against you seven times a day, and seven times a day turns back to you saying 'I repent', you will forgive (*afeseis*) him (Lk 17:3–4).[14]

In a famous parable, which only Matthew reports (Mt 18:23–35),[15] the need to pardon one's fellows is emphasized as a condition for

---

[12] Gnilka correctly recognizes that "the Lord's Prayer does not reflect post-Easter theology", and admits: "The Lord's Prayer's affinities with the Old Testament—Judaic conceptual world cannot be disputed. It is true that it could have been pronounced even by a Jew who did not know, or did not want to know, anything about Jesus" (*Das Matthäusevangelium I*, 216).

[13] J. Jeremias (*Das Vater-Unser*, 25–26) had the merit of underlining the specific nature of the second request of the Lord's Prayer (which makes God's forgiveness depend on men forgiving each other), even if it conflicted with his theory of salvation already now offered by Jesus Christ: the second request, writes Jeremias, "surprises us because, and this is the only time it happens in the Lord's Prayer, the reference is to human behavior. From this unique case one can argue just how important it was to Jesus to make this addition. [. . .] Jesus repeated several times that one cannot ask God for forgiveness, if we ourselves are not ready to forgive others" (*Das Vater-Unser*, 25). Jeremias however completely neglects to bring out the social consequences of the forgiveness that a person must grant to another person who has acted unjustly towards him/her.

[14] On the reconstruction of Jesus' original saying cf. G. Segalla, "Perdono «cristiano» e correzione fraterna nella comunità di «Matteo» (Mt 18,15–17.21–35)", in: G. Galli (Ed.), *Interpretazione e perdono* (Genova, Marietti, 1992), 35–36.

[15] Cf. Segalla, Perdono «cristiano», 31–35. 37–39; Gnilka, *Il Vangelo di Matteo*,

obtaining God's forgiveness. The narrative places this principle in a social context of interpersonal relationships ordered hierarchically, in which it is a master who first forgives an inferior. Although of superior degree, and without being under any constraint, he cancels a considerable debt of a slave placed beneath him in the social scale. But this slave does not cancel a small debt another slave owed him. The master is furious at this behavior:

> His master sent for him and said: You wicked slave. I forgave you all that debt because you pleaded with me. Should you not have mercy on your fellow slave, as I had mercy on you? And in anger his master handed him over to the guardians until he would pay his entire debt. So my heavenly Father will also do to every one of you, if you do not forgive your brother from your heart (Mt 18:32–35).[16]

Also in Luke's Gospel, in fact, the forgiveness of sins is compared to the cancelling of debts without repayment:

> A certain creditor had two debtors; one owed five hundred denarii and the other fifty. When they could not pay, he forgave (echarisato)[17] the debts for both of them (Lk 7:41–42).

214–223; Malina-Rohrbaugh, 1992, 119–20. From the point of view of the literary genre and of the history of the tradition, the parable (18: 23–34) has to be distinguished from the concluding saying (18:35). On how far both are to be attributed to Jesus, cf. Segall, *Perdono «cristiano»*, 37–38.38–39. Cf. also D.C. Duling, "The Matthean Brotherhood and Marginal Scribal Leadership", in: P. Esler (Ed.), *Modeling Early Christianity. Social Scientific Studies of the New Testament and its Context* (London, Routledge, 1955), 159–182.

[16] It is very important to realize that this parable is without christological content, too. J. Gnilka, *Das Matthäusevangelium II.Teil. Kommentar zu Kap. 14,1–28,20* (Freiburg, Herder, 1988), 147 tries to avoid this (which is a problem for him, given that he is concerned over a connection to the so-called post-Easter christology), declaring "Without its christological implication the parable remains colorless, and becomes a moral teaching". Of course this judgment depends entirely on Gnilka's theological ideas, that, frankly speaking, should not be allowed to transform the sense of the text. It is nevertheless important to notice that Gnilka has to recognize that, if there is a christological sense, it is only implicit. He tries to make it explicit by suggesting "Jesus had promised the *basileia* to the poor, he had welcomed them into his liberating communion, he had had meals with them, he had promised them the mercy of his Father. All this cannot fail to have consequences for them in their lifetimes". And the consequence would be that Jesus invites the poor not to maintain that it is "legal" to require the debtor to repay his debt, but to consider him "a man whom God has forgiven" (221). In actual fact, a certain kind of theology of grace is being forced into the parable's text, to make it fit into his preconceived idea of "christology". See also R. Penna, *I ritratti originali di Gesù il Cristo. Inizi e sviluppi della cristologia neotestametaria. I. Gli inizi* (Cinisello Balsamo, San Paolo, 1999).

[17] It should be noted that Luke uses different verbs to mean the cancelling of debts (*charizomai* in 7,42) and the cancelling of sins (*afiemi* in 7,42).

From these two passages in Matthew and Luke it turns out that the forgiveness of sins by God requires three conditions, together meant as a necessary premise: 1) repentance for one's own sins; 2) the cancelling of the debts of others without requiring repayment or compensation; 3) repentance by others.

To conclude, what distinguishes these passages is the fact that the forgiveness of sins depends on a debts-remission system. The system in some cases (Luke 7:41–42) is centered on an initial action by God who forgives spontaneously, and to everyone, any respective debt because no one is able to pay it back. Or else, in other cases (i.e. Mt 18:15–18; 32–35), the remission system is established in a circular way, starting from the remission by one man to another and ending with the remission by God to the man who forgave the other one. God's remission in this case operates as a consequence, depending on the first remission.

2. It is often asked whether it is God's forgiveness that takes priority in these texts, or the conversion or repentance of the man. It is a legitimate question, but overmuch conditioned by modern theological interests.[18] It neglects one basic aspect of the forgiveness of sins.

In the conception of the forgiveness of sins without expiatory sacrifice, a project or an ideal image of society's organization and

---

[18] Segalla, Perdono «cristiano», 41 concentrates mainly on this: "the subject of the forgiveness conceded to people was present in Judaic circles of the NT. However, the idea of the forgiveness of God as the event on which the duty of forgiveness should be based, never appears. That is specific to 'Christian' forgiveness and is rooted in the singular event of Christ, both the historical Christ and the Christ who died and was resurrected 'for the forgiveness of sins'". Here most of the conclusion depends on the concepts used: "Judaic" is opposed to "Christian". If "Judaic" means culture, in other words the whole set of patterns on which the conceptions, practices, institutions and material life of a society are based, then it is certainly difficult to argue that Jesus is not part of "Judaic" culture. Therefore any "singularity" (this is the concept Segalla uses) on Jesus' part, as of any other great Jewish religious leader of the epoch, cannot fail to be "Judaic". As a result "Judaic" cannot be opposed to the concept of "Christian", because Christianity at the time of Jesus' movement and of the very earliest Church is not a culture. To be able to talk about Christian culture means waiting for the Byzantine Empire, certain western medieval environments, and so on in later centuries. From the cultural point of view the conception that attributes primacy to God in the offer of forgiveness is wholly an integral part of Judaic culture. On the methodological problem of the incorrect opposing of "Christian" to "Judaic", cf. also E. Schüssler Fiorenza, *Gesù Figlio di Miriam, Profeta della Sofia. Questioni critiche di cristologia femminista* (Torino, Claudiana, 1996), 124–135.

of mankind itself is often implicit.[19] This is true both for the concept of transgression and for the concept of the forgiveness of sins.

With the word "transgression" we mean the violation of a norm, in its objective aspect. With the word "guilt", on the other hand, we mean the subjective aspect in which the transgressor feels inner responsibility for his/her transgression.[20] In every social or religious system, in fact, going against a norm creates disorder and a sense of insecurity, whether it concerns God or man. When the rules are broken and the customary relationships between individuals are no longer respected (for example in family life or in public institutions), the orderly pattern of existence is upset. The normal ideals and practice of social and religious life become less comprehensible, indeed obscure, or may be subject to corruption or degradation. Breaking a norm can set off regression in the ritual and religious life of a community, or the weakening of a community or people's beliefs. If an increasing number of individuals cease to respect a norm, confidence in it is socially weakened.

The cancelling or redressing mechanisms of transgressions and of guilt, have first of all the double function (a) of declaring a behavior transgressive as such, and, implicitly (b) of obtaining from the whole of society recognition of the validity of the norms. In many cases they also obtain (c) public recognition of guilt by the transgressor which, in this way, strengthens their double function. Secondly,

---

[19] On the social interpretation of Early Christianity, see A. Destro—Pesce M., *Antropologia delle origini cristiane* (Bari/Roma, Laterza 1997²); Id., *Come nasce una religione. Antropologia e esegesi del Vangelo di Giovanni* (Bari/Roma, Laterza 2000); Ph. Esler, *Community and Gospel in Luke-Acts. The Social and Political Motivations of Lucan Theology* (Cambridge, Cambridge University Press, 1987); Id., *The First Christians in Their Social World. Social-Scientific Approaches to New Testament Interpretation* (London and New York, Routledge, 1994); Id., *Modelling Early Christianity. Social-Scientific Studies of the New Testament in its Context* (London, Routledge, 1995); J.H. Neyrey (Ed.), *The Social World of Luke-Acts. Models for Interpretation* (Peabody Massachusetts, Hendrickson, 1991); R. Rohrbaugh (Ed.), *The Social Sciences and the New Testament Interpretation* (Peabody Massachusetts, Hendrickson, 1996).

[20] J. Assmann makes a distinction between three different conceptions of transgression that correspond to three types of religious conceptions. The first, based on the concept of shame, requires a technique of cancellation or compensation for the transgression, only if the latter occurred in the presence of witnesses. A second conception develops the concept of guilt. In this case the subject feels responsible for his act of transgression even if it passed unnoticed in the society in which he lives. The third conception is that of sin. Cf. "Confession in Ancient Egypt" in A. Destro and M. Pesce, *Ritual and Ethics. Patterns of Repentance* (New York, Global Publications, 2002), 41–60.

(d) they allow the transgressor to be excluded from normal social relations. He/she is therefore officially placed in a marginal or inactive position. Finally, the transgressor (e) can be reintegrated, but only after having recognized his/her own guilt and redressed his/her transgression. The procedures for the elimination of guilt, therefore, are essential for readmission into a religious community. In the cases in which religious systems tend to coincide with the overall social organization of a human group or people, such mechanisms also become procedures of reintegration in the civil community structures, instruments of the reconstitution of society itself.

3. With non-expiatory forgiveness we find ourselves outside every sacrificial area. We have here a forgiveness of sins system that is clearly an alternative to that of sacrifice.

In this context we can go over the essential points of the parable of the two slaves in Matthew (18:23–35), because they contain a clear appeal to the social order and to the world of real, intersubjective relationships. It is precisely the lord-slave relation (and then slave-slave), that illustrates the premise of the system. Paying back a debt in itself is a duty; not to pay it back quite rightly brings about punishment. Only the elimination of the debt eliminates the consequent punishment. In the parable, the master's behavior is that of the cancellation of a duty (paying back the debt), thereby changing the slave's position, freeing him/her from his/her debt without his/her having to do anything. This is done so that he/she will follow or re-apply the same principle towards others. The ideal to which the system tends is that of reciprocity between one person and another: no one should be bound by debts (or guilt) to another, but each should free the debtor without a compensation. We have here a chain reaction mechanism oriented to the re-establishment or to the creation of an ideal order. See also Mt 5:23–24:

> when you are offering your gift at the altar, if you remember that your brother has something against you, leave your gift at the altar and go first be reconciled to your brother and then come and offer your gift.

The central aspect of the cancellation of debts mechanism lies in enabling the debtor (i.e. the guilty person) to acquire once again the power to carry out free actions in his/her turn. In reality, the just repayment of the debt is not eliminated unconditionally, but on one condition: that the debtor in his/her turn sets off a cancellation of debts mechanism.[21] If this does not happen the master insists on the repayment of the debt he/she had earlier cancelled. In this case, in other words, God proceeds to punish the sinner: "And in anger his master handed him over to the guardians until he would pay his entire debt" (Mt 18:34). Here the relationship between the forgiveness of sins and God's last judgment ("So my heavenly Father will also do to every one of you") can be clearly seen. In Jesus' vision, there are two different moments in the succession of eschatological events. First comes remission, and then the last judgment.[22] This can also be seen in Mt 6:12.14: first comes remission among men, and then the eschatological forgiveness of God. Between the two there is the closest and most essential of relationships. In the imminence of the last judgment it is necessary to engage in a chain reaction of reciprocal collective pardon. If this reciprocal pardon is not made operational, people will undergo the punishment of the last judgment.

Basically, the punishment of guilt is really applied only if the person pardoned by God does not pardon others. The threat of punishment (strong in various passages: cf. Mt 11:21–24; 12:41–42; Lk

---

[21] On Mt 18: 23–35 cf. J. Gnilka, *Jesus von Nazareth. Botschaft und Geschichte* (Freiburg i.B., Herder, 1990), 98–102 who sees in this parable (as also the one in Luke 7, 41ss.) the intention to reveal the mercy of God "which goes beyond all the received categories of normal human behavior. This mercy gives without being asked [...] this mercy wishes to transform people" (102). First of all, it is not true that the mercy of God gives without being asked, because the slave begs the master to condone his debt ("I condoned your entire debt *because you begged me to*" Mt 18:32). It is true that the mercy of God wishes to transform people, but Gnilka 1) neglects the fact that the mercy of God requires the person to condone in his turn; 2) forgets to ask himself *which* transformation—according to Jesus—God would like to introduce into the lives of people. Sin is a social crime and requires, in every system of cancellation of sins, a social reintegration. Jesus does not create the conception of the mercy of God out of a cultural vacuum. God's mercy has cultural contents and social effects.

[22] Cf. J. Weiss, *La predicazione di Gesù sul Regno di Dio* (Napoli, M. D'Auria, 1993) (German: *Die Predigt Jesu vom Reiche Gottes. Zweite Auflage* [Göttingen, 1900]), 134: "Among the authentic sayings of Jesus, Mk 9:43s. expresses in the clearest way the link between judgment and the beginning of the kingdom of God. As always it is presupposed that the listener will still be alive at the coming of the kingdom. Two alternatives are offered: either enter into the kingdom (or into eternal life) with a mutilated member, or be thrown into hell with all one's members. Thus: the road to life or the kingdom passes via the judgment, with which the destiny of the individual is decided". We shall therefore have the following order of events: judgment, kingdom. The forgiving of sins is situated before the judgment. Cf. Jeremias, *Das Vater-Unser*, 25–26.

13:2–5)[23] in this way becomes an incentive to pardon others, to institute personal and social relations founded on the respect of one's fellows' liberty.

The question to ask at this point is the following: if the religious and social ideal that is implicit in Jesus' conception of the remission of sins is that of a circular procedure for the creation of an ideal social order, we have to ask ourselves whether this ideal is a creation of Jesus, or if it existed in the religious conceptions of his time. We think that this second hypothesis is the more probable. The society model that lies at the root of Jesus' words is inspired by certain aspects of the biblical ideal of the Jubilee—as it is to be found above all in chapter 25 of Leviticus (Lv 25:8–55).[24]

In the Jubilee of Leviticus 25 a set of rules aims to reorganize the people of Israel socially and religiously every fifty years. In the Jubilee year, the entire community of Jews—in the land of Israel—should be subjected to a form of restoration or new beginning of its fundamental social and religious structures. This mechanism of collective reorganization consists essentially of the fact that each individual member of the people has to regain his[25] own liberty if he was reduced to slavery, and has to regain possession of his house and land if he had had to give them up because of debts he had incurred:

> You shall proclame liberty throughout the land for all its inhabitants [. . .] each of you shall return to his holding and each of you shall return to his family (Lv 25:10).

The extraordinary meaning of collective re-ordering and social renewal that the Jubilee year had to have is underlined also by the great ritual of the sounding of the horn. The Jubilee is proclaimed with due solemnity. The *shofar* would have to be taken from village to village and from city to city in the form of a public proclamation of freedom:

> you shall bring the shofar throughout your land (Lv 25:9).

---

[23] G. Barbaglio G., *L'anno della liberazione. Riflessione biblica sull'anno santo* (Brescia, Morcelliana, 1974), 89–90.

[24] On the Jubilee in Leviticus cf. B.A. Levine, *Leviticus* (The JPS Torah Commentary), (Philadelphia, The Jewish Publication Society, 5749/1989); Ph.J. Budd, *Leviticus* (Grand Rapids, Eerdmans, 1996). For recent literature on Leviticus cf. in addition J.F.A. Sawyer (Ed.), *Reading Leviticus. A Conversation with Mary Douglas* (Sheffield, Sheffield Academic Press, 1996); A. Pitta, *L'anno della Liberazione. Il giubileo e le sue istanze bibliche* (Cinisello Balsamo, Edizioni San Paolo, 1998); M. Zappella (Ed.), *Le origini degli anni giubilari. Dalle tavolette in cuneiforme dei Sumeri ai manoscritti arabi del Mille dopo Cristo* (Roma, Piemme, 1998).

[25] The subject of Levitical rule is explicitly masculine (see the following quotation).

What is important, in the social project inherent in the Jubilee, is the mechanism of the reconstitution of the society of Israel, the process of return to an original situation. On the ideal plane, the Jubilee pattern corresponds to a regulating mechanism that reactivates the formative bases of a culture.

It may well be asked why Jesus connected this social ideal to that of the forgiveness of sins. The answer lies precisely in the book of Leviticus. The moment in which, according to Lv 25:9, the Jubilee year must be proclaimed, is of great significance. The redactor of the book of Leviticus established that the Jubilee had to be proclaimed on the tenth day of the seventh month, i.e. right at the start of the annual ritual of the Day of Atonement (*Yom ha-kippurim*). The coinciding of these two moments sheds light on the meaning and values implicit in the performances themselves. God's cancelling the sins of a people and the social reorganization of the people have to be connected because the expiatory ritual and the radical social renewal are thought of as necessarily consistent with each other: a return of the Jews to their original condition of parity and freedom required that a collective ritual of expiation and conversion should be set in action. Only conversion, that is essential to Leviticus' conception of the Day of Atonement, permits a radical social change.[26] At the same time, in the Jubilee year, the land of the people of Israel had to be regenerated or reintegrated, and therefore, as in the sabbatical year,[27] it should not be subjected to cultivation:

> the land shall yield its fruits and you shall eat your fill, and you shall live upon it in security. And should you ask, 'What are we to eat in the seventh year, if we may neither sow nor gather in our crops?' I will ordain my blessing for you in the sixth year, so that it shall yield a crop sufficient for three years. When you sow in the eight year, you will still be eating old grain until the ninth year, until its crops come in (Lv 25:19–22).

---

[26] Cf. G. Deiana G., *Il Giorno dell'espiazione. Il kippur nella tradizione biblica* (Bologna, Edizioni Dehoniane), 1995, 109; A. Destro—M. Pesce, "Il rito ebraico di Kippur: Il sangue nel tempio, il peccato nel deserto", in G. Galli (Ed.), *Interpretazione e Perdono* (Genova, Marietti, 1992), 47–73; "Conflits et rites dans le Temple de Jérusalem d'après la Mishna. Le rite de Yom Kippur (Traité Yoma) et l'ordalie des eaux amères (Traité Sota)", in: Ph. Bourgeau, A. de Pury (Eds.), *Le Temple, lieux du conflit. Actes du colloque de Cartigny 1988* (Centre d'Etude du Proche-Orient Ancien, Université de Genève), (Leuven, Éditions Peeters, 1995), 127–137.

[27] Moreover, the preceding year, that is the forty ninth year, coincided with a sabbatical year.

The Jubilee is therefore a return to origins not just of a social character, but also natural and cosmic. The connection between the Day of Atonement (and therefore remission of sins) and a social ideal obtained through respect for the social laws of the sabbatical year (help to the poor and cancelling of debts) may be found again in a text of Qumran: 1Q22.[28] This text clarifies the connection between an act cancelling debts that has to be practiced collectively, i.e. by the whole of society, and God's forgiveness of sins at the Day of Atonement. The connection is clear in the phrase:

> you will not ask restitution, because in this year [God will bless you, forgiving you your sins . . .] (1Q22 Col III 6–7).

For the form of Judaism that is expressed in this text, God's forgiveness of sins is connected to an act cancelling debts on the part of men. If one remembers that the Day of Atonement requires a concrete and inner conversion on man's part to be able to obtain God's forgiveness of sins, it is evident that this text expresses a religious ideal for which there can be no conversion and forgiveness on God's part unless concrete brotherhood and economic equality is reached.[29] The conversion and the forgiveness of sins require the reconstitution of a relationship of equality between the members of the people. The wealth of some and the poverty through debt of others cannot be tolerated. Both in 1Q22 and in Lv 25:8–55, there is an impressing theological vision in which God's action is at the center. It is naïve to think that we are faced with a "moral" or

---

[28] "In this year you shall grant a release. 5 [Every creditor] who [has lent something to] someone, or [who possesses something from his brother], will grant a re[lease to his fell]ow, for 6 [God], your [God, has proclamed the release. You are to demand restitution] from the fore[igner, but from your brother] you shall not demand restitution, for in that year 7 [God will bless you, forgiving you your si]ns . . .] 8 [. . .] in the year [. . .] of the month of [. . .] 9 [. . .] on this day [. . . Because your fathers] wandered 10 [in the wilderness until the tenth day of the month {the[. . . on the te]nth [day] of the month} 11 you shall refrain [from all work.] And in the tenth day of the month, you shall atone [. . .] of the month 12 [. . .] they shall take [. . .]" (1Q22 Col III 4–12). Translation of F. García Martínez, *The Dead Sea Scrolls Translated. The Qumran Texts in English.* Wilfred G.E. Watson Translator, Leiden, Brill, 1995), 267; cf also C. Martone, *Testi di Qumran. Traduzione italiana dai testi originali con note*, a cura di F. García Martínez (Brescia, Paideia, 1996), 456.

[29] On *Yom ha Kippurim* see Destro—Pesce, "Il rito ebraico di Kippur"; "Conflits et rites dans le Temple de Jérusalem d'après la Mishna"; M. Pesce, "La lavanda dei piedi di Gv 13,1–20, il Romanzo di Esopo e i Saturnalia di Macrobio", *Biblica* 80 (1999), 240–249.

"legal" vision from which Jesus (together with early Christianity), would distance himself, in favor of a more "spiritual" vision, or a "direct and personal relationship" with God.[30]

At this juncture, it must be remembered that in the Gospels the noun most often used to define the forgiveness of sins is *afesis*. For Greek-speaking Jews the term *afesis* evoked associations of great significance. *Afesis* is precisely the term defining Jubilee in LXX, the Greek translation used by the redactors of the Gospels. In Lv 25:10 the Hebrew word that indicates the Jubilee (*yovel*, which means "ram"[31] and in a derived way "trumpet made with a ram's horn") is translated by the LXX by "the year, signal of *afesis*" (*eniautós afeseos semasia*),[32] i.e. the time in which the signal was given—with the *yovel*—of the beginning of the fiftieth year. In Lv 25:30 the term *afesis* is used to translate *yovel* and therefore seems to be the usual term the Greek-speaking Jews adopted to indicate the Jubilee (cf. also Lv 25:28). In Leviticus (27:17–24), the Jubilee is also defined as "the year of *afesis*", and in the book of Numbers as "the *afesis* of the children of Israel" (Num 36:4).

At a general social level, in the Greek Bible the term *afesis* appears in a variety of meanings. In Exodus (18:12) it indicates the rejection of the wife in the sense of release from or freedom from the marriage bond.[33] In Lv 16,26 it indicates the sending or releasing of the goat in the desert. In Judith 11:14 it means "permission"; in Esther 2:18 "day of rest". In the first book of the Maccabees (10:28.30.34; 13:34) it indicates "exemption". For Isaiah in chapter 58:6 it means freedom for the imprisoned and translates the Hebrew *hofshi*, while in chapter 61:1 it is related to the liberation of prisoners of war

---

[30] This is also against G. Scheuermann, "Il Giubileo negli autori del Nuovo Testamento", in Zappella, *Le origini degli anni giubilari*, 160: "the two evangelists underline the moral, religious sin: Luke speaks explicitly of sins (*hamartias*)". Religion always has social presuppositions. The difference between Luke and Matthew should be stressed here.

[31] Cf. D. Cohen, *Dictionnaire des racines sémitiques ou attestées dans les langues sémitiques* II, (Leuven, Peeters, 1996), 485–486; n. 4 p. 485; L. Koehler, W. Baumgartner, *The Hebrew and Aramaic Lexicon of the Old Testament* (Translated and Edited under the Supervision of M.E.J. Richardson), (Leiden, Brill, 1995), 398. See also F. Bianchi, "Il giubileo nei testi ebraici canonici e post-canonici", in Zappella, *Le origini degli anni giubilari*, 84–85.

[32] Cf. P. Harlé—D. Pralon, *Le Lévitique. Traduction du texte grec de la Septante, Introduction et Notes* (Paris, Cerf, 1988), 198: «un an signal de la remission».

[33] In Hebrew the opposite term is *'agunah* which stands for the woman bound to a husband who has left her without dissolving the marriage bond.

(Hebrew: *deror*) and therefore return home, and the release. In Ezekiel 46:17 it indicates the year of the freeing (in Hebrew: *derór*) of the slave and in Jeremiah 34:17 it indicates the liberty of one's brother and fellow.[34]

Of course, *afesis* also means forgiveness of sins. But not, it should be noted, "expiation". Indeed, the Greek Bible uses a different verb for expiation/removal, i.e. *exilaskomai* ("expiate"), while for the act of concession of forgiveness of sins it uses the verb *afiemi*:

> the priest shall make expiation (Hebrew: *kipper*, LXX: *exilasetai*) for them and they shall be forgiven (Hebrew: *nislah*; LXX *afethesetai*) (Lv 4:20).

The *afesis*, the remission of sin is therefore the effect that follows on from the sacrificial ritual act, and not the ritual act in itself.

To conclude, the term *afesis* as used in the gospel texts not only indicates God's religious forgiveness, but also alludes to a vast set of principles very closely connected to personal liberty and social reordering.

4. In the light of these reflections, we can more easily understand another passage in the Gospels that certainly contains a nucleus going back to Jesus. It can be understood against the background of the social and religious ideal of the Jewish Jubilee, intended as the necessary consequence of God's forgiveness of sins.

According to Luke's Gospel, Jesus was inspired by the Jubilee freedom ideal right from his first preaching in the synagogue at Nazareth, the place "where he had been brought up" (Lk 4:16):

> The scroll of the prophet Isaiah was given to him. He unrolled the scroll and found the place where it was written:
> 'The spirit of the Lord is upon me; because he has anointed me,
> to announce to the poor, He has sent me
> to proclame liberation (*afesis*) to the captives
> and sight to the blind' [Is 61:1–2 LXX]
> 'to give liberation (*afesis*) to the oppressed' [Is 58:6 LXX],
> 'to proclaim the year of favor of the Lord' [Is 61:2 LXX] (Lk 4:17–19).

However, the announcement of a year of liberation in chapter 61:1 of the Hebrew text of Isaiah already recalls the proclamation of Jubilee year.[35] The quotation by Luke from Isaiah looks back to an

---

[34] Cf. Budd, *Leviticus*, 346; Levine, *Leviticus*, 171.
[35] Is 61:2 speaks of *liqr'* [. . .] *drwr* just like Lv 25:10: *qr'tm drwr*. On the link between Is 61:1–2 and Lev 25:8 ff., cf. also D. Monshouwer, "The Reading of the

ideal of liberation and remission that in Leviticus' scheme corresponds to the liberation of the children of Israel. The quotation from Isaiah, which brings together at least two different passages (Isaiah 61:1–2 and 58:6 LXX) goes back to the Gospel redactor or perhaps to a preceding tradition. The nucleus of historicity of the preaching in the synagogue at Nazareth certainly cannot be extended to the literary form of the quotation from Isaiah.

The overall theme of Is 61:1–9 is, however, that of a year of liberation as premise of the restoration of the nation, and of a primacy with respect to the other peoples, as the consequence of a new covenant with God "for all time" (Is 61:8). Hence the Jubilee ideal, also in this passage, forms part of a setting of overall social and religious renewal, in a succession of events in some way eschatological. The basic difference between Isaiah and Leviticus lies in the fact that Leviticus imagines a cyclical reconstitution of the society, while in Isaiah 61 the expectation of a particular event (in which the social and religious project conceived of in Leviticus comes into existence) seems to prevail.[36]

It is, though, very important to bear in mind that Is 58:1–12, from which the passage inserted in the Is 61:1–2 quotation is drawn,

---

Prophet in the Synagogue at Nazareth", *Biblica* 72 (1991), 90–99; Esler, *Community and Gospel in Luke-Acts*, 181–182. M. Prior, *Jesus the Liberator. Nazareth Liberation Theology (Luke 4.16–30)* (Sheffield, Sheffield Academic Press, 1995), 139–141 is against the hypothesis that Luke is making reference to the Jubilee year on the grounds that «Luke does not use the terminology peculiar to the Jubilee (no sowing, no pruning, no rest for the land, no day of atonement, and so on, although the *eis ten patrida autou*, 'each returning to his family' of Lv 25,10 LXX finds a resonance). Neither does he develop peculiarly Jubilee concepts in the course of his writing. Luke's own understanding of *aphesis* must be an important element in the discussion» (139). However, it is precisely the *afesis* and the reference to the Day of Atonement implicit in the quotation that prove the contrary. Besides, Prior ignores the fact that 11QMelch—as we shall see further on—offers an eschatological interpretation of the last Jubilee and connects the Jubilee of Lv 25, 8 to Is 61,1–2. So also his additional objection, that opposes the eschatological element characteristic of Luke's Jesus to the Jubilee theme (140), loses its validity. On the link between Is 61,1–2 and the Lv 25, cf. recently also Pitta, *L'anno della liberazione*, 55–56.56–62; S.H. Ringe, *The Jubilee Proclamation in the Ministry and Teaching of Jesus: A Tradition-critical Study in the Synoptic Gospels and Acts* (Diss. Union Theological Seminary, New York, 1981); Id., *Jesus Liberation and Biblical Jubilee: Images for Ethics and Christology* (Philadelphia, 1985); A. Trocmé, *Jesus and the Nonviolent Revolution* (Scottdale Pa, Herald Press, 1973); Bianchi, "Il giubileo", 126–128.

[36] Pitta, *L'anno della liberazione*, 56 rightly underlines that the cyclical characteristic, typical of Leviticus, is absent in Isaiah 61. But we believe he tends overmuch to construct a theology of progressive revelation, from the cyclical structure of Leviticus to a presumed expectation in Isaiah of a "definitive realization", to find eventually in Lk 4:17–19 the "fulfillment".

is itself a passage concerning precisely the Day of Atonement. It is argued there that besides fasting, an act of social justice that puts an end to the injustice practiced by each and every person, must be carried out:

> Is not this the fast that I choose? Says the Lord.
>   loose all the fetters of injustice; untie the cords of the pressing contracts; let the oppressed go in liberty and break every unjust contract.
>   Share your bread with the hungry; bring the homeless poor into your house; when you see the naked, cover him and do not ignore who lives in your home (Is 58:6–7 LXX).

We must always ask ourselves what overall social ideal underlies a text. It is not enough to restrict ourselves simply to observe, as for example Jeremias did,[37] that Luke omitted all reference to God's vengeance in the coming of the eschatological day according to Isaiah.[38] The Isaiah texts contain a good deal more. It contains the ideal of the Day of Atonement in relation to the Jubilee year (Is 61:1–2). The conversion, meaning also the redressing of social injustice (Is 58:6–7), and the restoration of Israel to its original state, are premises for a period of restoration of the nation and of its relationships with the peoples (Is 58:12; 61:4–9).[39]

In the first place, however, what comes to light in this passage in Luke, is similar to that which clearly appears from the passages in Matthew we quoted earlier. In them, Jesus places great emphasis on the debtors, on the slaves, and on those that through their debts may become slaves. The overall social pattern of the Jubilee, in Jesus' words, becomes one of the premises of his social ideal. The second factor is that the levitical conception of the Jubilee involves the liberation of Israel and therefore the reconstitution of a social unit,—a re-entering of the poor, of debtors, and of slaves into the rights and bonds of their original family and clan groups. In Matthew, Jesus is only addressing precisely:

> the lost sheep of the house of Israel (Mt 15:24).

Jesus' mission can therefore be explained as the reintegration of original interpersonal relationships among the members of the people.

---

[37] "The day of vengeance of our God" (Is 61:2). J. Jeremias, *Jesus Verheissung für die Völker* (Stuttgart, Kohlhammer, 1956).

[38] Cf. Prior's criticism of Jeremias in *Jesus the Liberator*, 94.

[39] However, it must be taken into account that the LXX of Is 61:1 adds a hint about the blind which is not there in TM, but is there in Is 35:5.

Just as the Jubilee means the reintegration of debtors, so the forgiveness of sins means the pacification and re-equilibrium among men and their reciprocal relationships. It is the ideal of the Jubilee that Jesus employs to plan the religious reunification of the nation. The forgiveness of sins or religious conversion on the one hand, and social reorganization on the other, seem to converge. Here the concept of religious Jubilee merges with that of the kingdom of God. Jesus' design is theological here.

We have therefore seen that the consecutive events of day of expiation and Jubilee year make up the background that explain why the forgiveness of sins is followed by eschatological events in Jesus: the last judgment and the kingdom of God.

The question to ask now is as follows. In Leviticus, the Jubilee year does not seem to be an eschatological event. In what way, therefore, can the Jubilee be the cultural matrix of an eschatological conception that is so essential and central to Jesus? The answer comes from a text discovered near Qumran, 11QMelchisedek[40] (which can be dated between the end of the second century and the first half of the first century before the Common Era).[41] This text not only explicitly contains the connection between the levitical Jubilee and Is 61,1–2 (cf. 11QMelchisedek 2.4.9) that we found in Luke 4,18–19, but above all demonstrates that the fiftieth Jubilee was (1) connected to the forgiveness of sins and (2) was considered the final eschatological event.[42]

1 "[. . .] your God [. . .]
2 [. . .] And as for what he said: *Lev 25:13* 'In this year of jubilee, [you shall return, each one, to his respective property', as it is written: *Dt 15:2* 'This is]
3 the manner (of effecting) the [release: every creditor shall release what he lent [to his neighbour. He shall not coerce his neighbour or

---

[40] Cf. C. Gianotto, *Melchisedek e la sua tipologia. Tradizioni giudaiche, cristiane e gnostiche (sec. II a.C.—III d.C.)* (Brescia, Paideia, 1984), 64–75; Id., "La figura di Melchisedek nelle tradizioni giudaica, cristiana e gnostica (sec. II a.C.—sec. III d.C.)", *Annali di Storia dell'Esegesi* 1 (1984), 137–152; Martone, *Testi di Qumran,* 253–255; J. Maier, *Die Qumran-Essener: Die Texte vom Toten Meer. Band I: Die Texte der Höhlen 1–3 und 5–11* (München, Reinhardt, 1995), 361–363; E. Puech, *La croyance des Esséniens en la vie future: immortalité, resurrection, vie éternelle? Histoire d'une croyance dans le Judaïsme ancien,* I vol. (Paris, 1993), 516–526; L. Moraldi, *I testi di Qumran* (Torino, UTET, 1971), 577–580.
[41] Cf. C. Martone, *Testi di Qumran,* 253; Maier, *Die Qumran-Essener.* I, 361. Puech, *La croyance.* I, 519–522.
[42] On the Jewish eschatology of the Second Temple see C. Gianotto, "Il millenarismo giudaico", *Annali di Storia dell'Esegesi* 15 (1998), 21–51.

his brother when] the release for God [has been proclaimed].
4 [Its inter] pretation for the last days refers to the captives, about
whom he said: *Isa 61:1* to proclaim liberty to the captives.' And he
will make
5 their rebels prisoners [. . .] and of the inheritance of Melchizedek,
for [. . .] and they are the inheri[tance of Melchi]zedek, who
6 will make them return. He will proclaim liberty (*deror*)[43] for them,
to free them from [the debt] of all their iniquities (*awonot*). And this
will [happen]
7 in the first week of the jubilee which follows the ni[ne] jubilees. And
the day [of atonem]ent is the end of the tenth jubilee
8 in which atonement will be made for all the sons of [God] and for
the men of the lot of Melchizedek. [And on the heights] he will decla[re
in their] favour according to their lots; for
9 it is the time of the 'year of grace' *[Is 6:2]* for Melchizedek, to exa[lt
in the tri]al the holy ones of God through the rule of judgment, as is
written
10 about him in the songs of David, who said: *Ps 82:1* 'Elohim will
stand up in the assem[bly of God,] in the midst of the gods he judges'.[44]

The connection between Dt 15:2 and Is 61:1 is made on the basis
of the fact that both verses use the same verb "proclaim" (*qr'*).
Forgiveness (*semitah*, that LXX translates *afesis*) that is to be proclaimed according to Dt 15:2 is—following 11QMelch—the liberation of slaves (*deror*, that LXX translates *afesis*) that will be proclaimed
in the (probable eschatological) Jubilee according to Is 61:1. Verse 2
of chapter 61 in Isaiah is connected, on the other hand, with the Day
of Atonement foreseen in the levitical Jubilee (Lv 25:9). So the succession of events would seem to be: first the realization of the social
and religious ideal of the sabbatical year (as it is seen in Dt 15:2)
and the Jubilee, and then the forgiveness of the Day of Atonement,
which will occur at the beginning of the fiftieth Jubilee, and which
is identified with the year of grace of Is 61:2.

Puech[45] writes as follows on this passage: "in 11QMelk ii 4 F
[. . .] 'the end of days' concerns the proclamation of the remission
of debts in the first week of the last of the ten jubilees [. . .]. The

---

[43] Here it can clearly be seen the way *deror* means both the remission of sins and
the cancellation of debts, just like *afesis*, because the same word is used.
[44] We follow the translation of F. Garcia Martinez See also Martone, *Testi di
Qumran*, 253–254; Puech, *La croyance*. I, 524–526; but translations differ a great deal,
cf. for example Gianotto, *Melchisedek*, 65–66.
[45] Cf. also Puech, *La croyance*. *I*, 516–526. On 11QMelch cf. also Gianotto,
Melchisedek, 64–75 with reference to the parallel texts on the eschatological Jubilee.

Day of Atonement is the end of the tenth Jubilee, when Melchisedek, the highest heavenly priest, will pronounce judgment. The expression is therefore synonymous with *b'hryt ha't* of 4QMMT C 31: 'so that you may rejoice at the end of time'. This last conception of the end of time in which the last judgment takes place in the tenth week is to be connected back to that of the Apocalypse of the Weeks in Enoch 93:1–10 + 91:11–17 + 93:11–14". "The conception of eschatology—Puech concludes—is in perfect agreement with the biblical notion of this subject and in direct line with the books of the Prophets, including the calculation of delays: 490 years or 10 jubilees in Dan 9 and 11QMelk".[46] In conclusion, 11QMelch makes the end of time coincide with the fiftieth Jubilee. The text foresees the following succession of events:

– proclamation of a liberation from sin in the first week of the Jubilee
– at the end of the Jubilee: expiation through the Day of Atonement
– year of grace for Melchisedek
– last judgment in which the judge is Melchisedek.

The succession of events does not seem to us to be very clear: a number of events and other functions and figures are named. What counts, however, is that the end of days is seen in the fiftieth Jubilee, and that it is connected to a remission of sins which does not coincide with the last judgment; and finally, that a connection between the Jubilee and Day of Atonement exists, even if it seems that the Day of Atonement occurs at the end of the Jubilee.

Conclusion

The most ancient stratum of the early Christian tradition shows us that Jesus imagined the forgiveness of sins without any need for expiation, in other words without the need for a victim, for the shedding of blood.

After Jesus' death, primitive Christianity was faced with the problem of giving a meaning to the death of Jesus. It is at this point that certain early Christian groups interpreted the death of Jesus and his resurrection in the light of the conceptions of the *qorban* of the

---

[46] E. Puech, "Messianisme, eschatologie et résurrection dans les manuscrits de la Mer Morte", *Revue de Qumran* 18 (1997), 264.

Temple at Jerusalem. It is very important to realize that the early Christian reading of the *qorban* is not an objective ethnographical description, but an interpretation that selects in the *qorban* only those elements that could be useful to the understanding of the religious significance of Jesus' death. In the *qorban* of the Temple some of the first Christian theologians saw above all the killing and the blood of the victim. Leviticus offered a theoretical explanation of the meaning of the use of blood:

> For the life of the flesh is in the blood, and I have given it to you to put it upon the altar for making expiation (*lekapper*) for your lives; for it is the blood that effects expiation (*jekapper*) as life (Lv 17:11).[47]

A later, Christian text, the *Letter to the Hebrews* (9,22) will affirm:

> without the shedding of blood (*aimatekchusia*) there is no remission (*afesis*) (Hebr 9:22).[48]

This sentence, however, cannot be taken to mean a description of the *qorban* of the Jewish temple, but rather the underlining of just one aspect which becomes important in the light of the fact that Jesus, dying, had shed his blood.

One final point: it is significant that Matthew's Gospel, despite having handed on the conception in which God's remission of sins happens simply after a reciprocal reconciliation between men, nevertheless affirmed that the Son of God had come:

> to give his life as a ransom for many (Mt 20:28).

And finally that the blood of Christ:

> is poured out for many, for the forgiveness of sins (Mt 26:28).

It is important to note that Matthew avoids claiming that the baptism of John the Baptist was practised "for the forgiveness of sins", as both Mark 1:4 and Luke 3:3 claim. The phrase "for the forgiveness of sins", suppressed in reference to the baptism of John, is shifted over to the reference to the Eucharist. This shift is very important from two points of view. In the first place, Matthew affirms that the forgiveness of sins happens through the death of Christ. Secondly,

---

[47] Cf. Budd, *Leviticus*, 247–249; Levine, *Leviticus*, 115.

[48] Cf. Harlé-Pralon, *Le Lévitique*, 32; P. Garuti, *Alle origini dell'omiletica cristiana. La lettera agli Ebrei. Note di analisi retorica* (Studium Biblicum Franciscanum Analecta 387) (Jerusalem, Franciscan Printing Press, 1995).

he conceives of the eucharist as a ritual in which the forgiveness of sins takes place. Matthew's Christian group hence possesses a ritual for the forgiveness of sins that differs from that of *Yom Kippur*.

The evolution from Mt 6:12 to Mt 26:28 is not only the passage from a non-expiatory forgiveness of sins to a forgiveness through the death of Jesus, but also one step in the passage from Jesus to Christianity.[49]

---

[49] One the same subject of this article see M. Pesce, "La remissione dei peccati nell'escatologia di Gesù", *Annali di Storia dell'Esegesi* 16 (1999), 45–76; A. Destro-M. Pesce, "Between Family and Temple. Jesus and the Sacrifices", *Hervormde Teologiese Studies* 58 (2002); A. Destro-M.-Pesce, "I corpi sacrificali: smembramento e rimembramento. I presupposti culturali di Rom 12, 1–2", in L. Padovese (Ed.), *Atti del VII Simposio di Tarso su S. Paolo Apostolo* (Roma, Pontificio Ateneo Antoniano, 2002).

EUCHARIST: SURROGATE, METAPHOR, SACRAMENT OF SACRIFICE

BRUCE CHILTON

Over the past ten years, I have developed an account of the development of eucharistic practices within primitive Christianity, beginning with the contributions of Jesus as a conscious practitioner of Judaism. The first book in this direction was *The Temple of Jesus*,[1] in which I engaged explicitly with the work of anthropologists of sacrifice in order to understand Jesus' position concerning the cultus in Jerusalem. Indeed, eucharist at the time I initially researched the book was not foremost on my mind. My principal concern had been to assess Jesus' attitudes toward and actions in the Temple itself. But in the course of that work, I saw the direct connection between Jesus' last meals with his followers and his action in the Temple. The eucharist emerged, then, as a surrogate of sacrifice. Encouraged by many scholars, notably Bernhard Lang, I then undertook in *A Feast of Meanings*[2] a properly exegetical study, in order to detail the evolution of the texts within the typical practices of the first Christians. That analytic work, in turn, was presented in a more accessible form, within a religion-historical framework, in *Jesus' Prayer and Jesus' Eucharist*.[3]

Here I wish briefly to explain the types of eucharist—especially as surrogates, metaphors, and sacraments of sacrifice—attested within the New Testament. But then I wish to return to a theoretical question, in order to be more precise about the moment eucharist emerged as a surrogate of sacrifice within Jesus' practice, because that appears to have been the moment generative of the other types.

---

[1] Bruce Chilton, *The Temple of Jesus. His Sacrificial Program Within a Cultural History of Sacrifice* (University Park: The Pennsylvania State University Press, 1992).

[2] Bruce Chilton, *A Feast of Meanings. Eucharistic Theologies from Jesus through Johannine Circles* (NovTSup 72; Leiden: Brill, 1994).

[3] Bruce Chilton, *Jesus' Prayer and Jesus' Eucharist His Personal Practice of Spirituality* (Valley Forge: Trinity Press International, 1997).

Introductory

The Mishnah, in an effort to conceive of a heinous defect on the
part of a priest involved in slaughtering the red heifer, pictures him
as intending to eat the flesh or drink the blood (*m. Para* 4:3). Because
people had no share of blood, which belonged only to God, the
thought of drinking it was blasphemous. To imagine drinking human
blood, consumed with human flesh, could only make the blasphemy
worse. So if Jesus' words are taken with their traditional, autobiographical meaning, his last supper can only be understood as a delib-
erate break from Judaism. Either Jesus himself promulgated a new
religion, or his followers did so in his name, and invented the last
supper themselves. Both those alternatives find adherents today among
scholars, and the debate between those who see the Gospels as literally true reports and those who see them as literary fictions shows
little sign of offering anything like progress. But in either case, the
question remains: if the generative act was indeed anti-sacrificial
(whether that act was literal or literary), how did the cycles of traditions and the texts as they stand come to their present, sacrificial
constructions?

There is another, more historical way of understanding how
eucharist emerged in earliest Christianity, an approach which takes
account of the cultural changes which the development of the movement involved. Interest in the social world of early Judaism, and in
how Christianity as a social movement emerged within Judaism and
then became distinct from it, has been growing for the better part
of a century. The result is that we are no longer limited to the old
dichotomy, between the "conservative" position that the Gospels are
literal reports and the "liberal" position that they are literary fictions.
Critical study has revealed that the Gospels are composite products
of the various social groups which were part of Jesus' movement
from its days within Judaism to the emergence of Christianity as a
distinct religion. When we place eucharistic practices within the social
constituencies which made the Gospels into the texts we can read
today, we can understand the original meaning Jesus gave to the
last supper, and how his meaning generated others.

The last supper was not the only supper, just the last one.[4] In
fact, the last supper would have had no meaning apart from Jesus'

---

[4] I owe the phrasing to Hershel Shanks, who in private correspondence used it

well established custom of eating with people socially. There was nothing unusual about a rabbi making social eating an instrument of his instruction, and it was part of Jesus' method from the first days of his movement in Galilee.

Meals within Judaism were regular expressions of social solidarity, and of common identity as the people of God. Many sorts of meals are attested in the literature of early Judaism. From Qumran we learn of banquets at which the community convened in order of hierarchy; from the Pharisees we learn of collegial meals shared within fellowships (*haburoth*) at which like-minded fellows (*haberim*) would share the foods and the company they considered pure. Ordinary households might welcome the coming of the Sabbath with a prayer of sanctification (*kiddush*) over a cup of wine, and open a family occasion with a blessing (*berakhah*) over bread and wine.

Jesus' meals were similar in some ways to several of these meals, but they were also distinctive. He had a characteristic understanding of what the meals meant and of who should participate in them. For him, eating socially with others in Israel was a parable of the feast in the kingdom which was to come. The idea that God would offer festivity for all peoples on his holy mountain (see Isa 2:2–4) was a key feature in the fervent expectations of Judaism during the first century, and Jesus was held to have shared that hope at an early stage, as may be seen in a saying from the source of his teaching known as "Q" (see Matt 8:11 = Luke 13:28, 29):

> Many shall come from east and west,
> and feast with Abraham, Isaac, and Jacob
> in the kingdom of God.[5]

Eating was a way of enacting the kingdom of God, of practicing the generous rule of the divine king. As a result, Jesus avoided exclusive practices, which divided the people of God from one another in his view; he was willing to accept as companions people such as tax agents and others of suspect purity, and to receive well-known

---

to help summarize my position; see "The Eucharist—Exploring its Origins," *Bible Review* 10.6 (December, 1994) 36–43.

[5] Because my interest here is in the traditional form of the saying, before changes introduced in Matthew and Luke, I give a reconstructed form; see *God in Strength: Jesus' Announcement of the Kingdom* (Studien zum Neuen Testament und seiner Umwelt 1; Freistadt: Plochl, 1979; reprinted Biblical Seminar 8; Sheffield: JSOT Press, 1987) 179–201. More recently, see *Pure Kingdom. Jesus' Vision of God* (Studying the Historical Jesus 1; Eerdmans: Grand Rapids and London: SPCK, 1996) 12–14.

sinners at table. The meal for him was a sign of the kingdom of God, and all the people of God, assuming they sought forgiveness, were to have access to it.

Jesus' practice of fellowship at meals caused opposition from those whose understanding of Israel was exclusive. To them, he seemed profligate, willing to eat and drink with anyone, as Jesus himself was pictured as observing in a famous saying also from "Q" (Matt 11:19 = Luke 7:34):

> A man came eating and drinking, and they complain:
> Look, a glutton and drunkard, a fellow of tax agents and sinners.

Some of Jesus' opponents saw the purity of Israel as something which could only be guarded by separating from others, as in the meals of their fellowships (*haburoth*). Jesus' view of purity was different. He held that a son or daughter of Israel, by virtue of being *of Israel*, could approach his table, or even worship in the Temple. Where necessary, repentance beforehand could be demanded, and Jesus taught his followers to pray for forgiveness daily, but his understanding was that Israelites as such were pure, and were fit to offer purely of their own within the sacrificial worship of Israel.

As long as Jesus' activity was limited to Galilee, he was involved in active disputes, but essentially inconsequential ones. (Slightly deviant rabbis in Galilee were far from uncommon.) But Jesus also brought his teaching into the Temple, where he insisted on his own teaching (or *halakhah*) of purity. The incident which reflects the resulting dispute is usually called the cleansing of the Temple (Matt 21:12–13 = Mark 11:15–17 = Luke 19:45–46 = John 2:13–17). From the point of view of the authorities there, what Jesus was after was the opposite of cleansing. He objected to the presence of merchants who had been given permission to sell sacrificial animals in the vast, outer court of the Temple. His objection was based on his own, peasant's view of purity: Israel should offer, not priest's produce for which they handed over money, but their own sacrifices which they brought into the Temple. He believed so vehemently what he taught that he and his followers drove the animals and the sellers out of the great court, no doubt with the use of force.[6]

Jesus' interference in the ordinary worship of the Temple might have been sufficient by itself to bring about his execution. After all,

---

[6] For a full discussion, see Chilton, *The Temple of Jesus*.

the Temple was the center of Judaism for as long as it stood. Roman officials were so interested in its smooth functioning at the hands of the priests whom they appointed that they were known to sanction the penalty of death for sacrilege. Yet there is no indication that Jesus was arrested immediately. Instead, he remained at liberty for some time, and was finally taken into custody just after one of his meals, the last supper. The decision of the authorities of the Temple to move against Jesus when they did is what made the last supper last. Why did the authorities wait, and why did they act when they did? The Gospels portray them as fearful of the popular backing which Jesus enjoyed, and his inclusive teaching of purity probably did bring enthusiastic followers into the Temple with him. But in addition, there was another factor: Jesus could not simply be dispatched as a cultic criminal. He was not attempting an onslaught upon the Temple as such; his dispute with the authorities concerned purity within the Temple. Other rabbis of his period also engaged in physical demonstrations of the purity they required in the conduct of worship. One of them, for example, is said once to have driven thousands of sheep into the Temple, so that people could offer sacrifice in the manner he approved of (see *b. Beṣ.* 20a–b). Jesus' action was extreme, but not totally without precedent, even in the use of force.

The delay of the authorities, then, was understandable. We may also say it was commendable, reflecting continued controversy over the merits of Jesus' teaching and whether his occupation of the great court should be condemned out of hand. But why did they finally arrest Jesus? The last supper provides the key; something about Jesus' meals after his occupation of the Temple caused Judas to inform on Jesus. Of course, "Judas" is the only name which the traditions of the New Testament have left us. We cannot say who or how many of the disciples became disaffected by Jesus' behavior after his occupation of the Temple.

However they learned of Jesus' new interpretation of his meals of fellowship, the authorities arrested him just after the supper we call last. Jesus continued to celebrate fellowship at table as a foretaste of the kingdom, just as he had before. But he also added a new and scandalous dimension of meaning. His occupation of the Temple having failed, Jesus said of the wine, "This is my blood," and of the bread, "This is my flesh" (Matt 26:26, 28 = Mark 14:22, 24 = Luke 22:19–20 = 1 Cor 11:24–25 = Justin, *1 Apology* 66.3).

In Jesus' context, one of confrontation with the authorities of the Temple, his words can have had only one meaning. He cannot have meant, "Here are my personal body and blood;" that is an interpretation which only makes sense at a later stage. Jesus' point was rather that, in the absence of a Temple which permitted his view of purity to be practiced, wine was his blood of sacrifice, and bread was his flesh of sacrifice. In Aramaic, "blood" and "flesh" (which may also be rendered as "body") can carry such a sacrificial meaning, and in Jesus' context, that is the most natural meaning.

The meaning of "the last supper," then, actually evolved over a series of meals after Jesus' occupation of the Temple. During that period, Jesus claimed that wine and bread were a better sacrifice than what was offered in the Temple: at least wine and bread were Israel's own, not tokens of priestly dominance. No wonder the opposition to him, even among the Twelve (in the shape of Judas, according to the Gospels) became deadly. In essence, Jesus made his meals into a rival altar, and we may call such a reading of his words a ritual or cultic interpretation.

The cultic interpretation has two advantages over the traditional, autobiographical interpretation as the meaning Jesus attributed to his own final meals. The first advantage is contextual: the cultic interpretation places Jesus firmly with the Judaism of his period, and at the same time amply accounts for the opposition of the authorities to him. The second advantage is its explanatory power in relation to subsequent developments: the cultic interpretation enables us to explain sequentially the understandings of eucharist within earliest Christianity. The cultic sense of Jesus' last meals with his disciples is the generative meaning which permits us to explain its later meanings as eucharistic covenant, Passover, heroic symposium, and Mystery.

Six types of eucharistic practice behind "The Last Supper"

The six types of practice may be succinctly reviewed now, on the understanding that they have been developed in exegetical terms in *A Feast of Meanings*, and in religion-historical terms in *Jesus' Prayer and Jesus' Eucharist*. Jesus joined with his followers in Galilee and Judaea, both disciples and sympathizers, in meals which were designed to anticipate the coming of God's kingdom. The meals were characterized by a readiness to accept the hospitality and the produce of Israel at large. A willingness to provide for the meals, to join in the fellow-ship, to forgive and to be forgiven, was seen by Jesus as a sufficient condition for eating in his company and for entry into the kingdom.

Jesus' view of purity was distinctive, and—no doubt—lax in the estimation of many contemporary rabbis. In one regard, however, he typifies the Judaism of his period: there was an evident fit between his practice of fellowship at meals and his theory of what was clean. Meals appear to have been a primary marker of social grouping within the first century in Palestine. Commensal institutions, formal or not, were plentiful. They included the banquets of Qumran, but also occasions of local or national festivity throughout the country. Any patron who mounted a banquet would appropriately expect the meal to reflect his or her views of purity, and guests would not be in a good position to militate in favor of other views. But meals need not be on a grand scale to be seen as important, and much more modest events might be subject to custom: a household might welcome a feast or Sabbath with a cup of sanctification (the *kiddush*), and bless bread as a prelude to a significant family affair (the *berakhah*). In addition, collegial meals shared within fellowships (*haburoth*) at which like-minded fellows (*haberim*) would share the foods and the company they considered pure would define distinct social groups.

Jesus' practice coincided to some extent with that of a *haburah*, but his construal of purity was unusual. Given the prominence accorded wine in his meals and the way his characteristic prayer emphasizes the theme of sanctification, we might describe the first type of his meals—the practice of purity in anticipation of the king-dom—as a *kiddush* of the kingdom. But his meals were not limited to households, so that there is already, in its simplest form, a metaphor-ical quality about this practice. Any analogy with the communal meals of Qumran would seem to be strained, unless the feedings of the 5,000 and the 4,000 are held originally to have been staged as massive banquets designed to instance Jesus' theory of purity and his expectation of the kingdom.

Indeed, there is practically no meal of Judaism with which Jesus' meals do not offer some sort of analogy, because the meal was a seal and an occasion of purity, and Jesus was concerned with what was pure. But both the nature of his concern and the character of his meals were distinctive in their inclusiveness: Israel as forgiven and willing to provide of its own produce was for him the occasion of the kingdom. That was the first type in the development of the eucharist.

Jesus himself brought about the final crisis of his career. His teaching in regard to the kingdom and its purity, including his communal meals as enacted parables, might have been continued indefinitely (for all the controversy involved) outside of Jerusalem. But he sought to influence practice in the Temple, where the purity of Israel was supremely instanced and where the feast of all nations promised by the prophets was to occur. A dispute over the location of vendors of animals for sacrifice was the catalyst in a raging dispute over purity between Jesus (with his followers) and the authorities in the Temple. The riot in the Temple which Jesus provoked may have been sufficient by itself to bring about his execution, given the importance of the Temple within both Judaism and the settlement with Rome. But he compounded his confrontation with the authorities by putting a new interpretation upon the meals people took with him in their expectation of the kingdom. As he shared wine, he referred to it as the equivalent of the blood of an animal, shed in sacrifice; when he shared bread, he claimed its value was as that of sacrificial flesh. Such offerings were purer, more readily accepted by God, than what was sacrificed in a Temple which had become corrupt. Here was a sacrifice of sharings which the authorities could not control, and which the nature of Jesus' movement made it impossible for them to ignore. Jesus' meals after his failed occupation of the Temple became a surrogate of sacrifice, the second type of eucharist.

The third type is that of Petrine Christianity, when the blessing or breaking of bread at home, the *berakhah* of Judaism, became a principal model of eucharist. A practical result of that development was that bread came to have precedence over wine. More profoundly, the circle of Peter conceived of Jesus as a new Moses, who gave commands concerning purity as Moses did on Sinai, and who also expected his followers to worship on Mount Zion. As compared to Jesus' practice (in its first and second stages), Petrine practice represents a double domestication. First, adherents of the movement congregated in the homes of their colleagues, rather than seeking the hospitality of others. Second, the validity of sacrifice in the Temple was acknowledged. Both forms of domestication grew out of the new circumstances of the movement in Jerusalem and fresh opportunities for worship in the Temple; they changed the nature of the meal and the memory of what Jesus had said at the "last supper." The application of the model of a *berakhah* to eucharist was a self-conscious metaphor, because the careful identification of those gathered in Jesus' name with a household was itself metaphorical.

The fourth type of eucharist, the contribution of the circle of James, pursued the tendency of domestication further. The eucharist was seen as a Seder, in terms of both its meaning and its chronology. So understood, only Jews in a state of purity could participate in eucharist, which could be truly recollected only once a year, at Passover in Jerusalem. The Quartodeciman controversy (concerning the timing of Easter) of a later period, fierce though it appears, was but a shadow cast by a much more serious contention concerning the nature of Christianity. The Jacobean program was to integrate Jesus' movement fully within the liturgical institutions of Judaism, to insist upon the Judaic identity of the movement and upon Jerusalem as its governing center. Nonetheless, there is never any doubt but that eucharist is not portrayed as an actual replacement of the Seder of Israel as such, and for that reason the language of metaphor is appropriate here, as well.

Paul and the Synoptic Gospels represent the fifth type of eucharist. Paul more vehemently resists Jacobean claims, by insisting Jesus' last meal occurred on the night in which he was betrayed (1 Corinthians 11:23), not on Passover. He emphasizes the link between Jesus' death and the eucharist, and he accepts the Hellenistic refinement of the Petrine type which presented the eucharist as a sacrifice for sin. That type is also embraced in the Synoptic Gospels, where the heroism of Jesus is such that the meal is an occasion to join in the solidarity of martyrdom. The Synoptic strategy is not to oppose the Jacobean program directly; in fact, its chronology is accepted (although not without internal contradiction). Instead, the Synoptics insist by various wordings that Jesus' blood is shed in the interests of the communities for which those Gospels were composed, for the "many" in Damascus (Matt 26:28) and Rome (Mark 14:24), on behalf of "you" in Antioch (Luke 22:20). The Synoptic tradition also provided two stories of miraculous feeding which symbolized the inclusion of Jews and non-Jews within eucharist, understood as in the nature of a philosophical symposium (see Mark 6:32–44; 8:1–10 and parallels). This willingness to explore differing meanings with eucharistic action attests that any such meaning, taken singly, was understood metaphorically.

The feeding of the 5,000—understood as occurring at Passover—is taken up in John 6 in a fully Paschal sense. Jesus himself is identified as the manna, miraculous food bestowed by God upon his people. The motif was already articulated by Paul (1 Cor 10:1–4), but John develops it to construe the eucharist as a Mystery, in which Jesus offers his own flesh and blood (carefully defined to avoid a crude misunderstanding; John 6:30–34, 41–58). That autobiographical reading of Jesus' words—as giving his personal body and blood in eucharist—had already occurred to Hellenistic Christians who followed Synoptic practice. The Johannine practice made that meaning as explicit as the break with Judaism is in the fourth Gospel. Both that departure and the identification of Jesus himself (rather than his supper) as the Paschal lamb are pursued in the Revelation (5:6–14; 7:13–17). The sixth type of eucharist can only be understood as a consciously non-Judaic and Hellenistic development. It involves participants in joining by oath (*sacramentum* in Latin, corresponding to *musterion* within the Greek vocabulary of primitive Christianity) in the sacrifice of the Mysterious hero himself, separating themselves from others. Eucharist has become sacrament, and involves a knowing conflict with the ordinary understanding of what Judaism might and might not include.

"The Last Supper" is neither simply Jesus' Seder nor simply a symposium of Hellenists to which the name of Jesus happens to have been attached. Such ideological regimens, which will have the Gospels be only historical or only fictive, simply starve the reader of the meanings which generated the texts to hand. The engines of those meanings were diverse practices, whose discovery permits us to feast on the richness of tradition. A generative exegesis of eucharistic texts may not conclude with a single meaning which is alleged to have occasioned all the others. One of the principal findings of such an approach is rather that meaning itself is to some extent epiphenomenal, a consequence of a definable practice with its own initial sense being introduced into a fresh environment of people who in turn take up the practice as they understand it and produce their own meanings. The sense with which a practice is mediated to a community is therefore one measure of what that community will finally produce as its practice, but the initial meaning does not determine the final meaning.

The meanings conveyed by words must be the point of departure for a generative exegesis, because those meanings are our only access to what produced the texts to hand. But having gained that access, it becomes evident that eucharist is not a matter of the development of a single, basic meaning within several different environments. Those environments have themselves produced various meanings under the influence of definable practices. Eucharist was not simply handed on as a tradition. Eucharistic traditions were rather the catalyst which permitted communities to crystallize their own practice in oral or textual form. What they crystallized was a function of the practice which had been learned, palpable gestures with specified objects and previous meanings, along with the meaning and the emotional response which the community discovered in eucharist. There is no history of the tradition apart from a history of meaning, a history of emotional response, a history of practice: the practical result of a generative exegesis of eucharistic texts is that practice itself is an appropriate focus in understanding the New Testament.

The moment of magical surrogacy

If Jesus is seen as generating eucharist as a surrogate of sacrifice, the question emerges: how can he have undertaken such an action, with such an understanding? In terms of circumstance, his failed occupation of the Temple provides an adequate occasion, but not a sufficient cause from the point of view of his motivation.

Some years ago, I taught a course to my students at Bard College with a professor of Asian religions.[7] Our purpose was to read through the group of theorists whose work has been formative of the discipline of the study of religion in the United States, including William Robertson Smith, James George Frazer, Emile Durkheim, Max Weber, Bronislaw Malinowski, Marcel Mauss, Victor Turner, Edward Evans Evans-Pritchard, Clifford Geertz, René Girard, and Catherine Bell. The point of focus we selected was magic, and I came to realize, particularly through our reading of Max Weber, that the myth of the magician as originator might be clouding our perception of that category.

Ralph Schroeder, has made an especially interesting contribution from this point of view.[8] Despite the criticism of Weber as an "intellectualist," Schroeder is attracted by Weber's linkage of magic, religion,

---

[7] My colleague, Laurie Patton, has pursued this interest in a study of mantra in domestic religious practices in early India.

[8] *Max Weber and the Sociology of Culture* (London: Sage, 1992) 33–71, a chapter entitled "The Uniqueness of the East."

and science: "In Weber's view, magic has a rational aim which is pursued by irrational means, whereas religion is characterized by an increasingly irrational aim and increasingly rational means to salvation."[9] Schroeder continues:

> The most undifferentiated form of magic, in Weber's view, is where magical power is thought to be embodied in a person who can bring about supernatural events by virtue of an innate capacity. This belief is the original source of charisma. 'The oldest of all "callings"' or professions, Weber points out, 'is that of the magician' (1981a: 8). From this point, charisma develops by a process of abstraction towards the notion that certain forces are 'behind' this extraordinary power— although they remain within the world (1968: 401).[10]

This leads to an analysis of magic as static:

> The inflexibility of the means employed with magic creates a static system of norms and ritual prescriptions which reinforces traditional conduct. Charisma, inasmuch as it is tied to concrete embodiments and tangible successes, easily becomes routinized. Moreover, the unchallengeable position of the magicians constitutes an obstacle to cultural change because by attaching sacred norms to economic, political, and other functions, the magician sanctions their traditional role as well.[11]

This contrasts sharply with the dynamic quality of religion:

> That is, the world as a whole must have a meaning outside of what is empirically given. It should be emphasized that this is a feature of all the great religions—again, Weber refers to them as *Kulturreligionen* (1980b: 367). This is notable because here we have what is, from the viewpoint of a sociology of culture, an answer to Weber's lack of a concept of 'society': the unity that this concept affords elsewhere is here taken on by the unity of 'culture' in the form of the *Kulturreligionen*.[12]

What Schroeder does not say, and yet may easily be inferred from his study, is that magic should not be seen as the foundation of religion, but as a specific manifestation of religion, when the entire system is held to be concentrated in an individual or individuals. Magic expresses more the crisis of a system than the presupposition of a system.

---

[9] *Max Weber and the Sociology of Culture*, 34.
[10] *Max Weber and the Sociology of Culture*, 37, citing *Wirtschaftgeschichte* (Berlin: Duncker and Humblot, 1981) and *Economy and Society* (New York: Bedminster, 1968).
[11] *Max Weber and the Sociology of Culture*, 38–9.
[12] *Max Weber and the Sociology of Culture*, 40, citing *Wirtschaft und Gesellschaft* (Tübingen: Mohr, 1980).

Such a description accords rather well with some of the figures Josephus calls false prophets, whose followers presumably called them prophets. There has been a tendency to class John the baptist with them. In fact, Josephus simply calls John a good man (*Antiquities* 18 § 117), and describes Bannus' similar commitment to sanctification by bathing in approving terms (*Life* § 11). Nothing they did (as related by Josephus) can be compared with what Josephus said the false prophets did: one scaled Mount Gerizim to find the vessels deposited by Moses (*Antiquities* 18 §§ 85–87), Theudas waited at the Jordan for the waters to part for him, as they had for Joshua (*Antiquities* 20 §§ 97–98),[13] the Egyptian marched from the Mount of Olives in the hope the walls of Jerusalem might fall at his command (*Antiquities* 20 §§ 169–172) so that he might conquer Jerusalem (*War* 2 § 261–263). If there is an act in the Gospels which approximates to such fanaticism, it is Jesus' entry into Jerusalem and his occupation of the Temple; apparently he expected to prevail against all the odds in insisting upon his own understanding of what true purity there was, in opposition to Caiaphas and the imposing authority of a high priest sanctioned by Rome. When Jesus is styled a prophet in Matthew 21:11, 46, that may have something to do with the usage of Josephus, but to portray John the baptist in such terms is incautious.

These acts of magic are not spontaneous or heroic foundations of new religions by means of Weberian charisma. Rather, each instantiates a response to a sense of crisis, the conviction that the entire religious system has gone wrong, and may only be retrieved by a magician who takes that system on to himself. Finding Moses' vessels, parting the Jordan, taking Jerusalem, and occupying the Temple are all examples of the attempt to right the system by seizing and manipulating its most central symbols. They are instances of magic as theurgy, the access of divine power in order to change and mold the ordinary structures of authority, whether social or natural.[14]

---

[13] According to Colin Brown, Theudas was inspired by John the baptist, whose program was not purification but a re-crossing of the Jordan; see "What Was John the Baptist Doing?" *Bulletin for Biblical Research* 7 (1997) 37–49, 48. That seems a desperate expedient to avoid the obvious connection with purification. The equally obvious obstacles are that crossing the Jordan is not a part of any characterization of Yohanan's message in the primary sources, and that Josephus does not association Yohanan with the "false prophets." For the context of John's immersion (and Jesus'), see Chilton, *Jesus' Baptism and Jesus' Healing. His Personal Practice of Spirituality* (Harrisburg: Trinity Press International, 1998).

[14] Such is the sense of magic which stands behind the works of Morton Smith,

It is in this context that I find Bernhard Lang's work (represented in this volume) as intriguing as I do.[15] I must admit that, when he first suggested precise connections between Jesus' last meals and normally sacrificial acts, I reacted with some reserve. Now, however, he has specified those connections in great detail, and—at the same time—the sense of such connections is clearer to me. In taking the Temple to his table, Jesus not only celebrated God's sovereignty and marked that celebration as an acceptable sacrifice; he also marked that magical surrogacy as the means of the fulfillment of Israel.

The Secret Gospel (New York; Harper and Row, 1973) and *Jesus the Magician* (New York: Harper and Row, 1977). Throughout, what is apparent is the influence of Hans Lewy, *Chaldean Oracles and Theurgy* (Cairo: Institut français d'archéologie orientale, 1956).

[15] See *Sacred Games. A History of Christian Worship* (New Haven: Yale University Press, 1997), and my adaption of these ideas in *Rabbi Jesus. An Intimate Biography* (New York: Doubleday, 2000).

THIS IS MY BODY: SACRIFICIAL PRESENTATION AND THE ORIGINS OF CHRISTIAN RITUAL

Bernhard Lang

> Qu'est-ce qui constitue le culte dans une religion quelconque? C'est le sacrifice. Une religion qui n'a pas de sacrifice, n'a pas de culte proprement dit. Cette vérité est incontestable, puisque, chez les divers peuples de la terre, les cérémonies religieuses sont nées du sacrifice.[1]
>
> François-René de Chateaubriand, 1802

In this paper we will argue that the Eucharist as instituted by Jesus and celebrated by his early followers belongs to the category of sacrifice or, more precisely, represents an alternative to animal sacrifice.[2] Jesus does not seem to have invented the ritual handling and consumption of a token piece of bread and the drinking of wine; arguably, what he did was transform a well-known and often practiced form of sacrifice celebrated at the Jerusalem Temple in his period. We will develop our argument in three stages. (1) First, we will offer a detailed description of a standard private sacrifice as it was celebrated at the Jerusalem Temple. (2) Then we will show how Jesus and his movement designed the Eucharist on the basis of some of the elements

---

[1] "What constitutes the ritual of any religion? Sacrifice! A religion without sacrifice has no proper ritual. This truth cannot be denied, for, among all the peoples of the earth, religious ceremonies derive from sacrifice." François-René de Chateaubriand, *Génie du Christianisme* [1802], in: *Oeuvres complètes* (Paris: Pourrat, 1836), vol. 16, 60 (part IV, "Explication de la Messe").

[2] Our fresh (and to some readers no doubt rather daring and surprising) reconstruction rests on earlier historical scholarship, especially on the solid work of H. Gese and B. Chilton. These two biblical scholars were the first to explain the Lord's Supper in terms of sacrifice. In so doing, they demonstrated that the origins of one of the central acts of Christian worship are not lost in the darkness of legendary accounts. See Hartmut Gese, *Essays on Biblical Theology* (Minneapolis: Augsburg, 1981) 117–40; Bruce D. Chilton, *The Temple of Jesus: His Sacrificial Program within a Cultural History of Sacrifice* (University Park: Pennsylvania State University Press, 1992) and *A Feast of Meanings: Eucharistic Theologies from Jesus through Johannine Circles* (Leiden: Brill, 1994). We have developed the argument in Bernhard Lang, *Sacred Games: A History of Christian Worship* (New Haven: Yale University Press, 1997) which includes a chapter on sacrificial notions in Christian interpretations of worship ("The Fourth Game: Sacrifice," 205–81).

of this Temple ritual. (3) A third section will present a hypothetical
account of the reasons why Jesus designed a new ritual.

1. *Private sacrifice in Jesus' time*

In order to thank God for benefits received—recovering from illness,
returning home safely from a long journey, and the like—Jews took
a lamb or a goat, went to the Jerusalem Temple, and presented themselves to a priest who then saw to it that the animal was slaughtered,
and certain parts burned on the altar. A feast was then arranged
for the sacrificer and the latter's guests. While this description may
give a first idea of what happens when a sacrifice is offered, it remains
too sketchy for our purposes. There are many more acts involved,
and biblical as well as some other sources can help us to reconstruct
some of the procedures and their arrangement as a sequence of
sacred acts. The insert that follows lists the most important acts
referred to in the ancient sources and tries to reconstruct the "ideal
type" of a private sacrifice. In order to sketch the full picture, we
also make an effort to fill some of the gaps in the historical record.

THE SIX STEPS OF SACRIFICIAL PROCEDURE
(PRIVATELY OFFERED SACRIFICE)

STEP I   *Preparation.* The sacrificer brings the animal and some other
             gifts, including bread and wine, to the Temple and presents
             them to a priest.

STEP II   *Slaughtering.* The priest slaughters the animal and separates
             "blood" and "body."

STEP III   *Offering of the blood at the altar.* The priest tosses the blood against
             all sides of the altar. We conjecture that before the blood
             is tossed, the priest presents it to God, pronouncing a for-
             mula: "This is N's blood," N being the name of the sacrificer.

STEP IV   *Presentation of the body and the bread at the altar.* The sacrificial
             material brought before the altar is presented and dedicated
             to God with a gesture of elevation. We conjecture that at
             the presentation at the altar, the priest pronounces these
             words: "This is N's body," N being the name of the sacrificer.

STEP V   *Disposal of the wine.* The priest presents the wine at the altar,
             elevating the cup and invoking the name of God. The con-
             cluding ritual act is the pouring out of the wine at the foot
             of the altar.

STEP VI   *Communal meal.* The sacrificer receives the body of the slaugh-
             tered animal back and prepares a feast to which guests are
             invited.

Sacrifice must be thought of as a costly meal in whose preparation priests are involved and which requires a particular sequence of acts taking place in the Temple. In the first stage, which we may term the preparation, someone takes an animal to the Temple and presents it to a priest.[3] The sacrificer declares which kind of sacrifice he or she wants to offer. The sacrificer also puts his hand (with force) on the head of the animal. Slaves and women were not allowed to perform the hand-leaning rite. In addition to the animal, the sacrificer also brings wine and four kinds of unleavened and leavened bread.[4]

The slaughtering of the animal (step II) follows immediately.[5] The priest or the priest's attendant slaughters the animal and separates "blood" and "body." The blood is collected in a bowl. The sacrificer watches from the "court of the Israelites," while the priest does the slaughtering in the sacrificial court. During the following steps, the sacrificer stays in the court of the Israelites.

The following two steps seem to be the culmination of the ritual. First comes the offering of the blood at the altar (step III).[6] The priest tosses the blood against all sides of the altar. We conjecture that before the blood is tossed, the priest presents it to God at the altar, pronouncing a formula: "This is N's blood," N being the name of the sacrificer. The sacrificer still watches. Then, the victim's body and some bread are presented at the altar (step IV).[7] The sacrificial material brought before the altar consists of part of the bread, the slaughtered animal's breast, and certain parts of the entrails (essentially the kidneys and the fat covering the entrails). All of this is presented at the altar and dedicated to God with a gesture of elevation. Then the entrail parts are thrown onto the pyre that burns on the altar, whereas the breast and the bread remain with the officiating priest who consumes them later. We conjecture that at the presentation at the altar, the priest pronounces these words: "This is N's body," N being the name of the sacrificer. The sacrificer watches.

---

[3] Lev 3:2; 7:12–13. Mishna Pesahim 5:2; Mishna Menahot 9:8.
[4] Bread is referred to in Lev 7:12–13, and wine in Num 15:10.
[5] Lev 1:11; Mishna Zebahim 2:1 and Mishna Pesahim 5:5.
[6] Lev 3:2.
[7] Lev 3:3–4; 7:12–14.30; 8:25–29; Num 15:8. The presentation of a live animal before God (i.e., before the altar) is referred to as an exception (Lev 16:10). On the correct understanding of the "elevation" gesture (Hebrew, *tenûpâ*), see Jacob Milgrom, *Numbers: The JPS Torah Commentary* (Philadelphia: Jewish Publication Society, 1990) 425–26.

After the offering of blood, meat, and bread, the priest takes a cup of wine, elevates it, utters an invocation to God, and then pours it at the foot of the alter (step V).[8] The sacrificer still watches.

After the priest has poured out the wine, he returns the slaughtered animal to the sacrificer for consumption. The communal meal that follows (step VI) no longer takes place at the altar, but nonetheless near the Temple. Since the meat has to be consumed on the day of sacrifice,[9] the sacrificer immediately prepares a feast to which guests are invited (people who had been present all along, together with the sacrificer watching the priest officiate). Bread and wine are also consumed.

The ritual as we have reconstructed it has a beautiful, symmetrical design with a beginning, a middle, and a conclusion. The preparatory stages (I and II) are followed by the offering of bread and the animal's body (IV), which is framed by two libations, first of blood (III) and then of wine (V). A joyous meal forms the conclusion (VI). The main sacrificial material is the slaughtered animal's blood and body, but this material is doubled in unbloody form with bread and wine.

For the words with which the priest presents the sacrificial gifts at the altar, no ancient sources are available.[10] Here our reconstruction relies on the words that Jesus used in his redesigned ritual: "This is my body" and "This is my blood."[11] Placed in a concrete ritual situation, these words lose their enigmatic quality and sound quite natural. In an earlier period, when the sacrificer, and not the priest, officiated at the altar, these could have been the formulae of sacrificial presentation. When the sacrificer approached the altar with his slaughtered animal, he uttered the words: "This is my body," i.e., here I bring my sacrificial body; it belongs to me and I place it on your altar. Similarly, when offering the victim's blood, he would say, "This is my blood," i.e., here I offer the blood of my sacrificial victim. Unfortunately, this interpretation must remain conjectural. Yet, we can point to three sacrificial formulae found or alluded to

---

[8] Num 15:10; Ps 116:13; Sir 50:15.—Ps 116 implies that sacrificers, not priests, present the wine, but by New Testament times, this apparently had changed.

[9] Lev 7:15.

[10] The Old Testament does not include any prayer texts or words of offering recited at sacrifices, but 2 Chr 30:21–22 implies the existence of such prayers.

[11] Matt 26:26.28 and parallel passages. For "body" (Greek *sôma*) and "blood" (*haîma*) as belonging to the sacrificial vocabulary, see Hebr 13:11.

in the Old Testament. The book of Deuteronomy prescribes a text to be pronounced by the peasant as he presents his harvest gifts to the Temple. It includes a presentation formula, to be said at the handing over of the basket to the deity, represented by a priest: "Now I bring here the first fruits of the land which you, Yahweh, have given me" (Deut 26:11). This example shows that the bringing of a gift to the temple involved a formal act of presentation in which it was customary to use certain prescribed words. Formulae pronounced by priests and related to the ritual use of blood bring us closer to "eucharistic" language. In the book of Exodus, there is an expression that Moses used when applying sacrificial blood to people: "Behold the blood of the covenant that Yahweh has made with you" (Exod 24:8). A third example comes again closer to the words spoken by Jesus. An Old Testament legend recounts how King David, during a war, makes a sacrifice to Yahweh in the abbreviated, substitute form of a libation. As no animal could be slaughtered, water serves as a substitute for blood. David pours out the water in the name of the men who in a daring act have fetched it from a cistern under the enemy's control. In the absence of an altar he pours the water out onto the ground and says: "This is the blood of the men who went at the risk of their lives" (2 Sam 23:17). Priests may have used similar expressions when tossing sacrificial blood at the altar, presenting the victim's breast or bread and wine, or when throwing parts of the victim into the fire burning on the altar. A sacrifice must be formally presented and the sacrificer identified. Actually, the presentation, and not the killing of the victim, seems to have been the central ritual act.

2. Jesus' new sacrifice

The earliest form of the Eucharist, as far as we can reconstruct it, consisted of three simple parts. First, a communal meal was eaten by a small number of people; here we may of course think of Jesus and his narrower circle of the twelve as mentioned in the gospels. Then, the presider presented some bread to God in a gesture of elevation, saying, "This is my body." Those present shared the token piece of bread offered to God. The third and concluding act repeated the bread rite with a cup of wine. Here again, the words of presentation were pronounced, "This is my blood," and the cup was

shared by those taking part in the celebration. What we have here
is patterned on private sacrifice as celebrated at the Temple. We
can best understand Jesus' new sacrifice as an abbreviated form of
the six-step ritual described above. One item remained essentially
unchanged: as in the Temple ritual, bread was presented to God
with the formula, "This is my body," and was then eaten (without
being burned on the altar). Other features were changed. Jesus introduced two main alterations: (1) He transferred the ritual to the realm
outside the Temple; as a consequence, every act involving the cooperation of a priest had to be omitted. Since no priest was involved,
no animal could be slaughtered, no blood could be sprinkled, and
nothing could be burned on the altar. (2) Jesus reduced the Temple
ritual to its unbloody part,[12] and here he reversed the order of the
various ritual acts: the meal no longer formed the conclusion, but
was now placed at the beginning and was followed by ritual gestures with bread and wine. There is some ambiguity as to the
sequence of these gestures. The gospel of Luke places the wine rite
first, whereas Mark and Matthew place it after the bread rite.[13] Both
sequences make sense. The sequence wine rite—bread rite may be
seen as replicating the original sequence of the animal sacrifice which
required the quick disposal of the victim's blood (which had to be
tossed against the altar before congealing). Those placing the wine
rite last no doubt simply imitated the priests who concluded sacrificial
celebrations with a libation of wine.

The new, unbloody ritual, while completely redesigned, still served
the same purpose of honoring God with a present and giving him
thanks for benefits received. Therefore Christians often called it by

---

[12] An interesting parallel to the Jesuanic omission of the "bloody" part of sacrifice
comes from India, where grain, originally a gift accompanying the sacrifice of a
goat, came to stand for the entire ritual. The Indianist Wendy Doniger O'Flaherty
compares this development with the eucharistic sacrifice in Christianity: "The
Eucharist thus stands at precisely the same remove from human sacrifice as the
'suffocated' rice cake in Hindu ritual stands at its own remove from the sacrifice
of a goat. Indeed, in both instances we have what is more precisely not the replacing of flesh by grain but the supercession of flesh by grain. That is, in the earliest
records of both the ancient Hebrew sacrifice and the ancient Vedic sacrifice, the
killing of the animal was accompanied by an offering of grain (rice and barley in
the Vedic sacrifice or, in the case of the Vedic stallion, balls of rice). These sacrifices
were thus ambivalent from the very start; they involved not only an animal surrogate for a human victim but the substance that first complemented and [eventu-
ally, B.L.] replaced that surrogate." Wendy Doniger O'Flaherty, *Other People's Myths*
(New York: Macmillan, 1988) 118. I owe this reference to Lawrence Zalcman.
[13] Wine—bread: Luke 21:17–19; bread—wine: Mark 14:22–23 and Matt 26:26–28.

its old name of *eucharistia*, the Greek term for thanksgiving.[14] The central rite by which God was honored consisted of a gesture of elevating bread and wine and presenting these gifts to God saying, "This is my body—This is my blood." Neither an accompanying prayer (as in later Christian worship) nor the eating and drinking formed the core. The sacrifice of Jesus consisted exclusively in the very rite of presentation, i.e., the elevation and the words accompanying this gesture.

Why should the abbreviated, unbloody sacrifice replace the elaborate, expensive, and time-consuming priestly celebration at the Temple? The idea of replacing a standard sacrifice by something else is not entirely new, but has precedents in actual ritual practice. In anthropological literature, the classical example of sacrificial lenience comes from the Nuer, a black cattle-herding people living in the Sudan.[15] When someone cannot afford to slaughter an ox, a tiny little cucumber will do as well, at least as a temporary expedient. The Nuer treat the cucumber as though it were an animal victim: it is presented and consecrated, an invocation said over it, and eventually slain by the spear. A similarly striking instance of sacrificial substitution can be quoted from ancient Egypt.[16] A priest or a scribe could honor a deity or a deceased person by pouring some water and uttering the formula: "A thousand loaves of bread, a thousand jugs of beer for N." The water replaced the large amount of bread and beer evoked by the sacrificer. In Israel, private sacrifice, like its public counterpart, normally required the killing and offering of a domestic animal. Frequently, the entire animal was burned "for the deity," so that the sacrificing individual or community did not have the benefit of a joyous meal. Only the well-to-do could afford frequent sacrifices. One Old Testament story contrasts the poor man, who owned only one little ewe lamb, with a rich person, who had very many flocks and herds.[17] We can see why the lower classes were excluded from frequent participation in private sacrificial worship.

---

[14] For an early reference to the Christian sacrifice as *eucharistia* "thanksgiving," see Didache 9 (ca. 110/160 CE). See also the verb "to give thanks" (Greek *eucharistein*) in the New Testament report on the Last Supper, Matt 26:27.

[15] Edward E. Evans-Pritchard, *Nuer Religion* (Oxford: Oxford University Press, 1956) 203.

[16] Hans Bonnet, *Reallexikon der ägyptischen Religionsgeschichte* (Berlin: de Gruyter, 1952) 425.

[17] 2 Sam 12:3.

In certain cases, they were allowed to offer a pair of pigeons or tur-
tledoves instead of a lamb; and if they could not afford to buy these,
an offering of some flour (about 4 kg—still a substantial gift) would
do as well.[18] The most common substitute for sacrifice, however, was
prayer, which ranked as a kind of "offering of the poor." Visitors
to the Temple were ideally expected to bring an offering to the
Lord, but if they came empty-handed they were at least supposed
to prostrate and utter a prayer. Such an understanding of prayer is
reflected in the book of Psalms, the collection of Jerusalem Temple
prayers.[19] Thus we find a supplicant asking that his prayer "be taken
like incense" before the Lord, and his "upraised hands" (that is, the
palms raised upward in a customary gesture of prayer) be accepted
"like an evening grain-offering" of the public cult. When the psalmist
says, "accept, O Lord, the free-will offering of my mouth," the poor
person actually expects his words to be as acceptable as an animal
sacrifice. When he declares that "a broken spirit is a sacrifice acceptable to God" and proclaims that God "will not despise a broken
and contrite heart," he has no intention of renouncing sacrifices as
such, but merely indicates the fact that a broken spirit, expressed in
song or prayer, is all he can offer. He expresses the hope that this
spirit will count for him as if it were a "real" sacrifice. A post-biblical Jewish text sums the matter up quite succinctly: "If a man has
a bullock, let him offer a bullock; if not, let him offer a ram, or a
lamb, or a pigeon; and, if he cannot afford even a pigeon, let him
bring a handful of flour. And if he has not even any flour, let him
bring nothing at all, but come with words of prayer."[20]

The last quotation seems to imply that an animal constitutes the
original and real sacrificial material, whereas everything else counts
as a substitute. However, not all Jews may have looked at it this

---

[18] Lev 5:11; 12:8.

[19] Ps 141:2; 119:108; 51:19. Our interpretation is indebted to Menahem Haran,
"Temple and Community in Ancient Israel," in M.V. Fox, ed., *Temple in Society*
(Winona Lake: Eisenbrauns, 1988) 17–25, see 22.

[20] Midrash Tanhumah Buber, Tsaw 8:9b, as quoted in G.C. Montefiore et al.,
A Rabbinic Anthology (New York: Schocken, 1974) 346. Lenience in Jewish sacrificial
practice is discussed in Gershon Brin, *Studies in Biblical Law* (Sheffield: Sheffield
Academic Press, 1994) 74–81. For alternatives to sacrifice among Second Temple
Essenes, Pharisees, and Christians, see also Dennis Green, "To '. . . send up, like
the smoke of incense, the works of the Law.' The Similarity of Views on an
Alternative to Temple Sacrifice by Three Jewish Sectarian Movements of the Late
Second Temple Period," in Matthew Dillon (ed.), *Religion in the Ancient World. New
Themes and Approaches* (Amsterdam: Hakkert, 1996) 165–175.

way. The French scholar Alfred Marx has suggested that in early Judaism there was an emphasis on the unbloody part of the sacrifice, and possibly certain circles saw it as more important than the actual animal sacrifice.[21] In the cultural world in which early Judaism developed, a certain opposition to animal sacrifice and its replacement by offering of bread and drink was known. This was the ritual option of some of the ancient Zoroastrians whose god Ahura Mazda was recognized as the state god of the Achaemenid empire. According to inscriptional evidence dating from ca. 500 BCE, Ahura Mazda was honored with daily gifts of bread and wine.[22] At least some Jews admired and emulated Zoroastrian monotheistic belief, insistence on ritual purity, and expectation of resurrection after death. They would even go as far as adopting a vegetarian diet. While the Zoroastrian connection with Jewish Temple ritual and its understanding by those who practiced it remains conjectural, there is evidence for the prominence of the libation rite that formed the conclusion to both the public and the private sacrifices. The oldest description we have of public sacrificial worship at the Temple refers to the high priest who "held out his hand for the cup and poured a drink offering of the blood of the grape; he poured it out at the foot of the altar" (Sir 50:15). The description seems to imply that the gesture of pouring out "the blood of the grape" was more visible and more solemn than the sprinkling of the animal blood (not mentioned at all in this source). One of the psalms refers to a private sacrifice of thanksgiving as follows: "I will lift up the cup of salvation and call on the name of the Lord . . . I will offer to you a thanksgiving sacrifice" (Ps 116:13.17). Here, the gesture of presenting the cup of wine can sum up the entire celebration.

3. Why did Jesus design this new form of sacrifice?

It is tempting to see Jesus as the prophet who wanted to bring the Temple ritual and its spiritual benefits within the reach of the poor who could not afford to buy and sacrifice a lamb. It is also tempting

---

[21] Alfred Marx, *Les offrandes végétales dans l'Ancien Testament* (Leiden: Brill, 1994) 143–65.

[22] Heidemarie Koch, "Zur Religion der Achämeniden," *Zeitschrift für die alttestamentliche Wissenschaft* 100 (1988) 393–405. The once popular idea that the prophet Zarathustra rejected animal sacrifice altogether is no longer maintained by scholarship.

to see Jesus as the legislator who abolished animal sacrifice, replacing it by simpler, unbloody gifts, thus (perhaps unknowingly) adopting Zarathustra's attitude and promoting the Persian prophet's ritual reform. However attractive these interpretations may be, they are based on ideas foreign to the mentality of Jesus and his early followers. We have to look for different reasons why Jesus felt he should design a new program of sacrifice.

While the well-known gospel legend places Jesus' birth in Bethlehem, a small town near Jerusalem, Jesus was a Galilean, born and raised in the northern part of Palestine. To be a Galilean meant being recognized by one's particular dialect, and by one's lack of interest in the priestly worship celebrated at the far-away Jerusalem Temple. Jesus seems to have belonged to those Galileans who refused to conform to the priestly demands. Horrified at the thought of expressing the relationship to God in a monetary transaction, he opposed the way public sacrifice was organized.[23]

Private sacrifices, by contrast, meant much for Jesus. During his lifetime, his followers, or at least those who listened to him, went to the Temple to offer their sacrifices. In one instance, after a healing, Jesus sent the healed person to the Temple: he did not tell him not to bother about sacrificing. Rather, he would instruct him: "Go, show yourself to the priest, and offer the gift that Moses commanded" (Matt 8:4). Jesus respected the law that prescribed a series of offerings that reintegrate a formerly "leprous" and "unclean" person into full membership of the community (Lev 14). He addressed all those who wished to sacrifice and insisted on a very particular preparation: the restoration of social harmony among people. This injunction is contained in a well-known passage from the Sermon on the Mount: "So when you are offering your gift at the altar, if you remember that your brother has something against you, leave your gift there before the altar and go; first be reconciled to your brother, and then come and offer your gift" (Matt 5:24–25). Disharmony would spoil the sacrifice, make it ineffective, and presumably offend God, provoking his wrath. Here the attitude of Jesus echoes the psalmist's conviction that only someone "who has clean hands and a pure heart" can legitimately sacrifice in the Temple (Ps 24:4).[24]

---

[23] This seem to be the implication of Matt 17:24–27; see Chilton, *The Temple of Jesus*, 129.

[24] In Ps 24:3, to "stand in the Lord's holy place" seems to be a technical expression for the sacrificing layman's presence in the Temple.

Jesus, as we saw, accepted the institution of animal sacrifice. He also endorsed the biblical legislation regulating it. But he had his own ideas about the personal situation of the sacrificer. He criticized the procedures involved with the actual offering at the Temple. His critical stance culminated in a dramatic action generally referred to as his "cleansing" of the Temple.

All four gospels report how Jesus, in an angry demonstration, disrupted the transactions at the Temple.[25] Mark's report is believed to be the oldest one:

> Then they came to Jerusalem. And he entered the Temple and began to drive out those who were selling and those who were buying in the Temple, and he overturned the tables of the money changers and the seats of those who sold doves; and he would not allow anyone to carry a vessel through the Temple. He was teaching and saying, "Is it not written, 'My house shall be called a house of prayer for all the nations'? But you have made it a den of robbers." And when the chief priests and the scribes heard it, they kept looking for a way to kill him; for they were afraid of him, because the whole crowd was spell-bound by his teaching. And when evening came, Jesus and his disciples went out of the city. (Mark 11:15–19)

While historians would generally agree that the report reflects a historical event, they are less sure about what actually happened and what Jesus' intention may have been. For readers unfamiliar with the cultural and religious world of ancient Judaism, the incident suggests that the market place had spilled over into the Temple in the way it often invaded the interiors of medieval cathedrals. In his dramatic action, Jesus restored the original function of the Temple, making it a house of prayer again. However, this reading ignores the cultural setting of the report. The "buying and selling" does not refer to just any transaction done in a market place; rather, we have to think of the buying and selling of sacrificial animals which include the pigeons mentioned in the passage. Does the report indicate, then, Jesus' rejection of sacrifice (for which animals had to be bought) and his preference for the more spiritual act of prayer?

Two facts militate against this interpretation, making us aware of quite different implications. As we have seen, Jesus was far from condemning private sacrifice as such; in fact, he endorsed and even recommended it. It also seems that the selling of animals had been introduced into the Temple precinct only recently and did not meet

---

[25] The four reports: Matt 21:12–13; Mark 11:15–19; Luke 19:45–48; John 2:13–17.

with general approval.[26] Caiaphas, high priest between ca. 18 and 36 CE, was apparently the first to authorize the sale of sacrificial animals within the Temple precincts, presumably within the outer court. What Jesus wanted, then, was to change what went on in the Temple, to bring it closer to the ideal of unmediated, direct worship of God. He invoked a passage found in the prophecy of Zechariah: "There shall no longer be traders in the house of the Lord of hosts" (Zech 14:21). His bold action may have appealed to popular sentiment, even among the Temple personnel, so that no one bothered or dared to take action against him. If they had indeed been offended, one would expect the Temple police to have taken immediate action, and Jesus would have been challenged and arrested on the spot.

We could stop here and admit that any further interpretation borders on mere speculation. Recent scholarship, however, seems to permit at least tentative suggestions about what Jesus had in mind when "cleansing" or "occupying" the Temple.[27] Although some details of our reconstruction may seem unusual, they can be put forward as at least plausible.

By Jesus' day, laypeople wishing to present a private sacrifice seem to have been reduced to the role of paying sponsors. They would pay, in the court of the Gentiles, for a sacrificial animal which was then handed over to the Temple personnel. Sponsors would probably wait for some time until they got certain parts of the slaughtered victim (in the case of so-called peace offerings and thank offerings). Paying, laying a hand on the animal's head, and receiving part of a slaughtered animal: this was all that happened in the foreground. Slaves and women sacrificers were not allowed to perform the laying-on of a hand.[28] The actual sacrificing—the slaughter, the collection of the blood, the ritual disposal of blood and fat, sometimes even the laying-on of a hand—happened far away, hardly visible to the sponsor. Not being permitted to enter the Temple's court of the priests (where the animals were slaughtered and where the altar was located), he or she stood in the "court of the Israelites" and simply watched: this was all that a sacrificing man or woman[29]

---

[26] Victor Eppstein, "The Historicity of the Gospel Account of the Cleansing of the Temple." *Zeitschrift für die neutestamentliche Wissenschaft* 55 (1964) 42–58 reconstructs how the selling of animals was introduced into the Temple.

[27] Chilton, *The Temple of Jesus*, 91–111, and *A Feast of Meanings*, 57–63.

[28] Mishna, Menahot 9:8.

[29] When a woman's sacrifice was performed, she had access to the "court of the

could do. This reduced, minimal involvement of lay people naturally made sense: it facilitated the performance of a large number of sacrifices by priestly specialists, especially on festival days when the Temple became crowded. The practice also kept non-Jews out of the sacred areas, while allowing their sacrificial gifts, simplified to payment or the handing-over of an animal, to be accepted. Now, Jesus objected to reducing the sacrificial procedure to a financial transaction in which someone would pay for a sheep and then have little to do with the actual sacrifice. In ancient times the actual slaughtering had been the task of the offering person himself; a priest would step in only if the offerer found himself in a state of ritual impurity.[30] For Jesus, God's people were pure,[31] and thus should have had more involvement with the sacrificial procedure than the Temple establishment granted them. People should first of all buy their animals on the Mount of Olives, where the market was located prior to its transferral to the Temple area itself. They should actually own their victim.

Sacrificers should also be present at the actual slaughtering and the ensuing ritual acts. Tradition acknowledges that someone's offering cannot be made "while he is not standing by its side."[32] But mere presence, in the eyes of Jesus and other teachers, would not suffice. We can invoke the Talmudic tradition of Rabbi Hillel, almost a contemporary of Jesus, who also objected to the impersonal, clericalized manner of sacrifice.[33] According to Hillel, offerings should not simply and informally be given to the priests for slaughtering. Rather, the owners should always, even during busy festival days, lay their hand on their animals' heads prior to handing them over to the officiating priest. This ritual gesture, prescribed by law (Lev 3:2), apparently indicated both the ownership of the lamb and served as a gesture of offering. Hillel's suggestion made such an impact on

---

Israelites": Tosefta, Arakhin 2:1—"A women would not be seen in the court [of the Israelites] except during the offering of her sacrifice."

[30] Lay slaughtering of sacrificial animal: Lev 3:2; priestly slaughtering in case of lay impurity: 2 Chron 30:17. While the Mishna (Zebahim 3:1) and Josephus' account of sacrificial practice in *Jewish Antiquities* 3:226–27 seem to imply that in the first century CE the layman killed his victim, Philo in *Special Laws* 2:145–46 denies this; presumably, practice varied.

[31] Mark 7:14–23.

[32] Mishna, Taanit 4:2.

[33] Babylonian Talmud, Betsah/Yom Tob 20a. As Jacob Milgrom pointed out to the author, this text implies the omission of the laying-on of a hand only in the case of private mandatory sacrifices offered during festivals.

one Baba ben Butha that he had large numbers of animals brought
to the Temple and gave them to those willing to lay a hand on them
in advance of sacrifice.

Jesus, like Hillel, wanted people to participate more in their offering.
As a theurgist involved with arcane sacramental procedures,[34] he had
a strong sense of the need to perform a ritual in the proper way.
If people bought their animals on the Mount of Olives (rather than
in the Temple area), they would actually own them and bring them
to the Temple themselves. Jesus may have been aware of the strict
rule governing the foremost private sacrifice, that of Passover. The
law prescribed that prior to offering the Passover lamb, the sacrificer
must own it for four days.[35] Owning the victim, then, must have
been important for Jesus. While we do not know anything about
Jesus' view of the laying-on of a hand on the animal's head, we can
at least speculate about a formula with which he wanted people to
designate a sacrifice as their own. Perhaps they should offer the various parts of the slaughtered and cut-up animal using the formula,
"This is my body," i.e., here I bring my sacrificial body; it belongs
to me and I place it onto your altar. Similarly, they should offer
their blood saying, "This is my blood," i.e., here I offer the blood
of my sacrificial victim.

The rest of the story about Jesus and the Temple is quickly told.
Jesus' occupation of the Temple did not lead to any changes in the
traditional ritual procedures. Everything stayed the way the priestly
establishment had determined. His action had no immediate impact;
like Hillel's, it remained an episode remembered by his disciples,
passed on orally, and eventually recorded in a few puzzling lines of
literature.

Although the priestly establishment may have disagreed with Rabbi
Hillel's view on the hand-leaning, we hear of no action against him.
Why, then, were the priests so enraged with Jesus that they wished
to kill him? The reason must be sought in another offense and not
in this one—an act that threatened their very existence.

Historians of early Christianity have long since argued that Jesus
was killed for having committed an act of provocative disobedience
to Israel's sacred law, an act of blasphemy punishable by death.

---

[34] I.e., baptism (John 4:1, v. 2 being a gloss) and initiation into meeting dead
prophets (Mark 9:2–6); see Lang, *Sacred Games*, 105–6.294–95.
[35] Exod 12:3.6.

Bruce Chilton has persuasively argued that this act had to do with Jesus' disillusionment with Temple sacrifice.[36] After realizing the impossibility of reforming the sacrificial procedure at the Temple, he came to oppose private sacrifice. He thought of it as procedurally deficient and hence ineffective and invalid. He was not the only one to protest against ritual abuses surrounding sacrifice: the Essenes rejected Temple worship as then practiced (though for reasons different from those of Jesus: they held the contemporary high priesthood to be illegitimate).

Unlike the Essenes, Jesus did not consider sacrificial worship as impossible to perform. Rather, he created his own substitute for it. He continued the already well-established tradition of joyous meals. These he shared with large crowds, with "publicans and sinners," with his wealthy sponsors, and with the narrower circle of his disciples. He began to introduce into these meals a new and unprecedented ritual action, one that involved the use of sacrificial language. Jesus declared the eating of bread and wine a new sacrifice. Bread would stand for the sacrificial body of the slaughtered animal and wine for the blood tossed at the foot of the altar. The declarative formulae, "This is my body" and "This is my blood," designate bread and wine as unbloody substitutes for private sacrifice. We must beware of reading any hidden meanings into this symbolic gesture. Bread and wine neither take on special, magical qualities, nor is there any link to the (sacrificial) death of Jesus. A simple and straightforward declaration said over bread and wine had, in the minds of Jesus and his followers, *replaced* private sacrifice as performed at the Temple.

The priestly establishment could have ignored a Galilean rabbi's private cult. Yet, they vented their anger at him and were successful in their plan to have him killed.

The rest of the story is known. Jesus introduced his new ritual in secret among the most intimate of his friends. He practiced it occasionally if not frequently, and the new ritual meal demonstrated his decision not to live in compromise with the Temple establishment of his day. The authorities got wind of it. Wishing to be sure about what was going on, they looked for a witness. A man called Judas betrayed his master's "sacrifice." Jesus had added to and indeed surpassed his earlier extravagant behavior, which had already led to accusations

---

[36] Chilton, *The Temple of Jesus*, 154, and "The Trial of Jesus Reconsidered," in Bruce Chilton and Craig A. Evans, *Jesus in Context* (Leiden: Brill, 1997) 481–500.

of blasphemy.[37] Now that the crime of blasphemy had been established definitively, the Temple authorities had little difficulty having Jesus executed by order of the Roman procurator, Pontius Pilate.

Our tentative reconstruction visibly departs from what we find in the gospels. This departure can hardly be avoided if what we are looking for is the true course of events. The account in the gospels blends reliable information with legendary accretions and shapes them so that they speak meaningfully to Christians of the second or third generation. Yet, there are enough historical facts that can be discerned in the gospel account of a "Last Supper" to suggest some kind of introduction of a new ritual. Viewed against the background of Jesus' original endorsement and eventual rejection of private sacrifice, his ritual of bread and wine makes sense.

In the early nineteenth century, Chateaubriand in his celebrated *Génie du christianisme* argued that "among all the peoples of the earth, religious ceremonies derive from sacrifice."[38] Stated in this very general way, Chateaubriand's claim will not convince contemporary specialists. As far as Christianity is concerned, however, he has made a valid point. In Christianity, "les cérémonies religieuses sont nées du sacrifice."

BIBLIOGRAPHY

Bonnet, Hans. *Reallexikon der ägyptischen Religionsgeschichte.* Berlin: de Gruyter, 1952, 424–26: "Libation."

Brin, Gershon. *Studies in Biblical Law.* Sheffield: Sheffield Academic Press, 1994.

Chateaubriand, François-René de. *Oeuvres complètes.* Paris: Pourrat, 1836, vol. 16.

Chilton, Bruce D. *The Temple of Jesus: His Sacrificial Program within a Cultural History of Sacrifice.* University Park: Pennsylvania State University Press, 1992.

———. *A Feast of Meanings: Eucharistic Theologies from Jesus through Johannine Circles.* Leiden: Brill, 1994.

———. "The Trial of Jesus Reconsidered," in Bruce Chilton and Craig A. Evans, *Jesus in Context.* Leiden: Brill, 1997, 481–500.

Eppstein, Victor. "The Historicity of the Gospel Account of the Cleansing of the Temple." *Zeitschrift für die neutestamentliche Wissenschaft* 55 (1964) 42–58.

Evans-Pritchard, Edward E. *Nuer Religion.* Oxford: Oxford University Press, 1956.

Gese, Hartmut. *Essays on Biblical Theology.* Trans. Keith Crim. Minneapolis: Augsburg 1981.

Green, Dennis. "To '. . . send up, like the smoke of incense, the works of the Law.' The Similarity of Views on an Alternative to Temple Sacrifice by Three Jewish

---

[37] Mark 2:7; 14:64.
[38] See above, n. 1.

Sectarian Movements of the Late Second Temple Period." In Matthew Dillon (ed.), *Religion in the Ancient World. New Themes and Approaches*. Amsterdam: Hakkert, 1996, 165–175.

Haran, Menahem. "Temple and Community in Ancient Israel." In Michael V. Fox (ed.), *Temple in Society*. Winona Lake: Eisenbrauns, 1988, 17–25.

Koch, Heidemarie. "Zur Religion der Achämeniden." *Zeitschrift für die alttestamentliche Wissenschaft* 100 (1988), 393–405.

Lang, Bernhard. *Sacred Games. A History of Christian Worship*. New Haven: Yale University Press, 1997.

Marx, Alfred. *Les offrandes végétales dans l'Ancien Testament*. Leiden: Brill, 1994.

Milgrom, Jacob. *Numbers: The JPS Torah Commentary*. Philadelphia: Jewish Publication Society, 1990.

Montefiore, C.G. et al. *A Rabbinic Anthology*. New York: Schocken, 1974.

O'Flaherty, Wendy Doniger. *Other People's Myths*. New York: Macmillan, 1988.

THE CHRISTIAN EXEGESIS OF THE SCAPEGOAT
BETWEEN JEWS AND PAGANS*

Daniel Johannes Stökl

> Do you not think it irreverent to liken the Lord to
> goats?[1]

1. *Introduction*

The sacrificial theory of René Girard, presented in his books *La violence et le sacré* and *Le bouc émissaire*, has been a focus of attention,
whether one agrees with his main theory, an amplification of the
Freudian myth, or not.[2] He surveys various rituals in various places
and at various times that treat a victim similar to the Levitical scapegoat and with a similar atoning function. In the book of Leviticus,
however, it is very clear that the ritual refers not to a human being
but to an animal, a goat. Strangely enough, most of Girard's scapegoats are not animals but *human* beings. Girard might have supposed
that the appellation 'scapegoat' would be more easily understood by

---

* I would like to express my gratitude to a number of people who read earlier
versions of this article and made valuable suggestions (without necessarily subscrib-
ing to its contents); Dina Ben Ezra, Katell Berthelot, Prof. Hans-Dieter Betz, Jeff
Brand, Prof. Cristiano Grottanelli, Dr. Jeff Hodges, Prof. Christoph Markschies,
Lukas Mühlethaler, Prof. Lorenzo Perrone, Dr. Seth Sanders, Dr. David Satran,
and Prof. Guy Stroumsa. I would like to thank especially Dr. Clemens Leonhard,
for discussing the Syriac texts. I am much indebted to Jennie Feldman and Evelyn
Katrak for correcting the English. Remaining mistakes were introduced after their
revisions. Last but not least, I would like to thank all the conference participants for
the very lively and constructive discussion following the presentation of this paper.
The preparation of this article has been generously sponsored by the Dr. Nelly
Hahne-Stiftung, and the Minerva foundation Germany. The article is related to my
Ph.D. thesis under the guidance of Prof. Guy Stroumsa on the topic "The Impact
of Yom Kippur on Early Christianity", which has just been completed and sub-
mitted to the Hebrew University.

[1] Εἶτα οὔ σοι δοκεῖ βλάσφημον τὸ τράγοις τὸν δεσπότην ἀφομοιοῦν; (Theodoret of
Cyrus, *Eranistes Dialogos* 3:253). I used the edition of the Greek text by Ettlinger (1975),
here pp. 210:19–20. The translation used here is by Blomfield Jackson (1892: 226).

[2] Girard (1982 and 1971). He was not the first to use the term "scapegoat" to
characterize certain rituals with human beings as victims—Sir James Frazer called
one volume of his 3rd edition of the *Golden Bough* "The Scapegoat." (see footnote 85).

a modern Western audience than for example the Greek term *pharmakos*, which *is* concerned with human victims.[3] He could be reasonably sure that the subsumption of human sacrifices under the scapegoat ritual would be acceptable to his readers, because 'scapegoat' has become a fixed term in Western thought. But since when? Given that Girard's central chapter talks about Jesus as scapegoat, one would expect that the analogy between the death of a human being (Jesus) and the scapegoat ritual was first drawn in the New Testament and through this entered the Western *imaginaire*, its collective repertoire of motifs. However, as is well known, the Christian canon does *not* refer to Jesus as scapegoat. When and how did the scapegoat enter the Western *imaginaire* as a category connoting a type of *human* atonement sacrifice, if not in the New Testament?

The present paper tries to answer this question by investigating the place of the Yom Kippur scapegoat ritual in Early Christian exegesis and its historical and ideological context. The special focus is a proposed explanation for the development of the Christian exegesis of the scapegoat in its changing Jewish and pagan context.[4]

1.1 *The temple ritual of the scapegoat*

According to the evidence of Philo and the rabbinic tract *Yoma*, Yom Kippur was the most important Jewish festival at the time of the Second Temple and thereafter.[5] Its details are complicated, but the main parts of the ritual consist of two clearly distinct movements of the two goats, the sacrificial goat and the scapegoat, one set against the other. The first movement is centripetal: The holiest and purest human being, the high priest, enters the purest and holiest spot on earth, the adyton of Jerusalem's temple, bearing the blood of the

---

Girard's controversial theory provoked a number of responses, both positive and negative; an overview of some of them, especially those of biblical scholars, can be found in North (1985).

[3] On this ritual see below.

[4] Following are some of the previous studies on patristic exegesis of the scapegoat: Sabourin (1959); Louf (1960); Signer (1990); compare also Lyonnet and Léopold (1970), pp. 182–184 and 269–289. Studies dealing with a part of the tradition are Prigent (1961); Perrone (1980), pp. 67–72; Zani (1982); Guinot (1988); Tampellini (1998), pp. 175–184. The unpublished dissertations by Norman H. Young (1973) and Scullion (1991) focus on biblical and inter-testamental sources, but they also have short appendices on a part of the patristic exegeses (Young 1973: 384 ff.; Scullion 1991:298–305). Finally, the following articles have been most inspiring for my research on this topic: Schwartz (1983); Grabbe (1987); and Versnel (1989).

[5] Philo, *de specialibus legibus* 2:193–194, *de congressu eruditionis gratia* 89. The name of the rabbinic tract for Yom Kippur is *Yoma*, i.e. *the* day.

sacrificial goat.[6] The second movement is centrifugal: the scapegoat is sent from the temple into the desert. The focus here is on this second part.

The biblical description is quite sketchy compared to the much more detailed rabbinic accounts.[7] Most of the details of the scapegoat ritual can be cross-checked with external evidence and can be accepted as reflecting a historical description of the Temple ritual.[8] The two goats had to be similar in appearance, height and value. After a lottery, the high priest put a red ribbon around the horn of the scapegoat and placed it in front of the tabernacle.[9] The sacrificial goat was slaughtered and its blood brought into the holy of holies.[10] The high priest then placed both his hands on the scapegoat, confessed the sins of his people and sent the scapegoat out into the desert, accompanied by a 'prepared man'. On its way out of the temple through the curious crowd, the scapegoat was apparently abused and cursed by some.[11]

---

[6] For a treatment of some mythopoeic aspects of the 'centripetal' part in Jewish and Christian sources of the Second Temple period see now Stökl (1999).

[7] Compare the rabbinic tract *Yoma* in the Mishna, the Tosefta and the Talmudim. For the Mishna I used the critical edition by Rosenberg (1995). Göran Larsson edited the first part of the Tosefta in his dissertation (1980). There is no critical edition of the Talmudic tracts, but Friedrich Avemarie's richly annotated German translation of the Palestinian Talmud (1995) is based on the best manuscripts.

[8] Lev 16; 23:26–32; Num 19:7–11; 1 Enoch 10:4–8; Josephus *Antiquitates Iudaicae* 3:240–243; Philo *de specialibus legibus* 1:186–188, 2:193–203, *de Plantatione* 61; mYom (esp. 4–6) and its parallels in the Tosefta, Sifra on Leviticus and the Talmudim; Barn 7. The literature on Lev 16 is vast. I refer only to the commentary by Jacob Milgrom (1994) and Giovanni Deiana (1994). Attempts to reconstruct the 'historical' temple ritual were made by Hruby (1965); and Tabori 1995 (Hebrew). Cf. also the very useful commentaries in Larsson (1980) and Avemarie (1995) and the valuable article by Safrai (1990). To the best of my knowledge Gedalyahu Alon (1967) was the only scholar to accept the information contained in the Early Christian traditions for a reconstruction of the Temple ritual (in Hebrew). On geographical *realia* see August Strobel (1987).

[9] Another part of the red ribbon was fastened to the sacrificial goat.

[10] Of course, the centripetal movement as a whole included also the burning of the incense and the sprinkling of the blood of the calf in the holy of holies.

[11] Philo *De specialibus legibus* 1:188 (ἐφ᾽ ἑαυτῷ κομίζοντα τὰς ὑπὲρ τῶν πλημμελησάντων ἀράς); cf. also Barn 7:7–9. The rabbinic sources relate, that either the Babylonians (mYom 6:4) or the Alexandrians (bYom 66b) pulled the hair of the goat and expressed the wish to send their sins away with it as fast as possible— טול וצא טול וצא; according to the Palestinian Talmud (yYom 6:43c [6:4]) the Alexandrians said: "How long are you going to keep the corruption (קלקלה) among us?" see Sokoloff (1990), *s.v.* Schwartz (1983: 263 footnote 15) refers to Genesis Rabba 20:3 (on Gen 3:14; Theodor-Albeck [183: 4–5]) as an example of a possible confusion between קלקלה (corruption) and קללה (curse).

The 'prepared man' led the scapegoat along a certain route to a precipice in the desert called *Beyt Haroro* or some similar name.[12] He took part of the red ribbon and fastened it to a rock and finally killed the scapegoat by pushing it over the precipice.[13] The man had to wait until the evening and to wash himself and his clothes before he could enter the city again. Such is my reconstruction of the ritual according to the account in the biblical and extra-biblical sources.[14]

1.2   *The transformations following the destruction of the temple*

With the destruction of the temple in 70 CE, the Temple ritual lost its natural geography. The centre of Jewish worship shifted from the destroyed temple to the synagogues, and its ritual was transformed into a bloodless service of liturgical memory.[15] The most Temple-centered ritual of Yom Kippur was dramatically re-enacted in the Yom Kippur ritual in the *Seder Ha'Avoda*.[16] The atoning force of the

---

[12] mYom 6:8; *Targum Pseudo-Jonathan Leviticus* 16:10, 21b–22. On the different spellings in the Mishna and the Talmudim cf. *Diqduqe Sofrim* 4:193–194 and Rosenberg (1995) Vol. 1 p. 76. For an interpretation of the similar names of the strange location Dadouæl / Doudaæl in *1 Enoch* 10:4 and the rabbinic בית חרורו / הרורו / הדורו / הדורי see already Geiger (1864), here: pp. 200 f; Charles 1912; cf. Milik's two etymological explanations of the name in *DJD* (1961) 2:111 f and in (1976), pp. 29 f; and the responses of Molenberg (1984), here p. 143, footnote 34) and Lester Grabbe (1987: 155, footnote 6) to his theses. Strobel rejects the identification of the two places (1987: 149–151).

[13] Cf. the sources cited in the preceding footnote and Philo, *de Plantatione* 61.

[14] According to a statement in *Massekhet Shevu'ot* the theological functions of the two goats were strictly distinct. While the sacrificial goat cleansed and rededicated the temple and its holy vessels from the impurity collected through various ritual violations, the scapegoat expiated the sins of the people (על זדון טומאה מקדש וקדשיו שעיר הנעשה בפנים ויום הכפורים מכפרין. ועל שאר עבירות שבתורה הקלוח והחמורות הזדונות והשגגות, הודע ולא הודע, עשה ולא תעשה, כרתות ומיתות בית דין שעיר המשתלה מכפר. [mShev 1:6]). In my opinion it is rather anachronistic to suppose that this statement was *the* understanding of the ritual of the goats *in the era of the Temple*, as Kraus supposes (1991A: 164–167).

[15] Of course, this transformation of the Temple cult was not all of a sudden and its beginnings are ascertainable much earlier, at least in Hellenistic Judaism, from the translations of the Septuagint starting in the third century BCE to its acme in Philo's writings.

[16] This formulation is Rabbi Ze'ev Gotthold's. For an analysis of the dynamics of the relation between myth and ritual in the *Seder HaAvoda* see Michael D. Swartz (1997). For an analysis of the hymns of the *SederHaAvoda* compare the (unpublished) dissertation by Maleakhi (Jerusalem 1974, in Hebrew). In the discussion of this paper at the 1999 Taubes Center Conference, Prof. Arthur Green suggested not to turn down *a priori* the possibility that the liturgical re-ritualization of the Temple service in the Piyut might be also in response to the development of Christian liturgy.

blood and the dignity of the high priest were transferred to the uttering of God's name and the power allegedly dwelling in the high
priest's garments.[17] One could call this radical transformation a twofold
revolution, hermeneutical and liturgical, with the two parts mutually
dependent.[18]

A parallel revolution, also hermeneutical and liturgical, took place
within developing Christianity, which 'cooked' the Old Testament
and 'spiced' it for Greek, Roman and other non-Jewish tongues.[19]
Yom Kippur, too, became part of the menu.

In the Christian exegesis of Leviticus 16, Jesus is usually depicted
in the two main movements mentioned above: First, as high priest
offering his own blood in the holy of holies; and second, as scapegoat cleansing the world by carrying away its sins. The first picture
is already found in the formative collection of Early Christianity, the
New Testament; as an elaborate description in the Epistle to the
Hebrews and as an allusion in Paul's Epistle to the Romans, two of
the most central passages for later Christian theology.[20] However,
while the scapegoat may stand in the background of some New
Testament passages, the New Testament never refers explicitly to
Jesus as 'scapegoat'.[21] Nevertheless, the absence of a canonical precedent did not prevent the Church Fathers from promoting the scapegoat as *typos* of Christ to a *topos*.

---

[17] Cf. the unpublished lectures of Michael D. Swartz in Jerusalem and Bar Ilan
1998; for the general theory of the priestly origin of early liturgical poetry see e.g.
Yosef Yahalom (1996, in Hebrew), pp. 56–58.

[18] Eventually, at the beginning of the Gaonic period the ritual of *Kapparot* became
popular, though controversial to this day, and re-introduced the element of blood
into Jewish worship. Cf. Lauterbach (1935).

[19] This expression should not be understood as having an anti-Christian conno-
tation, i.e. to forge the OT. For similar language cf. Origen *ComIoh* 10:18 (103–105).
For this text and the revolutionary character of Early Christian hermeneutics cf.
Stroumsa (1999).

[20] See especially Heb 9 and Rom 3:25. For a discussion of the relationship
between these passages and Yom Kippur compare Young (1973: 155–339), Kraus
(1991A:45–70, 168–193, 235–259; 1991B: 167–168) and the unpublished M.A. thesis of Daniel Stökl (1997).

[21] Young discusses Jo 1:29; Gal 3:13; 2 Cor 5:21; 1 Pet 2:24; and Rev (1973:
340–368). Daniel R. Schwartz (1983) suggests Gal 3:13. One might also consider
Heb 13:12–13.

In several of these passages it is difficult to distinguish between the influence of
Is 53 and the influence of the scapegoat. However, the two traditions may very
well be related. As Baruch Levine remarks, the concept of the Suffering Servant is
"the most dramatic application of the scapegoat phenomenon to humans"—Levine
(1985: 128). Cf. also Schwartz (1983: 262–263).

1.3   *The thesis*

The gap between the canonical and the exegetical tradition, i.e. the popularity of the scapegoat typology despite the absence of an explicit precedent in the New Testament, may be explained by the essence of the Christian hermeneutic revolution as a two-tiered proselytising movement, between the Jewish roots and the pagan audience.

First, Christians chose to prove the validity and antiquity of their faith by Christianising the Old Testament through typological and allegorical exegesis. Second, the recurrence of the annual Jewish day of atonement, the rabbinic transformation of Yom Kippur in the fast and the worship of the synagogue, attracted many Christians.[22] Consequently, the Church Fathers had to propagate and embellish their interpretation of Leviticus 16 in the framework of their theology of atonement—which was based on Christ's once-and-for-all sacrifice—as the proper spiritual understanding, as against the fleshly interpretation of the Jews. Third, the Church Fathers had to convince non-Jews in their own, unbiblical language regarding the reasoning behind the "foolishness of the cross", and had to make the rationale of Jesus' atoning death manifest. In doing this, these Christians continued the line of the first Greek ethnographers as scholars of religion using Greek parallels to Christian ideas to make themselves understood. Therefore, some Church Fathers compare Jesus' atoning death not only to the Levitical scapegoat but also to the well-known *pharmakos* ritual and related myths. Fourth, the Church Fathers had to fight a polytheistic interpretation of Yom Kippur put forward by Emperor Julian. Following his polemic opus *Against the Galileans*, most of the longer Christian exegeses emphasise the unity of the scapegoat's destiny with God.

In my opinion it was these four issues—the Christianization of the Jewish Bible, the 'dangerous' attraction of the Jewish Yom Kippur, the popularity of the pagan *pharmakos* ritual, and later also the reaction on the polytheistic interpretation by Julian—that motivated the Christian propagation of the scapegoat typology.

I will now deal briefly with the three main Christian exegeses as witnesses of the Christian *imaginaire* of the scapegoat. I will then try to pinpoint the place and development of the Christian interpretations between Jews and pagans. I conclude with comments on some of the implications.

---

[22] On this cf. also Stökl (2001).

2. *Scapegoat typologies in the Fathers*

2.1 *Types of exegesis*

I would like, at the outset, to clarify briefly the distinction I draw between typological and allegorical forms of exegesis. While allegory seeks to reveal deeper wisdom by translating concrete images to an ideal realm, typology connects the textual images of a canon to events in history.[23] Typological exegesis becomes *mythological* the moment that not only the *typos* is understood as prophesy of the historical event but the roles of the event and the *typos* are exchanged and the event is subjected to a *typos* of the mythological text. For example, there is an important difference between the following claims:

a) that the real meaning of Leviticus 16 is a prophecy of the atoning death of the Messiah,

b) that on his death Jesus entered the heavenly holy of holies with his blood.

A further hermeneutical subgroup of the typological form is the adoption of *eschatological* implications of the canonical image—in our example: from the moment of entering the heavenly holy of holies, Jesus has been interceding for our sake, and he will continue to do so until he leaves the *adyton* at the end of days.

2.2 *The Christian transformation of the scapegoat*

The 'holistic Christological' exegesis—Christ being simultaneously sacrificial goat and scapegoat

The first explicit scapegoat typology appears in the *Epistle of Barnabas*, probably around 100 CE.[24] The typology belongs to an earlier, probably Jewish-Christian testimonial source that also inspired Justin Martyr, Tertullian[25] and, on a different level, Hippolytus and Ishodad

---

[23] Compare the classical definition of Goppelt (1939: 18–19).

[24] The most recent introductory discussion to this date can be found in Carleton Paget (1994) and Hvalvik, (1996). For the history of tradition compare besides Prigent (1961) and Carleton Paget (1994) also Skarsaune (1987: 307–313). I could not consult Robert Kraft's unpublished dissertation (Harvard 1961), but most of its results should be included in Prigent and Kraft (1972).

[25] Barn 7; Justin *Dialogus cum Tryphone* 40:4–5 (Marcovich 1997); Tertullian *Adversus Iudaeos* 14:9–10 (CCSL 2/2) and *Adversus Marcionem* 3:7:7–8 (SC 399); Barnabas' scapegoat typology has been transmitted solely through Barnabas' source, and had no direct impact even on those exegetes who honoured the *Letter of Barnabas* as canonical, e.g. Clement of Alexandria or Origen.

of Merv.[26] Since the typology contains halakhic information, it has
usually been defined as a Jewish-Christian tradition.[27] This exegesis
is a typology in the 'Geertzian' sense in that it takes as its reference
not the biblical text, but a report about the ritual as it was practised in the temple.[28]

Justin and Tertullian compare the two goats to Jesus' two *parou-
siai*: in his passion and upon his glorious return.[29] On that account,
I would call this typology eschatological. The similarity of the goats
enables the Jews to recognise Christ at his second *parousia* as the
same person as the one whom they crucified. The abuse and cursing parallel Jesus' passion. The curious red ribbon functions as a
second means of recognition. It symbolises the crown of thorns of
Jesus' passion and the priestly scarlet robe on his return.[30]

---

[26] The red ribbon fastened to the scapegoat's head is found, too, in Hippolytus
In Prov. fragm. 75 and in an abridged version also in pseudo-Anastasius. This was
noted in Zani (1987), an article, that has remained unnoticed by the recent discussions on Barnabas. The fragment of Hippolytus (and the reference to pseudo-
Anastasius) has been translated and published by Richard (1966: 94). The red ribbon
is mentioned also in a tradition quoted (and rejected) by a Nestorian exegete of
the 9th century, Ishodad of Merv (see Ceslas Van den Eynde [1958] CSCO 179
p. 104 lines 11–15). Clemens Leonhard suggests that parts of Ishodad's anonymous
traditions (at least on Genesis and Psalms) may quote a lost commentary by Theodore
of Mopsuestia. On this important Syriac exegete, whose works contain a treasure
of otherwise lost traditions, cf. Leonhard (2000) and his dissertation, *Ishodad of Merv's
Exegesis of the Psalms 119 and 139–147. A Study of His Interpretation in the Light of the
Syriac Translation of Theodore of Mopsuestia's Commentary* (Diss., Vienna 1999, forthcoming in one of the coming supplement volumes to CSCO). According to Ishodad,
the Nestorian exegetes Mar Narsai (5th century) and his pupils John and Abraham
of Beth-Rabban propose the (good) archangel Michael as the personality behind
the pseudonym Azaz'el (Van den Eynde [1958] CSCO 179, pp. 102–3).
[27] See Alon 1967: 302–305.
[28] Compare Geertz 1973.
[29] For Justin and Tertullian the scapegoat signifies passion, and the sacrificial
goat the return of Jesus Christ. Barnabas' passage, often described as confusing (e.g.
Carleton Paget 1994:137) takes a goat, which according to him was eaten (!), as
referring to the passion and to the Eucharist (7:4–5), and the scapegoat as referring to the passion, too, and to the parousia (7:6–11). Barnabas speaks probably of
three goats, one eaten (cf. mMen 11:7), one burnt and one sent away—on this
question see Alon 1967: 305.
[30] On the importance of the priestly robe (ποδήρης) and the place of the high
priestly ritual of Yom Kippur in a reconstruction of the Early Christian priestly
Messianology cf. Stökl 1999. The differences between the witnesses are substantial
but point to a common source as their origin. While Tertullian certainly knew
Justin's writings, scholarship is divided on the question of his knowledge of Barnabas.
A knowledge of Barnabas is presumed by Tränkle (1964; pp. LXXVI–LXXXII).
Prigent (1968: 108) considers the texts as independent. See Prigent's and Carleton
Paget's (1994: 138–140) commentaries for a detailed analysis of the differences and
agreements. The parallels to the traditions of the *Gospel of Peter* as suggested by
Mara (1975: 21) and Crossan (1988: 115–233) require further investigation.

Various 'bipolar' readings—Origen of Caesarea

Origen expounds his theology of Yom Kippur in the 9th and 10th *Homilies on Leviticus* along three main ideas.[31] First, all sinners need a day of atonement.[32] Second, the *true* Yom Kippur started with Christ's atoning death on Good Friday and will conclude with the end of the world.[33] Finally, for the true Christian, every day is a *dies humiliationis*.[34] This is a development of Philo's concept of Yom Kippur. According to Philo, he who reaches the highest level of religiosity lives every day as if it were Yom Kippur.[35]

Since all of Origen's exegeses are based on an opposition between the bad scapegoat and the good sacrificial goat, I have called this type 'bipolar'.

Origen starts with an *internal ecclesiological allegory* comparing the two goats to two kinds of 'pure' people, i.e. two kinds of Christians.[36] While good Christians do good deeds and purify God's people through their martyrdom, bad Christians, not worthy of martyrdom, have to carry also the sins of the repentant and the penitent.[37] If all members of God's people were uniformly good, there would be no need for a scapegoat.[38]

In an *external ecclesiological allegory*, Origen takes the sacrificial goat and the scapegoat as symbolising the Church and its adversaries (*contrariae*

---

[31] I have used the numbering in the English translation by Barkley (1990) (= *HomLev*). I used the GCS-edition by Baehrens (1920: 417–445). Cf. also the annotated translation by Borret in Sources Chrétiennes (1981).

[32] *Die propitiationis indigent omnes qui peccaverunt* (9:1:1, Baehrens 417:23).

[33] *Haec est propitiationis dies; in qua data est nobis remissio peccatorum, cum 'pascha nostrum immolatus est Christus'* (1 Cor 5:7)" (*HomLev* 10:2:3, Baehrens 443:19–21). Consequently, this day is not only *the true* Yom Kippur but also the true Passover. The end of this Yom Kippur is the end of the world: *dies propitiationis manet nobis usque quo occidat sol, id est usque quo finem mundus accipiat* (*HomLev* 9:5:9; Baehrens 427:18–20). Cf. also *HomLev* 9:5:4, Baehrens 426:3f.

[34] *Omne tibi tempus apertum est totius anni* (*HomLev* 10:2:3; Baehrens 443:27–28). *Immo totius vitae tuae dies habeto ad humiliandam animam tuam* (*HomLev* 10:2:3; Baehrens 443:28—444:1). *Quando ergo non est tibi humiliationis dies, qui Christum sequeris, qui est humilis corde et humilitatis magister?* (*HomLev* 10:2:3; Baehrens 444:2–3).

[35] For this analysis of Yom Kippur in Philo compare Stökl 1997: 18–25. I could not consult Deiana (1987).

[36] Based on the observation that goats are 'clean', he refers to them as the baptized Christians—*HomLev* 9:4:4, Baehrens 424:1–7.

[37] *HomLev* 9:4:3, Baehrens 423:17–20; and *HomLev* 9:3:4, Baehrens 422:19–22 for the good Christians; and *HomLev* 9:4:3, Baehrens 423:20–24 and *HomLev* 9:3:3, Baehrens 422:8–19, 22–27.

[38] *HomLev* 9:3:2 "*Si esset omnis populus Dei sanctus et omnes essent beati, non fierent duae sortes super hircis . . . sed esset sors una et hostia una Domino soli*" (Baehrens 421:23–26).

potestates), i.e. "we" and "the others".[39] This allegory is closely related
to an understanding put forward by Philo, who distinguishes between
worshippers of the Creator and worshippers of the creation.[40] However,
Origen exemplifies this allegory as a *mythological typology* since he
chooses to illustrate the two kinds of people with the two sinners
crucified with Christ.[41] Like the goat of the Lord's lot is sacrificed
to God, martyred Christians come close to God and enter paradise.[42]
The prepared man guiding the scapegoat into the desert is compared to Christ who descending to hell banned "the principalities
and powers and rulers of this world".[43] This picture looks surprisingly similar to earlier Jewish eschatological myths based on Yom
Kippur when the evil forces are conquered by the Messianic armies,
however, Origen uses only the past tense.[44]

In another typological exegesis, Origen compares the two goats to
Barabbas and Jesus. Barabbas, the scapegoat, carried the sins into
the wilderness; Jesus, the sacrificial goat, atoned on behalf of his
believers; and Pilate was the prepared man, who cleansed himself
after the proceedings.[45]

In a *moral* form of this exegesis, Origen exhorts us to banish from
our hearts the bad thoughts and feelings that are Azazel's lot. The
homo paratus is the *ratio* educated in God's word and in his precepts.
Though *ratio* is seemingly defiled by dealing with evil thoughts, it is
nonetheless purified by expelling them. The good thoughts are
sacrificed on the altar and atone with God through the intercession
of Christ the High Priest.[46]

Interestingly, Emperor Julian's exegesis agrees on the ontological
opposition of the meanings of the two goats, one good and one evil.
Julian, however focusing on the destination of the two goats raises
their opposition to a theological level. While the sacrificial goat is

---

[39] *HomLev* 9:5:2, Baehrens 425:9–1–14. For the Philonic influence compare Louf
1961:273.
[40] *De Plantatione*, 61; *quis rerum divinarum heres sit*, 179.
[41] *HomLev* 9:5:2–4, esp. Baehrens 425:5–7. Cf. *cCels* 6:43 and *dePrinc* 3:2:1.
[42] *HomLev* 9:5:2 Baehrens 425:9–11.
[43] *HomLev* 9:5:4, Baehrens 425:26–29, for the quotation alluding to Col 2:15 and
Eph 6:12 cf. 425:23 (*principatus ac potestates et rectores mundi*).
[44] E.g. in *11QMelchizedeq*.
[45] *HomLev* 10:2:2. This exegeses is also found in pseudo-Hieronymus' commentary (6th century) on Mk 15:11. On this text see now Cahill (1998). On the medieval
influence of this exegesis compare Louf (1961: 274).
[46] *HomLev* 9:6, esp. Baehrens 428:28–429:3. Compare *HomIos* 23.

sacrificed to the supreme God, the scapegoat is an apotropaic gift
to chthonic deities.

> And now observe again how much Moses says about the deities that
> avert evil: "And he shall take two he-goats of the goats for a sin-
> offering, and one ram for a burnt offering. And Aaron shall bring also
> his bullock of the sin-offering, which is for himself, and make an atone-
> ment for himself and for his house. And he shall take the two goats
> and present them before the Lord at the door of the tabernacle of the
> covenant. And Aaron shall cast lots upon the two goats; one lot for
> the Lord and the other lot for the scape-goat" [cf. Lev 16:5–8] so as
> to send him forth, says Moses, as a scapegoat, and let him loose into
> the wilderness. Thus is sent forth the goat that is sent for a scape-
> goat. And of the second goat Moses says: "Then shall he kill the goat
> of the sin-offering that is for the people before the Lord, and bring
> his blood within the veil, and shall sprinkle the blood upon the altar-
> step, and shall make an atonement for the holy place, because of the
> uncleanness of the children of Israel and because of their transgres-
> sions in all their sins" [Lev 16:15]. Accordingly it is evident from what
> has been said, that Moses knew the various methods of sacrifice.[47]

*The revival of the holistic Christological type of exegesis in the fifth- and sixth-
century East*

Quite similar to the holistic Christological exegesis but independent
of it is an *economical Christological allegory*,[48] prominent in the fifth-century exegeses of Cyril of Alexandria,[49] Theodoret of Cyrus,[50] and
Hesychius of Jerusalem,[51] which greatly influenced later generations.[52]
The typology compares the two goats and their ritual to the two

---

[47] Translation of the fragments of *Against the Galileans* (on the basis of Neumann's
edition) by Wilmer Cave Wright in LCL *Julian* 3 (1959), pp. 404–7. Cf. also the
commentary of Masaracchia (1990) (non vidi).

[48] This exegesis is an example of an allegory that is simultaneously a typology.
The goats symbolise a historical figure, but their number and ritual point towards
the Christological economy.

[49] *Glaphyrorum in Leviticum liber* (PG 69:580 A–589 B); *Ep. ad Acacium Scythop.* (in:
Acta Conciliorum Oecumenicorum [ed. Schwartz 1928] Vol. 1:1:4 pp. 40–48 or PG 77:
201 C–221 A), *Contra Iulianum Liber* IX (PG 76:960 A–970 A). A critical edition
and translation of the latter work is now in preparation by an international group.
See Kinzig (1997). An introduction to Cyril's exegesis was written by Kerrigan
(1952). For this passage see p. 192.

[50] *Eranistes 3. Dialogue;* in Ettlinger 208:26–211:32 (PG 83:249 D–256 B) and
Quaestiones in Leviticum 22 in: Marcos and Sáenz-Badillos (1979), here 172:23–175:18
(PG 80:328 A–329 D). Compare Guinot (1995: 771–775).

[51] *Commentarius in Leviticum V* (PG 93:989–1002). Compare Tampellini's introduction to this work (1998).

[52] On the influence on medieval exegesis cf. Louf 1960.

natures of Christ. The passion and the human nature of Christ are symbolised in the sacrificial goat, while the scapegoat stands for the impassible divine nature that escaped into the desert, the solitary country, i.e. death, through which Christ passed for our sake.[53]

I would like to end this exposition with a hymn on the scapegoat, written in Syriac by Jacob of Sarug (+521).[54]

Jacob, like Cyril, Theodoret, and Hesychius, contests the interpretation of Azazel as demon, but, from a different starting point. His Bible, the Peshitta, adopted the Hebrew 'Aza'zel (עזאזל) but spelled it differently, using the divine eponym '-el' to form, ܥܙܐܙܝܠ ('Azaz'el), as in the Qumran fragment 4Q180 (עזזאל).[55] Jacob takes this as one of the many names of God, the strong ('aziz, ܥܙܝܙ) God, representing God's angry and zealous aspect vs. his mercy and pity. The strong aspect of God receives the goat.

> Why did he name the Lord and 'Azaz'el?
> ... he is the Lord and 'Azaz'el is the same
> that he is the Lord, and he is strong and at the same time God
> the names are different, there are not different gods placed in the lines
> (264).

That the goat is sent out into the desert is a reminder of God's deeds regarding Israel during the journey through the desert:

> He became strong (ܐܬܥܫܢ) in the country of the Pharaoh, being violent
>   in horrors and marvels and frightening <actions>, which he showed there,
> fire and hail-stones together with darkness and hard ulcer,
> the sea that was divided; the Pharaoh who was suffocated; the people
>   that was saved;

---

[53] Hesychius, however, puts forward a unique interpretation for the scapegoat's destination, 'solitary' meaning abandoned by all *evil*, and 'desert' therefore symbolising 'heavens', the place where Christ remains after his resurrection.—"*desertam terram, et solitariam, sive inviam nullatenus existimemus nunc in quolibet malo oportere accipi, neque per hoc piorum aures, hi qui ad impietatem legem trahunt, conturbent. Desertam enim a malo dicit, et solitariam, sive inviam, quae ab intelligibilibus hostibus ambulari non potest, in qua Deus habitat, et apparet ... Ergo desertum et invium, sanctum est, et Sancti sanctorum habitaculum, ubi in coelos divinitas tempore passionis abiisse dicitur, non de loco ad locum migrans, sed cohibens propriam virtutem ex humanitate, ut daret spatium passioni, in loco digno sibi, in sinu Patris videlicet manens*" (992A–B).

[54] The Syriac text was edited by Bedjan (1907: 259–283). Clemens Leonhard has now finished a preliminary translation, which he and I plan to publish with a commentary.

[55] For עזזאל cf. also bYoma 63b; Sifra Aharei Mot 2:8; Targum Pseudo-Jonathan to Leviticus 16:10, with an etymological explanation (the hardest of the mountains). Cf. Sh. Ahituv, "Azazel" in *Encyclopedia Judaica* 1:999–1002.

a cleft flood and a stone that is pouring out and gushes out floods;
and by means of that, he was strong (ܚ̈ܝܠ) as we said;
because of this, that he-goat was sent <out>
into the wilderness towards Azazel by the Levites (265)
. . . .
and for this desert, <the Lord> demanded a he-goat, which was sent
    to it/him[56]
in order that he reminded them of everything that happened there (266).

Jacob's real scapegoat is again Christ, who carries the crimes of the
whole country (272) and, by leaving it, sanctifies and purifies it from
uncleanness (275f). In a very anti-Jewish interpretation Jacob sees
the Jewish crucifiers in the role of the prepared man and in the
predators who tear apart the scapegoat (276–278).[57] They have to
wait outside the camp, unclean until the evening. Only then can
they enter the city and only after having washed themselves. This
manifests the power of baptism, which would have cleansed the sin
of the Jewish crucifiers, had they repented (279).

In sum, what, according to the reasoning of the Church Fathers,
was the reason God commanded the scapegoat to be *sent away*?
Barnabas, Justin, Tertullian, and Hippolytus would have answered
that the details of the ritual are a sign indicating to the faithful readers of the Bible that the Messiah to come is the crucified Jesus of
Nazareth. Another interpretation, found in Origen and Hippolytus,
compares the sending of the scapegoat into the desert with Jesus'
mission to the Gentiles.

According to Cyril, Theodoret, and Hesychius, these lines were
written to foreshadow the two natures of Christ. Jacob calls Moses
a prophetic painter who did not want to reveal the son openly but
hid him by painting all the sacrifices as portraits of the coming
Christ. In Jacob's eyes, the reason for sacrifices lies in their bringing
people to repentance. "While the offering was not necessary for God,
it attracted the offerer to ask for reconciliation" (269). The scapegoat
was a mere device for the high priests' confession (271), the 'real'
sacrifice. Accordingly, the confession or repentance of the people was
the central feature and aim of the ancient sacrifices, while the blood

---

[56] It is unclear if the desert or God is meant.
[57] A similar line of interpretation appears also in medieval Latin exegesis—Thomas
Aquinas (scapegoat = Christ), William of Auvergne († 1249) (scapegoat = sinners), and
Dionysus the Carthusian († 1472) (scapegoat = Christ), see Sabourin 1959: 62 f or
1970: 282 f.

of Jesus was only the means of atonement. Jacob's hymn ends with
a solemn admonition: "Aaron, do not again cast lots on the he-goats,
for the son carried the sins of the whole country and brought them
out" (283). In other words, the country has been cleansed.

2.3   Explaining the history of exegesis

I suggest five issues—one impediment and four causes—related to
this form of development in the Christian exegesis of the Yom Kippur
scapegoat.

Jewish mythologisation of the scapegoat before Christianity
The first issue is the question of why the Jewish authors of the New
Testament texts were generally reluctant to describe Jesus as scapegoat.[58]
The earliest followers of Jesus were not the first to use the powerful
images of Yom Kippur, especially the scapegoat in their mythological
language. We find earlier similar attempts to connect the fall of the
angels in the *Urzeit* with the day of their punishment in the *Endzeit*
in various examples of Jewish apocalyptic literature.[59] The sacrificial
goat did not play any role in these myths. Only the two other protagonists, the high priest and the scapegoat, were mythologically ele-
vated to leaders of the good and the evil forces, respectively.

By the first century BCE at the latest, Azazel had clearly become
a demon, a leader of the rebellious angels who introduced sin into
the world by teaching humanity the arts of magic and war.[60] Moreover,
the scapegoat of the Temple ritual could be perceived as Azazel's

---

[58] There is no *explicit* association of Jesus with the scapegoat in the earliest Christian
literature except the Jewish-Christian tradition behind the *Letter of Barnabas*. For
probable implicit allusions in the NT compare Young 1973, Schwartz 1983, Scullion
1991, and Stökl 1997.

[59] Cf. esp. Grabbe (1987); Hanson (1977); Nickelsburg (1977); and now Stökl
1999. See also the unpublished (Hebrew) dissertation of Devora Dimant (1974) and
her article (1978).

[60] Cf. 1 En 8–10, 13, 55:3 f; 69:2; 4Q203; ApocAbr 13, 14:6, 20:7, 23:11, 29. Cf.
Grabbe (1987) and Janowski (1995), columns 240–248. A demon Azazel prevails
also in later Jewish magic texts like the incantation bowls. Of course, the original
meaning of Azazel in the biblical text might already be the name of a demon,
probably in the appearance of a he-goat (cf. Lev 17:7; Is 13:21, 34:14, 2 Chron
11:15). On dating the introduction of the Yom Kippur ritual cf. Deiana (1994).
However, the evidence for dating Lev 16 is equally obscure as for 1 Enoch 10. If
Lev 16 is dated prior to 1 Enoch 10, we might be prisoners of a canonical reading of the Bible. Is it possible that we have to consider a reversed relationship of
the canonical and the apocryphal witness, i.e. a dependence of the biblical text and
ritual on a (supposedly older) myth of Azazel as described in 1 Enoch 10?

personification, too. This is shown through the mistreatment of the scapegoat in the description of the ritual according to the Rabbis, Philo, and Barnabas.[61]

The translators of the Septuagint preserved some of this chthonic aspect of Azazel by coining the term '*apopompaios*' related to *apopompê*, which is known in religious contexts.[62] Aquila and Symmachus, however, chose neutral paraphrases for the enigmatic Azazel.[63] The same is true for the Mishna, which prefers *HaSa'ir HaMishtaleach* (the goat, <that was> sent away) and does not mention Azazel even once. According to an anonymous presbyter quoted by Irenaeus, Azazel was the angel who inspired Marcus the magician.[64] And finally, Origen compares Christ's descent into hell to the victory over the Satan named Azazel.[65]

Regarding this demonization of Azazel, it was not at all an obvious move to use this suspect scapegoat as *typos* for Christ. For the Christian *imaginaire*, too, goats belonged to the realm of sin and usually symbolised evil people, as Matthew 25:31–46 demonstrates.[66] This problem of the negative image of goats in general and of the scapegoat in particular is best exemplified in a question by the doubtful one in the *Eranistes* by Theodoret of Cyrus: 'Do you not think it irreverent to liken the Lord to goats?' Theodoret's 'Orthodox' protagonist answers with a *Qal waKhomer*: Jesus himself used a serpent as *typos* and Paul dared to call the Saviour 'sin' and 'curse'.[67] The image of the goat remains negative, but it is reasoned that Jesus has to disguise himself in evil forms to save all men.

---

[61] Philo, *de Plantatione* 61.

[62] LXX 16:8.10a ἀποπομπαίος; 16:10b ἀποπομπή; 16:26:—ὁ χίμαρος ὁ διεσταλμένος εἰς ἄφησιν. For ἀποπομπή in Greek religious thought cf. Isocrates 5, *Philip* 117. Cf. Schlesier (1990A).

[63] Symmachus: 16:8.10b τράγος ἀπερχόμενος; 16:10a τράγος ἀφιεμένος. Aquila: 16:8 κεκραταιωμένος; 16:10 τράγος ἀπολυόμενος/ἀπολελυμένος. See Wevers, (1986); and Field (1871). See also the extensive footnote to Lev 16:8 in Harlé and Pralon (1988).

[64] *Adversus Haereses* 1:15:6. These lines are quoted in Epiphanius, *Panarion* 34:11 (GCS 31:23).

[65] *Contra Celsum* 6:43. Few Greek Christian texts mention the Hebrew Azazel. Besides Origen and the cited lines by Irenaeus, there are some biblical manuscripts of the LXX that transliterated ἀζαζήλ instead of translating it—Lev 16:10 in mss M, 18, 416; Lev 16:26 in mss M and 416.

[66] Moreover, the image of Christ as Lamb was known at least from the end of the first century CE (ἀρνίον in Rev 5:6.8, etc., and ἀμνός in John 1:29, 1 Pet 1:19) and Paul could describe Jesus as Passah (lamb) in 1 Cor 5:7.

[67] For the reference to the text see footnote 1.

The Christian adoption of Leviticus

The second issue is connected to the question of why indeed Christians of the second century returned to those parts of the Septuagint that had not been typologised or allegorised by the first generations, the authors of the New Testament.

In the context of a Roman empire, which held religious innovations in high disregard Christianity had to prove its antiquity. Some of the early Christians tried to foster their claim on the heritage of the Jewish Scriptures by offering Christian explanations of as many of the texts as possible.

The main figure of Early Christianity who did not refute the *novitas* of Christianity but on the contrary emphasised it as a central message was Marcion, who consequently tried to root out from his Christian canon any remembrance of Jewish tradition or thought. For him, therefore, any typology was heresy, and Christ could never be the Levitical scapegoat.

Most Christian thinkers, however, tried to lay claim to the Jewish texts of the Bible, and they adopted and developed sophisticated exegetical strategies to reinforce this claim. The Jewish interpretation was considered to be blind to the proper, spiritual meaning of the whole Old Testament, including the book of Leviticus, as books of prophecy.

Consequently, most of the Early Christian texts on Yom Kippur (Barnabas, Justin, Tertullian, Origen) appear in the framework of apologetic-polemical writings against Jews or Marcionites, juxtaposed with a long series of other typological readings. Tertullian's scapegoat typology, for example, appears twice, in almost identical versions—once in the *adversus Marcionem* and once in the *adversus Iudaeos*.

Moreover, the fight for legitimacy might very well have extended to the 'proper' understanding of Leviticus. The first Jewish commentary to Leviticus, the halakhic Midrash edited in the third century, was called *Sifra*, i.e. *the* book. This may explain why the first Christian homilies and commentaries on Leviticus by Origen of Caesarea emerged in this period.[68] It seems to have been crucial for those generations of Christians to include also the book of sacrifices in the Christianisation of the whole Old Testament.

---

[68] Origen's commentary on Leviticus did not survive. We know about two other Early Christian commentaries on Leviticus—one by Victorinus of Poetovio († ca. 304), the first Latin exegete, the other by Eusebius of Emesa († ca. 359). Victorinus'

Christian reaction against Christian participation in the Jewish Yom Kippur
The third issue is the particular preoccupation with the sixteenth
Chapter of Leviticus. Since the Epistle to the Hebrews had revealed
the proper understanding of Leviticus 16 and its canonical status had
been accepted, one would expect there to have been no need for any
further development of the Christian understanding of Yom Kippur.

It seems that the living presence of the transformed Jewish day
of atonement was an annual challenge to the Christian theology of
Christ's once-and-for-all atoning self-sacrifice. Many patristic state-
ments tell us that the Jewish version of a transformed day of atonement was seen as very attractive by a number of potential converts,
God-fearers, and Christians and was therefore a dangerous source
of unanswered queries regarding the Christian exegesis.[69]

In his *Homilies on Leviticus*, Origen complains about the meagre
attendance at prayers and warns his flock not to participate in the
Jewish fast.[70] Some 150 years later and much more furious, John
Chrysostom writes most of his notorious *Homilies Against the Jews* around
the 'dangerous season' of Tishrei's festivals, with a number of direct
attacks on Christians who fast on Yom Kippur.[71] Theodoret of Cyrus
and again John Chrysostom complain of the joyous character of the

---

commentary is most unfortunately lost. Eusebius' eclectic commentary survived in
its Armenian translation recently edited by the Mekhitarist Vahan Hovhannesian
(1980: 125–134). However, the commentary on Leviticus does not treat Leviticus
16. Ter Haar Romeny (1997: 114–119) suggests that Eusebius' opposition to allegory might explain his lack of interest in the sacrificial passages (p. 117).

[69] For this argument compare now Stökl (2001).

[70] Meagre attendance: 9:5:9 (*aut tu putas, qui vix diebus festis ad ecclesiam venis . . .,
quod possit <sors Domini> venire super te?*); Baehrens 428:2–3. Participation of Christians
in the fast: *HomLev* 10:2:1; Baehrens 442:10–11 (*qui putant pro mandato legis sibi quoque
Iudaeorum ieiunium ieiunandum*); cf. also *HomIer* 12:12 (ὅσοι τὴν νηστείαν τὴν Ἰουδαϊκὴν
ὡς μὴ νοοῦντες τὴν τοῦ ἱλασμοῦ ἡμέραν τηρεῖτε [τὴν] μετὰ τὴν Ἰησοῦ Χριστοῦ ἐπιδημίαν,
οὐκ ἠκούσατε τοῦ ἱλασμοῦ κεκρυμμένως, ἀλλὰ φανερῶς μόνον) (GCS 6; E. Klostermann,
Leipzig 1901, pp. 100: 15–17). The question stays open, if these Christians participated
in the fast in Jewish or in Jewish-Christian circles or if they were "private Judaizers."
In any event, the Jewish fast was attractive enough to be observed, and it was kept
by a number of people that was large enough to attract Origen's attention.

[71] E.g. *AdvIud* 1:1, 2:1, 4:1.3, 7:1, 8:1–2. Compare Wilken (1983: 35, 64f). Cf.
also the numerous interdictions in medieval legal texts against Christian participation
in Jewish fasts collected by Linder (1997). Especially N° 3 (Canons of the Apostles
70/Apostolic Constitutions 8:47) matches perfectly Chrysostom's local and chronological context. Note also 102, 103, 118, 121, 187, 353, 356, 357, 360, 370, 371,
949. However, they all partially depend on each other and—like all legislative
texts—some may represent simple repetitions of previous legislation without the
same context of Christians participating in the Jewish fast. Note the explicit reference to Chrysostom's Homilies in text N° 353, p. 176.

Jewish fast.[72] And finally, Jacob of Sarug confuses Yom Kippur with Succoth, probably because of their chronological proximity and the building of the booths, which are more conspicuous than the fast.[73] This would be less probable for a reader of Leviticus than for someone directly confronting living Judaism.

Greek parallels to the scapegoat and the mission of the Church

Next is the question of why and how the demonic character of the scapegoat came to be attenuated and how the scapegoat became so preeminent a *topos* in Christian thought and exegesis.

Here, one has to consider Greek and Roman parallels to Christ's atoning death, which show some similarity to the scapegoat ritual, i.e., the *pharmakos*. In Athens, for example, at the festival of Thargelion and in times of distress, two ugly men, one with black figs as purification for the women, one with white figs as purification for the men, were fed for a certain time and then killed or driven across the border. In Massilia in cases of epidemic, a poor man was fed and clothed expensively for one year and then led round the walls of the city and thrown from a precipice or chased away. Similar rituals existed in Abdera and Leukas. However, one must distinguish between the real ritual and the ideal myth as Jan Bremmer has pointed out.

> In historical reality the community sacrificed the least valuable members of the polis, who were represented however, as very valuable persons. In the mythical tales ... we always find beautiful or important persons, although even then these scapegoats remain marginal figures: young men and women, and a king.[74]

Some Church Fathers compare Jesus' death not only to the scapegoat and all other biblical sacrifices but also to legends about kings

---

[72] Theodoret of Cyrus, *Quaestiones in Leviticum 32* (Marcos-Sáenz Badillos 183:17–19). John Chrysostom *AduIud* 1:2. Compare mTan 4:8 and parallels about the dancing of the young Jerusalemite girls on Yom Kippur (לא היו ימים טובים לישראל כחמישה, עשר באב וכיום הכיפורים, שבהם בנות ירושלים יוצאות בכלי לבן שאולים, שלא לבייש את מי שאין לו ... ובנות ירושלים יוצאות וחולות בכרמים).

[73] Bedjan p. 263. The same confusion can be found in Plutarch, *Quaestiones Convivales*, 4:6:2. See Stern (1974–1984), Nº 258 = Vol. I, pp. 550–562, and his commentary on this passage on p. 561.

[74] See Bremmer (1983: 307). Moreover, most heroes of the Greek myths offer themselves voluntarily. For a comparison with earlier studies of the scapegoat see his excellent bibliography in footnote 2 p. 299. It may be interesting that an opposite relationship between myth and ritual practice exists between the Mishna *Yoma* ("the ritual") and *Leviticus* 16 ("the myth").

sacrificing their lives to avert epidemics or natural catastrophes, i.e. to avert evil. These mythical tales are closely connected to the *pharmakos* rituals.[75] Clement of Rome writes:

> Let us also bring forward examples from the heathen. Many kings and rulers, when a time of pestilence has set in, have followed the counsel of oracles, and given themselves up to death, that they might rescue their subjects through their own blood. Many have gone away from their own cities, that sedition might have an end. . . .[76]

And Origen answers Celsus:

> They (the disciples) dared not only to show to the Jews from the sayings of the prophets that he was the one to whom the prophets referred, but also showed to the other nations that he who was crucified quite recently accepted this death willingly for the human race, like those who have died for their country to check epidemics of plague, or famines, or stormy seas. For it is probable that in the nature of things there are certain mysterious causes which are hard for the multitude to understand, which are responsible for the fact that one righteous man dying voluntarily for the community may avert the activities of evil daemons by expiation, since it is they who bring about plagues, or famines, or stormy seas, or anything similar. Let people therefore who do not want to believe that Jesus died on a cross for men, tell us whether they would not accept the many Greek and barbarian stories about some who have died for the community to destroy evils that had taken hold of cities and nations. Or do they think that, while these stories are historically true, yet there is nothing plausible about this man (as people suppose him to be) to suggest that he died to destroy a great daemon, in fact the ruler of daemons, who held in subjection all the souls of men that have come to earth?[77]

In my opinion the rise of the scapegoat-typology was probably fostered by the fact that its rationale was easily understandable to non-Jewish converts, potential future candidates of the Christian mission and as well to opponents in the polemic struggle because of its comparability to their own cultural institution of *pharmakos* rituals and their aetiological tales, as we have seen in the testimonies of Clement of Rome and Origen. The crucified Messiah thus became less "foolish" to Greeks.

---

[75] See Bremmer (1983: 300–307).

[76] 1 Cl 55:1—Kirsopp Lake's translation in LCL. It was H.S. Versnel's fascinating article (1989, 185–189) that drew my attention to these passages. He refers to the very learned analysis by Ernst von Lasaulx (1854), to my knowledge von Lasaulx was the first to use these references in a comparative study.

[77] *Contra Celsum* 1:31.

A reaction to Julian's polytheistic reading

Finally, the reaction to Julian's pagan revival deeply changed the variety of the Christian interpretations of Yom Kippur. As we have seen, he understood the scapegoat as an apotropaic sacrifice to a chthonic deity, a reading not so different from Origen's exegesis of Azazel as a demon.

In their descriptions of the scapegoat ritual, Philo and Josephus use vocabulary that seems deliberately designed to resemble Greek ritual language in order to be more comprehensible to a non-Jewish audience: Philo calls the precipice over which the scapegoat is thrown *barathron*, the same term the Athenians used for the cliff from which the death candidates were thrown.[78] And Josephus (or one of his assistants) uses *apotropiasmos* as the designation for the scapegoat.[79] The very same root was used by Julian.[80] Texts from the Talmud and the Pirke de Rabbi Eliezer provide evidence that some Jewish exegetes knew a tradition according to which the scapegoat is a bribe to Azazel/Sammael, God's adversary.[81]

In Eastern Christian authors subsequent to Julian, we never find such attempts to liken the description of the scapegoat rituals to their Greek parallels. Moreover, the four important interpreters of the scapegoat after the time of Julian—Cyril, Theodoret, Hesychius, and Jacob—fervently stress that the scapegoat is a sacrifice to the one God. Consequently, the atoning sacrifice to the one God is identified with Christ.[82]

3. *Summary*

To summarize: The Jewish authors of the New Testament refrained from using the scapegoat as a type of Christ because it was identified or connected with a demon. Early Christian authors, however, did develop a range of various typologies of the scapegoat as part of the

---

[78] *De Plantatione* 61. Cf. Liddell and Scott's dictionary on βάραθρον.

[79] Josephus *Antiquitates Iudaicae* 3:240–1. Cf. Liddell and Scott, s.v. Cf. Schlesier (1990B).

[80] Julian: ἀποτρόπαιος LCL 3 (Wright) p. 402 (299A).

[81] Pirke deRabbi Eliezer 46 (Friedlander pp. 363–364).

[82] Jerome, too, interprets the scapegoat as a type of Jesus unlinked to evil powers. *Dialogus adv. Pelag.* 1:35 (CCSL 80:45:78–86).

Christianisation of the Old Testament, as an answer to the attractive Jewish version of Yom Kippur, and probably as a vehicle, parallel to the Greek *pharmakos*, to promote Christian ideas. The Christian authors of the 5th century limited the range of possible interpretations in reaction to the interpretation of Emperor Julian.

4. *Implications: The place of the scapegoat in the* imaginaire *of early Christianity and of modern scholarship*

The mythological connotations of Yom Kippur in the apocalyptic literature place the ritual of the temple in the context of the cosmological myth as to how evil entered the world in the *Urzeit* and will leave the world again in the *Endzeit*.[83] In this light, the annual temple ritual is a prefiguration of the eschatological scenario of the future and not a dramatic re-enactment of the past. The apocalyptic mythologisation does not propose an *alternative* to sacrifice; in contrast, it substantiates an eschatological *rationale*.

The Christian understanding of Yom Kippur and the scapegoat ritual is a re-mythologisation, a new creation of a formative myth. Some medieval liturgists interpreted the Mass as a re-ritualisation of the Christian Yom Kippur, with Christ as High Priest and as scapegoat—but a discussion of this topic is beyond the scope of the present paper.[84]

The Christian canon included only the centripetal part—the entry of Christ, the High Priest, into the holy of holies—as typologized in the Epistle to the Hebrews or, differently, Christ as *hilastêrion* (כפורת) in Paul's Epistle to the Romans. Unlike Leviticus 16, these texts from the New Testament became part of the regular liturgical readings. Nevertheless, the genre of some texts on the scapegoat clearly reveals that they had a liturgical function: The exegeses of Origen and perhaps also Hesychius were parts of homilies on Leviticus, presented in the church. Also, the hymns by Hippolytus and by Jacob of Sarug point to a liturgical *Sitz im Leben*.

---

[83] For the relevant texts and studies see footnotes 59 and 60.

[84] E.g. Ivo of Chartres (+ 1116), *de convenientia veteris et novi sacrificii* (PL 162:535–562), for a typological reading of Yom Kippur and the Mass cf. esp. 553–561; or Hildebert († 1133), *versus de mysterio missae* (PL 171:1177–1194), here esp. 1183–1190 and Petrus Pictor (= Ps-Hildebert) *liber de sacra eucharistia* (PL 171:1195–1212), here esp. 1212.

But the Christian transformation of Yom Kippur and its scapegoat into a Christian myth exceeded canon and liturgy. Christ as a
scapegoat became a central part of the Christian *imaginaire*, its collective repertoire of motifs. Scholars of religious studies have compared the Greek *pharmakos* rituals, Jesus' death, and the scapegoat
without referring to the crucial difference between goat and man.
The success of the exegesis of the Church Fathers can be mea-
sured by the ease with which we use the term 'scapegoat' for Jesus.
Because of the Church Fathers, we consider in a single category the
different phenomena *pharmakos*, Jesus' self-sacrifice, and scapegoat rituals. René Girard could call his book *Le bouc émissaire* even though
most of his scapegoats are not animals but human beings. He can
call Jesus a scapegoat even though the New Testament does not.
Pharmakos would have been a more reasonable title for Girard's book
were not the 'scapegoat' the central term in our—i.e. the modern
Western—*imaginaire*, as a result of the Church Fathers' propaganda.[85]

Bibliography

Ahituv, Sh. "Azazel" in *Encyclopedia Judaica* 1:999–1002.
Alon, Gedalyahu. "HaHalakha be'Iggeret Bar Naba'" (= The Halakha in the Barnabas-
   Letter) in: *Mekhqarim beToledot 'Israel (= Studies in Jewish History)* (2 vols.; HaKibbuz
   HaMe'ukhad 1967) (Hebrew).
Avemarie, Friedrich. *Yoma—Versöhnungstag* (Übersetzung des Talmud Yerushalmi Bd.
   2/4; Tübingen: 1995).
Baehrens, W.A. *Origenes Werke, sechster Band: Homilien zum Hexateuch in Rufins Übersetzung.*
   Erster Teil: Die Homilien zu Genesis, Exodus und Leviticus (GCS 29; Leipzig 1920).
Barkley, Gary Wayne. *Origen. Homilies on Leviticus 1–16* (Washington, D.C.: Catholic
   University of America Press 1990).
Bedjan, Paulus. *Homiliae Selectae Mar-Jacobi Sarugensis, Tomus III* (Paris/Leipzig:
   Harrassowitz 1907).
Blomfield Jackson. *Theodoret of Cyrus: Eranistes* (Nicene and Post Nicene Fathers Second
   Series, Vol. 3, [reprint Grand Rapids, Michigan 1983 = 1892]).
Bremmer, Jan N. "Scapegoat Rituals in Ancient Greece," *Harvard Studies in Classical
   Philology* 87 (1983) 299–320.
Cahill, Michael. *The First Commentary on Mark: An Annotated Translation* (New York
   and Oxford: Oxford University Press 1998).
Cancik, Hubert and Burkhard Gladigow and Matthias Laubscher (eds.), *Handbuch
   Religionswissenschaftlicher Grundbegriffe* (Stuttgart, Berlin, Cologne: Kohlhammer 1988 ff).
Carleton Paget, James. *The Epistle of Barnabas: Outlook and Background* (WUNT 2:64;
   Tübingen: Mohr 1994).

---

[85] Frazer wanted to call the volume, which today bears the title "The Scapegoat",
"The Man of Sorrows". He did not change his mind "until the very eve of the
publication of the relevant section of the third Edition." See Fraser (1990: 142).

Charles, R.H. *The Book of Enoch or 1 Enoch: Translated from the Editor's Ethiopic Text* (reprint Jerusalem 1973 = 1912).

Crossan, John. *The Cross That Spoke*, (San Francisco 1988).

Deiana, Giovanni. "Il giorno del Kippûr in Filone di Alessandria," in: F. Vattioni (ed.), *Sangue e Antropologia V* (Roma 1987) 891–905.

———. *Il giorno dell'espiazione: Il* kippur *nella tradizione biblica* (Supplementi all Revista Biblica 30; Bologna: EDB 1994).

Dimant, Devora. "1 Enoch 6–11: A Methodological Perspective," *SBL.SP* (1978) 323–339.

———. *Mal'akhim sheKhatu' biMgilot Midbar Yehuda waSefarim haKhizonim haQrovim Lahen (= The Fallen Angels in the Dead Sea Scrolls and the related Apocrypha and Pseudepigrapha)* (Jerusalem 1974) (in Hebrew).

Ettlinger, G. *Theodoret of Cyrus: Eranistes* (Oxford: Clarendon 1975).

Field, Frederic. *Origenis Hexaplorum Quae Supersunt; sive Veterum Interpretum Graecorum in Totum Vetus Testamentum Fragmenta*, vol. 1 (Oxford: Clarendon 1871).

Fraser, Robert. *The Making of the* Golden Bough: *The Origins and Growth of an Argument* (London: Macmillan 1990).

Geertz, Clifford. "Deep Play: Notes on the Balinese Cockfight," in: *The Interpretation of Culture: Selected Essays* (New York 1973), pp. 412–453.

Geiger, Abraham. "Zu den Apokryphen," *Jüdische Zeitschrift für Wissenschaft und Leben* 3 (1864) 196–204.

Girard, René. *La violence et le sacré* (Paris: Grasset 1971; ET: Baltimore: John Hopkins 1977).

———. *Le bouc émissaire* (Paris: Grasset 1982; ET: Baltimore: John Hopkins 1986).

Goppelt, L. *Typos, die typologische Deutung des Alten Testaments im Neuen* (BFCT 2/43; Gütersloh 1939; reprint Darmstadt: Wissenschaftliche Buchgesellschaft 1969).

Grabbe, Lester L. "The Scapegoat Tradition: A Study in Early Jewish Interpretation," *JSJ* 18 (1987) 152–167.

Guinot, Jean-Noel. *L'exégèse de Théodoret de Cyr* (Théologie historique, 100; Paris: Beauchesne 1995).

———. "L'exégèse du bouc émissaire chez Cyrille d'Alexandrie et Théodoret de Cyr," *Augustinianum* 28 (1988) 603–630.

Hanson, P.D. "Rebellion in Heaven, Azazel and Euhemeristic Heroes in 1 Enoch 6–11," *JBL* 96 (1977) 195–233.

Harlé, P. and D. Pralon. *La Bible d'Alexandrie, III, Le Lévitique, traduction du texte grec de la Septante, introduction et notes* (Paris: Cerf. 1988).

Hovhannesian, Vahan. *Eusébe d'Emèse, 1. Commentaire de l'Octateuque* (Venice: St. Lazare 1980).

Hruby, Kurt. "Le Yom Ha-Kippurim ou Jour de l'Expiation," *L'Orient Syrien* 10 (1965) 41–74, 161–192, 413–442.

Hvalvik, R. *The Struggle for Scripture and Covenant, the Purpose of the Epistle of Barnabas and Jewish Christian Competition in the Second Century* (WUNT 2:82; Tübingen: Mohr 1996).

Janowski, Bernd. "Azazel," in Karel van der Toorn, Bob Becking, and Pieter W. van der Horst (eds.), *Dictionary of Deities and Demons in the Bible* (Leiden: Brill 1995), columns 240–248.

Kerrigan, Alexander (O.F.M.). *St. Cyril of Alexandria: Interpreter of the Old Testament* (Analecta Biblica 2; Rome: Pontificio Istituto Biblico 1952).

Kinzig, Wolfram. "Zur Notwendigkeit einer Neuedition von Kyrill von Alexandrien, *Contra Iulianum*" in *Studia Patristica* 29 (1997) 484–494.

Kraft, Robert. *The Epistle of Barnabas: Its Quotations and Their Sources* (unpubl. diss, Harvard 1961).

Kraus, Wolfgang. "Der Jom Kippur, der Tod Jesu und die <Biblische Theologie>: Ein Versuch, die jüdische Tradition in die Auslegung von Röm 3,25f einzubeziehen," in Ingo Baldermann et alii (eds.), *Jahrbuch für Biblische Theologie 6, Altes Testament und christlicher Glaube* (Neukirchen-Vluyn: Neukirchener 1991A, pp. 155–172).

―――. *Der Tod Jesu als Heiligtumsweihe. Eine Untersuchung zum Umfeld der Sühnevorstellung in Römer 3,25–26a.* (WMANT 66; Neukirchen-Vluyn 1991B).

Larsson, Göran. *Der Toseftatraktat Jom hak-Kippurim, Text, Übersetzung, Kommentar, 1. Teil, Kapitel 1 und 2* (Lund: 1980).

Lasaulx, Ernst von. *Die Sühnopfer der Griechen und Römer und ihr Verhältniss zu dem einen auf Golgatha; ein Beitrag zur Religionsphilosophie (Vortrag zur Feier des Namensfestes seiner Majestät des Königs am 25. August 1851)* (Würzburg: Voigt and Mocker 1854).

Lauterbach, Jacob Z. "The Ritual for the Kapparot Ceremony," in his *Studies in Jewish Law, Custom and Folklore* (New York: Ktav, 1970 = 1935) pp. 133–142.

Leonhard, Clemens. "Tradition und Exegese bei Ishodad von Merv (9.Jh.) am Beispiel der Opfer von Kain und Abel (Gen 4,2–5a)" in: M. Tamcke and A. Heinz (eds.), *Zu Geschichte, Theologie, Liturgie und Gegenwartslage der syrischen Kirchen. Ausgewählte Vorträge des deutschen Syrologen-Symposiums vom 2.–4. Oktober 1998 in Hermaansburg.* (Studien zus Orientalischen Kirchengeschichte 9; Münster, Hamburg, London: MIT 2000), pp. 139–179.

―――. *Ishodad of Merv's Exegesis of the Psalms 119 and 139–147. A Study of His Interpretation in the Light of the Syriac Translation of Theodore of Mopsuestia's Commentary* (Diss., Vienna 1999, forthcoming in one of the coming supplement volumes to CSCO).

Levine, Baruch A. "René Girard on Job: The Question of the Scapegoat," *Semeia* 33 (1985) 125–33.

Linder, Amnon. *The Jews in the Legal Sources of the Early Middle Ages: Edited with Introductions, Translations and Annotations* (Detroit and Jerusalem: Wayne State University Press and The Israel Academy of Sciences and Humanities 1997).

Louf, Andreas. "Caper emissarius ut typus Redemptoris apud Patres," *Verbum Domini* 38 (1960) 262–277.

Lyonnet, Stanislav. "The ceremony of the Scapegoat," in idem and Léopold Sabourin, *Sin, Redemption and Sacrifice: A Biblical and Patristic Study* (Analecta Biblica 48; Rome: Biblical Institute Press 1970), pp. 182–184.

Maleakhi, Zwi. *Ha'Avoda leYom haKippurim, 'Ofyha, toldoteyha, veHitpatkhuta baShira ha'Ivrit* (= The 'Avoda' for Yom Kippur, Its Characteristics, History and Devel-opment in Hebrew Poetry) (unpubl. diss.; Jerusalem 1974, in Hebrew).

Mara, M.G. *Evangile de Pierre: Introduction, texte critique, traduction,* (SC 201; Paris 1975).

Marcos, N. Fernández and A. Sáenz-Badillos. *Theodoreti Cyrensis Quaestiones in Octateuchum* (Madrid 1979).

Masaracchia, Emanuela. *Giuliano Imperatore—Contra Galilaeos: Introduzione, testo critico, traduzione* (Testi e Comenti/Texts and Commentaries 9; Rome 1990).

Milgrom, Jacob. *Leviticus 1–16: A New Translation with Introduction and Commentary* (Anchor Bible 1994).

Milik, J.T. *The Books of Enoch: Aramaic Fragments of Qumrân Cave 4* (Oxford 1976).

Molenberg, Cornelia. "A Study of the Roles of Shemihaza and Asael in 1 Enoch 6–11," *JJS* 35 (1984) 136–146.

Nickelsburg, G.W.E. "Apocalyptic and Myth in 1 Enoch 6–11," *JBL* 96 (1977) 383–405.

North, Robert. "Violence and the Bible: The Girard Connection," *CBQ* 47 (1985) 1–27.

Perrone, Lorenzo. *La Chiesa di Palestina e le controversie cristologiche, dal concilio di Efeso (431) al secondo concilio di Constantinopoli (553)* (Brescia: Paideia 1980).

Prigent, Pièrre and Robert Kraft. *Epitre de Barnabé: Introduction, traduction et notes* (SC 172; Paris: 1972).

Prigent, Pièrre. *Les testimonia dans le christianisme primitif: L'épitre de Barnabé I–XVI et ses sources* (Etudes Bibliques 47; Paris 1961).

Richard, M. "Les fragments du commentaire de S. Hippolyte sur les Proverbes de Salomon," *Le Muséon* 79 (1966) 65–94.

Rosenberg, Yehoshua. *Mishna 'Kippurim'—Mahadura Bikortit beTseruf Mavo'* (2 vols.; unpublished dissertation; Jerusalem 1995).

Sabourin, Léopold. "Le bouc émissaire, figure du Christ?" *Sciences Ecclésiastiques* 11 (1959) 45–79.

———. "The Scapegoat as 'Type' of Christ in the History of a Doctrine," in idem and Lyonnet, Stanislav, *Sin, Redemption and Sacrifice: A Biblical and Patristic Study* (Analecta Biblica 48; Rome: Biblical Institute Press 1970), pp. 269–289.

Safrai, Shmuel. "Der Versöhnungstag in Tempel und Synagoge," In: Hanspeter Heinz (ed.), *Versöhnung in der jüdischen und christlichen Liturgie* (QD 124; Freiburg im Breisgau 1990; pp. 32–55).

Schlesier, Renate. "Apopompe," in Cancik et alii (1990A) Vol. 2:38–41.

———. "Apotropäisch," in: Cancik et alii (1990B) Vol. 2:41–45.

Schwartz, Daniel R. "Two Pauline Allusions to the Redemptive Mechanism of the Crucifixion," *JBL* 102 (1983) 259–268.

Scullion, James Patrick. *A Traditio-Historical Study of the Day of Atonement* (unpubl. diss.; Washington, D.C.: Catholic University of America 1991)

Signer, Michael. "Fleisch und Geist: Opfer und Versöhnung in den exegetischen Traditionen von Judentum und Christentum," in: Hanspeter Heinz (ed.), *Versöhnung in der jüdischen und christlichen Liturgie* (QD 124; Freiburg im Breisgau 1990); pp. 197–219.

Skarsaune, Oskar. *The Proof from Prophecy* (S.NT 56; Leiden: Brill 1987).

Sokoloff, Michael. *A Dictionary of Jewish Palestinian Aramaic of the Byzantine Period* (Ramat Gan: Bar Ilan University Press 1990).

Stern, Menahem. *Greek and Latin Authors on Jews and Judaism. Edited with Introductions, Translations and Commentary* (3 Vols.; Jerusalem: The Israel Academy of Sciences and Humanities 1974–1984).

Strobel, August. "Das jerusalemische Sündenbock-Ritual: Topographische und landeskundliche Erwägungen zur Überlieferunsgeschichte von Lev 16,10.21f", *ZDPV* 103 (1987) 141–168.

Stroumsa, Guy G. "The Christian Hermeneutical Revolution and Its Double Helix," in: *Barbarian Philosophy. The Religious Revolution of Early Christianity* (WUNT 112; Tübingen: Mohr Siebeck 1999), pp. 27–43.

Stökl, Daniel. "The Biblical Yom Kippur, the Jewish Fast of the Day of Atonement and the Church Fathers" *Studia Patristica* 34 (2001) 493–502.

———. "Yom Kippur in the Apocalyptic *imaginaire* and the Roots of Jesus' High Priesthood: Yom Kippur in Zechariah 3, 1 Enoch 10, 11QMelkizedeq, Hebrews and the Apocalypse of Abraham 13," in Jan Assmann and Guy G. Stroumsa (eds.), *Transformations of the Inner Self in Ancient Religions* (Studies in the History of Religions [*Numen* Book Series] 83; Leiden, Boston, Köln: Brill 1999), pp. 349–366.

———. *Jom Kippur im frühen Christentum. Das Verständnis von Jom Kippur bei Philon, im jüdisch-apokalyptischen* imaginaire *und im Antiken Christentum nach den Auslegungen bis zum Ende des Zweiten Jahrhunderts* (unpubl. MA-thesis, Jerusalem: Hebrew University 1997).

Swartz, Michael D. "Ritual about Myth about Ritual: Towards an Understanding of the 'Avodah' in the Rabbinic Period," *JJTP* 6 (1997) 135–155.

Tabori, Yosef. *Mo'adei Israel biTkufat haMishna vehaTalmud* (= Israel's Festivals in the Mishnaic and Talmudic period), Jerusalem 1995 (Hebrew).

Tampellini, Stefano. *Introduzione allo studio del* Commentarius in Leviticum *di Esichio di Gerusalemme* (unpublished dissertation, Bologna 1998).

ter Haar Romeny, R.B. "Early Antiochene Commentaries on Exodus," *Studia Patristica* 30 (1997) 114–119.

Tränkle, Hermann. *Q.S.F. Tertulliani Adversus Iudaeos mit Einleitung und kritischem Kommentar* (Wiesbaden: Franz Steiner 1964).

Van den Eynde, Ceslas. *Commentaire d'Išodad de Merv sur l'Ancien Testament. II. Exode— Deutéronome* (Text: CSCO 176 = SS 80; Translation: CSCO 179 = SS 81; Louvain: Peeters 1958).

Versnel, H.S. "Quis Athenis et Hierosolymis? Bemerkungen über die Herkunft von Aspekten des 'Effective Death'," in: J.W. van Henten (ed.), *Die Entstehung der jüdischen Martyriologie* (Studia Post Biblica 38; Leiden: Brill 1989) pp. 162–196.

Wevers, John William. *Leviticus*, (Septuaginta: Vetus Testamentum Graecum Auctoritate Academiae Scientiarum Gottingensis editum vol. 2:2; Göttingen: Vandenhoeck 1986).

Wilken, Robert. *John Chrysostom and the Jews: Rhetoric and Reality in the Late 4th Century* (The Transformation of the Classical Heritage 4; Berkeley, Los Angeles and London: University of California Press 1983).

Yahalom, Yosef. *'As be'Eyn Kol: Seder ha'Avoda ha'Eretz-'Isra'eli haQadum leYom haKippurim* (= Priestly Palestinian Poetry: A Narrative Liturgy for the Day of Atonement) (Jerusalem: Magnes Press 1996, in Hebrew).

Young, Norman H. *The Impact of the Jewish Day of Atonement upon the Thought of the New Testament* (unpubl. diss. Manchester 1973).

Zani, A. "Tracce di un'interessante, ma sconosciuta, esegesi midrašica giudeo-cristiana di Lev 16 in un frammento di ippolito," *Bibbia e Oriente 24* (1982) 157–166.

THE BODY AS TEMPLE IN THE HIGH MIDDLE AGES[1]

JENNIFER A. HARRIS

In the second chapter of the Gospel of John, Jesus strides into the Jerusalem Temple, over-turns the tables of the money-changers, and creates quite a scene (Jn 2:13–17; synoptic accounts in Mt 21:12–13; Mk 11:11–25; Lk 19:45–48). The meaning of this event, commonly called the 'cleansing of the Temple,' is hotly debated in modern scholarship, but in the patristic and medieval periods it was perfectly clear: Jesus declares here that his body has replaced the Temple. He says "Destroy this Temple and in three days I will raise it up" (Jn 2:19), and from then on this phrase was understood as clearly referring to the "temple of his body" (Jn 2:21). Thus began the association of the body with the Temple in the Christian tradition. In this paper we shall examine the way in which the biblical equation of Jesus's body with the Jerusalem Temple was incorporated into eleventh- and twelfth-century ideas about the nature of the body and the self.[2] To do so, we shall first look briefly at the developing idea of the Temple in the early Christian tradition, and then, more extensively, explore the idea of the body as temple in the High Middle

[1] I should like to thank Al Baumgarten and Bar-Ilan University for organizing and sponsoring the colloquium at which this paper was first presented. Earlier drafts of this paper were read and commented upon by many people to whom I owe thanks: of these, I would like to single out in gratitude Brian Stock for his careful guidance, as well as Joseph Goering, Robert Sweetman, and Isabelle Cochelin for their comments and encouragement in the development of these ideas. I should also like to thank Pauline Thompson, Oren Falk, Greti Dinkova-Bruun, and Wendy Greyling for their helpful suggestions concerning format, style, and content. I extend special thanks to Elisheva Baumgarten, a generous scholar and friend throughout the evolution of this project. Translations of Latin texts, unless otherwise indicated, are my own.

[2] A brief, yet comprehensive study of the Christian use of the Temple in the Middle Ages is Hugh Nibley's influential article, "The Christian Envy of the Temple," *JQR* 50.2–3 (1959/60) 97–123, 229–40. In this seminal work, Nibley overlooks the equation of body and Temple in the New Testament and in the medieval tradition. I have just completed my doctoral dissertation, "The Place of the Jerusalem Temple in the Reform of the Church in the Eleventh Century," in which I offer a fuller discussion of the various uses of the Temple in the medieval Christian imagination.

Ages.[3] We shall use, as our point of departure, one sermon by a neglected twelfth-century author, Adam of Dryburgh, in which Christian traditions about the Temple are neatly summarized.[4] We shall examine, in particular, how this idea of the body as temple developed from the identification of the Temple with Jesus' body to an association with Mary's body and, finally, with the bodies of all believers. En route, we shall also look at the way in which the identification of body and temple influenced and was in turn influenced by church architecture, liturgical customs, and popular devotions.[5]

1. *The idea of the Temple*

From the outset of the Christian tradition, Jesus was portrayed as God's earthly dwelling place; in the Gospel of John, Jesus' cosmic genealogy culminates in the dramatic restatement of creation itself, "And the Word became flesh, and dwelt among us" (Jn 1:14). Jesus as divine presence was soon followed by Jesus as Temple, as we have seen in his 'cleansing' of the Temple. Apart from Jesus' own statement, the text suggests the popular response to Jesus' action: witnesses to the event treat Jesus as though he were the new temple; as Matthew reports it, "the blind and the lame came up to him in the temple, and he healed them" (Mt 21:14).

Perhaps it is in his death that Jesus is most clearly identified with the Temple. At the moment of his death, it is noted that "the curtain of the Temple was torn in two, from top to bottom" (Mt 27:51; Mk 15:38; Lk 23:45). One stream of the interpretive tradition, beginning with the Epistle to the Hebrews 9, suggests that this fact ensured unmediated access to God by means of the High Priesthood of Jesus.

---

[3] The early Christian traditions about the Temple are adequately explored elsewhere and shall only be referred to in passing here. Paul von Naredi-Rainer, *Salomos Tempel und das Abendland* (Cologne: Dumont, 1994), 9–43, provides historical background for the changing uses of the Temple in later medieval and Renaissance Europe. See also Heinz-Martin Döpp, *Die Deutung der Zerstörung Jerusalems und des Zweiten Tempels in Jahre 70 in der ersten drei Jahrhunderten nach Christum* (Tübingen: Francke, 1998) for the Early Christian interpretation of the destruction of the Temple.

[4] PL 198.363–72.

[5] A word about terminology: when referring to the Jerusalem Temple, I shall use 'Temple;' when referring to the concept of the temple, including notions of God's earthly dwelling place, I shall use 'temple.'

Another tradition reads the event as signalling the departure of God from the old sanctuary now that the new temple has been established in Jesus. Both suggest that the life and death of Jesus had in some way overshadowed the Temple as the dwelling place of God.

The apostle Paul makes explicit the supersession of the Temple by the incarnate God. In his Letter to the Colossians, he writes, "In him, the fullness of God was pleased to dwell" (Col 1:19). Paul likens Jesus to the temple that joins all peoples into one household; he is the cornerstone of a new edifice which is "the holy temple in the Lord" (Eph 2:21).[6] Paul also extends the significance of the temple to include the faithful. Of the community of believers, he writes "you (pl.) are built . . . into a dwelling place for God in the Spirit" (Eph 2:22), and "[you are] the temple of the living God" (2 Cor 6:16). Of each and every Christian, Paul writes, "don't you know that you are God's temple and that God's spirit dwells in you?" (1 Cor 3:16); of their bodies, he stresses that "your body (sing.) is a temple of the Holy Spirit within you . . ." (1 Cor 6:19).[7] Despite Paul's insistence, the somatic temple of every believer was a neglected doctrine for the first millennium of the Christian tradition. In the intervening centuries, the Temple was most often used as a metaphor for the Church,[8]

---

[6] It is unimportant for my point that the Pauline authorship of Colossians and Ephesians is a matter for modern scholarly debate; my use of 'Paul' conforms with medieval usage, and is for convenience here.

[7] Bruce Chilton points out that in the earliest MSS of the Greek New Testament the text of 1 Cor 6:19 speaks of "body" (*sôma*) in the singular, whereas after the fifth century, the "bodies" (*sômata*) in question are plural. This suggests that the association between the individual body and the Temple was effaced on the eve of the Middle Ages. In the Latin tradition, Jerome's Vulgate translation reflects the text of his day and translates "your members" (*membra vestra*). The correction to the singular "your body" (*corpus vestrum*) was made during the ninth-century Carolingian renaissance; we note its use by many ninth-century authors, but it is not until the eleventh century that the singular usage is again used, and even then it is not frequent.

[8] Pope Gregory I often uses the Temple as an ecclesiological metaphor (e.g., *Homiliae in Hezechielem*, ed. M. Adriaen. CChr, Series Latina 142 [Turnhout: Brepols, 1971]; see Thomas Renna, "Bernard of Clairvaux and the Temple of Solomon," in *Law, Custom, and the Social Fabric in Medieval Europe*, ed. Bernard S. Bachrach and David Nicholas [Kalamazoo: Medieval Institute Publications, 1990] 77 for his discussion of this text). Gregory's ecclesiology is not institutional and encompasses the collective of faithful believers; his use of the Church as Temple reflects concern for the moral development of its members. In his commentary on the book of Job, Gregory portrays the conscience of all believers as a "house of God" (*domus Dei*), an internal judge (see *Moralia in Iob*, ed. M. Adriaen, CChr, Series Latina 143 [Turnhout: Brepols, 1979] 4.31, 61 and 24. 8, 18).

the soul or mind,[9] and heaven. Only around the year 1000 did Christians begin thinking again about the earthly body of Jesus and the implications of his corporeality for their own embodiment.

2. *The body as Temple*

The revived association of the body with the Temple is nowhere clearer than in the work of a neglected twelfth-century writer, Adam of Dryburgh (ca. 1140–1212). Adam was a Praemonstratensian (Augustinian) canon; he lived at Dryburgh Abbey in Scotland until he became a Carthusian hermit.[10] At Dryburgh around the year 1185, he composed a sermon entitled "On the exercise of religious conversion" (*De exercitio religiosae conversationis*). The sermon explicates Jesus' presentation in the Temple as an infant. More specifically it addresses the presence of the prophetess Anna who, according to Luke's account, "never left the Temple but worshipped there with fasting and prayer night and day" (Lk 2:36–38).[11] In his sermon, Adam offers eight biblical representations of the Temple from which Anna did not depart: the body of Christ, Mary, the Church, the believers, the human body, the mind, the human and angelic intellect, and heaven.[12] Of interest for our study are Adam's views of the Temple as Christ's body, as Mary, and as the human body.

---

[9] Bede compares the mind of believers to the Temple in his treatise *De Templo* (ed. D. Hurst, CChr Series Latina 119A [Turnhout: Brepols, 1969] 1.14, 2). The Christian mind is like the imagined Temple, replete with images derived from the Scriptures; recalling these mental images habituates the viewer to the moral life. Bede's conception of this Temple as a "hall of memory" in service of the Church is important for our study. The interior temple as the locus of memory will become an integral part of the high medieval tradition about the body as Temple (see Mary Carruthers, *The Book of Memory* [Cambridge: Cambridge University Press, 1990] 72 for her discussion of the "halls of memory").

[10] The classic biographical article on Adam of Dryburgh is André Wilmart, "Magister Adam Carthusiensis," in *Mélanges Mandonnet* (2 vols.; Paris: J. Vrin, 1930) 2.145–61. For an excellent recent article which places Adam within the Augustinian tradition yet exposes his innovations, see J.F. Worthen, "Adam of Dryburgh and the Augustinian Tradition," *Revue des études augustiniennes* 43 (1997) 339–47.

[11] The use of Anna as a theological figure was not common in the Middle Ages, but we note her use in the acts of the Synod of Arras (*Acta Synodi Atrebatensis*, ca. 1025). Anna is there associated with the sanctity of the Church as Temple (see s. III: *De sancta ecclesia quae est domus Dei*, PL 142.1284D–1285A). The Synod affirmed the Temple-like sanctity of Christian churches, thus provides the first explicit argument for sacralized Christian space. See Dominique Iogna-Prat, *Ordonner et exclure* (Paris: Aubier, 1998) 164–69, for the slow development behind this claim.

[12] See PL 198.364D–365B.

a. *Jesus' historical body as Temple*

Adam begins with the Temple as the body of Christ, which signifies both the incarnate body of the historical Jesus and his eucharistic body. Adam says that, like Anna,

> we should remain with one mind, and by no thought or desire should you depart. For to remain with the mind in that temple, which we have called the body of Christ, is a pious devotion as well as a fruitful experience. Certainly it is the fullness of every piety to discern the human body in the Word; [and to discern] the flesh in divinity, the man in God.[13]

The importance of the human and bodily life of Jesus is one of the pillars of twelfth-century spirituality, of which Adam is an eloquent exponent.[14] But interest in the incarnate body of Christ may be traced back two centuries, and seems to have been well underway by the turn of the first millennium. The use of visual images of the suffering God began at the turn of the ninth century, even though this iconography did not become preponderant until the eleventh century.[15] It has been suggested that the millennial expectations of people living in the tenth century increased their interest in, and contributed to their identification with, the human, suffering Jesus.[16] While eschatological expectations are too evanescent to trace with ease, it is safe to say that a number of converging factors in the tenth century may have contributed to this new interest, including devotions to the Cross and the Crucifix,[17] interpretations of biblical apocalyptic books such as Revelation, Daniel and 2 Thessalonians,

---

[13] *ut in uno quoque mente immoremini, et a nullo cogitatione et desiderio discedatis. Nam in templo illo, quod Christi esse corpus diximus, mente immorari sicut pium ad devotionem, sic et fructuosum quantum ad utilitatem: plenum siquidem omni pietate est, humanum in verbo cernere corpus: et in divinitate carnem, hominem in Deo.* PL 198.365B–C

[14] Giles Constable, *The Reformation of the Twelfth Century* (Cambridge: Cambridge University Press, 1996) 278–9.

[15] Marie-Christine Sepière, *L'Image d'un Dieu souffrant: aux origines du crucifix* (Paris: Cerf, 1994) 15–8, 165–75, 225–33.

[16] See Johannes Fried, "Endzeiterwartung um die Jahrtausendwende," *Deutsches Archiv für Erforschung des Mittelalters* 45.2 (1989) 453–4.

[17] One of the earliest material examples of the new devotion to the suffering Christ is the Gero Crucifix of Cologne fabricated ca. 980, see John Beckwith, *Early Medieval Art* (New York: Praeger Publishers, 1965) 150. Fried, "Endzeiterwartung," 449–52, dates the Crucifix to 976 and notes the earlier introduction of widespread devotion to the Cross in the liturgy of the Mass, at the 'te igitur' prayer prior to the Offertory (a practice also noted by Sepière, *L'image*, 177–9); Fried, "Endzeiterwartung," 455, points to texts on the devotion to the Cross such as Odo of Cluny's *Occupatio* VI (ca. 927–42) where the sign of the Cross is a protection from sin.

which engendered concern about an historical Last Judgement,[18] the
widespread use of the *Anno Domini* dating system, which focussed on
the millennial anniversary of the Incarnation and Resurrection and
the anticipated battle between Christ and Antichrist at the end of
history,[19] and, finally, the historicized account of the life of Antichrist
written ca. 950 by Adso of Montier-en-Der.[20]

The increased focus on an imminent historical judgement likely
bred a new consciousness of sin and, in turn, both an identification
with the suffering Saviour and the need for clearer mechanisms of
forgiveness.[21] One of the most effective extant means of penance was
pilgrimage; the noticeable rise in Holy Land pilgrimage in the second half of the tenth century suggests not only increased access, but
also an increased search for forgiveness.[22] Pilgrimage to the Holy
Land in turn promoted the historical sites of Jesus's life and works.
Pilgrims returning from the Holy Land brought back to Europe
numerous relics of the Cross and, after its partial destruction in 1009,
of the Holy Sepulchre.[23]

Not surprisingly, interest in the life and works of the historical
Jesus inspired developments in the doctrine of the Incarnation. The

---

[18] Fried, "Endzeiterwartung," 393–412, finds early development of historical concern, especially in Aquitaine, Lorraine and Burgundy; for the opposing view, see
E. Ann Matter, "The Apocalypse in Early Medieval Exegesis," in *The Apocalypse in
the Middle Ages*, ed. Richard K. Emmerson and Bernard McGinn (Ithaca: Cornell
University Press, 1992) 47–50; Guy Lobrichon, "L'ordre de ce temps et les désordres de la fin," in *The Use and Abuse of Eschatology in the Middle Ages*, ed. W. Verheke,
D. Verhelst and A. Welkenhuysen (Leuven: Leuven University Press, 1988) 224–5,
236–41.

[19] Richard Landes, "Lest the Millennium be Fulfilled: Apocalyptic Expectations
and the Pattern of Western Chronography 100–800 CE," in *Use and Abuse of Eschatology*,
178–81; Bernard McGinn, "Portraying the Antichrist in the Middle Ages," in *Use
and Abuse of Eschatology*, 13–5.

[20] Adso of Montier-en-Der, *Libellus de ortu et tempore Antichristo*, ed. D. Verhelst,
CChr, Continuatio Medievalis 45 (Turnhout: Brepols, 1976).

[21] See H.E.J. Cowdrey, "The Genesis of the Crusades: the Springs of Western
Ideas of Holy War," in *The Holy War*, ed. T.P. Murphey (Columbus: Ohio State
University Press, 1976) 21–4, and Jonathan Riley-Smith, *The First Crusaders* (Cambridge:
Cambridge University Press, 1997) 25–8 on the confusing state of the means of for-
giveness in the late tenth and early eleventh centuries.

[22] Paul Alphandéry, *La Chrétienté et l'idée de croisade* (2 vols.; Paris: Éditions Albin
Michel, 1954) 1.10–27 sees this need for forgiveness rooted in the eschatological
expectations of the time.

[23] Geneviève Bresc-Bautier, "Les imitations du Saint-Sépulcre de Jérusalem (IXe–
XVe siècles): Archéologie d'une dévotion," *Revue d'histoire de la spiritualité* 50 (1974)
322–3 on the importance of the Holy Sepulchre and its relics in western devotion;
see also Riley-Smith, *First Crusaders*, 30–35.

eleventh century marked a turning point in theological concerns from the purely christological (on the nature of the second person of the Trinity) to the incarnational (on the divine and human implications of Jesus's embodiment).[24] At this time, the Eucharist became linked with the Incarnation; together they stood as the two manifestly enduring facts of God's purpose in salvation.[25] At the end of the eleventh century, Anselm of Canterbury (1033–1109) wrote the first major treatise on the Incarnation, entitled "Why God became Man" (*Cur Deus Homo*), which in turn inspired many others.[26] Anselm explicated in contemporary theological terms the meaning of God's incarnation, the implications of which soon began to shape the signification of the Temple.

Rupert of Deutz (ca. 1075–1129), a Benedictine monk writing shortly after Anselm, displays the broadening concern for the life and works of Jesus in his study of Solomon's Temple. In Rupert's exposition every detail of the building represents a part of Jesus' body or an event in his life. He writes,

> The door in the side of the Temple is the wound in the side of the dominical Body pierced by the lance, without which there is no entrance, there is no door or portal by which one may enter, in order to stand before God wherever he wishes. For from that side, when it had been struck by the lance, flowed water and blood (Jn 19), by which sacrament the sin of the world is destroyed, [and] in which we also are baptized.[27]

The simple vision offered by Rupert reflects the epistemological realism of contemporary orthodoxy,[28] whereas Adam of Dryburgh's is shaped by the 'hermeneutic epistemology' of the later twelfth

---

[24] Jaroslav Pelikan, *The Christian Tradition*, vol. 3: *The Growth of Medieval Theology (600–1300)*, (Chicago: University of Chicago Press, 1976) 3.

[25] Gary Macy, *The Theologies of the Eucharist in the Early Scholastic Period* (Oxford: Clarendon Press, 1984) 33, 44–5. Macy cites the works of the ninth-century Paschasius Radbertus and Durand of Fécamp (ca. 1060) as examples of the incarnational view of the Eucharist.

[26] Anselm of Canterbury, *Cur Deus Homo* in *Opera Omnia*, ed. F.S. Schmitt (6 vols.; Rome, 1940) 2.39–133. See below, 247–248, for discussion of this text.

[27] *Ostium lateris templi vulnus est in latere lanceato Dominici corporis, praeter quod non est aditus, non est ostium, vel janua qua intret quis, ut in quovis ordine coram Deo stare possit. Nam ex illo latere, cum lancea percussum esset, sanguis et aqua profluxit* (Joan. XIX), *quo sacramento deletum est peccatum mundi, in quo et baptizati sumus). De Trinitate et operibus eius,* ed. H. Haacke, CChr, Continuo Medievalis 22 (Turnhout: Brepols, 1972) 3, 10. 443–50.

[28] We note that Rupert was also the first undisputed historicizing reader of the

century.[29] Adam's Jesus is a comprehensible object of contemplation and interpretation that must be recalled and meditated upon; one does not so much enter this temple as construct it within by means of memory. The importance of memory for the construction of the interior is a theme to which we shall return when we look at the human body as temple.[30]

b. *Christ's Eucharistic body as Temple*

Adam turns from the Temple as incarnate body of Jesus, conceived historically, to the eucharistic body of Christ, conceived theologically. He considers both to be objects of memory and salvation. Thus he writes,

> We who have been formed by the divine institution and admonished by the salutary precepts often celebrate the sacrifice of the salvific host, even we who often die sinning, for are we not restored to life when recalling to memory the death of our Redeemer in the holy sacrament, and does He not increase the effect of our salvation with our frequent celebrations of the mystery?[31]

This identification of Christ's body with the eucharistic sacrifice is central to our understanding of the Christian uses of the Temple in the Middle Ages, as well as for the body as temple.

Book of Revelation, see Bernard McGinn, "Symbols of the Apocalypse in Medieval Culture," *Western Quarterly Review* 22 (1983) 215–83, reprinted in *Apocalypticism in the Western Tradition* [Aldershot: Variorum, 1984] 277–9.

[29] The distinction in epistemological outlook between naive realism and critical realism (a 'hermeneutic epistemology') is important to make in assessing the positions of our authors. In general, earlier writers, e.g., Gregory I, embrace a naive epistemological realism with respect to objects, that is, they accept that the truth about an object inheres in it and can be apprehended directly: the truth about the soul is that it *is* the temple of God. As we turn to the twelfth century, we find critical realists such as Adam of Dryburgh who assert that what can be known about an object requires interpretive interaction between the knower and the object: that the soul is a temple is not known apart from one's interpretation of the terms involved and one's contemplation of them. The act of knowing becomes the act of interpreting, hence of construction and interiorizing. Knowing about the interior temple is part of the process of constructing that temple. On 'hermeneutic epistemology,' see Brian Stock, *The Implications of Literacy* (Princeton: Princeton University Press, 1983) 241–325.

[30] See below, 245–253.

[31] ... *oblationem hostiae salutaris saepe celebrare praeceptis salutaribus moniti, et divina institutione formati solemus; nisi ut qui saepe peccando morimur; revocata ad memoriam in sacramenta sancta Redemptoris nostri morte, vivificemur, et eum frequentatione mysterii crescat nostrae salutis effectus?* PL 198.366C.

The use of Temple analogies when discussing the nature of the Eucharist, its ministers, and the churches in which it is confected becomes a detectable trend as early as the fourth century. The physical separation of clergy and laity in church buildings began then with the introduction of a separate area for the clergy.[32] At this time, Christian ministers were first called 'priests' (*sacerdotes*, that is, Temple priests), rather than simply 'elders' (*presbyteros*).[33] Coincident with these developments, the Eucharist came to be understood as the *sacrificium Christi*, that is, the sacrifice of Christ by and for the Church, in addition to the existing understanding of the Eucharist as a sacrifice of praise or of gifts offered by the people to God.[34] With the increased sacralization of the Eucharist and its ministers came the use of veils and screens to separate the altar from the laity; these increasingly elaborate dividers in some cases evoked the interior of the imagined Tabernacle and Temple.[35]

The movement of altars and clergy behind protective screens, however, was not merely a recreation of the Jerusalem Temple; the use of the Temple analogy was early testimony to the new locus of sanctity in the Christian imagination: the sacrificial host (and its communicants) as the dwelling places of God. Clearly the equation of Jesus' body and the Temple in John's Gospel was realized in the weekly (if not daily) celebrations of Christ's sacrificial offering of his body to the Church. By the sixth century, the rite of dedication of the church building clearly presents the church structure as a new Temple.[36] But the church as Temple is only thus because of the

---

[32] F.B. Bond and B. Camm, *Roodscreens and Roodlofts* (2 vols.; London: Pitman and Sons, 1909) 1.12–5; see also Joan R. Branham, "Sacred Space under Erasure in Ancient Synagogues and Early Churches," *Art Bulletin* 74 (1992) 375–94.

[33] Dan Donovan, "The Levitical Ministry in the Early Church," (Ph.D. diss., University of Münster, 1970) 571–6.

[34] R.P.C. Hanson, "Eucharistic offering in the Pre-Nicene Fathers," *Proceedings of the Royal Irish Academy* 76 C (1976) 89–91.

[35] See Bond and Camm, 1.4–8; also 1.22–3 for the three-fold division of churches used to recreate the structures of the Tabernacle and Temple. Rood screens and lofts eventually became fixed structures in numerous medieval churches. In one particularly interesting example, the eleventh-century reconstruction of the Benedictine priory of Christ Church in Canterbury undertaken by Archbishop Lanfranc (ca. 1070–7) contained a rood beam at the top of the screen which represented two cherubim as guardians of the inner sanctuary, a scene reminiscent of the guardians of the ark of the covenant; see Aylmer Vallance, *Great English Church Screens* (London: B.T. Batsford, 1947) 28.

[36] See *Le Sacramentaire gregorién*, ed. Jean Deshusses (3 vols.; Fribourg: Éditions universitaires, 1971–82) 3.176–212. This identification only increased over subsequent

prior conceptualization of the Eucharist as Christ's body, a portable, ingestible temple. The sacralization of the Eucharist and its ministers is perhaps the single most important post-biblical development in our study of the body as temple.

Thereafter a simple logic developed concerning the body, the Eucharist, and the temple: since Jesus' body is a Temple, and the Eucharist is his Body, then the Eucharist is both Body and temple. This three-fold association of body, temple, and Eucharist was explored in the liturgical commentary of Amalarius of Metz (ca. 775–ca. 850), "Book of Ecclesiastical Offices" (*Liber officialis*). Jesus' bodily sacrifice in the Mass is explicated within the context of a christianized Temple.[37] The ninth- and eleventh-century debates about the nature of the Eucharist were conducted under the influence of this kind of liturgical praxis and commentary. The resulting doctrines exhibited a wide range of meaning, yet increasingly functioned under the rubric of the Incarnation. New importance was placed on the shared nature of the sacrificial Host and humanity commingled in the eucharistic feast; by eating Jesus' bodily sacrifice as Eucharist, believers take God within, and their bodies are renewed and transformed into temples.[38] William of St. Thierry (1085–1148?), a Cistercian monk, succinctly describes the result,

> [The believer] eats and drinks the Body and Blood of his Redeemer, the heavenly manna, the bread of angels, the bread of wisdom, and while eating it [the believer] is transformed into the nature of the food he eats. For to eat the Body of Christ is nothing other than to be made the body of Christ and the temple of the Holy Spirit . . . and dedicated by the rite of dedication . . . it can receive . . . no dweller other than the God who created and fashioned it.[39]

Adam emphasizes the transformative value of the eucharistic body of Christ. In the interior temple, one contemplates the historical body

---

centuries, see my doctoral dissertation, chapter two "The Place of the Temple in the Christian Imagination."

[37] *Amalarii episcopi opera liturgica omnia*, ed. J. Hanssons (2 vols.; Vatican City: Bibliotheca apostolica vaticana, 1948–50) 2.3, 35: *Triforme est corpus Christi*. I am grateful to John Gibaut for first pointing me to Amalarius's commentary.

[38] For example, Macy notes that in Durand of Fécamp, "Christ specifically took on flesh in order that we might be joined to his Godhead through consuming that flesh," 45 (see Durand, *De corpore et sanguine Christi*, PL 149.1383B–C).

[39] *Manducat et bibit corpus et sanguinem Redemptoris sui, manna caeleste, panem Angelorum, panem sapientiae; et manducans transformatur in naturam cibi quem manducat. Corpus enim Christi manducare, nihil est aliud quam corpus Christi effici, et templum Spiritus sancti? Templum*

of Christ as temple and is renewed, in soul and body, by the eucharistic body of Christ. For Adam, even the act of priestly celebration of the sacrament offers comfort and redemption. Adam reveals the complete Christian transformation of the idea of the temple into the sacrificial body of Christ: it is in the eucharistic communion that one encounters the tremendous presence of God.[40] Christ's body, the temple, and the Eucharist have become inseparable aspects of the faithful life.

c. Mary's body as Temple

The second 'body' that Adam identifies with the Temple is Mary. Her body is the temple because her womb was the original earthly dwelling place for the Incarnate God. In the twelfth century, Mary's body as the habitation for Christ represented God's earthly dwelling place in the medieval imagination as clearly and as often as did Jesus, perhaps even more so.[41] Adam of Dryburgh's string of pious addresses to Mary as "temple of God" (templum Dei) and as effective intercessor for Christian prayer were clearly characteristic of his time. He writes,

> She herself is our Lady and our advocate. She is our sweetness and life, our hope and mediatrix. She is the mother of God, the queen of the angels, the lover of humans, defeater of demons, refuge of the wretched, comfort of orphans, helper of the infirm, strength of the weak, confirmation of the just, the raising up of the fallen, forgiveness for the sinner, joy of the blessed. She is the tabernacle of the Father, the chamber of the Son, the arbour of the Holy Spirit, the resting

autem hoc cum ornatum fuerit praescriptarum positione virtutum, et supradicto dedicandi ordine dedicatum, nullos ulterius alienos titulos potest suscipere,nullum habitatorem, nisi Deum qui condidit illum et creavit. De natura et dignitate amoris. PL 184.403B; trans. The Nature and Dignity of Love (Kalamazoo: Cistercian Publications, 1981) 100. I would like to thank my colleague Teresa Pierre for directing me to William.

[40] Devotion to the Eucharist would become, in the thirteenth century and later, a pillar of popular devotion. But, as Miri Rubin has shown, 'official recognition' of eucharistic devotion was slow to emerge, which suggests its prior grounding in popular practice, see Corpus Christi: the Eucharist in Late Medieval Culture (Cambridge: Cambridge University Press, 1990) 164–212.

[41] See Hilda Graef, Mary; a History of Doctrine and Devotion (2 vols.; London: Sheed and Ward, 1963) 2.162–264 for the section on medieval devotions to Mary. References to Mary's body include "temple of God" (e.g., in Eadmer, De conceptione beatae Mariae virginae, PL 159.305D: quod ipse sibi parabat templo in quo corporealiter habitaret, et de quo in unitate suae personae perfectus homo fieret . . .), and "the ladder of heaven" (e.g., in Ambrose Autpert, Sermo in assumptione Mariae, PL 39.2133: facta est certe humilitas Mariae scala coelestis, per quam descendit Deus ad terram).

place of the Trinity, the celestial habitation, the home of the incarnate Word, the temple of God.[42]

The story of Mary's connection with the Temple goes back to the legend concerning her childhood dedication. In the *Protoevangelion of James*, Mary is an infant oblate to the Temple (6.2; 7.2),[43] and as a dedicated virgin she weaves the sacred veil of the Temple, which later tears at the crucifixion of Jesus (10.1).[44] The presentation of the infant Mary in the Temple became a festival in the eastern Church in the eighth century and by the eleventh century moved into the western Church as well.[45]

Ambrose of Milan (d. 397) was perhaps the first Latin Christian author to equate Mary with the Temple because she bore the Incarnate God in her womb.[46] References to Mary as the "temple of God" (*templum Dei*) or the "temple of the Lord" (*templum Domini*) are thereafter found in the homilies and prayers of such influential authors as Bede, Peter Damian (1007–72), and Anselm of Canterbury.[47] Devotion to Mary as temple grew steadily throughout the early Middle Ages, picking up its pace around the turn of the millen-

---

[42] *Ipsa domina nostra, et advocata nostra; dulcedo et vita nostra: spes et mediatrix nostra. Ipsa Dei genitrix, regina angelorum, amatrix hominum, superatrix daemonum, refugium miserorum, solamen pupillorum, auxilium infirmorum, robur debilium, confirmatio justorum, erectio lapsorum, absolutio peccatorum, laetitia beatorum. Ipsa patris tabernaculum, filii cubiculum, Spiritus sancti umbraculum, Trinitatis reclinatorium, coeleste habitaculum, incarnati Verbi domicilium, Dei templum.* PL 198.367C–D.

[43] *La Forme la plus ancienne du Protévangile de Jacques*, ed. E. de Strycker (Brussels: Societé des Bollandistes, 1961); for bibliography, see W. Schneemelcher, ed., *Neutestamentliche Apokryphen*, (2 vols.; Tübingen: J.C.R. Mohr, 1959–64) 2.277–90 (English trans. *New Testament Apocrypha*, rev. ed. [2 vols.; Philadelphia: Westminster Press, 1991] 2.421–39).

[44] Peter Brown, *The Body and Society* (New York: Columbia University Press, 1988) 273 notes that Mary's enclosure in the Temple became the model for all later descriptions of consecrated women.

[45] Yves Congar, *The Mystery of the Temple* (Newman Press, 1962) 254, note 2. Mary's presentation in the Temple is not to be confused with Jesus' presentation by Mary (2 February).

[46] *De Spiritu Sancto* 3.80. Ambrose also likened Mary to the shut gate of Ezekiel's vision (Ez 44:2) in his *de institutione virginis* 8.54 (cited in Brown, *Body*, 354–5). See also Jerome, *Epistola ad Eustochium* 22 (23) on virgins, in general, as the temples of God. I thank my colleague Liesl Smith for pointing out the broader connection between virgins and the *templum Dei*.

[47] See Bede, *Homiliae*, Liber III, LXXXI (*ad sanctas omnes*), PL 94.452; Peter Damian, *De Beata Maria, ad sextam*, in *Lateinische Hymnendichter* (*Analecta hymnica* 48), ed. G. Dreves (Leipzig: R. Reisland, 1905), #25, p. 36; PL 145.921B; Anselm of Canterbury, *Oratio* LV, PL 158.962A.

nium.[48] At this time, the four Marian great festivals became extremely popular,[49] with the feast of the Assumption of Mary becoming one of the major festivals of the Church year.[50] Mary's corporeal assumption into heaven relied upon her physical status as the undefiled *templum Dei*,[51] and this doctrine was increasingly accepted during the tenth and eleventh centuries.[52] Mary's perpetual virginity was then represented in images of the Temple, such as the closed east-facing gate of Ezekiel's temple vision (Ez 44:1–3).[53]

The association of Mary's body with the Temple was an essential step on the way toward conceiving of the human body as God's temple. Mary was the human being most worthy of imitation and as temple she was an example, the obedient recipient of the divine call for all humanity to become God's earthly dwelling places. The great popularity of Marian devotion assured wide transmission of the idea of the body as temple.

d. *The believer's body as Temple*

We have seen how the identification of Jesus's body with the Temple evolved slowly over the course of many centuries, and how it influenced even the shape of churches. As well, we have seen how a parallel development equated Mary's body with the Temple. Devotions to the Body of Christ and to Mary transcended the social boundaries

---

[48] Penny Schine Gold, *The Lady and the Virgin* (Chicago: University of Chicago Press, 1985) 43; see also Éric Palazzo and Ann-Katrin Johansson, "Jalons liturgiques pour une histoire du culte de la Vierge dans l'Occident latin (V^e–XIe siècles)," in *Marie: le culte de la Vierge dans la societé médiévale*, ed. D. Iogna-Prat, É. Palazzo and D. Russo (Paris: Beauchesne, 1996) 18–9.

[49] Palazzo and Johansson, "Jalons liturgiques," 23–4. The four Marian festivals are the Nativity, Annunciation, Purification, and Assumption.

[50] See Palazzo and Johansson, "Jalons liturgiques," 34.

[51] Graef, *Mary*, 2.179 points out three sermons on the Assumption attributed to Ildephonsus that are likely the work of Paschasius Radbert. In one of these sermons, Mary is assumed into heaven because she is God's temple: *sicque Ecclesiam una cum matre reduxit ad superos, quoniam ipsa est Dei templum, et arca novi testamenti . . .* (PL 96. 238A).

[52] See Palazzo and Johansson, "Jalons liturgiques," 36; also Graef, *Mary*, 2.203–11.

[53] Betty al-Hamdani, "The Burning Lamp and other Romanesque Symbols for the Virgin that come from the Orient," *Commentari* XVI. III–IV (1965) 174–8. The image that al-Hamdani notes is the *porta clausa* in a manuscript of Ildephonsus of Toledo's *De virginitate perpetua S. Mariae adversus tres infideles*, dated 1067, and now found in the Laurentian Library, Florence, ms Ashburnham 17. Rupert of Deutz also refers to Mary as this gate: *Porta sanctuarii quae est, nisi Virgo, per quam primo patuit janua sanctuarii exterioris, sanctuarii coelestis . . .* (PL 167.1493C).

between popular and elite members of the Church. It is important
to note that these devotional innovations preceded the renewed association of the individual believer's body with the Temple, to which
we now turn. Adam's discussion of the human body as temple is
quite brief and focuses on "those things which pertain to the
sanctification of your body," such as fasting, prayer, alms-giving, seri-
ousness of appearance, and chastity.[54] In order to understand how
creative this new use of the Temple was, as well as the importance
of Adam's short statement about spiritual exercises, we must look
briefly at the changing role of the body and its capacity for renewal
in the Christian tradition.

In the Greek patristic tradition the material body was believed to
be at best a garment covering the spiritual body, or at worst a regret-
table consequence of sin and the Fall.[55] In either case, the material
body obscured the image of God (*imago Dei*), the locus of human
redemption. While the material body was problematic, eastern
Christians centred their notion of salvation on the Incarnation of
Christ rather than on the Passion and Resurrection, an emphasis
which did not come to the West until the central Middle Ages.[56]

Among the Latin Fathers, the most influential on the topic of the
body for the Middle Ages was Augustine of Hippo (354–430).[57] For

---

[54] "We have called your body the fifth temple. Do not depart this temple, that
is, do not neglect those things which pertain to the sanctification of your body.
Take care to feed the hungry and to give drink to the thirsty, to dress the naked,
to greet the stranger, to go to the incarcerated, to visit the sick. In these six works
of mercy, we ought to meet the needs of our neighbours according to (our) abili-
ties, but [also we ought] to be willing to do good according to our powers (Mt.
25:35)." (*Quintum templum assignavimus corpori tuo. Noli et de hoc templo discedere, id est noli
ea, quae ad sanctificationem corporis tui pertinent, negligere. Cura cibare esurientem, potare sitien-
tem, nudum vestire, hospitem colligere, venire ad incarceratum, visitare infirmum. In sex opera mise-
ricordiae, quibus indigentiae debemus proximorum juxta vires occurrere, sed prodesse etiam juxta
vires velle*). PL 198.369A.

[55] See Gregory of Nyssa, "On the Making of Man" (*de hominis opficio*) as discussed
in Gerhart B. Ladner, "The Philosophical Anthropology of Saint Gregory of Nyssa,"
DOP 12 (1958) 58–94, reprinted in *Images and Ideas in the Middle Ages* (2 vols.; Rome:
Edizioni di storia e letteratura, 1983) 2.825–65. See Origen, "On First Principles" (*Peri
archôn*) as discussed in Brown, *Body* 164–9 (on Origen) and 293–6 (on Gregory). See
also Kallistos Ware, "'My Helper and my Enemy': The Body in Greek Christianity,"
in *Religion and the Body*, ed. Sarah Coakley (Cambridge: Cambridge University Press,
1997), 96–100.

[56] Gerhart B. Ladner, "St. Augustine's Conception of the Reformation of Man
to the Image of God," *Augustinus Magister, Congrès International Augustinien, Paris 21–24
September 1954*, 867–78, reprinted in *Images and Ideas in the Middle Ages*, 2.595–6.

[57] Augustine's contemporaries, Ambrose and Jerome, were less optimistic about
the body than Augustine.

him, both epistemological and anthropological barriers stood between
the human person and the original *imago Dei*. These barriers were
the result of the Fall when the mortal body and the rational mind
were disconnected from one another in the primeval act of disobedience.[58] The Fall resulted in the disordering of mind and body and
the human being's inability to glory in the status of divine image-
bearer.[59] These barriers were, however, believed to have been sur-
mounted, in part, by the saving acts of Crucifixion and Resurrection.
More importantly, Augustine saw the material body as bearing the
enduring *imago Dei*, freed through the Crucifixion to be fully revealed
in the general resurrection.[60] Augustine recognized that the disordering of mind and body would be a factor in the human condition until the final resurrection; until which time, the grace of free-will
remains distorted by sin, personal change cannot be perfectly willed,
knowledge of the truth stands behind the horizon of the darkened
human intellect, and the human body, despite bearing the *imago Dei*,
is the problematic junior member of the psychosomatic union.[61]
Despite his apparent pessimism about the present human condition,
Augustine maintained a stubborn hope for the transformation of the
human individual and society in the present.[62]

By the tenth century, as we have already seen in passing, western Christians began to invest much greater importance in the human
body of Jesus; by extension their own material bodies came to be
seen as sharing the same human nature as Jesus.[63] The renewal of
incarnational theology in the West coincided with the growing popular interest in Jesus' life and works, which resulted in Anselm of
Canterbury's systematic reflections on the implications of the Incarnation for the human person in "Why God Became Man" (*Cur Deus
Homo*). Anselm was rooted in the Augustinian tradition, yet moved

---

[58] Andrew Louth, "The Body in Western Catholic Christianity," in *Religion and
the Body*, 116–19.
[59] Brown, *Body*, 397–407.
[60] Ladner, "Augustine," 597–602.
[61] Brown, *Body*, 416–22 and 429–46.
[62] Ladner, "Augustine," 602–7.
[63] It is possible that John Scotus Eriugena (ca. 810–ca. 877) transmitted Greek
ideas about the soteriological importance of the Incarnation into the Latin West,
thereby renewing the debate about the material body. In his "On the Division of
Nature" (*Periphyseon*), Eriugena pitted eastern ideas (namely, Gregory of Nyssa's 'spiritual body') against those held in the West (especially, Augustine's emphasis on the
material body as the locus of the *imago Dei*), and in so doing created the beginnings of a synthesis.

beyond his mentor's cautious anthropology. For Anselm, sin is the false likeness to God which the human will has chosen in its wickedness. Anselm implies that the will that takes on a false image can, with the aid of the Son, regain the enduring image of God in the present life.[64] For Anselm, there is no anthropological barrier to redemption; by the light of reason and the Incarnation, the epistemological barrier is also lessened. Anselm believes, like his Greek predecessors, that the Incarnation overcomes the monstrous disorder of the Fall. Thus humanity gains a toe-hold in redemption on a tiny theological ledge and the human body, associated with divinity in the Incarnation, fed on the eucharistic body of Christ, and bearing the image of God, takes up a more important position in the economy of salvation.

Bernard of Clairvaux (1090/1–1153), writing some thirty or forty years after Anselm, embraces the new possibilities for the body. In his sermons on the dedication of the church at Clairvaux, Bernard states

> For what of sanctity can belong to these dead walls on account of which they should be honoured with a religious solemnity? They are undoubtedly holy, but it is because of your bodies. For indeed does anyone doubt that your bodies are holy, which are the temple of the Holy Spirit? (1 Cor 6:19)[65]

The church building is sanctified by the bodies of its monks because they are the "temple of God." Bernard is particularly attuned to the potential of the body in human redemption. For him, the body "has maintained the likeness to God lost by the soul in the Fall;"[66] this

---

[64] ". . . both man, for whom the Son was to pray, and the devil, whom he was to defeat, had taken wilfully upon themselves false likeness of God. Hence they had sinned, as it were, more specifically against the person of the Son, who is believed to be the true likeness of the Father." (*Homo pro quo erat oraturus, et diabolus quem erat expugnaturus, ambo falsam similitudinem dei per propriam voluntatem praesumpserant. Unde quasi specialius adversus personam filii peccaverant, qui vera patris similitudo creditur). Cur Deus Homo* 2, 9; trans. Janet Fairweather in *Anselm of Canterbury: the Major Works* (Oxford: Oxford University Press, 1998) 324–5.

[65] *Quid enim lapides isti potuerunt sanctitatis habere, et eorum sollemnia celebremus? Habent utique sanctitatem, sed propter corpora vestra. An vero corpora vestra sancta esse quis dubiet, quae templum Spiritus Sancti sunt (II Cor 6, 9). In dedicatione ecclesiae, sermo primus, Sancti Bernardi Opera*, ed. J. Leclercq and H. Rochais (8 vols.; Rome: Editiones cistercienses, 1957–77) 5.370–1; trans. a priest of Mount Melleray, *St. Bernard's Sermons for the Seasons and Principal Festivals of the Year* (3 vols.; Dublin: Browne and Nolan, 1924) 2.385; see Renna, "Bernard and Solomon's Temple," 80–2 for his discussion of this text.

[66] John R. Sommerfeldt, *The Spiritual Teachings of Bernard of Clairvaux* (Kalamazoo:

is why the exercises of daily life, which he calls "bodily observances" (*observationes corporeas*), are essential to the restoration of one's internal life.[67] The restoration of the individual monk extends to the monastic community. Bernard writes,

> Therefore, dearest brethren, let us endeavour with all ardour of desire and with all thanksgiving to build a temple to the Lord in us. Let it be our first solicitude that He dwell in each of us singly, and then let us induce Him to make His abode in us as a community also.[68]

For Bernard, the body of the monk as God's dwelling place is a building block for the monastery as divine habitation.

Bernard acknowledges that this present body is only a temporary dwelling for God; what lies ahead is the eternal body in the permanent dwelling place of God in heaven. Attention to the earthly body in the twelfth century made the prospect of its dissolution problematic. As a result, there was at this time an increasing use of static images, such as a rebuilt statue or temple, rather than 'organic' images to represent the resurrection body.[69] Changelessness was a desired bodily state associated with the resurrection body and the Temple was a sign of that state. The importance of changelessness makes the discussion about the body of the individual believer as temple all the more poignant. Clearly, the present body will dissolve, yet some believed that it too could partake of the heavenly promise of changelessness before the resurrection. The Desert Fathers in the early Church certainly felt that they could achieve a measure of

---

Cistercian Publications, 1991) 24 (see 24–31 for his discussion of Bernard's view of the body).

[67] "I do not mean by this that external means can be overlooked, or that the man who does not employ them will become quickly spiritual. Spiritual things are certainly higher, but there is little hope of attaining them or receiving them without making use of external exercises" (*Neque hoc dico, quia haec exteriora negligenda sint, aut qui se illis non exercuerit, mox ideo spiritualis efficatur, cum potius spiritualia, quamquam meliora, nisi per ista, aut vix, aut nullatenus vel acquirantur, vel obtineantur). Apologia ad Abbatum Guillelmum, Sancti Bernardi Opera*, 3.94.

[68] *Itaque, fratres, toto cum desiderio et digna gratiarum actione studeamus ei templum aedificare in nobis, primo quidem solliciti, ut in singulis, deinde ut in omnibus simul inhabitet, quia nec singulos dedignatur, nec universos. In dedicatione ecclesiae, sermo secundus, Sancti Bernardi Opera* 5.377; trans, 2.397.

[69] Caroline Walker Bynum, *The Resurrection of the Body* (New York: Columbia University Press, 1995) 130–6 and 224–5, suggests that earlier models of the human body "growing" into its resurrection state (hence "organic" imagery) are replaced in the twelfth century (by authors such as William of Saint-Thierry and Hugh of Saint-Victor) with inorganic images: rebuilt statues and the rebuilt Temple.

changelessness in their extreme ascetic practices: by eating and sleeping little, the body slowed and they regained some of the blessed-
ness of the pre-lapsarian body of Adam.[70] Even the ascetic food
practices of some medieval women were attempts to transcend their
bodily limitations, to reach beyond the present body and partake of
the heavenly body.[71] William of Saint-Thierry, as we have seen, perceived a link between eating the Eucharist and bodily stasis: for him
the temple of peace is built within by eating the body of Christ.
Eating God inoculates the body against decay and accelerates the
possibility of enjoying true sanctity on earth.[72] These are themes that
Adam reiterates at the century's end; but, as we shall see, in Adam
it is spiritual exercises more than food practises that sanctify the
body and offer a glimpse of the heavenly stasis.

Preoccupation with the resurrected body suggests that the body
in the High Middle Ages, besides being the locus of mortality and
decay, was also the locus of personal identity. In this context the
corporeal self is seen as the locus of the spiritual practices of reading, meditation, and remembering, and the place in which the interior temple of God is constructed. Augustine already wrote of
interiorizing the temple in prayer, reading, and interpretation in the
fifth century.[73] For him, as for later authors, interiorization is an
intellectual and cultural process that is disciplined and voluntary; it
is not a datum about the self.

We noted above that when Adam speaks of internalizing the Body
of Christ, he assumes the use of memory as the central tool for this
task.[74] He writes,

> Therefore I hasten to the body which has not committed (any) sin in
> order that the sin which I have committed through the body be remit-
> ted. Because if the flesh in me lusts against the Spirit (Gal 5:17); if
> the vices of the flesh have a grip on me; if its titillating goads vex
> (me), is it not then the more necessary for me to hasten back to my
> firm and only refuge, the body of my Jesus, in order that the concu-
> piscense of my body be extinguished, the temptations be overcome,

---

[70] Brown, *Body*, 220–5.

[71] Caroline Bynum, *Holy Feast, Holy Fast* (Berkeley: University of California Press,
1987) 189–218.

[72] Bynum, *Resurrection*, 222.

[73] See, e.g., *De Magistro* 1.2; *De doctrina Christiana* 3.14.22; *Confessiones* 13.15; *De diver-
sis quaestionibus* 20; *Enarrationes in Psalmos* 64.8; *De trinitate* 1.6.13 and 7.3.6.

[74] See above, 240–243.

and the goads be blunted? For what is more efficacious an aid for obtaining a victory of this kind than pure and serene meditation on his body?[75]

Meditation on the human body of Jesus elevates the body of the one contemplating through identification with the Incarnate God's body. By virtue of this identity, Jesus' historical body can be internalized in memory and there form a shield against sin.

Hugh of St. Victor (1096?–1141), an Augustinian canon and an explicit source in Adam's writings, explores techniques for stilling the 'restless heart' and building a house for God in one's own heart in his treatise "On the Moral Meaning of Noah's Ark" (*De arca Noe morali*).[76] The faculty for the construction of the interior house of God is the memory. Hugh writes,

> First we must specify the place wherein the Lord's house must be built; then we must tell you of its material. The place is the heart of man, and the material is pure thoughts. Let no one make excuse, let no one say: 'I cannot build a house for the Lord, my slender means are not sufficient to meet such great demands. Exile and pilgrim I am, and dwelling in a country not my own, I lack even a site. This is work for kings. This is work for many people. How should I build a house for the Lord?' O man, why do you think like that? That is not what your God requires from you. He is not telling you to buy a piece of land from someone else, in order to extend His courts. He wants to dwell in your own heart—extend and enlarge that![77]

One reads the Bible to train the memory, thus internalizing the biblical text, and converting it into the story of one's own life, a moral

---

[75] *Sic ergo curro ad corpus, quod non fecit peccatum: ut et mihi remittatur, quod per corpus feci, peccatum. Quod si in me caro concupiscit adversus Spiritum (Gal. V, 17); si me carnis vitia tentant; si stimuli ejus titillantes infestant: nonne et tunc mihi magis recurrendum est, ad solum et solidum refugium meum, Jesu mei corpus, ut corporis mei concupiscentia exstinguatur, superentur tentationes, stimuli hebetentur? quod enim tam efficax auxilium ad obtinendum hujusmodi triumphum, quam pura et defaecata meditatio corporis ejus?* PL 198. 366D–367A.

[76] PL 176.617–80. Noah's Ark is cognate with the Temple; Hugh uses the Ark to present the shape of one's interior world. I am grateful to Jeremy Worthen for pointing out Hugh's use of this metaphor in other works, including *De vanitate mundi*, in his unpublished article, "For the Love of God: Hugh of St. Victor and Biblical Exegesis."

[77] *Primum designandus est locus, in quo aedificari oporteat domum Domini. Deinde scribenda materia. Locus est cor hominis, materia cogitationes mundae. Nemo se excuset. Nemo dicat, non possum aedificare domum Domino, non sufficit tantis impendiis tenuis paupertas mea, cui et ipse locus deest exuli, et pergrino, et in terra aliena degenti. Hoc opus est regnum, hoc multorum est opus populorum. Ego vero quomodo aedificabo domum Domino? Cur sic cogites homo? Non hoc exigit a te Deus tuus. Non dicit tibi, ut fundum emas alienum ad amplificanda atria sua. Cor*

narrative of scripture rooted in the believer's heart, or memory.[78]
Through this process, the individual enlarges the heart and constructs God's interior dwelling place, and the internal narrative shapes
the ethical life of the believer.

The corporeal nature of the ethical self is also explored by Hugh's
contemporary, Peter the Venerable (1092–1156), the abbot of Cluny.
In a sermon preached in Paris on the eve of the Second Crusade
in 1147, entitled "In Praise of the Lord's Sepulchre" (*De laude sepulchri dominici*), Peter transfers the meaning of the Temple as God's
dwelling place to Christ's tomb where his body rested for three days
and was then resurrected.[79] Peter follows the developing discourse
about God's interior dwelling place; he praises the building in the
Holy Land, but the sepulchre that interests him is the quiet resting
place that every Christian constructs in his or her heart through
memory and meditation. The heart that Peter speaks of is clearly
the memory, as he says,

> [Christ] is the one who 'abides in my breast,' at no time ever will he
> be separated from the memory of my bosom or heart, because he
> claims for himself within my breast a place in the middle of my body.
> In this respect I will even imitate his tomb . . . by retaining in my
> heart . . . a perpetual memorial of him.[80]

---

tuum inhabitare vult, hoc amplifica, dilata. . . . PL 176. 663B; trans. in *Hugh of Saint-Victor:
Selected Spiritual Writings* (London: Faber and Faber, 1962) 122–3.

[78] Carruthers, *Book of Memory*, 44 on the heart as a metaphor for memory.

[79] "If therefore the temple of God, constructed for the pouring out of prayers to
God, is called holy, is not the tomb all the more holy, which contains within itself
the temple of God, that is Christ, in whom God reconciled the world to himself,
[and] who said concerning himself: 'Destroy this temple, and in three days I will
raise it up'? If the altar of God, on which the corpses of animals are offered to
God, is holy, is not the tomb of the Lord, in which rests the sacrificed body, offered
to God, of the Lamb of God who takes away the sins of the world, all the more
holy?" (*Si igitur templum Dei ad preces Deo fundendas constructum, sanctum dictum est,
nonne sepulchrum in se continens templum Dei, id est Christum, in quo Deus erat mundum rec-
oncilians sibi, qui de seipso ait: 'Solvite templum hoc et in tribus diebus excitabo illud', mul-
tomagis sanctum est? Si altare Dei cadavera animalium oblata Deo suscipiens sanctum est, nonne
sepulchrum Domini, in quo corpus Agni Dei qui tollit peccata mundi Deo oblatum requievit, mul-
tomagis sanctum est?*), "De laude sepulchri domini," ed. Giles Constable, *Rbén* 64 (1954)
235.

[80] *Qui 'inter ubera mea commorabitur', quia a memoria pectoris vel cordis mei, quod inter
ubera etiam in corpore meo medium sibi locum vendicat, nullo unquam tempore separabitur. Imitabor
et in hoc sepulchrum eius quod velut in medio terrae positum continuit corpus eius, retinendo in
corde meo, quod quasi inter ubera mea medium est, perpetuam memoriam eius.* "De laude,"
243.15–21.

Incarnational memory transforms the reader's knowledge of Christ's life, death and resurrection into a personal narrative which shapes the moral life of the believer. Once a sepulchre for Christ is constructed within this interior temple, its remembered inhabitant shapes the ethical self of its host. Peter makes few references to the soul or even the mind in his reflections on the Lord's sepulchre. Instead, he addresses his own flesh exhorting it to become the sepulchre of Christ. It is the memory in the body no less than the memory of the Body that constructs the interior temple.

Adam adopts Hugh's (and possibly Peter's) insights into memory and the house of God and with them shapes the memory of the Incarnate God that one must employ in order to construct Christ's bodily temple within. Adam's brief text on the body as temple suggests, however, that the construction of an interior temple is not an end in itself; the goal of Adam's discourse is to point his readers toward "the things that sanctify the body," that is, charitable acts such as giving to the needy. Adam gives explicit attention to the desired outcome of moral guidance from the interior temple, an implicit theme in the work of Hugh and Peter. As with the priestly act of celebrating the Eucharist, Adam seeks to locate the interior temple, as constructed through memory, prayer, and devotion, in the larger world.

The use of the interior temple to signify the shaping of the self in the High Middle Ages proves appropriate because it contains within its very nature the idea of construction (*aedificare*, "to build"), both of the self and, by extension, of the world.[81] This notion of voluntary interiorization gained increased application in the twelfth century when monks and canons alike were instructed in making their bodies temples through reading, memory, and self-knowledge. This novel approach was dependent upon prior developments in theology, popular devotions, anthropology, and epistemology; it is ultimately founded

---

[81] This idea is clear in Hugh of Saint Victor's *De arca* where building the temple of God within is a spiritual exercise of self-construction. He writes, "God dwells in the human heart after two modes—namely, by knowledge and love . . . There seems however to be this difference between them, that knowledge erects the structure of faith by its knowing, whereas love like the adorning colour embellishes the building by its virtue" (*Duobus modis Deus cor humanum inhabitat, per cognitionem videlicet et amorem, una tamen differre videtur, quod scientia per cognitionem fidei fabricam erigit, dilectio autem per virtutem quasi colore superducto aedificium pingit*), *De arca* 1, 2. PL 176.621D.

in the Pauline texts that we discussed at the outset of this article. The high medieval use of the Temple as a metaphor for the body was a celebration of God's presence within the community and bodies of the faithful, and, by their presence, in the world; it was a profound spiritual invention which gave great currency to ideas about the reform of the individual and the world. In this respect, there is no Christian envy of the Temple; the Christian idea of the body as Temple concerns democratized access to the sublime, and the pious deeds such access inspired.[82]

BIBLIOGRAPHY

Adam of Dryburgh. *De exercitio religiosae conversationis (Sermo XL)*. Patrologia Latina 198.363–72. Paris: J.-P. Migne, 1855.

Adso of Montier-en-Der. *Libellus de ortu et tempore Antichristo*. Edited by D. Verhelst. Corpus Christianorum, Continuatio Medievalis 45. Turnhout: Brepols, 1976.

Al-Hamdani, Betty. "The Burning Lamp and other Romanesque Symbols for the Virgin that come from the East." *Commentari* 16.3–4 (1965): 167–85.

Alphandéry, Paul. *La Chretienté et l'idee de croisade*. 2 vols. Paris: Éditions Albin Michel, 1954.

Amalarius of Metz. *Liber officialis*. In *Amalarii episcopi opera liturgica omnia*. Edited by J. Hanssons. Vol. 2. Vatican City: Bibliotheca apostolica vaticana, 1948.

Anselm of Canterbury. *Cur Deus Homo*. In *Sancti Anselmi Omnia Opera*. Edited by F.S. Schmitt. Vol. 2. Rome: n.p., 1940.

Anselm of Canterbury. *Anselm of Canterbury: the Major Works*. Oxford: Oxford University Press, 1998.

Beckwith, John. *Early Medieval Art*. New York: Praeger Publishers, 1965.

Bede. *De Templo*. Edited by D. Hurst. Corpus Christianorum, Series Latina 119A. Turnhout: Brepols, 1969.

Bernard of Clairvaux. *Sermones in dedicatione ecclesiae*. In *Sancti Bernardi Opera*. Edited by J. Leclercq and H. Rochais. Vol. 5. Rome: Editiones cistercienses, 1968.

Bernard of Clairvaux. *Apologia ad Abbatum Guillelmum*. In *Sancti Bernardi Opera*. Edited by J. Leclercq and H. Rochais. Vol. 3. Rome: Editiones cistercienses, 1963.

---

[82] On account of necessary limits, we are unable to discuss here the transference of the Temple traditions to the Holy Sepulchre and its imitations in the West. For discussion of these highly relevant topics, see Bianca Kühnel, "Jewish Symbolism of the Temple and the Tabernacle and Christian Symbolism of the Holy Sepulchre and the Heavenly Tabernacle," *Jewish Art*, 12/13 (1986/7) 150–2; Sylvia Schein, "Between the Temple Mount and the Holy Sepulchre: The Changing Traditions of the Temple Mount in the Central Middle Ages," *Traditio* 40 (1984) 175–95; Robert Ousterhout. "The Temple, the Sepulchre, and the *Martyrion* of the Savior," *Gesta* 29 (1990) 44–53. For the imitation of the Holy Sepulchre in western European architecture, see Bresc-Bautier, "Les imitations du Saint-Sépulcre;" Carol Heitz, "Le modèle du Saint-Sèpulcre," in *Guillaume de Volpiano et l'architecture des rotondes*, ed. M. Jannet and C. Sapin (Dijon: Éditions universitaires de Dijon, 1996); Guy Stroumsa, "Mystical Jerusalems," in his *Barbarian Philosophy: The Religious Revolution of Early Christianity* (Tübingen: Siebeck, 1999).

St. Bernard's Sermons for the Seasons and Principal Festivals of the Year. Translated by a priest of Mount Melleray. 3 vols. Dublin: Browne and Nolan, 1924.

Bond, F.B. and B. Camm. *Roodscreens and Roodlofts*. 2 vols. London: Pitman and Sons, 1909.

Bresc-Bauthier, Geneviève. "Les imitations du Saint-Sépulcre de Jérusalem (IXᵉ–XVᵉ siècles): Archéologie d'une dévotion." *Revue d'histoire de la spiritualité* 50 (1974): 319–42.

Brown, Peter. *The Body and Society*. New York: Columbia University Press, 1988.

Bynum, Caroline Walker. *The Resurrection of the Body, 200–1336*. New York: Columbia University Press, 1995.

Bynum, Caroline Walker. *Holy Feast and Holy Fast: the Religious Significance of Food to Medieval Women*. Berkeley: University of California Press, 1987.

Carruthers, Mary. *The Book of Memory*. Cambridge: Cambridge University Press, 1990.

Congar, Yves. *The Mystery of the Temple*. Westminster, MD: Newman Press, 1962.

Constable, Giles. *The Reformation of the Twelfth Century*. Cambridge: Cambridge University Press, 1996.

Cowdrey, H.E.J. "The Genesis of the Crusades: the Springs of Western Ideas of Holy War." In *The Holy War*. Edited by T.P. Murphy, 11–28. Columbus, OH: Ohio State University Press, 1976.

Donovan, Dan. "The Levitical Priesthood in the Early Church." Ph.D. diss., University of Münster, 1970.

La Forme la plus ancienne Protévangile de Jacques. Edited by E. de Strycker. Brussels: Societé des Bollandistes, 1961.

Fried, Johannes. "Endzeiterwartung um die Jahrtausendwende." *Deutsches Archiv für Erforschung des Mittelalters* 45.2 (1989): 385–473.

Gold, Penny Schine. *The Lady and the Virgin: Image, Attitude, and Experience in Twelfth-century France*. Chicago: University of Chicago Press, 1985.

Graef, Hilda C. *Mary; a History of Doctrine and Devotion*. 2 vols. London: Sheed and Ward, 1963.

Gregory the Great. *Homiliae in Hezechielem*. Edited by M. Adriaen. Corpus Christianorum, Series Latina 142. Turnhout: Brepols, 1971.

Gregory the Great. *Moralia in Iob*. Edited by M. Adriaen. Corpus Christianorum, Series Latina 143. Turnhout: Brepols, 1979.

Hanson, R.P.C. "Eucharistic Offering in the Pre-Nicene Fathers." *Proceedings of the Royal Irish Academy* 76 C (1976): 75–95.

Hugh of Saint-Victor. *De arca Noe morali*. Patrologia Latina 176.617–80. Paris: J.-P. Migne, 1880.

Hugh of Saint-Victor: *Selected Spiritual Writings*. London: Faber and Faber, 1962.

Ladner, Gerhart B. "St. Augustine's Conception of the Reformation of Man to the Image of God." In *Augustinus Magister, Congrès International Augustinien, Paris 21–24 Septembre 1954*. Paris: Études augustiniennes, 1954–5; reprinted in *Images and Ideas in the Middle Ages*. Vol. 2. Rome: Edizioni di storia e letteratura, 1983.

Ladner, Gerhart B. "The Philosophical Anthropology of Saint Gregory of Nyssa." *Dumbarton Oaks Papers* 12 (1958): 58–94; reprinted in *Images and Ideas in the Middle Ages*. Vol. 2. Rome: Edizioni di storia e letteratura, 1983.

Landes, Richard. "Lest the Millennium be Fulfilled: Apocalyptic Expectations and the Pattern of Western Chronography 100–800 CE." In *The Use and Abuse of Eschatology in the Middle Ages*. Edited by W. Verheke, D. Verhelst and A. Welkenhuysen, 137–211. Leuven: Leuven University Press, 1988.

Lobrichon, Guy. "L'ordre de ce temps et les désordres de la fin." In *The Use and Abuse of Eschatology in the Middle Ages*. Edited by W. Verheke, D. Verhelst and A. Welkenhuysen, 221–41. Leuven: Leuven University Press, 1988.

Macy, Gary. *The Theologies of the Eucharist in the Early Scholastic Period*. Oxford: Clarendon Press, 1984.

Matter, E. Ann. "The Apocalypse in Early Medieval Exegesis." In *The Apocalypse in the Middle Ages*. Edited by R.K. Emmerson and B. McGinn, 38–50. Ithaca: Cornell University Press, 1992.

McGinn, Bernard. "Portraying the Antichrist in the Middle Ages." In *The Use and Abuse of Eschatology in the Middle Ages*. Edited by W. Verheke, D. Verhelst and A. Welkenhuysen, 1–48. Leuven: Leuven University Press, 1988.

——. "Symbols of the Apocalypse in Medieval Culture." *Western Quarterly Review* 22 (1983): 215–83; reprinted in *Apocalypticism in the Western Tradition*. Aldershot: Variorum, 1984.

Nibley, Hugh. "The Christian Envy of the Temple." *Jewish Quarterly Review* 50.2–3 (1959/60): 97–123, 229–40.

Palazzo, Éric and Ann-Katrin Johansson. "Jalons liturgiques pour une histoire du culte de la Vierge dans l'Occident latin (Vᵉ–XIᵉ siècles)." In *Marie: le culte de la Vierge dans société médiévale*. Edited by D. Iogna-Prat, É. Palazzo and D. Russo, 15–44. Paris: Beauchesne, 1996.

Pelikan, Jaroslav. *The Christian Tradition*. Vol. 3, *The Growth of Medieval Theology (600–1300)*. Chicago: University of Chicago Press, 1976.

Peter the Venerable. *De laude dominici sepulchri*. Giles Constable, ed. "Petri Venerabilis Sermones Tres." *Revue bénédictine* 64 (1954): 232–54.

Riley-Smith, Jonathan. *The First Crusaders*. Cambridge: Cambridge University Press, 1997.

Rubin, Miri. *Corpus Christi: the Eucharist in Late Medieval Culture*. Cambridge: Cambridge University Press, 1990.

Rupert of Deutz. *De Trinitate et operibus eius*. Edited by H. Haacke. Corpus Christianorum, Continuatio Medievalis 21–24. Turnhout: Brepols, 1971–2.

Le Sacramentaire gregorién. Edited by Jean Deshusses. 3 vols. Fribourg: Éditions universitaires, 1971–82.

Schneemelcher, Wilhelm, ed. *Neutestamentliche Apokryphon*. 2 vols. Tübingen: J.C. Mohr, 1959–64; English translation: *New Testament Apocrypha*. Rev. ed. 2 vols. Philadelphia: Westminster Press, 1991.

Sepière, Marie-Christine. *L'Image d'un Dieu souffrant: Aux origines du crucifix*. Paris: Cerf, 1994.

Stock, Brian. *The Implications of Literacy: Written Language and Models of Interpretation in the Eleventh and Twelfth Centuries*. Princeton: Princeton University Press, 1983.

Vallance, Aylmer. *Great English Church Screens*. London: B.T. Batsford, 1947.

William of Saint-Thierry. *De natura et dignitate amoris*. Patrologia Latina 184.379–408 Paris: J.-P. Migne, 1854.

——. *The Nature and Dignity of Love*. Kalamazoo, MI: Cistercian Publications, 1981.

Wilmart, André. "Magister Adam Carthusiensis." In *Mélanges Mandonnet*. Vol. 2. Paris: J. Vrin, 1930.

Worthen, Jeremy F. "Adam of Dryburgh and the Augustinian Tradition." *Revue des études augustiniennes* 43 (1997): 339–47.

FIRSTFRUITS IN THE QURAN*

JONATHAN BENTHALL

A green parable

The Quranic parable of the People of the Garden is told in the Surah called 'The Pen' (Q. 68:17–33) which is thought to have been one of the earliest revealed to the Prophet Muhammad, at a time when he was confronting detractors in Mecca. God tells how he tested a group of men who resolved to collect the fruits of a garden in the morning, but they failed to make the reservation 'If it be God's will', *In sha' Allah*. A terrible storm came down at night and destroyed the garden while they were sleeping. At dawn, they called out to one another, 'Get up early if you want to gather the fruits', and they set off with confidence, whispering furtively to one another that no paupers must be allowed to break in on the garden and claim any of the fruit that day. When they saw the dark and desolate garden, they said 'We've surely lost our way' and then 'We're dispossessed!' But one of them, a relatively just man, said 'Did I not say to you, why don't you glorify God?'. They all said, 'Glory to our Lord! We have really done wrong!' Then they started to blame each other. They said 'Alas for us! We've behaved outrageously. Maybe our Lord will give us in exchange a better garden than this, for we turn to him in remorse.' The Surah goes on to state that the punishments of this life are nothing compared to the punishments in the hereafter, whereas gardens of delight are reserved for the righteous.

Though the parable does not explicitly mention firstfruits, I will follow Christian Décobert who says it must refer to them (1991: 196). They are certainly fruits which the owners of the garden

* Acknowledgments.

Thanks are due to John Bowen, Mary Douglas, Arthur Hertzberg, Emanuel Marx, Sarah Stroumsa, Arlette Tadié and Ameur Zemmali for help and advice, as well as to the convenors and participants in the Bar Ilan conference. I am also grateful to the Royal Anthropological Institute for giving me six months' sabbatical leave for January to June 1996; and to the Nuffield Foundation for a research grant.

intended to pick first thing in the morning, which is considered an auspicious occasion throughout the region (Westermarck 1926: ii, 252–253, Jaussen 1948: 364–365). According to Hebraic teaching, which deeply if often obscurely underlies the Quran, the firstfruits, like the firstborn of a family and the firstlings of animals, belong to God and are subject to sacrifice.[1] Another passage in the Quran says that 'dues' (ḥaqq) must be paid on the day of harvest (6:141).

Fruits are frequently mentioned both as signs of God's abundance on earth and as the principal sustenance in the gardens of Paradise. Like the bad gardeners in the parable, the people of Saba' or Sheba were once surrounded, according to 34.15–16, by gardens, but they turned from God and he flooded their gardens so that only bitter tamarisks and thorny lote-trees would grow there.[2]

Discursive fields of ritual giving

In the Hebraic Pentateuch, the three themes of ceremonial sacrifice (whether of animals or vegetables), tithing, and provision for the poor seem to occupy discursive zones which hardly overlap. Ilana Silber[3]

---

[1] As Leach (1983: 52–53) and others have noted, the sacrifice of firstborn children was widespread in the geographical context of the Old Testament. Leach follows Frazer in emphasizing the apotropaic or evil-preventing role of this form of sacrifice, and it is true that a pattern of preference for the second son as the sacred heir (Abel, Isaac, Jacob) runs through the biblical narrative. However, vegetable sacrifice was also a marked feature of the Near Eastern historical background, as in Egypt (MacCulloch 1913, van der Toorn 1995: 2053), though there is comparatively little evidence from the Levant as opposed to North Africa, where the custom has survived into modern times (for Algeria, see Doutté 1908: 491, 493).

On firstlings in Hebraic religion, W. Robertson Smith argued that these had less in common with firstfruits than with the first three years' produce of a new orchard which was not to be eaten as it was 'as if uncircumcised to you' (Leviticus 19:23— Smith 1927: 240–241, 462–465, see also notes by his editor Stanley A. Cook 583–584). The semiotic connections between circumcision, blood-sacrifice and the cutting of fruit are beyond the scope of this paper.

The Quran mentions in scathing terms the pre-Islamic custom of burying young girls (wa'd al-banat, Q. 16:58–59, 81:8–9), which was interpreted by Robertson Smith (1885: 279–285) as a form of human sacrifice, though not by all the Arabic sources.

More generally, the biblical background to Quranic teaching about tithing for the poor was recognized by some classical commentators such as the great Persian scholar of the early 12th century, Zamakshari. (I am grateful to Professor Sarah Stroumsa for the preceding two points in this note.)

On Muslim birth rituals, see Aubaile-Sallenave 1999.

[2] This is said to refer to the breakdown of the irrigation system of the Yemen or the Marib dam.

[3] See her paper in the present collection (291–312). Traditional biblical scholar-

has proposed a more general tripartite comparative classification—gifts to gods, gifts to religious officials, and gifts to the needy—which seems to correspond to this specific biblical pattern. There are many injunctions in the Pentateuch to provide for the poor, but the only overlap with tithing that I can find is in Deuteronomy 14:28–29. Whereas the annual tithes went to the priests, Levites (members of a priestly tribe) or to fund ceremonial feasting (Num. 18:21–27, 28:26–27, Deut. 12:17–19, 14:22–27; 18:4; Neh. 10:38–40), also singers and doorkeepers (Lev. 13:5–15), a special triennial tithe was prescribed for Levites but also for widows, orphans and resident aliens. Otherwise, these beneficiaries were provided for by the right to annual gleanings, and owners of fields and orchards were enjoined not to strip the entire crop (Lev. 19:9, 23:22). As for sacrifice, the Pentateuch provides for a rich variety of sacrifices and offerings—some simple gifts with no presentation at an altar, others involving complex cooking and rituals (Marx 1994, Rogerson 1980), with a preference for Abel's offering of ovine firstlings over Cain's arable produce (Gen. 4:1–7). But tithing seems to be a separate matter.

In the Quran, by contrast, the three fields are thematically connected. Let us take first the major sacrifices of camels and cattle which are retained in Islam, even though some minor rites—such as the dedication and loosing for free pasture of a she-camel after someone has recovered from an illness—are condemned as pagan superstitions (Q. 5:103). It is clear that the Great Feast or Feast of Immolation is not only a ceremony but a practical means of providing for the needy: 'Then eat thereof and feed the distressed ones in want' (Q. 22:28). Again: 'When [the camels] are down on their sides [after slaughter], eat ye thereof, and feed such as [beg not but live in contentment], and such as beg with due humility' (Q. 22:36)—the point being that the most importunate beggars are not necessarily those most in need.

As for the Quranic tithe or *zakat*, which I have discussed at some length elsewhere (Benthall 1999a), this is aimed to benefit the poor far more emphatically than the Hebraic equivalent. The connection between *zakat*, which is mentioned many times, and animal sacrifice, which is mentioned sparingly, is not made explicitly, but both are closely associated with prayer: *zakat* frequently and sacrifice occasionally,

ship was however uncertain as to the separation between tithes and firstfruits (Strahan 1913).

e.g. 108: 1–2: 'To thee we have granted the fount [of abundance]. Therefore to thy Lord turn in prayer and sacrifice'.

The main references to animal sacrifices seem, as we would say today, to accept their materiality (no question of converting it into mere metaphor) while asserting that they are 'symbols'—*sha'āir*—of God (Q. 22:32, 22:36). For 'It is not [the camels'] meat nor their blood. that reaches Allah: it is your piety [*taqwā*] that reaches him: He has thus made them subject to you, that ye may glorify Allah for his guidance to you' (22:37).

In many parts of the world, Muslims still perform the sacrifice of a camel, sheep, cow or goat on the day of the Great Feast, *'Id al-Kabīr*, to commemorate Abraham's sacrifice of the ram instead of his son (Q. 37:99–106, Bonte 1999, Brisebarre 1998). According to a dominant Muslim tradition, the son was Ismā'īl, his eldest by Hagar, who in the Genesis narrative (16:16, 21:5) was 14 years older than Isaac. (An alternative Muslim tradition identifies Isaac as the son; cf. Bonte 1999: 23, Dagorn 1981: 357). Abraham and Ismā'īl are held to have founded the Ka'bah in Mecca and to have been Muhammad's ancestor, while Isaac was the forefather of the Jews. Some Muslim commentators argue that the biblical version (Gen 22:1–18) must be an erroneous overlay because Isaac was never the *only* son of Abraham, whereas he is so called in verse 2 ('Ali 1989: 1148–1151). In both versions, Abraham's intention to carry out the sacrifice satisfies God, and finally an animal replaces the son. However, in the biblical version, Abraham seeks (at least on a naive reading of the text) to deceive Isaac when he asks where the sacrificial beast is, saying that God will provide it, whereas in the Quranic version the son, who has reached the age of working with his father, consents to the proposed act. Later rabbinic traditions assert that Isaac was told by his father that he was to be the sacrificial victim and assented (Hayward 1980). Abraham's interrupted sacrifice deeply underpins the theology of all three Semitic monotheisms, so deeply that we have had to wait till 1998 to read a thoroughgoing critique, by the feminist anthropologist Carol Delaney, of the patriarchal values which she claims have legitimated this disturbing narrative over more than two millennia. Why, she argues, cannot love of God be expressed *through* love of one's children, rather than in spite of it? And she argues that Freud was unable to analyse the Abraham narrative clearly, displacing it by a dubious palaeontological story of the sons stoning their father to death, and claiming universality for the Greek myth of Oedipus which but for Freud would have remained within the preserves of classical scholarship (Delaney 1998, cf. Benthall 1999b).

The Parable of the Garden brings the three themes together. Christians are also enjoined in the New Testament to say 'If it be the Lord's will' before embarking on a project, but Arabic theology has a special name for the reservation, *istithnā*, deriving from this passage (v. 18). The gardeners' first error is therefore to forget the firm principle, Quranic but shared by the other two Abrahamic monotheisms, that all wealth belongs to God. Their second error, if we accept Décobert's interpretation, is to refuse to offer the firstfruits. And their third is to seek to exclude needy people from the gleanings.

Purity and danger in the Quran

Décobert also makes a connection between a key Quranic term *zakat* and Mary Douglas's theorizing on purity (based on her early *Purity and Danger* rather than her later work on the Bible)—for it is derived from the Hebrew-Aramaic *zakût* (Décobert 1991: 198 ff), which had connotations of purity, rectitude and thriving, but not of alms. Here we must be careful. Many students of the Quran have made much of the etymological and philological approaches to which Arabic, with its system of derived forms of root verbs, so readily lends itself. However, the same cautions must apply to Arabic as to other languages: that arguments based on etymology are often merely reviving dead metaphors or in other ways underestimating the element of historical contingency in all language. The 'root fallacy', exposed as such by Barr (1961: 100 ff) in his critique of interpretation of the Hebrew Bible, must surely be also one that the Arabist can succumb to: that is to say, the assumption that there is for every root a meaning which is effective through all the variations given to the root by affixes and formative elements. Furthermore it is often hard to determine when a given Arabic word is being used in the Quran in what was a normal sense, and when it should be deemed to have been divinely 'transferred' (*naqala*) as a technical theological term (Izutsu 1965: 69, 1964: 13–17). To these caveats must also be added the point that meaning inheres in the things which writers say in sentences, not the words they say them in (Barr 1961: 270). But it is surely legitimate to build up a pattern of semantic fields of force cumulatively.

Mary Douglas's extensive publications on the Hebrew Bible are developments of her key insight that: 'The Bible classes together defilement of corpses, idolatry and all lies, deceits, false witness and bloodshed' (Douglas 1993: 152). Again:

> One may think of it like a rift in existence: on the one side there is God and everything he establishes, on the other side, inevitably and necessarily, there is impurity. For the Bible, and in the whole region, the destructive effect of impurity is physical, like a lightning bolt or disease. Nothing less than divinely instituted rites of purification will defend against it. (ib., 23).

The same may be said of the Quran, but we can also invert the signs and group together the opposite of these categories: ritual purity, acknowledgment of the Oneness of God and Islam, and faithfulness to promises. As Décobert has argued, there is a clear semantic overlap between the idea of alms and that of rectitude via the word *ṣadaqa* (1991: 199 ff), which is closely associated with *zakat* and combines the two connotations.

The unfortunate gardeners confess to *ṭaghā*, which means breaking boundaries like a swollen river. In the same Surah we find others castigated for calumniousness, arrogance, mocking of the Prophet, denying the Oneness of God, and other violations which we may see as interrelated.

Décobert argues that *zakat* is fundamentally a way to conceptualize the lineage—for relatives are entitled to much more than alms: *nafaqa* or 'expenditure' includes support or maintenance of kindred as well as *ṣadaqa* or alms (ib.: 216–227). He contests the claim by Watt (1953: 165–169, and see Izutsu 1959: 190) that Muhammad's teaching succeeded in the transfiguring of pagan taboo-thinking into a supposedly higher conception of ethical sincerity. According to Sunni orthodoxy, *zakat* purifies both the donor's wealth and his or her own state of mind. Islam as it developed was certainly founded on the idea of lineage, but this aspect was held in tension with the principle of voluntary election and openness to all candidates. In this respect the Quranic principle of purity is similar to what Douglas finds in Leviticus and Numbers, that is to say, contagion comes from the body or from moral failure, not from contact with foreigners or the lower classes as in many societies studied by anthropologists. Indeed, just before the Parable of the Garden we read a blistering attack on one of the Prophet's slanderers who despite his 'wealth and numerous sons' (v. 14) will soon be branded on the snout like an animal.

Contagion also emanates from idolatry on which much has been written in the tradition of Jewish scholarship. For instance, Halbertal and Margalit (1992: 215) explore a marital metaphor of God as husband, and idols as lovers. Kochan (1997: 5) states that worshipping gods other than the God of Israel is the only transgression which can be committed by a mere verbal expression of intent as opposed to action.

The Quranic concept of *shirk* is related—and also belongs explicitly with the sin of adultery or fornication (Q. 24:3)—but different. Whereas this word—'association', from a root that means 'sharing'—is often glossed as a synonym for paganism or polytheism (e.g. Glassé 1991: 370), modern scholarship suggests that this is imprecise. Kister has argued that 'the Jâhiliyya [pre-Islamic, literally time of 'barbarism' or 'ignorance'] tribes cannot be said to have been straightforward polytheists; they were *mushrikōn*, i.e. while accepting and admitting the existence and supreme authority of God, they associated other deities with Him' (Kister 1990: I.48, see also Henninger 1981: 12). More recently, Hawting has suggested that the accusation of *shirk* is part of an intra-monotheist polemic, directed against groups who regarded themselves as monotheistic, and that it provides us with no evidence of the actual beliefs of the pre-Islamic Arabs (Hawting 1999). In an article entitled 'The Pure Religion', Ringgren analyses the term *mukhliṣ*, applied several times in the Quran to followers of Islam and meaning 'pure and spotless'; he argues that the primary figurative meaning in the Quran is that of exclusive devotion to the One God (Ringgren 1962, see also Izutsu 1959: 189). Wansbrough too sees the underlying motive of Islamic 'election history' as a 'reaffirmation and restoration of original purity', that of the original theophany and Islamic community. This is a reversal of biblical salvation history which was essentially anticipatory and teleological (1980: 147–148).

Faith and works in Islam

Some Western students of Islam have argued that the religion insists on orthopraxy (correct conduct) as opposed to orthodoxy (correct doctrine), and it is true that in some versions of Islam, the theological debate focuses more on practice than on belief, as perhaps it does more generally in Judaism. Malcolm Ruel, in an important anthropological paper which claims that the concept of 'belief' is specific to the Christian and post-Christian tradition (Ruel 1982), concedes that the Islamic concept is similar. The Quran repeatedly emphasizes *īmān* or inner conviction, and, whereas analysis of the various modalities of belief in different religions must be left to philosophical anthropologists, it would be perverse to read the Quran without acknowledging its interest in mental states as well as actions. During the early history of Islam, a sectarian dispute arose which broadly, if not in detail, adumbrated the later disagreements in Christian theology as to the relative importance of faith and works (Izutsu 1965). The Murji'ites held that serious sins are offset by faith, and that good works (*'amal*) are secondary. The Kharijites downgraded faith and held that major sins forfeited salvation. So salient are the Quran's injunctions to good deeds on the one hand, and its celebration of God's attributes, especially mercy, on the other, that it is not surprising that mainstream Islam settled down to teaching that faith and works are mutually intertwined. *Zakat* is therefore both an act of social solidarity and also an affirmation of faith. The famous *hadith* or prophetic utterance 'Actions are according to their intentions' [*niyyah*], inscribed over a gate at Al-Azhar University in Cairo, is well supported in the Quran (e.g. Q. 33:5). Actions and thoughts are integrated in the Quranic terms for piety and God-fearing, *birr* and *taqwa* (Q. 2:177 and cf. Izutsu 1959: 210 ff, 1965: 73–74), while hypocrisy and lip-service are excoriated with the terms *fisq* and *nifāq*. The Quran developed late-antique traditions of piety, but did not shun the world as did the Christian and Manichaean ascetics—rather, piety was enjoined within the context of this world—and it also urged Believers to adopt an activist or militant stance in promoting piety around them (Donner 1998: 71–74).

> The emphasis on being godly and God-fearing thus appears in the Qur'ân in many guises, and is such a persistent theme that we must conclude it to have been the very essence of Muhammad's message. It is far more prevalent, for example, than any emphasis on Muhammad's role as prophet, although that is also present. To judge from the Qur'ân, then, Islam began as a movement of uncompromising, indeed militant, piety, perhaps initially inspired by Muhammad's fear that the Last Judgment was imminent (ib.: 75).

Problems of interpretation

A number of the scholars I have cited have tried to improve our understanding of the ideological system underpinning the rise of early Islam. This is similar to Mary Douglas's anthropological aim in her study of the Bible, and she considers the society represented in Leviticus and Numbers as a type of egalitarian enclave (not, of course, egalitarian as regards gender relations).[4] A similar argument could be advanced about the early Meccan period before Islam developed immense expansionary ambitions. The difficulty is that there is very little external, that is to say non-Muslim, historical or archaeological evidence relating to the origins of Islam until the end of the eighth century CE or about 150 years after the traditional date for the Prophet's death in 632 (Waines 1995: 268–279). One of the new school of revisionist Western scholars arrived at the conclusion that the Quran itself as we have it was compiled not by the Caliph 'Uthman less than twenty years after the Prophet's death, as tradition tells us, but by the Prophet himself (Burton 1977). Another however has contended that the Quran was assembled over time in a milieu of Judaeo-Christian sectarian polemics, with such a strong element of post-rationalization that it can bear no weight at all as a factual historical source (Wansbrough 1977, 1978; see also Berg 1997; Madigan 1995). A consensus now seems to be emerging that extreme versions of sceptical revisionism rely on some hypotheses for which there is no evidence, such as the existence, in the community of Believers, of an orthodox authority sufficiently centralized to promulgate a unitary doctrine (Donner 1998: 25–31); and that it is implausible that enough was known at this time in the region about technicalities of literary composition for the obvious differences between the literary style of the Meccan and the later Medinan Surahs to have been retrospectively fabricated (Berg op. cit.: 13).[5]

---

[4] Since this paper was first drafted, I find that Mary Douglas's ideas have already been applied by at least one scholar to the study of the Islamic law of ritual purity. Marion Holmes Katz argues that 'purity is associated in the Qur'an with the motif of the covenantal community and the preservation of boundaries', but this emphasis is replaced in later Muslim legal writings by more universalistic concerns (Katz 1999: 46).

[5] Since drafting of this paper, an extremely useful summary and anthology of the 'revisionist', post-Wansbrough trend of analysis has been published (Ibn Warraq: 2000; for a balanced review, see Irwin 2001). For instance, the existence of two

Great sacred texts cannot be analysed simply as texts from which information about the societies which generated them can be read out. The founders of each of the successful religions of the Middle East must have been cultural anthropologists *avant la lettre*, engaged in a project to make the new system acceptable; as Wansbrough puts it, selecting appropriate 'insignia' of confessional identity from the 'monotheist compendium' which included rites, membership rules and catechisms (1978: 99–100). History is crammed with examples of sectarian movements which did not make it. Mary Douglas contends that much of the Pentateuch is cast in a rustic or pastoral idiom by compilers who were in fact versed in the learning of ancient civilizations (1993: 90–91). It is possible that some of the more prominent features of the Quranic text may have been intentionally injected into it in order to provide a kind of primordialist local colouring. What could have been more anthropologically sensitive than the Quranic revelation's careful hierarchization of celestial entities or angels, and wayward local spirits or jinns, within the overarching 'chain of being' of *tauḥīd* or monotheism?[6] or than the qualified toleration of the Jews, Christians and Sabians? If *shirk* was held in such horror this was perhaps because it was a categorical anomaly defying this hierarchy, as well as because the new Islamic community's survival depended on suppression of the traditional forces which threatened it. Meanwhile, the animal sacrifices were preserved but transmuted into symbols of piety and unselfishness. The same themes can be found in some passages in the Old Testament, such as Psalms 51:16–17—'My sacrifice, O God, is a broken spirit; a wounded heart, O God, thou wilt not despise'—but their interpretation is controversial (Rogerson 1980: 52). The Jews ceased to offer sacrifices around 70 CE, while Pauline Christianity claimed that God's sacrifice of his Son made further sacrifices redundant except for the recapitulation of God's sacrifice in the Eucharist.

---

different styles in the Quran is undisputed, but the assignment of one set of surahs to Mecca and the other to Medina is no longer. The fact that the editor has had to publish under a pseudonym underlines the point made in my final paragraph about the hostility of some believers to rationalist approaches to Islam.

Ibn Warraq (Editor). 2000. *The Quest for the Historical Muhammad*. New York: Prometheus Books. Irwin, Robert. 2001. In the Full Light of History. *Times Literary Supplement*, 26 Jan., p. 13.

[6] However, the Devil being both an angel (Q. 2:34) and a jinn (Q. 18:50), it is possible that the distinction between angels and *jinn* is blurred (Hawting 1999: 53).

Thematic interpretation

A current, if not undisputed, trend among Muslim scholars is towards 'thematic interpretation' (Hanafi 1996), according to which the fact that all textual interpretations are inevitably geared towards the reader's current agenda is embraced rather than repressed. Among some Christian theologians, the Sermon on the Mount and some of Jesus's parables now stand out as a universal message of Christianity, whereas the narrative of his torture and execution, made to bear an immense burden of sacrificial meaning in traditional doctrine, is conceded to be a historical contingency and/or fulfilment of prophecy. Perhaps the Parable of the Garden and similar passages in the Quran are the Islamic equivalent of the Sermon on the Mount?

Such topics are still inflammatory. A number of Islamic scholars have recently been killed (since as Mahmoud Muhammad Taha in Sudan in 1985) or forced into exile (such as Nasr Aby Zayd in Egypt in 1995) as a result of their re-examinations of the Quran and Sunna. Anthropology is of no interest to fundamentalist Muslims, who believe that Islam is the only true anthropology. But with its tradition of respect for cultural sensitivities, and as the only social science which systematically subjects its own presuppositions (as well as others') to continuous questioning, anthropology may have an important role as an intellectual mediator.[7]

BIBLIOGRAPHY

'Ali, 'Abdullah Yûsuf. 1989. *The Meaning of the Holy Qur'ân*. Beltsville, MD.: Amana Publications.

Aubaile-Sallenave, Françoise. 1999. 'Les rituels de naissance dans le monde musulman' in Bonte, Pierre and Anne-Marie Brisebarre and Altan Gokalp (editors), *Sacrifices en islam: Espaces et temps d'un rituel*. Paris: CNRS Editions, pp. 125–160.

Barr, James. 1961. *The Semantics of Biblical Language*. Oxford: OUP.

Benthall, Jonathan. 1999a. Financial Worship: The Quranic Injunction to Almsgiving. *JRAI*, 5.1, March. Pp. 27–42.

——1999b. Two Takes on the Abraham Story (review article on Brisebarre 1998 and Delaney 1998). *Anthropology Today*, 15: 1. February. Pp. 1–2.

Berg, Herbert. 1997. The Implications of, and Opposition to, the Methods and Theories of John Wansbrough. *Method and Theory in the Study of Religion*. 9:1, 3–22.

Bonte, Pierre. 1999. 'Sacrifices en islam. Textes et contextes', in Bonte, Pierre and Anne-Marie Brisebarre and Altan Gokalp (editors), *Sacrifices en islam: Espaces et temps d'un rituel*. Paris: CNRS Editions, pp. 21–61.

---

[7] An informative work of collaboration with such a goal in mind, focused on contemporary Iran, is Fischer and Abedi (1990).

Brisebarre, A.-M. et al. 1998. *La fête du mouton: Un sacrifice musulman dans l'espace urbain*. Paris: CNRS Editions.

Burton, John. 1977. *The Collection of the Qur'an*. Cambridge: CUP.

Dagorn, René. 1981. *La Geste d'Ismaël d'après l'onomastique et la tradition arabes*. Geneva: Librairie Droz.

Décobert, Christian. 1991. *Le Mendiant et le Combattant*. Paris: Seuil.

Delaney, Carol. 1998. *Abraham on Trial*. Princeton: Princeton U.P.

Donner, Fred M. 1998. *Narratives of Islamic Origins: The Beginnings of Islamic Historical Writing*. Princeton, NJ: Darwin Press.

Douglas, Mary. 1993. *In the Wilderness: The Doctrine of Defilement in the Book of Numbers*. Sheffield: JSOT Press.

Doutté, Edmond. 1908. *Magie et religion dans l'Afrique du Nord*. Algiers: Typographie Adolphe Jourdan.

Fischer, Michael M.J. and Mehdi Abedi. 1990. *Debating Muslims: Cultural Dialogues in Postmodernity and Tradition*. Madison: University of Wisconsin Press.

Glassé, Cyril. 1991 (2nd ed.) *The Concise Encyclopaedia of Islam*. London: Stacey.

Halbertal, Moshe and Avishai Margalit. 1992. *Idolatry*. Cambridge, MA.: Harvard U.P.

Hanafi, Hassan. 1996. 'Methods of Thematic Interpretation of the Qur'an' in Wild, S., *The Qur'an as Text*, Leiden: Brill.

Hawting, G.R. 1999. *The Idea of Idolatry and the Emergence of Islam: from Polemic to History*. Cambridge: CUP.

Hayward, C.T.R. 1980. 'Appendix: The Aqedah [Binding of Isaac]' in *Sacrifice*, ed. M.F.C. Bourdillon and M. Fortes, London: Academic Press.

Henninger, Joseph. 1981. 'Pre-Islamic Bedouin Religion' in *Studies on Islam*, trans. and ed. Merlin L. Swartz. New York: OUP.

Izutsu, Toshihiko. 1959. *The Structure of the Ethical Terms in the Koran*. Tokyo: Keio Institute of Philological Studies.

—— 1965. *The Concept of Belief in Theology: A Semantic Analysis of Îmân and Islâm*. Tokyo: Keio Institute of Cultural and Linguistic Studies.

Jaussen, A. 1948. *Coutumes des Arabes au pays de Moab*. Paris: Maisonneuve.

Katz, Marion Holmes. 1999. 'Purified Companions: The Development of the Islamic Law of Ritual Purity.' Abstract of prizewinning dissertation (Humanities), 1998 Malcolm H. Kerr Dissertation Award. *Middle East Studies Association Bulletin*, 33.1, Summer, p. 46

Kochan, Lionel. 1997. *Beyond the Graven Image: A Jewish View*. London: Macmillan.

Leach, Edmund. 1983. *Structuralist Interpretations of Biblical Myth*. Cambridge: CUP.

MacCulloch J.A. 1913. 'Firstfruits' in *Encyclopaedia of Religion and Ethics* (ed. J. Hastings), Edinburgh: Clark.

Madigan, D.A. 1995. Reflections on some Current Directions in Qur'anic Studies. *Muslim World*, 85: 345–362.

Marx, Alfred. 1994. *L'Offrande Végétale dans l'Ancien Testament*. Leiden: Brill.

Ringgren, Helmer. 1962. The Pure Religion. *Oriens*. XV: 93–96.

Rogerson, J.W. 1980. 'Sacrifice in the Old Testament: Problems of Method and Approach' in *Sacrifice*, ed. M.F.C. Bourdillon and M. Fortes, London: Academic Press.

Ruel, Malcolm. 1982. 'Christians as Believers' in J. Davis (ed.), *Religious Organization and Religious Experience*, London: Academic Press.

Smith, W. Robertson. 1885. *Kinship and Marriage in Early Arabia*. Cambridge: University Press.

—— 1927 (3rd edition). *Lectures on the Religion of the Semites*. London: A.& C. Black).

van der Toorn, Karel. 1995. 'Theology, Priests, and Worship in Canaan and Ancient Israel.' In Sasson, Jack M. (editor). *Civilizations of the Ancient Near East*, New York: Scribner's, pp. 2043–2058.

Strahan, J. 1913. Firstfruits: Hebrew' in *Encyclopaedia of Religion and Ethics* (ed. J. Hastings), Edinburgh: Clark, VI: 41–45.

Waines, David. 1995. *An Introduction to Islam*. Cambridge: CUP.

Wansbrough, John. 1977. *Qurʾanic Studies: Sources and Methods of Scriptural Interpretation*. Oxford: OUP.

—— 1978. *The Sectarian Milieu: Content and Composition of Islamic Salvation History*. Oxford: OUP.

Watt, W. Montgomery. 1953. *Muhammad at Mecca*. Oxford: Clarendon Press.

Westermarck, Edward. 1926. *Ritual and Belief in Morocco*. London: Macmillan.

REESTABLISHING SACRIFICE IN TIMES OF TROUBLE?
SOMA MORGENSTERN'S *BLUTSÄULE* AS
NEGATIVE SACRIFICOLOGY

GESINE PALMER

> There is a kind of pressure in humans to take what-
> ever is most beloved by them and smash it. Reli-
> gion calls the pressure piety and the smashed thing
> a sacrifice to God. Prophets question these names.
> What is an idol? An idol is a useless sacrifice, said
> Isaiah.[1]

Presuppositions, notions, embarrassing wordings

Reestablishing Sacrifice: Presupposes that there has been an end to
sacrifice. That we have a communicable idea of what sacrifice means.
That most of us do not like sacrificing. That we might have to face
tendencies to reestablish sacrifice. That some of us might be tempted
to join endeavours to reestablish sacrifice because they think, it has
not been disestablished of right.

In Times of Trouble: Presupposes that the tendency just discovered
might have to do with troublesome events in history. That dises-
tablishing sacrifice was the project of comparatively good times. That
it might get lost as an achievement in worse times. That sacrifice
has been abandoned because people learnt to stand the meaningless
of the meaningless—whereas it returns as an attempt to make sense
of the senseless in cases of overwhelming senselessness and suffering.

Soma Morgenstern's *Die Blutsäule*, עמוד הדמים, *The Third Pillar* (the
English translation had to avoid the title *The Pillar of Blood* because
of a criminal novel bearing the same title) can be qualified as a
Jewish myth, a polyphonic one, though written by one man. Its subject is the *Shoah* and the end of exile. The formal idea was to write
in the language of those who hardly knew more than the Hebrew
Bible and the Ashkenazi tradition, as was true of a great many of

---

[1] Anne Carson, *Glass, Irony and God*, Toronto 1995.

the genocide's victims. The text is divided into 543 paragraphs, divided into 24 chapters.[2] Morgenstern, born in 1890 in Tarnopol, died in 1976 in New York. *The Third Pillar*, written in German in the years between 1946 and 1953, is an epilogue to his great novel in three volumes entitled *Funken im Abgrund* (finished in 1943, translated into English as *Sparks in the Abyss*).[3] Passages from *Die Blutsäule* have become part of the liturgy of *Yom HaKippurim* according to the conservative *Mahzor for Rosh Hashanah and Yom Kippur*, as edited by Rabbi Jules Harlow.[4]

Negative Sacrificology: The term is, of course, coined by analogy to the classical term "negative theology". The latter means, in short, a) there is a God or, at least, a notion of God; b) this notion cannot be qualified in positive terms, there are no attributes of God. It is, therefore, possible to speak about God only in negative terms: you can say what He is not, but you never can say what He is like; c) nevertheless, the fundamental impulse in negative theology is to make sure that it be possible to speak about God, while avoiding the sin of pretending to know more about God than one can know. The analogy, negative sacrificology, as I derive it from Morgenstern's epos, functions as follows: there is, a) a notion of *Qiddush HaShem* in a sense of sacrificing oneself (or a most beloved "thing") for the sake of God's name; b) traditional interpretations, classifications, and exaltations of this kind of sacrifice have become awkward and do not seem fit to describe the sacrificial events that might be seen in what has been called the holocaust; c) Still Morgenstern does describe the *Shoah* as a sacrifice. But we should find out who and what is being sacrificed, and what for. Children are described as sacrifices for the sake of Torah, but somehow, in order to make sense of their deaths— or in order to face their senseless deaths, on this point the text is highly ambiguous—another sacrifice is offered almost unambiguously: the cow. What cow?

---

[2] In two of the manuscripts to the book the paragraphs are numbered. Only later, Morgenstern seems to have refrained from this further allusion to Biblical style, but insisted on separating paragraphs by an extra line, cf. Ingolf Schulte, "Editorische Anmerkungen", in: Soma Morgenstern, *Die Blutsäule*, hrsg. v. Ingolf Schulte, Lüneburg 1997, p. 194 (in the following the text will be quoted without title according to this edition; the "Nachwort des Herausgebers" will be quoted as: Schulte 1997; translations into English are mine).

[3] Cf. Schulte 1997, 175.

[4] *Mahzor for Rosh Hashanah and Yom Kippur. A Prayer Book for the Days of Awe*, ed. by Rabbi Jules Harlow, New York (The Rabbinical Assembly) 1972, 565, cf. also Schulte 1997, 193.

Chapter I
The third pillar

The plot is in short: in a little city in the Ukraine at the time of the last battles between the Red Army and the retreating Wehrmacht, three customs men discover a wooden box, carrying an inscription they are unable to read. Two of them smell an attractive flavour and hope for food. The third one, later turning out to be a traitor of hidden Jews, feels repelled by an evil smell, but joins their attempts to open the box. All three of them do not succeed in their endeavours. Feeling threatened by the approaching Russian army they decide to hide the box close by, and choose the old Synagogue as a place fit for expecting the end of the battle. The Germans, after committing a massacre in the days of Yom Kippur, had desecrated the synagogue by turning it into a brothel. They painted the Northern wall with two images of crucified Jews, one of them grown up, the other a boy of about thirteen years, both of them with the red soviet star in the place of their hearts. German men, in medieval clothing and fully armed, dance with naked Jewish women around the crucifixes. In Gothic letters the painting is entitled "the Bloodwedding at the Sereth". This synagogue is the place where a final trial of the Nazis is being held. Several miracles take place around the box, the painting, in connection with some Nazis and, later on, some Russians showing up there. The court consists partly of spiritual personnages: a "messenger" from the world above, who pronounces the beginning of the trial; a narrator judge, who gives details about the story of the local Jewish community, including the perils of a couple of messianic twins (Nehemia and Jochanaan, born to Zacharja HaKohen, the Torah-scribe, and his aged wife Scheva) and their female counterparts, a couple of twins their age, and including the omens foreshadowing the community's end, the massacre in the synagogue; there is also an accusing judge, whose task is to summarize the crimes of the murderers who committed the massacre in normative language; and there is an Ab Bet Din, who presides over the trial and declares in the end that this court does not sentence other than by knowledge (*"ein Erkenntnis"*).[5] The defense is being argued in vain by

---

[5] "Dieses Gericht hat nicht die Macht, ein Urteil zu vollstrecken. Das Urteil dieses Gerichts ist im wahren Sinne dieses Wortes: ein Erkenntnis. Doch wird es Kraft und Geltung haben, wenn es dem Urteil des Oberen Gerichts entspricht, das zu gleicher Zeit tagt und unser Urteil gewärtigt." (128).

a messenger from hell, who reports Satan himself to feel offended
by the German crimes. Some of the survivors appear as witnesses,
accompanied by two local priests and the customs men, one of whom
had cared for a group of surviving Jews in the cellars of the synagogue. In the end, Nehemia, the surviving one of the messianic twins,
gets the task of proclaiming the sentence: salvation for Israel, final
curse and punishment for anything that might remember the mur-
dering Germans in the flesh or in the spirit, extinguishing of the
same from the book of life, punishment for all the passive witnesses
as well as for those who pardon the murderers too quickly, and
Atchalta D'G'ula for those Jews, who refuse to even write an epilogue
on the book of Europe, which is considered to be closed.

Morgenstern, a devout Jew, wrote realistic novels, painting in warm
colours the life of Jews in Eastern Europe. He was acknowledged
for his rich description and precise style by Robert Musil, Stephan
Zweig, Joseph Roth and others. After the Second World War every
thing "European" had become impure in his eyes, but he felt that
the only language in which he could cleanse himself from this impurity was German. He lost his mother and his brother in concentra-
tion camps, and even lost his language for several years following
the events to whose visual documents he exposed himself with immense
consequence, during his first years in New York. He performed his
personal act of ritual purification by writing a new messianic myth
that seems to display many characteristics of traditional Jewish ideas
concerning the messianic age, one of them being that it will come
slowly, as a little transformation in all things.[6] In elaborating this
myth, Morgenstern tries to correct some points in the Jewish religion as well as in Christianity: mainly regarding sacrifices.

---

[6] Cf. "Wie schon ein grosser Rabbi lehrte: Die Erlösung wird allmählich eintreten
als eine Verwandlung aller Dinge. Die Erlösung wird nicht einsetzen als ein Sturm mit
Blitz und Donner. Was krumm ist, wird gerade werden. Jegliches Ding in falscher
Lage wird seine Lage ein wenig verändern, um in die rechte Lage zu kommen, und
das wird die Erlösung sein." (147) This sentence resembles the following from Walter
Benjamin's essay on Kafka in a striking way: "Dies Männlein [das bucklicht Männlein]
ist der Insasse des entstellten Lebens; es wird verschwinden, wenn der Messias
kommt, von dem ein grosser Rabbi gesagt hat, dass er nicht mit Gewalt die Welt
verändern wolle, sondern nur um ein Geringes sie zurechtstellen werde", Walter Benjamin, *Gesammelte Schriften*, hrsg. von Rolf Tiedemann und Hermann Schweppenhäuser,
Frankfurt am Main 1977, II,2, 432. But while Benjamin seems to give to Gershom
Scholem the title of a great Rabbi, I suppose Morgenstern referred to Maimonides,
who, in his *Moreh Nevuchim* declared that the only difference made by the beginning of the messianic age would be the following: Israel would not be enslaved to
the other peoples. I owe this idea to Dr. Itta Shedeltzky in Jerusalem.

Chapter II
Negative sacrificology

On a first level, Morgenstern seems to read the violent death of European Jews as a sacrifice by the very motive of his title: The pillar of blood is a symbol that combines the Biblical tradition of a pillar of cloud and of a pillar of fire that guided the Israelites through the wilderness (as a motto he quotes Ex. 13,21) with the prophet Joel's visions of three miraculous signs that announce final judgement over the nations and salvation for Israel. These signs will be, (according to Joel 3,3) blood, fire and smoke/steam.

> Like the pillar of fire by night, like the pillar of cloud by day, said Nehemia, this pillar of blood will guide us through all deserts to the Holy Land. *Atchalta de ge'ula!* Redemption has begun. Next year in Jerusalem.[7]

With this, an interpretation of the murders as part of a salvation story (*Heilsgeschichte*) might be intended, with all the problems associated with such an interpretation, namely: a) it tends to ignore individual pain by subsuming it under the service to a great idea; b) it seems to find at least a reason of sorts, if not a guilt, with the victims of the monstrous crime and so makes, though unwillingly, common case with the murderers. I quote: "one and a half million children fell as *Opfer* for the Torah. For our children are our pledge."[8] In many places, the word *Opfer*, when being used in an august sense, seems to mean victim. But in this place, for example, the meaning is supposed to be expressly a sacrificial one: that something beloved to the highest degree is being given up, offered, for something higher. But what for?

The answer given in *The Third Pillar* seems to be unambiguous, far too unambiguous: it was for the sake of the return of the People of Israel to the Holy Land. In many respects—and this is the reason for my employing the term negative sacrificology—Morgenstern's myth can be read as an attempt to recapture for Jewish tradition all the concepts of judgement and execution which Christian tradition seems to have purloined from Judaism. And to recapture it in such a way that various motives which appear in the New Testament

---

[7] "Wie die Feuersäule bei Nacht, wie die Wolkensäule bei Tag,? sprach Nehemia, "so wird uns diese Blutsäule über alle Wüsteneien in das Heilige Land führen. *Atchalta d'ge'ula.* Die Erlösung hat angefangen. Kommenden Jahres in Jerusalem!" (146).

[8] 147.

are put in a different context and are turned emphatically against their Christian interpretation. Negative sacrificology is the inner core of this construction: while—according to Christian doctrine—Jesus Christ died for the sins of all men, i.e. for Jews and heathens alike, Morgenstern's Jochanaan (who has all the characteristics of Christ's harbinger of the same name in the Gospel according to St. John) has to die a senseless death, brought upon him by the gentiles, and thus bringing his blood upon them. Morgenstern writes expressly that the heathens extinguished the very light that had been destined for their salvation.

St. John writes, concerning the Baptist: "There was a man sent from god, whose name was John. The same came for a witness, to bear witness of the Light, that all men through him might believe. He was not that Light, but was sent to bear witness of that light" (Jo 1,6–8). Jochanaan,[9] as a counter figure to the Christian John the Baptist is in many ways overdetermined: He is the son of an old barren couple, Secharja HaKohen and Scheva (John the Baptist, according to St Luke 1 was born to Zacharia the priest and his aged wife Elisabeth). But Morgenstern's Jochanaan has a twin, Nehemia, who was also miraculously conceived. In the Bible, messianic twins were announced by the prophet Zachariah (4,11–14). They reappear in the revelation of St John (11,3–6).[10] The mother of Morgenstern's twins is called Scheva: this name indicates her connection with the mother of John the Baptist, Elisabeth, whose Hebrew name was Elisheva, and with Isaac's mother Sarah. She must laugh like biblical Sarah when she hears the announcement of a twin birth at her age.

Another reference to the Biblical idea of messianic twins is given in an otherworldly ability of Morgenstern's dedoubled heroes: According to St John's Revelation, both of the Lord's Anointed have the power to let fire come from their mouth and burn their enemies. This quality comes to the fore in the dramatic highlight of the massacre in

---

[9] During the 1999 Taubes Center conference, Paul Mandel asked me why the name is spelled in such a strange way: I guess this has to do with the name's spelling in Johann Strauss' opera Salome.

[10] The motive of two messiahs, split into the Messiah ben David and the Messiah ben Joseph, is, of course, well founded in rabbinic and later Jewish tradition. Here, in order to understand Morgenstern, however, stress should be laid on the motive of twinship and kinship and dedoubling of the messianic figure as two of the same origin.

the synagogue, as it is told by the narrator judge: the murder of Rahel. Rahel is one of a female couple of twins who had been intended to be married to Jochanaan and Nehemiah before the German invasion. She is the one whom Jochanaan chose as his bride. In spite of all restrictions ordered by the judge prohibiting elaborating the details of the cruelties, in this case the narrator judge gives most cruel details of some significance: An elderly German warrior asked to bring Rahel to her mother, picked her up with his bayonet, piercing her breast, and threw the dying child on her dying mothers belly. Seeing this, Jochanaan cried out: "Murderer, a flash of lightning will burn you!" The murderer was then hit by fiery spittle which charred his face; later it becomes clear that it was Nehemia who spit at the murderer, while another warrior killed his brother.

Nehemiah's name hardly demands an explanation: it is the name of the Jewish leader who rebuilt the "state" at the end of the first Babylonian exile. In addition, the root *nhm* which is the basis for the name might allude to the name of the Messiah ben Joseph, which is: Menahem, the comforter. According to tradition, however, this Menahem is bound to die in the final battle with the heathens. Morgenstern's Nehemia sees this destiny fulfilled by his brother. At court—the court over the heathens (that has been announced in the Book of Joel)—Nehemia—spells out the word "pillar of blood"/*Blutsäule*. He gives this name to the soap-figure, into which the mortal remains of his brother have been transformed. It was this figure—the figure of the one who came to enlighten the Heathens, preceded his brother in cursing them and was killed as a martyr for the sake of Torah—that turned out to be the content of the miraculous box, that could only be opened during the trial.

I shall return to some of the motives and their possible meanings later on. About the sacrifices which were made before an end of the *Galut* and a beginning of the *Geula* could be achieved, the following has to be said: First, the murdered children are considered sacrifices, but (unlike victims of the crusades in the Rhineland) they were not sacrificed by the Jews themselves, and nowhere is there even the slightest hint of an attempt to offer up the children for the sake of the Torah. But since the grown-ups cannot protect themselves, they cannot protect their children either. Second, according to the classical sacrificial notion, the children themselves should offer the sacrifice uncomplainingly and willingly. But though the two children who act as guarantors in this story, are innocent, they are also defiant, even militant. They have more to do with Job, who insists on his innocence, than with Jesus, who takes death upon himself for the sin of others. Nor is the sacrifice of one of the children a triumph of the Torah or a law, but on the contrary: The children die as sacrifices for the Torah. Nehemia therefore receives the Torah, and the figure of Jochanaan, the blood pillar, is wrapped in the Torah mantle and receives the Torah crown. It is the teaching of Israel considered to be embodied by the children of Israel which is fought by the heathens, but it is also the teaching, the Torah of Israel, which is stronger than all heathen enemies: not love and not faith, no not faith at all! It is the divine law which provides the basis for Nehemia's challenge to his angel:

> And N. took the figure from the table of the judge, as the Torah is taken after the reading, and he turned with his face and the face of his brother Jochanaan to the messenger, and he said: In the name of my brother Jochanaan, slain as blasphemy of the name, in the name of all the children of Israel who were slain as blasphemy and desecration of the name, in the name of the one and a half million names who fell to death for the observance of the One Name, I say Creator of all worlds, the measure of the suffering for your name has become full and more than full. . . . We want to ask for and plead for the end of exile. And if we do not ask for it, if we cannot plead for it, we will obtain it by sheer defiance. (141 ff)

The law, however, has changed. It is no longer a law that demands death for the name of God. When the innocent law-lover Nehemia challenges the angel Gabriel and feels himself weakening, the angel's twin, Mechzio, Michael, calls out to him: "Do not leave the messenger, Nehemia!" Wrestling with the angel like Jacob, Nehemia denies the Deity every right to blame the crimes of the Nazis as a punishment on the Jews. (In a letter to a friend Morgenstern wrote "that the Jews cannot have committed so many sins as to have deserved Hitler.") Not even Satan, a former Jewish Angel, not even his abhorrence at the child slaughterers that has him renew his claim to be called *Malach Hashammaim*, not even his return, can justify the deaths of the children.

The Russian officer of the liberating troops, sarcastically claiming to expect resurrection, finally shoots the crucified grown-up in the soviet star. With this a door in the wall opens and the bass player Awrejmel, who is half dead with exhaustion, falls through it and dies. After his death, the Russian General, clearly professing his Jewish origin according to the blood and his being non-Jewish according to belief, makes himself available to the *Minyan* for the Kaddish for the murdered Torah scribe. Now, in the end, after all variations of blood guilt, of blood-wedding and Blutgemütlichkeit etc. as characteristics of the murderers have been shown, there is the blood of the victims and the blood of the ancestors who together constitute surviving Israel. Awrejmel is described as one whose limbs look like a child's, overcome with hunger and exhaustion. Before dying he can tell his story. But the bass player himself cannot become the one for whom all waited in order to complete the minyan.

I summarize: Insofar as sacrifice is an interpretation of the children's deaths, the primary negations of classical sacrificology as we may be accustomed to it from the Bible (Hebrew Bible and New Testament), are the following: the sacrifice is not being demanded by a good God. Nor is it demanded by law, as a punishment for transgressions. It is not being offered willingly. Nevertheless—or because of this—the sacrifice is being rewarded. But taking upon themselves Torah and the end of *Galut* the Nehemian Jews have to bury their father Awrejmel = Abraham (whose name could be understood as the basso continuo of Jewish-Christian history), thus putting an end to sacrifice.

In the Biblical story of the *aqedah*, God demands the sacrifice of Isaac. He is satisfied at the very moment he sees that Abraham really is willing to slaughter his most beloved son. He then gives Isaac back, as a reward, perhaps, for unconditioned confidence and obedience. Abraham receives Isaac back even though (as Avieser Tucker remarked) Abraham did not propose to have himself slaughtered instead of his son: as he did, when Sodom was at stake, as even David did, when he found himself victorious over his own son Absalom. Isaac does not speak, but tradition names the God that demanded that sacrifice "Isaac's Terror" (פחד יצחק). It also adds a story in which God is said to just have been waiting for Abraham to say "no".

In Morgenstern's story, an evil that is worse than the devil demands the sacrifice of children. One is being murdered, against the express will of his parents, but he has a twin that survives. The twin saves the angel and perhaps God himself from their own cruelty by demanding from them the reward for a sacrifice he never wanted to offer. He stresses that he has been forced to suffer his brother's death.

What he wants, is life. This is all the opposite of Christian sacrificology. In Christian doctrine, the son decided to have himself sacrificed, and to pardon his murderers. Nevertheless, the reward, his resurrection, has no visible traces. In the extremes of Christian dogma a Christian must believe in the resurrection, but may not desire it. A true Protestant, who strives for his own salvation, exposes himself to the suspicion of so-called "Heilsegoismus". In terms of sacrifice: the only true sacrifice fulfills all the criteria of absolute confidence, belief and obedience and does not even speculate on a spiritual reward. In Morgenstern's text, all these terms are being turned upside down as a consequence of his idea of the last blood: confidence, belief and obedience in his sense are expressed by the power of the surviving twin to protest Israel's sufferings. These sufferings exceed any right of the deity to demands.

The prophets criticized sacrifices because they saw them as human attempts to escape the demands of God and the Torah. Morgenstern criticizes the sacrification of the children because God, by allowing them, seems to escape his own law. Performing the trial over the murderers, is God's only chance to return to his law, and perhaps it is God whom the Ab Bet Din wants to edify when he exclaims: We say, however, judge! For it is written: *Kol d'rochow mischpat* (כל דרכיו משפט)—all his ways are the law. Judge, for you will be judged. (Which is, of course, an inversion of the maxim of Jesus (Mt 7:1 and parallels) elaborated by Paul (Rom 2:1): "Judge not, that you not be judged." Morgenstern has thus made his point forcefully. The children's sacrifice is declared to be at its end. The second step of negative sacrificology seems to be completed.

However, at the beginning, I said that there is a somewhat hidden impulse to speak about sacrifice affirmatively. Indeed, there is one sacrifice that is offered willingly, a sacrifice that perhaps does turn the pillar of blood, the figure of Jochanaan into an idol, a useless sacrifice, as Ann Carson's Isaiah put it. As a blood-pillar, dressed in the Torah-mantle, Jochanaan has some features in common with another thing, that, all through the history of religions, like him is at one and the same time a sacrifice and the power to which people offer their sacrifices: cattle.

Chapter III
Cattle and the killing of children

Two mottos:
First by a prophet:

sovchey adam ;agalim yishakoon (זבחי אדם עגלים ישקון)?[11]

Second by a German novelist who wrote about his childhood during the War:

> I stuck to this innocence, this look of innocence,
> this not enlightenable look until 1945 because I knew,
> if I prepare him according to the expectations of the
> present Zeitgeist regarding this time, then I destroy
> my Johann. The question how one should have behaved
> then, does not interest me for a second, because that's
> what I do know. I want to tell why people then behaved
> the way they behaved. And to anybody who comes to say:
> Auschwitz is missing there, I can only say: hey, you are
> smashing my Johann. If in a book, where the Johann is
> ruling, the word "Auschwitz" appears, I can throw him away.[12]

In this chapter, I hope to make some other sense of the religious idea of child-sacrifice, and I hope to return to some of the questions that have been left open in the attempts to explain my title. I therefore switch to another system of symbols and representations, to be correlated with the Biblical symbols employed by Soma Morgenstern. I will take up psychoanalytical suggestions to substitute a permanent, a strictly symbolic child sacrifice, even in times of troubles in order not to prolong the troubles by offering other sacrifices in the flesh. This idea has been best expressed by the Lacanian psychoanalyst Serge Leclaire and presupposes a postfreudian

---

[11] Hos 13,2: Those who sacrifice human beings will kiss calves.

[12] In German: "Ich habe diese Unschuld, diesen Unschuldsblick, diesen nichtaufklärbaren Blick bis ins 45 hinein durchgehalten, weil ich gewusst habe, wenn ich den herrichte nach den heutigen Erwartungen des Zeitgeistes an diese Zeit, dann mach ich den Johann kaputt. Mir ist die Frage zutiefst fremd, wie man sich damals hätte benehmen sollen, das interessiert mich keine Sekunde, as weiss ich ja. Ich will erzählen, warum man sich damals so benommen hat, wie man sich benommen hat. Und jedem, der da kommt und sagt: da fehlt Auschwitz, dem kann ich nur sagen, Junge, du machst mir den Johann kaputt. Wenn in einem Buch, in dem der Johann dominiert, das Wort "Auschwitz" vorkommt, kann ich ihn wegwerfen." Martin Walser, *Tages-Anzeiger* 10.10.1998 Gespräch mit Andreas Isenschmid über seinen Kindheitsroman "Ein springender Brunnen".

interest in primary narcissism. I cannot enter the details of his construction here. What I can do, is quote some significant sentences
concerning the basic idea, and make some remarks as to its value
for understanding old and new myths:

> Psychoanalytic practice is based upon bringing to the fore *the constant
> work of a power of death—the death of the wonderful (or terrifying) child who,
> from generation to generation, bears witness to parent's dreams and desires. There
> can be no life without killing that strange, original image in which everyone's birth
> is inscribed.* It is an impossible but necessary murder, for there can be
> no life, no life of desire and creation, if we ever stop killing off the
> always returning "wonderful child."[13]

The Johann just quoted, who has aroused an ongoing debate in
Germany, is such a child. He is properly being brought to the fore,
if we think in psychoanalytical terms, being aware of the fact that
these terms are normative as well as descriptive. A certain maturity
demands that one knows about the wonderful child one tries to be,
and it demands that one tries time and again to kill this child within
oneself. The maturity itself, however, is only to be demanded, and
striving for it, as we see, can be refused. This refusal, however, comes
with a price, a price that is not always being paid by those who
refuse to strive for maturity. The killing of the wonderful child within
oneself is the killing of innocence itself. The refusal of this killing
demands the killing of innocent others, or, if we remain in the symbolic sphere, the killing of our own love towards others, even the
killing of our ability to love others, even perhaps our ability to act.
In this respect, psychoanalytical theory does not claim anything else
than most systems of belief, wisdom or philosophy which tell us that
we cannot act without becoming guilty. Guilt, however, may relate
to at least two notions: one is the notion of law: you are guilty of
transgressing the law. Then, as long as the law persists, you have a
chance to repair your relation to the law: atonement for a certain
guilt is possible by following the rules that law itself prescribes in
cases of transgression. This was the legal sense given to sacrifices all
over the Hebrew Bible. The other notion guilt can be related to is
the notion of innocence. Of course, it is difficult to imagine active,
individual guilt without a passage from innocence to guilt.

---

[13] Serge Leclaire, *A Child is being Killed. On Primary Narcissism and the Death Drive*,
translated from the French by Marie-Claude Hays, Stanford 1998, 2. Italics by
Leclaire.

The idea of fate, of fatual guilt, saves the idea of innocence, but sacrifices the idea of individual guilt. There is no individual transgression, when sin is inherited and thus unavoidable. Paul, by contrast, sacrificed the law in order to maintain an absolute idea of innocence: only law itself arouses the notion of guilt. In order to free oneself from guilt and to repair the state of innocence, law itself must be crucified in order to crucify sin, in order to regain the state of innocence for all possible sons. The German novelist Martin Walser, quoted above, seems to see speaking about Auschwitz as a representation of sin-producing law, that demands the killing of his innocent Johann. He does not want to have him killed and, perhaps, blames his heartfelt urge to do so, on anyone who dares to remind him of others that have been killed while his innocent Johann grew. Perhaps the guilt thrown on him by the deeds of his parents and their people might be so very unbearable that he retreats himself to a general negation of the need of guilt and insists upon his right to have been innocent. With this, he might be right and wrong at the same time: right insofar as he refuses to accept as his personal guilt something imposed upon him by his parents. Wrong insofar as he refuses to kill the concept of innocence which nurtures his "wonderful child".

Innocence as a form of helplessness can be felt as unbearable as well and can have similar consequences for the individual. Under attack, it can be easier to find the reasons for the attack within oneself than to bear the idea of being helplessly exposed to a threat from without. The dramatic search by victims of attacks for reasons within themselves, must be understood as the search for their own chance to change the events, though not always a very fruitful one. For some, however, the idea of innocence may provide a source of energy. In *The Third Pillar*, Nehemia only receives the power to challenge the angel from his security that all his sins and those of his people must have been forgiven. He himself has proved to be the wonderful child, and his brother, the other wonderful child, even has been killed. With this, all possible sin and guilt went to the murderers, and he is free, in the end, to write and to go on living. Although he lives as a wonderful child, slain but strong, Nehemia is still only half alive if one compares this text to those to which it is an epilogue.

As I said in the beginning, *The Third Pillar* is an epilogue to Morgenstern's novel in three volumes, entitled *Sparks in the Abyss*. Both,

the great novel and the epilogue, have a common, a Morgensternian,
but also a Biblical subtext, a story underlying the description of
Jewish life in Eastern Europe as well as the report of the court which
tried the destroyers of Jewish life in Eastern Europe. This story, coming to the fore time and again in the novel and in the myth, is a
story of cattle. In the battlefield of myths that is opened in *The Third
Pillar*, cattle are a symbol of great significance, and cattle play a
significant part in the novels of the trilogy. By the way, it reappears
as a personal obsession in Morgenstern's memoirs as well. *The Third
Pillar* begins as follows:

> It happened in that part of the world, where no true religion, worthy
> of this name, could ever grow; where all religions, worth this name,
> were spoiled, died. It happened in that part of the world, that derives
> its name from a woman [*Weib*], which, according to myth [*Sage*] in
> the figure [*Gestalt*] of a cow found some favour in the eyes of a high-
> est deity of this part of the world: in Europe."[14]

Of course, the original myth of Europe is different: The deity, Zeus,
fell in love with the princess of Phoenicia. In order to seduce her,
Zeus appeared as a white bull on the seashore, where Europe spent
some time playing and bathing with some other girls. He behaved
very gently, the girls liked him, and when Europe climbed on his
back, he began to run and took her to Crete.

So why did Morgenstern say that she was a cow? Among other
reasons, this is a first sounding of the trumpet, the first sentence of
his judgement over Europe: A deity who finds favour with a cow
can himself be nothing but a bull. By choosing the image of a cow
as the figure which gave its name to Europe, the godlessness of the
continent is being exposed. A god who has sexual desires might be
possible, though not the purest. A god who desires an animal, a
cow, can hardly be a God. A continent that derives its name from
a cow and glories in its ability to seduce one of its highest deities
can only be rotten. And this is how Morgenstern sees the development of Europe, finding its destiny foreshadowed in the very origins

---

[14] In German: "Es geschah in jenem Teil der Welt, wo keine wahre Religion,
dieses Namens wert, je gewachsen ist; wo alle Religionen, dieses Namens wert, ver-
darben, starben. Es geschah in jenem Teil derWelt, der seinen Namen von einem
Weib ableitet, das der Sage nach auch in der Gestalt einer Kuh einer höchsten
Gottheit dieses Weltteils wohl gefiel: in Europa." To Annemarie von Klenau,
Morgenstern wrote on October 27, 1948: "Was mich betrifft, kann ganz Europa
zum Teufel gehen, wo es ja längst hingehört."

of its eponymous myth (as he reads it): It has "moved from human-ism to nationalism to bestiality".[15] It received its name from a beast, and the beast was female. The male part is that of a beast claim-ing to be a God, but obviously becoming a murderous beast because of sexual desire.

Cattle are important all over the world, for pagans as well as Jews. Cattle are sacrificed to the gods, as well as they are deified: there is a heavenly cow in Egypt and holy cows in India. There are mon-sters and heroes whose bodies are partly human, partly those of bulls. A little bull is the symbol of paganism to which Israel sacrifices during the absence of Moses, but even the Jewish God, who always cared to be strictly unlike any human or beastly being, has his wrath compared to that of a bull, who pushes the nations to the ends of the earth. Efraim, while being untrue to God, is compared to a wild cow that must be forbidden to run among the peaceful lambs. The Israelites of the Northern Kingdom sin by worshipping calves at Bethel and Dan. Efraim was a young cow, but God will put a yoke on her beautiful neck, so Jacob will plow and Judah harvest: the cow, who used to seduce them, will have to serve them.

In chapter 19 of the book of Numbers, the sacrifice of a cow is prescribed: the cow has to be reddish and without blemish, she must be one that never felt a yoke on her neck, and everyone who touches her ashes and her blood, will be unclean. The first thing Abraham offers before God makes a covenant with him, promising return from Exile and inheritance of the land, is a three-year-old cow, cut in the middle (Gen 15,9). If one finds a slain man in the land that God has promised the people, and nobody knows who killed him, the people in the town closest to the corpse take a cow that never felt a yoke on her neck, guide her to a barren valley and break her neck. They wash their hands over her and deny that the blood of the guiltless has been shed by Israel (Dt 21, 1–9). Egypt is compared by Jeremiah to a beautiful young cow, but her slaughterer will come from the north. The rich in Samaria are mocked as fat cows by Amos.

---

[15] Cf. Dan Morgenstern: "The Holocaust, he felt, proved that Western History had moved from humanism to nationalism to bestiality. [...] But the Good Samaritan was also there. My father cherished and loved this Good Samaritan, the decent Christ-ian Witness who daily risked his life for unknown Jewish victims." D. Morgenstern, *Jazz—The Jewish-Black Connection*, in: *Creators and Disturbers, Reminiscences by Jewish Intellectuals of New York*, drawn from Conversations with Bernard Rosenberg and Ernest Goldstein, New York 1982, 109, quoted according to Schulte 1997, 189.

What do the famous red cow, the fat cows and the beautiful wild cows have in common, what do they have in common with calves? They are all bound to be slaughtered, or, sometimes, only to be forced under a yoke, while they themselves seem to live in illusions as to their destiny. In the Hebrew Bible, the female cattle bound to be slaughtered, and able to become a purifying sacrifice that prevents the bloodshed from coming over the people, still resembles the motherly deity that had a bull with her in archaic cults. Bulls and earth mothers are somewhat threatening deities. Their children, their sons, who purify by shedding the blood of cattle, are benefactors of mankind.

Morgenstern intended to expose the blasphemous acts of the Germans, at the same time as he reconstructed Judaism with the last blood of the victims and the surviving blood of the ancestors. In the process, he gives us a strong renewal of a fearful mythical connection between blood, sexuality and the desire to be a pure child in the use he makes of the image of cattle. The murderers in *The Third Pillar* have necks like bulls. The man who fights the Nazis as the only strong one, Mechzio, is the angel Michael. In the trilogy, he figures as the ox-eyed servant Mechzio. The ox-eyed, before transforming into Michael, the angel that served Isaac, has to fight his own temptation. Afterwards he has to fight a Jewish sinner in the flesh. His temptation is a beautiful young cow. He watches her in the meadows, but successfully suppresses his rising lust to be in the place of a young bull cavorting with her. This gives him the power to overwhelm another, stronger bull-necked man, who fell prey to his lust and sported with a female horse.

These scenes are written in high prose, full of sympathetic and understanding irony: Mechzio overwhelms both the giant horse-lover and his own temptations. Another scene shows a young Viennese Jew, the son of the lost son to a family of Eastern Chassidim, spending some time in the village of his grandfather. He falls in love with a young Ukrainian woman and meets her sometimes in the woods. The kisses of her lips are described as the kisses of a calf's mouth, and that seems to render the whole thing joyful to the highest degree. After a while the girl almost disappears, though there is never an official end to the affair. But all the heartiest interest of the boy transfers to the little boy Lipusch, the wise boy, the bright one, well educated in Jewish tradition and marvelously gifted in learning everything else. Lipusch has nothing to do with cows; he is pure. One of his joys, however, is to go to a little pool and to watch the stork = *Chassida*: the bird that brings the babies to those who don't know the sexual, the cattlish ways of having children. Lipusch is slain by an Ukrainian mob, an innocent victim. Mechzio who witnessed Lipusch's death and tried to save him, disappears thereafter, only to return as Michael in *The Third Pillar*.

Mechzio helps Nehemia to restore the Jewish people. Nehemia remains the wonderful child, while bemoaning his twin. We remain with the impression of a split story, that tries to stick to the idea of a sacrifice of innocent children and, at the same time, to protest against this very idea. The only unambiguous notion is the rejection of the sexual and the beastly by connecting it to murder. This material therefore presents us with a very rich example of a fresh way to deal with the idea of "once-and-for-allnes", and to understand the latter as a traumatic idea.

Conclusion

There seems to have been a long period of sacrificing animals, humans or other very good things to God. Monotheistic tradition seems to have developed the project of overcoming this practice and tried to disestablish sacrificing. But while its philosophers try to minimize the meaning of vestiges of sacrificial ritual in monotheistic traditions and tend to downplay them as not serious, merely pedagogic and so on, believers tend to draw heavily precisely on the painful or severe aspects of sacrificial traditions.

From the prophets to Maimonides to Freud the idea prevailed that better knowledge of oneself, of God's demands or the demands of cultural progress would render sacrifices superfluous. An *Erkenntnis*, a knowledge, a better understanding of the world—and be it the world with the abysses of the unconscious—could overcome that inner impulse of man to smash those things that are most beloved to him. Paradoxically, reality has moved in the opposite direction. This impulse is now recognized not only as a disease, but also as a recurring pattern, even as a demand.

At a certain point, accepting the impossibility of progress, is to achieve modest progress. Let us ignore the unavoidable effect of running against the wall of logic with this paradox for a moment. As long as psychoanalysis itself functions according to the scheme of progress and salvation-history (which, I would argue is the case with huge parts of the Freudian oeuvre), it has to tell a story of *Triebopfer*: sacrifice of desire (among other things). And it remains engaged in a project of overcoming superstition or idolatry from Moses to Freud. As soon as it opens its concepts to normativity and permanent struggle (which is the case with the concept of a necessary and impossible murder of the "wonderful child" that everybody has within him or herself according to Serge Leclaire), it can open a new room beneath the temples and churches and synagogues: a room to express and to understand the fears, panics and labors that search for their expressions in various reflected and unreflected sacrificologies. Scientific discourse on sacrifice, though perhaps motivated by these same impulses, and though not always aware of its own normative implications, seems rather to join the efforts of playing down the bewildering aspects of "hard-core sacrificing" (as Al Baumgarten formulated the notion).

In a last step I wish to go beyond Morgenstern's three-stepped negative sacrificology and also beyond simply joining the Leclairian recommendation to think about a spiritual permanent killing of the wonderful child. As I said already, I take the urge for once-and-for-allnes to be a traumatic one. If something unbearable has happened, it is a natural impulse to ask for reasons in order to avoid repeating. Those who believe they can overcome a fault responsible for great disaster, *once and for all*, may be those who have an advantage in their attempts to live on after a disaster. But catastrophes, in spite of their reputation to bring to the fore the truth about man, most times do more to repress that truth, and to force their victims into regressive tendencies.

Without the destructive shock of the *Shoah*, the fourth part of Morgenstern's novel (that he was planning) might have seen Lipusch mourned and the surviving Viennese boy find some ideals to fight for. In fact, as narrated in the extant works, there is only a very tiny hint to the possibility, a little subversion of Morgenstern's elaborated will to be a pure child that sacrifices the wild cow together with the murderous bulls. This little subversion might be discovered in the little love-story of two couples of twins, as told by the narrator judge. Jochanaan likes Rachel and Nehmia likes Ester. While both boys are described as neat and clean and wise and innocent, the two sisters are different: Ester is soft and pure, but Rachel has something provocative about her, like archmother Rachel perhaps, who, sitting on stolen idols, refuses to get up to have her saddle bags examined, pretending that she is bleeding in the female way (Gen 31,35). Nehemia, when wrestling with the angel, could be understood to imagine himself in the place of Jacob, who loved Rachel and was her beloved. That could have been a hopeful beginning. But its elaboration would presuppose a possibility of living in peace.

ECHOES OF SACRIFICE? REPERTOIRES OF GIVING IN THE GREAT RELIGIONS

ILANA F. SILBER

I. *Introduction*

Research on sacrifice has provided for a rich arena of intersection and mutual fructification between anthropological research and the history of religions (Bourdillon and Fortes 1980; van Baal 1975; Burkert 1996; Detienne and Vernant 1979; Vernant 1975; Evans-Pritchard 1956; Godelier 1996; Gusdorf 1948; de Heusch 1986; Linders and Nordquist 1987; Loisy 1920; Milbank 1995; Freud 1912; Girard 1972; Robertson W. Smith 1899; Tarot 1996; Testart 1993; Tylor 1871). Beyond the welcome multiplication of analyses of distinctive forms of sacrifice in specific historical and religious contexts, this has also resulted in much effort at comparative interpretation and typological distinctions (see Rivière 1997), as well as in a range of broader theories concerning the place of sacrifice in the long-term historical development of societies and civilizations (see Milbank 1995).

Within that corpus, one important line of interpretation has focused on aspects of sacrifice that bear a strong analogy to gift-giving, and may perhaps even justify seeing it as a form, or sub-type of the gift. Scholars adopting that perspective would tend to assert for example that both sacrifice and the gift entail some expectation of return from the gods, and that sacrifice constitutes, by and large, a vertical and more dramatic, amplifying or intensifying form of the gift. I mainly have in mind here a rich strand of analysis starting with Edward B. Tylor, passing through Marcel Mauss, and receiving new and diversified expression in the work of Walter Burkert, van Baal, Jonathan Parry, (more marginally) Claude Rivière, and most systematically perhaps (since for him this is only one more step in the elaboration of a more general "gift paradigm"), Alain Caillé.

This is only one strand among others, however, and it has to be seen as part and parcel of a burgeoning and complex set of debates arguing over the relative primacy of sacrifice vs. gift and the precise analytical, ontological and even historical relation between the two. In this perspective, the nagging question is whether sacrifice is derived from the gift, a subcategory of it; or is sacrifice the primary phenomenon, from which the gift is only a specific derivative? (see especially Anspach 1995; Caillé 1995).[1]

Much of this debate, however, has tended to remain on a very general conceptual and theoretical level, and to operate with an overly monolithic conception of both sacrifice and gift. Scholars partaking in it have in fact repeatedly called for more ethnological, anthropological or historical research on sacrifice of the kind necessary to give some kind of "empirical" basis to any and all of the alternative stances. Yet no less important and much less acknowledged an obstacle, I wish to argue, is the suprising shortage, in fact quasi-absence, of typologically and comparatively oriented research on the gift itself.

This shortage may seem suprising indeed, given the long and rich tradition of research on the gift in anthropology, and the relatively favorable inclinations to comparativism normally characteristic of that discipline. Yet the fact is that gift-giving has triggered much less comparative-typological or comparative-historical analysis than sacrifice (see Silber 1995 and Silber forthcoming). Even more crucial, for present purposes, there has been an even greater lack of comparative attention and conceptualization geared to the many forms of religious giving that have developed historically in the context of the so-called "great," or "other-worldly" religions.[2]

This relative neglect of comparative analysis of the gift in general and of religious giving in particular may be shown to have roots in the writings of Marcel Mauss, who wrote what are still among the most renowned and influential texts on both sacrifice and the gift— the earlier "Essai sur la nature et la fonction du sacrifice," co-authored

---

[1] Not surprisingly, such debates have been especially fostered in the framework of a journal whose main editor, Alain Caillé, argues for the paradigmatic primacy of the gift—at least in the sophisticated interpretation of the latter he has been elaborating for some years—as part of a more general, systematic critique of the impact of utilitarian and rational-choice approaches in the human sciences.

[2] Within that framework, moreover, there is again another important imbalance, resulting from a heavy preference—probably rooted in the history of anthropology itself—for the study of religious giving in the context of the Buddhist and Hindu traditions of India and southeast Asia, and the contrasting, nearly total neglect of religious giving in the context of the three monotheistic religions. It is thus only very recently, and in part thanks to the work of medieval historians influenced by anthropology, that some pioneering efforts in the field of Christianity can be recorded. See, in different veins, Bijsterveld; Silber 1995; Tarot).

in 1898 with Henri Hubert, and the later 1925 "Essai sur le don."[3] Both essays, admittedly, are comparatively oriented, and gather evidence taken from a multiplicity of historical and cultural contexts. Yet while the essay on sacrifice takes into account and even labors at making sense of the empirical diversity and multiplicity displayed by the object of its research, the essay on the gift tends on the contrary to bracket it out or at least eject it beyond its pale of analysis.

Yet even the *Essai* on the gift, I shall try to show, happens to give away some hints, or perhaps rather signals, of the need for a more historicizing and comparative approach, and to do so in a way that may have relevance for current discussions of sacrifice.

II. *Religious Giving in Mauss's* Essai sur le Don

Marcel Mauss's central argument in the *Essai* is that the gift is a "necessary form of exchange," and a "permanent form of contractual morality," "one of the human rocks upon which are built our societies." (*ESLD*: 148). His main concern, in other words, was to expose the generic features and principles of operation of the gift as a universal social phenomenon, displaying an impressive evolutionary continuity and an essentially similar nature across the most diverse historical periods and cultures. This heavy (and for him, it should be stressed, otherwise highly uncharacteristic) concern with continuity and similarity does not mean that Mauss never hinted at differences, or different forms and expressions of gift-giving. But even when he did, it is only in a marginal and subdued fashion, and never so as to challenge the mainly essentializing and homogenising thrust of his argument (see Silber 2000 and Silber forthcoming).[4] The gift may thus vary in specific details, expressions, or even scope of importance, but it is not assumed to vary in its basic underlying character and driving animus.

This one-sided emphasis on the generic similarities of the gift in

---

[3] Although I shall not have the time here to demonstrate that point, a similar lacuna can be shown to have reproduced itself among more recent studies of the gift in general and religious giving in particular.

[4] Far from being representative of Mauss's work at large, such a thrust is in fact at variance with the rich sensitivity to cultural and empirical variability that is otherwise associated with Mauss's writings, and is now even better understood to have often led him to deviate from Durkheim.

diverse contexts also explains the way in which the *Essai* only very briefly and insufficiently addressed the subject of *religious* giving specifically, in the confines of a section a mere six or seven pages long, entitled "gifts made to men and gifts made to gods" (Mauss 1973 [1923–4]: 164–171). Mauss himself is in fact the first to recognize this insufficiency: "Nous n'avons pas fait l'étude générale qu'il faudrait pour en faire ressortir l'importance . . . Nous nous bornons donc à quelques indications." (Mauss 1973 [1924]: 164).

Surprisingly brief and unsatisfactory indeed for a scholar steeped in the history of religions and already the co-author in 1898 with H. Hubert of a study on sacrifice, this part of the *Essai* is nevertheless highly significant here. What he terms "gifts to men in view of (i.e. intended to) the gods or nature" are introduced at first, strangely enough, as a "fourth theme" (the hint of a fourth obligation, supplementing the famed series of three obligations—to give, receive and return?) (*ESLD*: 164).[5]

While this would seem to indicate a first impulse to treat religious giving as somehow a "catégorie à part," Mauss's contrasting but finally winning preference is to nevertheless reincorporate it within the homogeneizing flow of his overall argument by stressing again and again the basic similarity and even interpenetration between giving to the gods and other forms of gift. At the origin of this similarity, in Mauss's mind, seems to be the fact that men had first to contract with the spirits of the dead and gods: after all, these were understood as the true owners of all human possessions. He also sees a certain kinship between the type of destruction of wealth entailed in potlatch-like forms of agonistic giving, and the one associated with sacrifice. And above all perhaps, he underscores a basic similarity of intent in gifts to men and gifts to the gods: both aim to obtain peace with the gift's recipient, and both entail the same principle of expected return, of *do ut des*. Contractual sacrifice, in sum, both presupposes gift-institutions, and is itself their heightened expression; the difference between them, in fact, seems to be only one of scale.[6] Moreover,

---

[5] Mauss presents this theme as one "qui joue un rôle dans cette économie et cette morale des présent," strengthening thus the sense of an operational (functional?) relation to the other three obligations. Godelier relates to this theme indeed as Mauss's "fourth obligation." (Godelier 1996: 44).

[6] Refusing a simple homology between gift and sacrifice, in contrast, see Godelier 1996: 46.

many ceremonies are presented as multifunctional, serving to articulate relationships and circulate gifts both among men and between men and gods; which thus further reinforces the sense of a deep affinity and interpenetration, even mutual embeddment of the two kinds of gift-processes.

Significantly, Mauss does not try at all to replicate in the *Essai* the basic conceptual strategy he had applied to the study of sacrifice in the earlier essay he wrote on that topic with H. Hubert, and in which he gave much more attention to the problem of concrete and historical diversity. (This is only the more striking since that study can be said to presage some important features of Mauss's later analysis of the gift, such as the emphasis on the mix of interestedness and disinterestedness, or abnegation and selfishness).[7]

Starting from the apparently baffling concrete diversity of rites of sacrifice in both forms and ends, Mauss and Hubert criticized previous attempts to subsume these all under one arbitrary and incomplete interpretation, such as seeing them all as emerging from one and the same primitive form (Tylor or Robertson Smith),[8] or to distinguish between a minimal number of basic types (e.g. sacrifices with an emphasis on expiation, thanksgiving, request).[9]

Aptly rendered by Evans-Pritchard (in his introduction to the 1968 English translation) as a sort of "grammar" of sacrifice the elements of which can appear in various mixes and combinations, Mauss and Hubert's strategy aimed at exposing the unity of the sacrificial with the help of a conceptualization abstract and flexible enough to be able to account for much of the diversity. In the *Essai sur le Don*, in contrast, Mauss is mostly concerned with articulating the unifying principle (mainly, the triple obligation to give, receive, return) and never explicitly addresses himself to issues of diversity. At no point does he try to conceptualize how that unifying principle, grammar-wise perhaps or else, could perhaps give us the ingredients or components whose diverse mixes and combinations could help account

---

[7] Another important feature, of course, is the emphasis on the contractual aspects of sacrifice.

[8] In Tylor's case, the gift was made by primitive men to supernatural beings with whom they needed to ingratiate themselves; for Robertson Smith, it was rooted in the ritual reaffirmation of totemic communion.

[9] However, Mauss and Hubert themselves offer some useful distinctions, dividing sacrifices for example into personal/objective (p. 13); regular/occasional (p. 14).

for the multiple and diverse expressions of the gift, religious or else, in various cultural contexts.[10]

However, it is also here—or more precisely in a page-long subsection that deals with alms-giving ("l'aumône") and is simply entitled "autre remarque"—that Mauss hints for the first and only time, and by way of a few sentences merely, to the fact that the gift might also have undergone some major historical developments and transformations.

Two historical phases of transformations are thus briefly alluded to. A first phase, which Mauss sees evinced in the early stages of development of the Jewish notion of *zedakah* and what he calls the "Arab" *sadaka*, saw the gift transformed into a principle of justice. Underpinning this transformation is the confluence of a "moral notion"—or what we would rather term now a process of "ethicization"—of gift-giving and wealth on the one hand, and of sacrifice on the other: the affluent had to be willing to rid themselves of some of their excess of riches to compensate, through their gifts, for the inequality of wealth and fate among men; and the gods had to agree to this new usage of wealth that used to be previously offered to them in fruitless sacrifices. For present purposes, it is worth underlining here the hint of a model claiming a historical relationship, and more specifically an inverse, sort of zero-sum or "see-saw" historical relationship, between sacrifice and charity, sacrifice having to decline in order for charitable giving to be able to rise.

Following upon this first phase of transformation, Mauss alludes to a second phase, which engendered a further metamorphosis of the gift, this time from a principle of justice into one of charity and alms-giving. No further clue is given, however, as to what was precisely meant by such distinctions and to what was entailed in that second phase of transformation. Alluding that the change entailed was of rather momentous import, though, Mauss limits himself to underscoring the broad diffusion that awaited the new "charitable" principle, as it would be fostered by the world expansion of Christianity and Islam.

Not only are these suggestions of important historical developments of the gift left undeveloped (thus cancelling the possibility of a confrontation with aspects of his basic conception which they might have contradicted); but they also remain limited to what he calls the

---

[10] See Caillé 1996, in contrast, for the recent articulation of such a more flexible "gift-paradigm."

"semitic" religions and are now more commonly addressed as the three monotheistic religions, i.e. Judaism, Christianity and Islam. More generally speaking, they fail to address, or even just reckon with the complexity and diversity of religious giving in either these or other religious traditions. Later chapters of the *Essai* that deal with topics such as Roman and Hindu ancient systems of law, moreover, do not explore any further the theme of historical stages or transformations, and cannot be said to provide us with any additional insights into the specific dynamics of religious giving or its diverse possible expressions.[11]

III. *For a differentiated approach to religious giving*

Even when critical of Mauss in other ways, current treatments of religious giving have very much remained within the confines of Mauss's framework, and kept imparting what seems to me an overly monolithic approach to that field of study. Little attention has thus been paid to the idea of historical transformations of religious giving, and even less to the idea, faintly suggested by Mauss, of a sort of dialectical, inverse historical relationship between sacrificial and charitable giving, the first having somehow to decline to allow the second to rise.

In contrast, and for reasons that may have to do with broader trends in the social sciences and with the impact of a Western, "economistic" form of ideology, research on religious giving has displayed a sustained, even obsessive preoccupation with issues of reciprocity and interestedness.

Most interpretations of giving to the gods have thus approached religious giving as just another variant of gift-exchange and reciprocity,

---

[11] Somewhat curiously, however, it is precisely on the basis of research on religious giving in India that the first signs of dissatisfaction with Mauss's approach have begun to appear, together with a novel interest in historical processes and developments; while no effort was made to pursue the subject in the context of the monotheistic religions, where Mauss did explicitly start addressing the gift's distinctive processes of historical transformation. In fact, as already amply underscored by Trautmann (1986) and Parry (1986), Mauss appears to have somehow "blinded himself" to the significance of a major feature of the Brahminic ideology of giving—namely, the importance of non-reciprocity—of which he was evidently aware (see Mauss 1973[1924]: 249), but which could only collide with his own emphasis on the obligation to return as one of the universal principles of operation of the gift across historical periods and civilizations.

basically in line (whatever the particulars) with the three-fold sequence of obligations (the obligation to give, to receive, to return) that was so fundamental to Mauss's approach to the gift. This is emphatically the case for example of Walter Burkert's recent volume *The Creation of the Sacred* (1996);[12] and it is also the case with many authors who have more specifically focused on sacrificial giving.

True enough, this emphasis on the principle of reciprocity and exchange has been counteracted by a number of studies which have started putting greater emphasis on the contrary upon the "asymmetrical" features of religious giving, such as the hierarchical distance between donor and recipient or the incommensurability of gifts and expected returns characteristic of giving to the gods (Van Baal 1975; Parry 1986; Caillé 1995; Godelier 1996; Rivière 1997). Building mainly upon the case of donations to funeral Brahmins in the city of Benares in India, for example, Jonathan Parry has argued that this type of donations entails a radical denial of reciprocity that sharply contradicts Mauss's well-known emphasis on the obligation to return the gift. Generalizing this idea, moreover, he sees this break in reciprocity as symptomatic of an ideology of "disinterested," "charitable" or "pure" giving that is characteristically fostered by all the other-worldly oriented, "great" religions and could not be found, indeed represents a sharp break with the type of gift-exchange found in more archaic settings.

I shall not enter here any deeper into the intricacies and problems posed by Parry's provocative argument.[13] It suffices to point out here, simply, that his formulation still tends to approach the issue of *religious* giving, specifically, from what remains a very gen-

---

[12] Religious giving, as Burkert sees it, basically conforms to a fundamental, biological principle of homeostatic balance and reciprocity, diffusely applied by human beings in their interaction with their human and physical environment, and naturally extended to their relation to the sacred.

[13] See Silber 2000. Two general reasons are brought up by Parry for this impact of "other-worldly" oriented religions: 1. other-worldly orientations entail a devalorization of material goods, that makes it easier as well as spiritually rewarding and religiously meritorious to transcend one's attachment to material wealth by giving it away. 2. charitable giving constitutes a minor exercise in and imitation of the kind of more advanced and systematic practices of renunciation and asceticism highly valued by other-worldly religions. As Parry himself points out, however, there are other ways of explaining the break in reciprocity between donor and Brahmin, which seem to have in fact rather little to do with disinterestedness and "charity" and to be anchored rather, or at least equally in conceptions of the economy of sinful and polluting substances and impurity.

eral point of view, no less general and monolithic in fact than approaches that emphasized exchange and reciprocity. Gifts to religious specialists such as Brahmins, and the category of "charitable" giving which Parry brings up in the process of generalizing his argument beyond India may perhaps better be understood as very different kinds of religious giving, entailing different material and symbolic dynamics, and not easily accounted for by one simple and unified model or theory. Significantly, moreover, Parry does not explicitly address himself to either sacrifice or giving to the gods—the type of religious giving which was the target, precisely, of models more attentive to features of exchange and reciprocity.

Finally, the same tendency to a monolithic treatment of the gift in general and of religious giving in particular has dominated recent discussions (whatever other important differences between them) of the relation between sacrifice and the gift (e.g. Anspach 1995, Caillé 1995, Scubla 1995), or as it is sometimes differently stated, giving to the gods and giving to men (e.g. Godelier 1996). However sophisticated and challenging in many other respects, this line of work has neither tried to distinguish nor compare between sacrifice and other types of religious giving.

Steering away thus from the dominant, overly generalizing and monolithic approach to religious giving and from the focus on issues of either reciprocity and disinterestedness that has often accompanied it, I propose to distinguish here between at least three broad types of religious giving: giving to the gods (including but not exhausted by sacrifice),[14] giving to religious institutions or religious specialists (coined here, awkwardly enough and for lack of a better word, "sacerdotal" giving)[15] and giving to the poor and needy (charitable giving).

---

[14] I have in mind here mainly the distinction between sacrifice (commonly believed to entail a degree of violence done to a sacrificed victim) and other types of non-violent tributes and offerings.

[15] It is significant that this category of giving is not as easily identifiable and does not have as well-known a designation as sacrifice or charity. "Sacerdotal" giving is a bit misleading, since it bears with it connotations of the ritual role of priests in sacrifices, or of roles of priestly mediation of access to salvation more generally. Patterns of giving corresponding to that category however cannot be assumed to be all made as a way of obtaining (or as Weber wrongly thought "buying") priestly help in the access to salvation, and can also be made to religious elites fulfilling no definite "priestly" or sacerdotal function. Although there may be some conceptual and practical overlap (an issue which reasons of space prevent me from expanding

Religious traditions or different historical periods of one and the same religious traditions may well vary in the kind of religious giving which they tend to encourage most, or most elaborate in doctrine and ideology. And there is no a priori reason to assume that these various types of religious giving display the same essential dynamics, or a same emphasis on either reciprocity or non-reciprocity.

Undoubtedly, these remain very rough distinctions, and would demand further conceptualization and perhaps some attempt at further sub-differentiation within each broad type (there may be more), as well as a more refined exploration of their mutual relations. Moreover, distinguishing between forms of religious giving in terms of the nature of the gift's recipient is not meant to exclude the possibility of other fruitful criteria of typological distinction. But as I shall try to illustrate, it does provide a fruitful and strangely unexplored heuristic strategy for the comparative analysis of both diverse forms of religious giving and diverse religious traditions.

To begin with, and as indicated by the very absence of a readily accepted label, much more attention has been paid to sacrifice and charity than to what has been more awkwardly addressed here as "sacerdotal" giving. Both analytically and phenomenologically, therefore, one advantage of our typology is that it argues the need to better explore the differences between charitable giving, i.e. giving as a way to provide for the usually basic and largely material necessities of the poor and other needy on the one hand, and "sacerdotal giving"—giving as a way to sponsor, promote, pay tribute, testify or in any other way relate to, a religious institution or spiritual-cultural elite geared to some form of supra-material, transcendent reality on the other. Within sacerdotal giving, one may want to further distinguish between giving for the funding of religious activity, personnel or institutions—what Timothy Brook (1993) for one, chooses to call religious patronage—in a way that emphasizes the latter's need for material support (thus partly converging with giving to poor and other needy) on the one hand, and giving as the expression of a distinctive form of spiritual relationship on the other. While these dimensions of religious patronage—the more instrumental and spiritual-expressive—are often intertwined, they need to be kept

---

upon here), sacerdotal donations are to be distinguished from tithes (obligatory, tax-like contributions, also mainly to religious institutions).

analytically distinct. On the spiritual-expressive side, this may entail expressing one's acknowledgment of certain religious ideals or practices and willingness to sponsor their individual or institutional representatives, whether materially "in need" or not, for the sake of or in name of an ultimate "religious" principle (God or gods possibly being one of them). The spiritual-expressive dimension, moreover, entails a tributary, testimonial or reverential orientation towards the gift's recipient (in the sense of the gift being a tribute to the latter's superior spiritual worth) which may also be found in sacrifice.[16] And like in sacrifice again, there may be a mix of reverential with propitiatory and/or expiatory orientations—of a kind much less likely to develop or much more indirectly so, in contrast, in the case of charitable giving.[17]

Far from being mutually exclusive, in any case, the three major types of giving so distinguished should be understood as possibly coexisting, with varying importance and degrees of mutual differentiation or interpenetration, in the context of discrete "repertoires" or "fields" of giving, shaped by the impact of diverse and historically evolving religious traditions.

Using such a framework, I prefer to eschew the issue of relative "primacy", either conceptual, ontological, or historical-archeological, of sacrifice and gift. My general assumption, rather, will be that the relation between them, or as it is rephrased here, the specific relation between sacrifice and other types of religious giving may not follow the same general and universal or "ontological" formula, and may very much vary across religions and historical eras.

IV. *Some synchronic and diachronic illustrations*

Simple and rough as this basic three-fold distinction may be, it is surprisingly useful in mapping and comparing in a synchronic fashion the repertoire of giving in various religious traditions and civilizations.

---

[16] In the case of sacrifice, this tributary, reverential orientation has received less attention than its communicative, propriatory or expiatory aspects, and seems to be referred to by Chauvet as part of the positive pole of intentionality of sacrifice (Chauvet 1995: 285).

[17] Whatever propitiatory or expiatory orientations are present in the case of charity, they are not geared to the gift's recipient (the poor and needy) as such, but based on the belief in a third, superior party (principle or power) able to assess and reward the act of charity.

To begin with, it helps bring into light a major and intriguing contrast between the repertoire of giving shaped by the impact of the broadly designated "Indian" religions and that of the three monotheistic religions. Occupying the center stage in the repertoire of religious giving in the Indian traditions is the gift by laymen (including kings) to religious specialists and religious institutions—"sacerdotal giving"—to the point of powerfully overshadowing and pushing to the margins (if certainly never cancelling) charitable giving to the poor and needy. Perhaps the most clear-cut case of this kind is the repertoire of giving characteristic of societies where Theravada Buddhism has been prevalent: in such context offerings (*dana*) to the order of monks (the *sangha*) have become so dominant as to totally overshadow all other types of religious giving, including both giving to the gods (sacrificial or not) and (central ideals of universal compassion, generosity and loving-kindness notwithstanding) charitable giving to the poor.[18] By contrast, and as indeed already intuited by Mauss, charitable giving to the poor becomes a much more central ideological motif and institutional practice in all monotheistic religions, where conversely, donations to religious specialists and institutions recede in relative soteriological importance.

These very crude contrasts, obviously enough, are not absolute and there may be important fluctuations in time: I have produced a detailed analysis of the specific convergence of contextual forces which enabled donations to monasteries in the medieval West to thrive on an enormous scale for a number of centuries despite the absence of any early doctrinal groundings calling for it (Silber 1995). This development is only the more impressive indeed given the very strong emphasis on charity otherwise characteristic of earlier phases of Christianity. Playing a supportive part in this process, however, were medieval tendencies to view monks as the truest Christian "poor" or alternatively, as the appropriate dispensors of charitable giving—or in other words to fuse or blur the distinction between the two types of giving distinguished above. Albeit far from so explicit, a similar ambiguity in the understanding of religious elites or specialists—as spiritually/ritually superior and yet also materially poor

---

[18] See also Lohmann (1995) for a similar observation and more reservedly, Guruge and Bond (1998).

and in need of "charitable" support—may be found in Indian contexts as well.[19]

These tendencies to overlap and fusion between analytically distinct, ideal-typical patterns of "sacerdotal" and "charitable" giving notwithstanding, historical shifts in their relative importance tend to further confirm the distinction between them. It is striking, for example, that the golden age of donations to monasteries seems not to have been favourable to more clearly differentiated "charitable" endeavours. And it is perhaps not incidental that the latter happen to have enjoyed an impressive efflorescence precisely at a time when donations to monasteries underwent a drastic decline.

As such fluctuations indicate, the approach just outlined can be put to use as a tool of not only synchronic but also diachronic analysis. This may even allow us in fact to reach for a more elaborate version of Mauss's idea, however faintly suggested in his hint of a relation between the historical decline of sacrifice and the rise of charity, of a whole arena of historical transformations and interplay among different and historically successive forms of religious giving.

Focusing on the historical trajectory of sacrifice, for present purposes, one interest of the idea of repertoires of giving developed above is that it encourages us to look for influences of sacrifice upon, or its displacement by, other forms of giving rather than (as is more commonly done), other forms of liturgical practices or ritual worship.[20] In the process it also may lead to assessments of historical developments that happen to deviate from the more accepted or usual interpretation of such developments in various religions.

---

[19] Largely latent in classical Brahminical ideology, it thus seems to flare up in the changing climate of the late-sixteenth century Nayaka period in south India, witnessing a new, emphatic preoccupation of kings with the lavish offering of food—rather than the more traditional royal gift of land—to large numbers of deprived Brahmins (Narayana Rao, Shulman and Subrahmanyam, 1992).

[20] Privileging the relation to ritual worship tends to highlight that aspect of sacrifice that entails, as Hubert and Mauss had already sensed, a way of communicating with the sacred; and later, alternative forms of ritual worship are seen as corresponding to more interiorized patterns of spiritual "communication". Focusing on the relation to other forms of religious giving does not cancel that aspect—perhaps more obviously present though in sacerdotal than charitable giving—but may highlight other aspects, such as the donor's capacity to disconnect from material goods or his restricted range of choice in doing so (sacrifice often entailing a more ritually defined offering to the one or few exclusively valid recipients), in contrast to other/later forms of giving allowing the donor more freedom to choose what, how much and to whom to give.

In the context of Judaism, for example, it is prayer, rather than either charitable or sacerdotal giving that is generally understood as a substitute for sacrifices in a context where sacrifices could not be practiced any more after the Destruction of the Temple and the Exile. In agreement with Mauss's very sparse remarks, however, and although he probably was not aware of it, it is also precisely in such a context that charity, Zedakah, quickly rose to a position of dominance in the repertoire of giving of Jewish communities. Contrary to what Mauss seems to imply, however, charitable giving was far from being a novel development in the Jewish tradition and already coexisted in earlier periods both with sacrifices on the one hand, and sacramental giving to a priestly class of ritual specialists on the other. In such earlier phases, in fact, it may well have itself to be understood as a "sacralized" transformation of earlier, non-religious models of charity to the poor already extant in other civilizations.[21] Yet all this does not prevent us from seeing this new rise to dominance of Zedakah in the post-Exilic period as also facilitated by the decline of sacrifices and perhaps even in part, and together with prayer, as a sort of substitute, or replacement for it.

Significantly though, neither notions of sacrifice nor self-sacrifice (in as much as it existed for example in the Jewish concept of *kiddush ha-shem*, i.e. sanctification of God's name through martyrdom) seem to attach to or otherwise shape the understanding and practices of Jewish charity in either earlier or later periods of Jewish history. Excessive, self-sacrificial charitable giving is in fact repeatedly discouraged. And as I have started to show elsewhere, extant attempts to establish a hierarchy of charitable giving adopt criteria of relative valorization which are much more governed by the idea of protecting the recipient's feelings (for example by hiding the identity of both donor and recipient) than by any concept of self-sacrificial "disinterestedness" (see Silber 2000).

This absence, or at least striking weakness of "echoes" of sacrifice in the ideals and practices of Jewish charity brings into relief the need to carefully distinguish between two distinct issues: the actual presence or absence of sacrifice within the repertoire of religious giving at a specific point of time, vs. the diverse capacity of sacrifice in different religions to still symbolically impinge upon and shape

---

[21] See Assmann 1992: 69 for the idea of Sakralisierung der Ethik.

conceptions and practices of other types of religious giving, even when itself otherwise obliterated at that time.

In the context of Christianity, in sharp contrast to Judaism, there have been powerful carry-over effects from one period to the next, confirming that sacrifice may still have a practical and ideological impact even in periods when it seems to have disappeared from the repertoire of "active" religious practices. This is of course the largely accepted version of the all-radiating effect of Jesus' primordial self-sacrifice upon other aspects and later periods of Christian religion.[22] Once again, one has to trace the relation of sacrifice not only to other patterns of worship and liturgy, but also to other modes of giving. Far from seeing the continuing impact of sacrifice limited to the growing importance of the eucharist in liturgical worship, indeed, Jesus's sacrificial gift of himself has combined with the no less foundational notion of God's free, gratuitous gift of grace in stamping other forms of giving, and charitable giving in particular with a whole range of interrelated connotations such as expiation, asceticism, renunciation, self-denial, selfless love, martyrdom, humility, common poverty. Central to Catholicism's overall "economy of grace," the self-sacrificial effects of *imitatio Christi* have remained powerful enough to shape the hierarchy of Christian ideals and practices of giving throughout the centuries (Pitt-Rivers 1992, p. 235; Tarot 1992; Neusch 1994; Chauvet 1994). So powerful in fact as to have been criticized for having biased early anthropological and sociological understandings of sacrifice with an undue attention to elements of abnegation and renunciation (Detienne and Vernant 1979; de Heusch 1986; see also Chauvet 1994); and as to even and still find surprisingly powerful echoes in more modern Western notions of the gift (Gagnon 1997; Derrida 1991; 1992).

This, however, is perhaps an only partial, and indeed perhaps overly sacrificial, rendering of the history of Christianity itself. Confirming the usefulness of our original three-fold distinction, this sacrificial bias becomes especially clear if one decides to pay closer attention, precisely, to the historical trajectory of our two other categories of religious giving, i.e. giving to the poor and giving to

---

[22] To some extent, the Christian stance (in fact more complex and multilayered than can be adequately conveyed here) developed indeed out of self-conscious opposition to the more ritualistic and "interested," or "functionalistic" aspects of Jewish sacrifices (themselves in fact far from uncontroversial even from within the Jewish tradition).

religious institutions or specialists. Already in the context of early Christianity in fact, there is by now greater awareness of competing and fluctuating conceptions concerning the rejection of Jewish sacrifices, the impulse to nevertheless worship God through some other form of offerings, the importance of ascetic renunciation, common poverty, charitable donations for the needy, and the precise role of a rising stratum of priestly leaders (as recipients, priestly sacrifiers and/or redistributors?) in all these.

This last issue, for present purposes, is precisely revealing of some important uncertainties: are the early Christian bishops or presbyters invested with a sacrificial role (itself defined differently as time goes on and eventually culminating in the sacramental reenactment of Jesus's sacrifice in the Eucharist) or also, and perhaps primarily, deemed responsible for the reception and the redistribution of charitable gifts to the needy?; relatedly, what is the nature of the offerings of the faithful just before or after the presentation of the Eucharist: are these offerings to God or charitable gifts destined to the needy— in part perhaps, as Justinus thought, for example, because God by definition is not in need of any gifts? (See esp. Magne 1975; and note the telling convergence, in this volume, with the contributions of Bernhard Lang and Adriana Destro).[23] Nothing at this stage, in sum, indicated yet any necessary dominance and all radiating impact of sacrifice and self-sacrifice over other expressions of religious giving.

Further into the Middle-Ages, sacrificial effects seem to have been temporarily counterbalanced by the rise to dominance for the span of some six centuries (6th to 12th) of an alternative pattern of religious giving already mentioned above—donations to monasteries. Significantly, not only did this new and influential pattern of "sacerdotal" giving lack any clear grounding in early doctrines, but it also was couched in an explicitly reciprocal, transactional idiom of exchange and reciprocity between donors and recipients which showed little trace of the self-sacrificial gift paradigm.

Confirming the heuristic interest of positioning sacrifice relatively to other forms of religious giving in both a synchronic and diachronic

---

[23] Charity may well have first gathered momentum more out of the practical dynamics of a life of total renunciation and common poverty (Magne 1975), than under the impact of either sacrificial or self-sacrificial conceptions. Abnegating, doloristic conceptions of sacrifice are themselves not the only possible Christian point of view (see Chauvet 1995).

fashion, another pattern yet has evolved in the context of Buddhism, which from the very start entailed a component of protest against the ritualistic and elitist aspects of sacrifice and gifts to the Brahmins in the Hindu tradition. Offerings to gods have not been excluded from the repertoire of active practices but are simply tolerated to proliferate as part of the whole realm of worldly actions and orientations belonging to the "lower" planes of kammatic and especially lay religiosity, while being denied any soteriological role or significance in the access to ultimate enlightenment. Overwhelmingly central from the earliest stages instead is a distinctive form of "sacerdotal" giving—offerings to the community of monks, the Sangha—bearing some major similarities to offerings to brahmins (both monks and brahmins being mandatory recipients of gifts, and not expected to reciprocate) and as already mentioned above, pushing to the margins charitable giving to the poor. Notwithstanding their same appellation (*dana*), and an otherwise rich world of shared cosmological and religious conceptions, neither offerings to monks nor charity to the poor bear any imprint of either Vedic or Hindu notions of sacrifice.[24] While all forms of generosity and benevolence, and offerings to all needy and/or deserving recipients are repeatedly praised and valorized, there is also a sharp tendency to grade them in terms of their contribution to the donor's accumulation of merit and access to salvation. Ultimately, however, nibbanic Buddhism (in the Theravada tradition more especially) undermines the soteriological importance not only of sacrifice but in fact of all giving that is only motivated by the accumulation of positive karma deemed necessary for a better life and better rebirth (themselves paradoxically important though on the path to salvation from the cycle of rebirths).[25] Upheld as exemplars instead are those more ideals forms of giving (in fact of offerings to the Sangha) indicative of the most extreme degrees of generosity and renunciation—such as propounded in the legendary

[24] Nor for that matter do notions of sacrifice find any echoes in monastic discipline and the practice of renunciation—contrary to the Brahmanic pattern, where important symbolic linkages between sacrifice and renunciation obtained, seeing in renunciation an interiorized, lasting form of sacrifice (see Biardeau and Malamud 1976; Cahn 1994; Heesterman 1964).

[25] To that extent, it may well be that undermining the status of sacrifice ultimately means undermining the status of all forms of religious gifting, in tune perhaps with an ultimate devalorization of all worldly human action and social order more generally.

stories of Prince Vessantara's or the wealthy merchant Anathapindika's unbounded acts of giving—i.e. giving geared to the search for supreme enlightenment through the disciplined cultivation of renunciation.[26] This also explains why teaching the path to salvation, a task normally belonging to monks, is often mentioned as the highest form of giving—*dhammadana*—ranked superior thus to all forms of lay donations to the Sangha. For present purposes, in any case, it is striking that neither the more ordinary forms of giving nor such excessive and selfless or even self-sacrificial forms of more "nibbanically-oriented" giving bear any imprint or "echoes" of sacrifice.

V. *Conclusion*

Discussions of the relation between gift and sacrifice have tended to suffer from an overly generalizing and monolithic approach to the gift in general and religious giving in particular. Arguing for a more differentiated approach, I have proposed to distinguish between three broad types of religious giving: giving to the gods (including but not exhausted by sacrifice), giving to religious institutions or religious specialists ("sacerdotal" giving) and giving to the poor and needy (charitable giving). If applied to the analysis of the repertoire of religious giving in the Jewish, Christian and Buddhist traditions from both a synchronic and diachronic point of view, this three-fold distinction defeats any single general and universal or "ontological" formula of relation between sacrifice and gift. Moreover, it helps bring into focus important variations in the relative importance of alternative types of religious giving across religions and historical eras that deserve a more sustained comparative exploration.[27]

---

[26] I would thus slightly modify the strong emphasis in Guruge and Bond (1998) on a smooth continuity between all forms of giving in Theravada Buddhism, all similarly valorized because of their ultimate relation to renunciation and the nibbanic search for enlightenment; and rather emphasize if certainly not a sharp dichotomy, at least a degree of tension between the more kammatic aspects and forms of *dana* more oriented to the accumulation of merit, and those more intimately associated with the ideal of renunciation and supreme salvation (replicating in fact the form of relation but also tension between karma/dharma/nirvana that is pervasive to all Buddhism more generally). Such extreme, even excessive forms of generosity would seem thus to be the closest to Parry's ideology of the "pure" gift. Parry's version of the pure gift however, includes the more common religious giving that does expect some form of ultimate soteriological reward even if it expects no reciprocity.

[27] I have not tried here to explain such important variations, but just to record them.

As such, the approach articulated here happens to converge with a similar move away from unitary, universal definitions that has emerged in recent modes of structural approaches to both gift and sacrifice (Caillé 1996; Chauvet 1994b).[28] Trying to take into account and conceptualize the rich diversity in empirical and historical expressions of these two phenomena, such modular, flexible approaches are more in continuity with Hubert and Mauss's grammar-like definition of sacrifice than with Mauss's search for the law-like universal principles of operation of the gift.

More comparative-historical in its general thrust, however, the research strategy suggested here may help enrich and modify extant grand theories concerning the place of sacrifice in the historical development of human civilizations. Most such developmental schemes tend to endow sacrifice with major importance in the earliest phases of development (to some minds even seeing in it the original and dynamic "fons" or motor of all things), while expecting it to lose this initial, foundational importance and eventually disappear in subsequent phases.[29] To the extent that the issue is addressed at all, this process of gradual waning is understood to naturally culminate in the thorough devalorization and marginalization of sacrifice in modern, "secularized" settings (for a contrary argument, however, see Nicholas 1996). And often suggested as the main motor of such developments is a process of gradual interiorization of religious action and spirituality, basically inimical to the grossly concrete, exteriorized and even violent aspects of sacrifice.

Our analysis, in contrast, has the effect of drawing more attention

---

[28] In Caillé's approach to the gift, there is place for a varying importance and combination of the three gift obligations (giving, accepting, returning a gift) and of four basic possible "facets" of the gift (briefly, ritual obligation; spontaneity/generativity; agonistic desire/self-presentation; love/harmony) in diverse cultural settings. Chauvet argues for a basic structure of sacrifice composed of four analytical "agents" (sacrifier, sacrificator, sacrified, destinatary; an oscillation between positive and negative poles; the negotiation of human space between animals and gods) and characterized by a distinctive set of polarities (such as life/death; debt/redemption; sacred/desacration; sacrifice/ethics) also varying in their precise concrete definition, importance and combination in different cultural settings.

[29] It is worth remembering, however, that not all societies have or ever had sacrifice (Woodburn in Bourdillon and Fortes 1980; Godelier 1996: 251). The assumption that sacrifice is a feature of the earliest, simplest or most "primitive" societies is itself debated. In R.N. Bellah's well-known article on religious evolution (1964), for example, sacrifice is introduced as a feature of the second, "archaic" stage only, still absent in the more fluid first, "primitive" stage and still present but already losing much of its significance in the third, "historic" stage.

to the vast expanse of the "great" religious traditions intermediary
to "primitive" and "modern" civilizations. In such a broad context,
moreover, it tends to suggest a number of diverse possible trajecto-
ries of sacrifice, in complex interplay with the rise and decline of
alternative forms of religious giving. Rather than only focusing on
the relative rise or decline in actual practices of religious giving,
moreover, one has to also explore their more subtle symbolic effects
or "echoes," at times powerful enough to reverberate across very
long stretches of time.

Notwithstanding the varying importance of a pole of utter spir-
itualization of the gift (such as in the gift of love, or of oneself), it
remains crucial to stress the ever concrete and material aspect of
the three types of religious gifting. None of the symbolic echoes or
absence thereof we were able to trace would obtain, indeed, if not
for the concrete, material nature of the object or wealth given away.
It is this concrete movement of matter, after all, that underpins the
gift's operation as a meaningful gesture and symbolic operator; and
that may well constitute, in final analysis, the only if also surprisingly resilient element of continuity between gift and sacrifice.

BIBLIOGRAPHY

Anspach, Mark 1995. "Le sacrifice qui engendre le don qui l'englobe," *La revue du
    M.A.U.S.S.* 5: 224–247.
Assmann, Jan 1992. *Politische Theologie Zwischen Aegypten und Israel*. München: Carl
    Friedrich von Siemens Stiftung.
Bataille, G. 1967. *La Part Maudite*. Paris: Minuit.
——— 1973. *Théorie de la religion*. Paris: Gallimard.
Bellah, R.N. 1964. "Religious Evolution," *American Sociological Review* 29: 358–374.
Biardeau, Madeleine and Charles Malamud (1976). *Le sacrifice dans l'Inde ancienne*.
    Paris: Presses Universitaires de France.
Bijsterveld, Arnoud-Jan 2001. "The Medieval Gift as Agent of Social Bonding and
    Political Power: A Comparative Approach," in Esther Cohen and Maike B.
    de Jon (eds.), *Medieval Transformations: Texts, Power and Gifts in Context*. Leiden:
    Brill, 123–156.
Bourdillon, Michael and Meyer Fortes (1980). *Sacrifice*. New York: Academic Press.
Brook, Timothy 1993. *Praying for Power: Buddhism and the Formation of Gentry Society in
    Late-Ming China*. Cambridge: Harvard University Press.
Burkert, Walter 1996. *Creation of the Sacred: Tracks of Biology in Early Religions*. Cambridge,
    Mass.: Harvard University Press.
Cahn, Annie 1994. "Le sacrifice dans l'hindouisme," in M. Neusch (ed.), *Le sacrifice
    dans les religions*. Paris: Beauchesne, 181–202.
Caillé, Alain 1996. "Ni holisme ni individualisme méthodologique. Marcel Mauss
    et le paradigme du don," *Revue du M.A.U.S.S* 8: 12–58.
——— 1995. "Sacrifice, don et utilitarisme: notes sur la théorie du sacrifice," *La
    revue du M.A.U.S.S.* 5: 248–294.

Chauvet, L.-M. 1994a. "Le 'sacrifice' en christianise: une notion ambigüe," in M. Neusch (ed.), *Le sacrifice dans les religions*. Paris: Beauchesne, 139–156.

———— 1994b. "Le sacrifice comme échange symbolique," in M. Neusch (ed.), *Le sacrifice dans les religions*. Paris: Beauchesne, 277–304.

Derrida, J. 1991. *Donner le temps*. Paris: Editions Galilée.

———— 1992. "Donner la mort", in Rabaté, Jean-Michel et Michael Wetzel eds., *L'éthique du don: Jacques Derrida et la pensée du don*. Paris: Metaille-Transition.

Détienne, Marcel et Jean-Pierre Vernant. 1979. *La cuisine du sacrifice en pays grec*. Paris: Gallimard.

Dumezil, G. 1924. *Le festin d'immortalité*, Paris: Geuthner.

Evans-Pritchard, 1956. *Nuer Religion*. Oxford: Clarendon.

Gagnon, Eric 1997. "De la pureté du don: contribution à un débat," *Anthropologie et sociétés* 21, 1: 9–24.

Girard, R. 1972. *Violence et sacré*. Paris: Grasset.

Griaule 1948. *Dieu d'eau*. Paris: Chêne.

Guruge A.W.P. and G.D. Bond, 1998. "Generosity and Service in Theravada Buddhism," in Warren F. Ilchman, Stanley N. Katz and Edward L. Queen II (ed.) *Philanthropy in the World's Traditions*. Bloomington: Indiana University Press, 79–96.

Gusdorf, Georges 1948. *L'expérience humaine du sacrifice*. Paris: PUF.

Heesterman, J.C. "Brahmin, Ritual and Renouncer." *Wiener Zeitschrift für die Kunde Süd- und Ostasiens* 8: 1–31.

Heusch, L. de 1986. *Le sacrifice dans les religions africaines*. Paris: Gallimard.

Loisy, Alfred, 1920. *Essai historique sur le sacrifice*. Paris: Nourry.

Magne, J. 1975. *Sacrifice et Sacerdoce*. Paris: Origines Chrétiennes.

Mauss, Marcel 1950. [1924]. "Essai sur le don: formes et raisons de l'échange dans les sociétés archaïques." In M. Mauss, *Sociologie et Anthropologie*. Paris: Presses Universitaires de France.

Mauss, Marcel and Henri Hubert 1898. "Essai sur la nature et la fonction du sacrifice," *L'Année* 2, 29–138 (Mélanges d'histoire des religions 1–130 et Oeuvres 1, 93–307). Transl. W.D. Halls with Introd. by E.E. Evans-Pritchard, *Sacrifice: its Nature and Function*. Chicago: The University of Chicago Press.

Milbank, John 1995. "Stories of Sacrifice: From Wellausen to Girard," *Theory, Culture and Society* 12: 15–46.

Narayana Rao Velcheru, David Shulman and Sanjay Subrahmanyam 1992. *Symbols of Substance: Court and State in Nayaka Period Tamilnadu*. Delhi: Oxford University Press.

Nicholas, Guy 1995. "Résurgences contemporaines du don sacrificiel," *La revue du M.A.U.S.S.* 5.

———— 1996. *Du don rituel au sacrifice suprême*. Paris: La Découverte.

Neusch, Marcel (ed.) *Le sacrifice dans les religions*. Paris: Beauchesne, 1994.

Rivière, Claude 1997. "Approaches comparatives du sacrifice," in F. Boespflug and F. Dunand, *Le Comparatisme en Histoire des Religions*. Paris: Cerf, 279–289.

Revue du M.A.U.S.S. 5, 1995. *A quoi bon (se) sacrifier?: sacrifice, don et intérêt*. Paris: La Découverte.

Scubla, Lucien 1995. "Vengeance et sacrifice: de l'opposition à la réconciliation," La *revue du M.A.U.S.S.* 5: 204–223.

Silber, I.F. 1995. "Gift-Giving in the Great Traditions: The Case of Donations to Monasteries in the Medieval West," *European Journal of Sociology* 36, 2: 209–243.

———— 2000. "Beyond Purity and Danger: Gift-Giving in the Monotheistic Religions," in T. Vandevelde (ed.), *Gifts and Interests*. Louvain: Peeters, 115–132.

———— forthcoming. "Le champ du don: pour une perspective historique comparée," in Marcel Fournier (ed.), *L'Héritage de Marcel Mauss*. Montréal: Presses de l'Université de Montréal.

Smith, W. Robertson 1899. *The Religion of the Semites*. London: Black.
Tarot, Camille 1992. "Repères pour une histoire de la naissance de la grâce," in *La Revue du M.A.U.S.S.* 1: 90–114.
——— 1996. "Christianisme et inconditionnalité," *La revue du M.A.U.S.S.* 7: 338–366.
Testart, A. 1993. *Des dons ou des dieux*. Paris: Colin.
Tylor, E.B. 1871. *Primitive Culture*. London, Murray.
Van Baal, J. 1976. "Offering, Sacrifice and Gift," *Numen* 2–3: 161–178.
Van der Leeuw, G. 1933. *Religion in its Essence and Manifestations*. (German).
Vernant, Jean-Pierre 1975. "Greek Religion, Ancient Religions." Paris, Collège de France 1975. Also in Froma I. Zeitlin (ed.) Jean-Pierre Vernant 1991, *Mortals and Immortals: Collected Essays*. Princeton, N.J.: Princeton University Press, 269–289.
——— [1981] 1991. "A General Theory of Sacrifice and the Slaying of the Victim in the Greek Thusia." ibid., 290–302.

CONTRIBUTORS

Tzvi Abusch
Department of Near Eastern & Jewish Studies, Brandeis University, Waltham, MA 02254 U.S.A.
e-mail: abusch@binah.cc.brandeis.edu

Albert Baumgarten
Department of Jewish History, Bar Ilan University, Ramat Gan, Israel 52900
e-mail: baumgaa@mail.biu.ac.il

Nicole Belayche
55 Rue Jean Jaures, F-92170 Vanves, France
e-mail: n.belayche@wanadoo.fr

Jonathan Benthall
212 The Grove, Hammersmith, London W6 7HG, England
e-mail: jonathanbenthall@hotmail.com

Bruce Chilton
Department of Religion, Bard College, Annandale, NY 12504 U.S.A.
e-mail: chilton@bard.edu

Adriana Destro
Dipartimentio di Studi Linguistici e Orientali, University of Bologna, Via Zamboni 16, 40125 Bologna, Italy
e-mail: destro@spbo.unibo.it

Jennifer Harris
Programme in Christianity and Culture, St. Michael's College, 81 St. Mary's Street, Toronto, Ontario M5S 1J4, Canada
e-mail: jeharris@chass.utoronto.ca

Peter Herz
Universität Regensburg, Universitätsstrasse 31, D-93053 Regensburg, Germany
e-mail: peter.herz@geschichte.uni-regensburg.de

Albert de Jong
Faculty of Theology, Leiden University, Postbus 9515, 2300 RA Leiden, The Netherlands
e-mail: afdejong@rullet.leidenuniv.nl

Bernhard Lang
Universität Paderborn, Warburger Strasse 100, D-33098 Paderborn, Germany
e-mail: alang1@hrz.uni-paderborn.de

Jacob Milgrom
13 Jabotinsky, Jerusalem, Israel
e-mail: milgrom@ha.hum.huji.ac.il

Gesine Palmer
Ansbacher Str. 61, D-10777 Berlin, Germany
e-mail: gpalmer@zedat.fu-berlin.de

Mauro Pesce
Dipartimento di Discipline Storiche, University of Bologna, Piazza S. Giovanni in Monte 2, 40125 Bologna, Italy
e-mail: pesce@spbo.unibo.it

Susan Sered
Center for the Study of World Religions, Harvard University, 42 Francis Avenue, Cambridge MA 02138 U.S.A.
e-mail: ssered@hds.harvard.edu

Ilana Friedrich Silber
Department of Sociology and Anthropology, Interdisciplinary Graduate Program in Hermeneutics, Bar Ilan University, Ramat Gan, Israel 52900
e-mail: ifsilber@mail.biu.ac.il

D. Stökl
Department of Comparative Religion, The Hebrew University, Jerusalem, Israel 91905
e-mail: msstoekl@mscc.huji.ac.il

Theo Sundermeier
Wissenschaftlich-Theologisches Seminar, Kisselgasse 1, D69117
Heidelberg, Germany
e-mail: t.sundermeier@t-online.de

Michael Swartz
Department of Near Eastern Languages and Cultures, Ohio State
University, Botany and Zoology Building, 1735 Neil Avenue, Columbus,
OH 43210 U.S.A.
e-mail: swartz.69@osu.edu

INDEX OF NAMES AND SUBJECTS*

---

* This index was prepared by Mr. Nitai Shinan of Jerusalem.